PUBLICATIONS

OF THE

NAVY RECORDS SOCIETY

VOL. 142

THE SUBMARINE SERVICE,
1900–1918

The NAVY RECORDS SOCIETY was established in 1893 for the purpose of printing unpublished manuscripts and rare works of naval interest. The Society is open to all who are interested in naval history, and any person wishing to become a member should apply to the Hon. Secretary, Department of War Studies, King's College London, Strand, London WC2R 2LS. The annual subscription is £30, which entitles the member to receive one free copy of each work issued by the Society in that year, and to buy earlier issues at much reduced prices.

———————————

SUBSCRIPTIONS and orders for back volumes should be sent to the Membership Secretary, 5 Goodwood Close, Midhurst, West Sussex GU29 9JG.

———————————

THE COUNCIL OF THE NAVY RECORDS SOCIETY wish it to be clearly understood that they are not answerable for any opinions and observations which may appear in the Society's publications. For these the editors of the several works are entirely responsible.

THE SUBMARINE SERVICE, 1900–1918

Edited by

NICHOLAS LAMBERT, M.A., D.Phil.

PUBLISHED BY ASHGATE
FOR THE NAVY RECORDS SOCIETY
2001

Published by
Ashgate Publishing Limited
Gower House
Croft Road
Aldershot
Hants GU11 3HR
England

Ashgate Publishing Company
131 Main Street
Burlington, Vermont 05401-5600 USA

Ashgate website: http://www.ashgate.com

British Library Cataloguing-in-Publication data

The submarine service, 1900–1918. – (Navy records series; no. 142)
  1. Great Britain. Royal Navy. Submarine Command – History
  2. World War, 1914–1918 – Great Britain – Naval operations
  I. Lambert, Nicholas
  359.9′33′0941′09041

Library of Congress Card Number: 00–110765

ISBN 0 7546 0294 X

Printed on acid-free paper

Typeset in Times by Express Typesetters Ltd, Farnham, Surrey and printed in Great Britain by MPG Books Ltd, Bodmin, Cornwall

v

CONTENTS

ACKNOWLEDGEMENTS

Thanks are owed to the following:

Brian Head; Captain Peter Hore, R.N.; Captain Jeremy Read, R.N.; Commander Jeffrey Tall, R.N.; Lieutenant-Commander W. J. R. Gardner, R.N.; Jenny Wraight; Michael Simpson.

INTRODUCTION

During most of the nineteenth century, the Admiralty dismissed submarine-boats as being unworthy of serious attention. Proposals to develop underwater warships were ridiculed. But in fact, the public declarations of Britain's naval high command masked an attention to the potential of submarines as effective instruments of war. Acting discreetly, the Admiralty sent officers to inspect and report on every experimental submarine built in British yards, and instructed the Naval Intelligence Department to keep close watch on progress made by foreign inventors, especially across the Channel in France. British naval officers may even have made clandestine inspections of submarine-boats built overseas. Accurate plans of submarine-boats employed by the Confederate Navy during the American Civil War, for example, can be found in British naval archives. The Victorian Navy, in other words, generally kept itself well informed about submarine development.[1]

At the beginning of the twentieth century, the Admiralty remained committed 'to do nothing to justify or encourage' rival powers from sponsoring submarine development despite indications that at least one foreign navy had mastered the art of underwater navigation. In 1899, the naval attaché in Paris, Captain Henry Jackson, warned that the French navy had developed a mechanically reliable vessel that could manoeuvre underwater safely and remain stable while launching torpedoes. Although this report was circulated within Whitehall, and did excite at least one important officer, the Board of Admiralty took no action. Over the next twelve months, naval lobbyists in the press and Parliament learned of French progress and warned that Great Britain was falling dangerously behind the French in the development of underwater warfare. Despite these shoals of criticism,

[1] See 'Projects for Annoying the Enemy (torpedoes, etc.)', C-in-C North America: copy of letter requesting Mr McClintock to proceed to England, 20 December 1872, ADM 12/897; 'Submarine boat invented by Mr McClintock reported on by Captain Nicholson and Mr Ellis (chief Engineer HMS *Royal Alfred*) and report of Adm. Inglefield', ADM1/6236; 'Report No.4 of 1872', by Adm. Inglefield, ADM 1/6236 part 2. I am indebted to Capt. Peter Hore for these references.

the First Lord of the Admiralty refused to change course. Or so it seemed.

In fact, the Admiralty had already taken action. In February 1900, the officers of the Naval Intelligence Division had been instructed to increase their efforts to learn about French progress. In April, the Board authorised the lifting of a ban on the use of contact mines as a first step towards the development of an antidote to the submarine. And later that month the Captain of the torpedo school (HMS *Vernon*) was instructed to launch an anti-submarine weapons (ASW) programme. In May, however, the Captain of the *Vernon* protested to the Admiralty that he could not begin until he was given some idea of the capabilities of submarine-boats, such as for how long they could proceed underwater, how far and how fast. The point was valid and later that month the Controller, Rear Admiral Sir Arthur Knyvet Wilson, recommended that the Royal Navy purchase an underwater boat for anti-submarine experiments. The First Lord and his senior adviser concurred and before the year was out the Admiralty had negotiated a contract with Messrs. Vickers, Sons & Maxim to supply five craft. Although built in Britain, these craft, known as 'Holland-boats' after the Irish-American submarine pioneer John Holland, were designed by the American Electric Boat Company and assembled under their supervision.

According to most history books, not everyone at the Admiralty was happy with the decision to purchase submarines.[1] In an often quoted – but rarely understood – paper written in January 1901, Rear Admiral Sir Arthur Knyvet Wilson went so far as to condemn all underwater warfare as 'underhanded'.[2] He was reputed also to have advocated a policy of hanging all crewmen of submarines captured in battle. Naval historians are mistaken, however, in interpreting these remarks as evidence of Wilson's opposition to the Vickers contract and the acquisition of the Holland-boats. (After all, it had been Wilson who had first suggested that the Navy purchase submarines!) It is equally wrong to suggest that he dismissed the significance of the submarine-boat – his analysis included an explicit warning that the French would use them against British merchantmen with deadly effect. The Controller wrote his memorandum, in fact, as a response to a suggestion by Mr H. Oakley Arnold-Forster MP (the new Parliamentary and Financial Secretary to the Admiralty) that the Royal Navy accelerate its

[1] Most recently by Dan van der Vat, *Stealth at Sea: the history of the submarine* (London, 1994), pp. 33–4.

[2] Admiral Sir Reginald Bacon, *From 1900 Onwards*, Hutchinson: London, 1940, pp. 50–51.

submarine programme. Wilson's argument was that the Admiralty should not yet abandon the policy (and in public the language) of discouraging foreign powers from investigating the possibilities of submarine warfare. He believed that the Royal Navy's purchase of submarines could and should be kept secret. Significantly, the majority of the Naval Lords endorsed the thrust of his arguments, though the Senior Naval Lord conceded that perhaps his presentation had been too forceful. But after winning the opening round, Wilson then overplayed his hand by subverting Arnold-Forster's efforts to buttress the case for development by recruiting expert consultants from outside Whitehall. In March 1901, he was removed from the post of Controller for his dogmatism on this and other matters. Wilson's departure, nevertheless, did not produce any immediate shift in submarine policy. Not until the replacement of Vice Admiral Arthur Moore as Second Naval Lord in early 1902 did the balance of opinion at the Admiralty at last shift towards cautious enthusiasm for the submarine.

In March 1901, the new Controller appointed Captain Reginald Bacon his special assistant and gave him the responsibility for overseeing the construction of the submarine-boats on order. Ten years earlier Bacon had been involved with the development of surface torpedo craft. In addition, he was a qualified torpedo officer known to have a bent for technical subjects. Bacon's first action was to question the wisdom of buying the Electric Boat design. While he did not doubt that the Holland-boats could dive, run submerged, and return to the surface, he suspected they would be poor sea-boats and consequently would prove to have little military value when tested under combat conditions. More generally he also feared that their low freeboard would prove dangerous when running on the surface with hatches open. He was also concerned about their safety when running on the surface. After the Admiralty legal department blocked his recommendation to halt their construction and allow him to remedy the most obvious design flaws, Bacon persuaded his superiors that it was necessary to order from Vickers an additional (sixth) submarine-boat of his own design. About May 1901, Bacon's status at the Admiralty was changed. He was granted the title of Inspecting Captain of Submarine-boats and given his own office inside Whitehall. At the same time his responsibilities were extended to cover all aspects of organising the submarines for the forthcoming programme of ASW experiments; finding an antidote to the submarine was still very much the Admiralty's primary objective. Later that summer the Admiralty called for volunteers to assist Bacon and in August six junior Lieutenants were selected including

Frank D. Arnold-Forster, the nephew of the Admiralty's Parliamentary Secretary. The successful candidates were sent to the Vickers yard at Barrow-in-Furness where the Holland-boats were under construction.[1]

His Majesty's Submarine-boat Number One was launched in October 1901, but an accident on the slipway delayed her completion until the new year and she did not make her first dive at sea (under the command of Lieutenant Arnold-Forster) until 6 April 1902. Anxious to recoup lost time, Captain Bacon consented to running the builders' and Navy's acceptance trials simultaneously. At the same time, the 'Number One' boat was used to train crews for the nearly completed second and third Holland craft. In August, the first three Holland-boats were finally handed over to the Royal Navy – though the exact status of the submarine-boats during this period remained nebulous as they were neither commissioned nor, by Admiralty decree, named. Bacon immediately moved 'Two' and 'Three' to Portsmouth to allow crew training to continue without interference from the builders. 'One', meanwhile, was handed over to the Torpedo School and used as a target to test the practicality of a variety of anti-submarine weapons. Much to everyone's surprise – and in certain quarters some annoyance – 'Holland One' survived the course (which included the detonation of 200 lb underwater explosive charges less than 80 yards from her hull) and in November was returned to Barrow for rebuilding.

Bacon spent the remainder of 1902 organising his embryonic 'submarine section' for further experiments and making preparations for further expansion. He bought himself this free time by convincing the Admiralty to postpone using the Holland-boats as 'clockwork mice' for training destroyers in anti-submarine techniques until he had first ascertained 'the value and capabilities of submarines' as a weapon of war. He also secured funding for a submarine depot ship, several tenders and some additional personnel. Remarkably, the Admiralty gave him everything he requested without so much as a murmur.[2] Bacon even

---

[1] The first applicants were: Lieutenants R.F.H. Mahon, Murray Sueter, H.F.C. Sinclair, F.G. Brooks, Herbert Richmond, F 'Del' Arnold-Forster and W.J.B. Law. For the first Officers and men appointed to the Submarine Service, see Appendix 1.

[2] Speculation is useless as to exactly why Bacon's requests were given such consideration by the Admiralty. Possibly, the expeditious manner in which his demands were processed reflected the Admiralty's determination to get ahead in submarines development as soon as possible. It is equally possible that Bacon's position within the Admiralty allowed him put his dockets at the head of the queue. Also, because he technically belonged to the controller's department and had an office at the Admiralty, he may have consulted his superiors and obtained their consent before he submitted his requests for additional equipment in writing – not bothering to submit requests that had been already denied – thus creating the impression that he was always successful in getting what he asked for. Probably we shall never know the reason why.

asked for and was given a better anchorage inside Portsmouth Harbour! The magnitude of the concessions given him should not be underestimated. The extra money spent on the submarine section during 1902–03 was equivalent to the Royal Navy's entire annual budget for gunnery fire-control equipment. In any case, by 30 January 1903, the material foundations of the submarine service were in place. The five Holland-boats were at last alongside their depot ship at Portsmouth and ready to commence preliminary tactical trials, with the number six boat (later designated HMS A1) nearing completion at Barrow.

* * *

In 1903, Admiralty woke up to the idea that submarine-boats could potentially be of great value to the service not just militarily but also politically. At the beginning of that year, the Prime Minister – Arthur James Balfour – established a special Cabinet sub-committee under the Duke of Devonshire to make a comprehensive review of imperial defence policy. The committee was charged with first determining the military requirements of the Empire, and then recommending where retrenchment could be safely made. The overriding aim was to save money. Since the end of the nineteenth century, the British State had been teetering on the brink of fiscal crisis. Expenditure in all areas of government activity was surging, while at the same time it was believed to be politically impossible to raise the rate of taxation. The slide into a situation where budget shortfalls became chronic was partially masked by the Boer War (1899–1902). During this period the government was able to suspend the 'balanced budget principle' and resort to borrowing. Within three years the annual cost of servicing the national debt increased by a quarter. At the end of hostilities, however, in 1902, the yoke of fiscal orthodoxy was reimposed and the Treasury obliged to balance the budget. Two factors complicated the Chancellor of the Exchequer's task: first, the refusal of the majority of the Conservative Party to consider raising extra revenue by imposing tariffs on imports; and second, a demand from the electorate – echoed by many back-bench Members of Parliament – for a cut in the rate of income tax. Given these constraints, the only possible way to balance the budget was to make deep cuts in defence spending, which at this time consumed over 50 per cent of total revenues. Hence Balfour's resolve to conduct a defence review.

The Cabinet Defence Committee began taking evidence in January 1903. First on the agenda was a consideration of the possibility of an invasion of the British Isles. As both Army and Navy claimed primacy in this area, to Balfour it seemed likely there must exist some duplication of effort. The committee established that preventing an invasion depended upon thwarting any attempt by the aggressor to seize one of 37 ports in the country. Without a deep-water port, the enemy could not land artillery, cavalry or supplies to support an assault force of infantry. The War Office opened their case by claiming that these ports were already protected by 'observation' mines offshore (ground mines placed and controlled by the Royal Engineers) and batteries of coastal artillery. The role of these forces was to buy time for a field army strong enough to repel the invaders to concentrate behind the port. While the generals admitted that the defences at some ports did need modernising and extending, they advised that the amount of extra money required would be trifling.

In reply the Admiralty argued that security from invasion rested upon the supremacy of the Royal Navy. So long as the fighting fleet remained in being, the admirals retorted, no hostile power would ever dare pass an invasion convoy across the sea. Rather than try to make port defences impregnable, the naval representatives argued, any extra money should be spent on strengthening the war fleet to ensure that the port defences would never even be tested. The debate on how best to defend the country from invasion subsequently degenerated into a squabble between the two armed forces as to which one should be given the greater slice of the defence budget. Very quickly, however, the Admiralty became concerned that members of the Cabinet found their arguments too difficult to understand. Moreover, testifying before the Cabinet Defence Committee in January, the Director of Naval Intelligence, Captain Prince Louis of Battenberg, inadvertently strengthened the War Office hand by conceding that some 'direct protection' of major ports was necessary to fend off 'minor raids' by up to 5 000 men that might conceivably slip past the Navy's patrols, and that this could be done most efficiently by the Army. The War Office representatives seized upon this slip to demand additional money from the Cabinet for updating and improving the coastal artillery and Royal Engineers mining organisation.

At about this time, it occurred to a number of junior officers at the Admiralty that perhaps the major ports could be shielded more efficiently and more cheaply by 'navy' submarines rather than the 'army' mines and guns. The chief proponent of this idea was Captain Henry Jackson, now serving as an assistant to the Director of Naval Ordnance. Jackson's idea was supported by the Captain of the Torpedo School, George Egerton. Although the Director of Naval Intelligence acknowledged the merit of the idea, he opposed it on the grounds that the Navy was a blue-water force and should have nothing to do with fixed defences. Battenberg subsequently tried to bury the idea by arranging for an interdepartmental committee to sit upon the question. However, this knavery failed to kill the idea. In October, Mr H. Oakley Arnold-Forster MP was promoted from the number two position at the Admiralty to become head of the War Office. Arnold-Forster, readers will recall, was an enthusiast for the submarine. Accordingly, one of his first acts as Secretary of State for War was to write 'unofficially' to his former chief at the Admiralty, Lord Selborne, proposing that the responsibility for port defences should be transferred to the Navy and that the mines be replaced by submarines. Arnold-Forster's proposal was not only extremely radical – this cannot be overstated – it also provoked fierce opposition from parties with vested interests inside both the naval and military bureaucracies.

During the winter of 1903, Arnold-Forster's idea rapidly gained support inside the Admiralty, first from the Senior Naval Lord, then the Controller, and then, curiously in view of the position he took earlier, the Director of Naval Intelligence. In November, the first steps were taken. Captain Bacon was instructed to survey the army mining establishments at Portsmouth, Devonport and Sheerness with a view to converting them into bases for submarines. The following month the Royal Navy agreed to take over Fort Blockhouse in Gosport. From February 1904, this became the home of the submarine service for the next 90 years. Also in December, in anticipation of a large expansion in the submarine fleet, Bacon demanded and was eventually granted help from the Constructor's department in designing a new and improved type of submarine. At this point the pace of reform faltered. Majority opinion inside the War Office and Admiralty solidified to prevent any further progress. At the same time Lord Selborne was persuaded to withdraw his support for Arnold-Forster's scheme after discovering that the devious War Minister had been secretly urging Balfour to saddle the Admiralty with responsibility for all coast defence batteries and maritime fortresses in addition to control of the corps of submarine miners.

The idea of using submarines in a key strategic role might have been stillborn if not for the efforts of two men. The patron of the 'Submarine Service' was Arthur James Balfour, the Prime Minister. During the summer of 1903, he executed a Cabinet reshuffle and appointed himself chairman of the Cabinet Defence Committee investigating the possibility of home invasion. For reasons that are still not entirely clear because of lack of documentary evidence, Balfour quickly became fascinated by the submarine. Throughout his political career he had always possessed a keen interest in naval and military technologies. In November 1903, the Prime Minister steered the Defence Committee into investigating the possibility of employing submarines to protect Britain's naval bases across the globe. The Admiralty representatives hesitated to approve this line of enquiry, by now having cause to be wary of politicians with big ideas. Balfour received much more powerful support, however, from the other 'god-father' of the 'Submarine Service', Admiral Sir John Fisher.

In September 1903, Admiral Fisher – or 'Jacky' as he was popularly known – was appointed Commander-in-Chief at Portsmouth. This made him Captain Bacon's superior officer and thus placed him in a position to read the secret reports on the progress with submarines and to consult the Inspecting Captain of Submarines. At the same time, Fisher was chosen as one of the three members of a special committee set up to consider how to overhaul the bureaucratic system at Army head-quarters. This placed him in contact with the Prime Minister and other members of the Cabinet interested in defence-related matters. Very soon thereafter, Fisher and Balfour entered into correspondence about the implications of submarine warfare and the impact these craft would have upon the conduct of naval strategy. Their letters show that by the beginning of 1904 both men had come to believe that the submarine had a central role to play in imperial defence, and that this idea was rapidly gaining hold in the minds of other influential experts in the field such as Lord Esher. They also shed important light on the evolution of Fisher's radical ideas on the application of naval force – theories he applied as Head of the Navy between 1904 and 1910. Also while serving at Portsmouth, Fisher ensured that submarines were given a fair chance in fleet manoeuvres by preventing certain senior officers from slanting the rules of engagement too far in favour of battleships. After the first series of exercises were cut short in March 1904 by the accidental loss of HM Submarine A1, Fisher loudly contradicted an assertion made by Admiral Wilson that the submarines had failed the test, and caused a more favourable report written by the junior umpires to be printed and circulated to the fleet.

In October 1904, Admiral Sir John Fisher assumed the post of Senior Naval Lord – he immediately changed the title to 'First Sea Lord' – and shortly afterwards persuaded the rest of the Board to approve (albeit with reservations) his vision of the role of the submarine. Within a fortnight the Admiralty advised the Committee of Imperial Defence (the reconstituted Cabinet Defence Committee) that it now endorsed the adoption of the submarine as the chief protection for naval bases throughout the empire. The Admiralty's sudden change of stance caught the generals at the War Office flat-footed and spluttering for a reply. Before the year ended, Fisher's skill in committee subsequently allowed the Navy to claim victory in the CID debate over which service should exercise primary responsibility for home defence. When the Cabinet's axe finally fell on the defence budget, therefore, the brunt was borne by the Army. The victory in the CID also justified a large increase in the number of submarines in the fleet, which in turn necessitated an expansion in the number of personnel required to man them.

Actually, Fisher had no intention of scattering submarines across the globe to defend the Navy's bases and coaling stations. Shortly after becoming First Sea Lord, 'radical Jack' revealed to Lord Selborne his new theory of naval warfare – the concept of flotilla defence. Fisher wanted the Royal Navy to abandon its traditional strategy of relying upon its strength in battleships to deter invasion and instead look chiefly to the flotilla (comprising destroyers and submarines) to 'deny' the narrow seas around the British Isles to all hostile warships. Relying upon the flotilla, he reasoned, would also free capital ships for deployment overseas thus enabling the Admiralty to regain the power to apply naval force in distant waters. In any case, he insisted, employing the battle fleet in home waters was impractical because of the dangers from enemy submarines and torpedo craft. Attrition of battleships cruising the narrow seas was certain to occur and with potentially disastrous consequences. In 1905, Fisher predicted that in the next war no large fleet would dare cruise the narrow European seas.

Lord Selborne was not convinced of the merits of flotilla defence. But his opposition proved to be of little consequence. In March 1905, he was replaced at the Admiralty by Lord Cawdor. The new First Lord was much more amenable and he allowed Fisher to reallocate new construction resources away from big ships towards the building of more flotilla craft and especially submarines. By 1907, sufficient numbers were available to implement the strategy of flotilla defence. In April that year, the Fisher Board executed a major redistribution of the fleet which resulted in ten battleships and eleven large armoured cruisers being placed in reserve and their crews turned over to man the flotilla. The change created a storm of protest at what was perceived to be a weakening of the fleet. For political reasons, however, Fisher refused to explain to his critics the exact purpose of the redistribution. The main reason for his silence was that he knew the majority of naval officers, had the concept of flotilla defence been explained to them, would not have approved of such a departure from traditional naval strategy. As a result he was barred from publicising that the reductions in the battle fleet had allowed the number of flotilla craft in commission to be increased, and that in his opinion the result was an overall strengthening of Britain's naval defences. Even those supporters who were privy to this knowledge were themselves divided over the wisdom of introducing the change so quickly. Unfortunately the one officer who had to be told of the new strategic policy – the fleet commander-in-chief, Lord Charles Beresford – was violently opposed. Beresford subsequently refused point blank to accept any war orders from the Admiralty that prescribed a flotilla defence strategy. The dispute between Beresford and Fisher over strategic policy became more and more acrimonious and in the end resulted in both being forced into early retirement – the former in March 1909 and the latter in January 1910.

The Personnel

The Admiralty's first call for volunteers to join the Submarine Service met with a disappointing response. Just thirteen Lieutenants applied for the six available slots for officers of which only one, F.D. Arnold-Forster, was qualified in Torpedo. And within a year he asked for and was given a transfer back to general service. Among enlisted men the response was even less enthusiastic. There were sufficient volunteers to crew only three of the five Holland-boats. When submarine-boats 'Four' and 'Five' began their trials at Barrow during the winter of 1902, therefore, the Admiralty was forced to draft men from the battleship *Jupiter* to bring the submarine section up to establishment.[1] In the new year measures were taken to make service in submarines appear more attractive to volunteers. From 1903, officers and men on the books of submarine depot ships were entitled to draw submarine pay – or 'hard lying money' as it was called. Officers in command of submarines were in addition authorised to draw 'command pay' – an allowance that effectively doubled their take-home pay. Bacon insisted this extra incentive to officers was necessary because he anticipated a high rate of turnover among submarine captains. He believed that the burden of commanding these vessels would be so great that officers would be able to stand the strain for no more than two years, and would then have to be returned to general service. If he was correct then turnover would indeed be high and the Submarine Service would require a constant flow of new men. Bacon thus hoped that the prospect of receiving command pay would ensure an adequate supply of volunteers. Readers might note, however, that Bacon's successors were to hold exactly the

[1] HMS *Jupiter*: 'Majestic'-class battleship (14 900 tons), laid down Clydebank October 1894 and completed 1897. Four 12-in. and twelve 6-in. guns. 18 knots.

opposite view and tried to keep experienced officers for as long as possible.

The Admiralty never intended the payment of hard lying money to remain permanent. Back in the 1880s, similar incentives had been offered to crews of the first torpedo boats but had been swiftly withdrawn once the craft were no longer regarded as dangerous and experimental. Thereafter, service in the torpedo fleet was regarded by the lower deck as no more onerous than a commission in a large warship. Service in submarines, however, never came to be regarded in the same light. Numbers of volunteers among enlisted men did not rise to a level where the extra incentives could be discontinued. Furthermore, in direct contrast with his views on officers, Captain Bacon became convinced that retention of already trained enlisted personnel, especially the skilled higher rates, was far more important than recruiting new volunteers. They did not want a constant flow of new recruits, in other words. They feared that payment of hard lying money could not be withdrawn without the risk of provoking an exodus of trained Petty Officers and Engine Room Artificers from the submarine service.

Pay Scales in 1906

(a) Officers' Gross Daily Pay in shillings (before deductions).

Rank	Basic Pay	Additional submarine pay	Additional pay for command of submarine	Total pay in submarines	Total pay in destroyers	Total pay as Lieutenant of battleship
Lieutenant (4 years' seniority)	10/0	6/0	3/9	19/9	10/0	10/0
Lieutenant (T) (4 years' seniority)	11/0	6/0	3/9	20/9	16/3[a]	13/ to 15/0[b]
Lieutenant (8 years' seniority)	12/0	6/0	3/9	21/9	17/3[a]	12/ or 14/6[c]

a With command pay.
b Lieutenants (T) received additional pay ranging from 2/0 to 4/0 per day.
c Senior Lieutenant of armoured warship entitled to additional 2/6 per day.

(b) Ratings' Gross Daily Pay in shillings (before deductions).

Rank	Basic pay	Submarine pay	If in charge of engines	Total pay in submarines	Total pay in destroyers
Chief Petty Officer (2 years)	2/8	2/6		5/2	3/2
Petty Officer (2 years)	2/2	2/6		4/8	2/8
CERA (2nd class)	7/0	2/6	1/0	10/6	8/6
ERA (4th class)	5/6	2/6		8/0	6/0
Stoker	2/0	2/0		4/0	2/4$^1/_2$
Able Seaman	1/7	2/0		3/7	1/11$^1/_2$

Successive Inspecting Captains of Submarines were of the opinion that the safe operation of submarine-boats depended upon minimising the possibility of human error. This required men that were not only highly skilled but also highly trained. Stringent standards were maintained by accepting only those volunteers who were assessed as 'above average' during the initial acquaintance course and afterwards submitting them to a period of intense training. Even then, the new men were incorporated into the service only very slowly. Inspecting Captains were careful not to dilute existing crews with too many recruits at once. As much as possible, they tried to keep experienced crews together and to accept only enough volunteers to replace natural wastage plus a margin to allow for expansion. Captain Bacon encountered many difficulties in keeping his best men. First and foremost he had to persuade them to remain in what was an unhealthy and hazardous occupation. This was accomplished most easily by continuing to pay hard lying money. In addition, there are indications that Bacon and his successors deliberately fostered a less formal, and therefore more attractive, working environment than existed elsewhere in the Navy. Dress regulations on board submarines and depot ships, for instance, were much more relaxed. Sports facilities (soccer pitches) were laid out close by on shore and the men encouraged to use them – though it is true that there were medical benefits to this practice. Informality between officers and the lower deck was tolerated to a degree that would have been unthinkable in a surface ship. Perhaps most importantly, men were usually allowed to go home after 4 p.m. The significance of this was that the majority of submariners were drawn from the Portsmouth division (where the submarines were based) and that a large proportion of the higher rates was married. The additional money for serving in submarines, indeed, allowed many officers and seamen to get married – or, according to legend, buy a motorcycle instead! (Motorcycles, perhaps, were found easier to maintain and offered a less bumpy ride.) In any case, submariners were given the money and time to indulge their interests.

Second, Bacon had to fight the civil servants running the Admiralty's M (manning) branch. Keeping men in one place was administratively complicated because, amongst other reasons, men in submarines were unavailable for rotation overseas. According to regulations, indeed, submariners were not part of the seagoing fleet; on paper, all submarines were attached to Portsmouth command as part of the reserve. So long as the numbers of men involved remained small, the headache of administering two personnel lists was manageable. But once numbers rose above 500, the civil servants began to protest. Bacon also had to fight with the Admiralty bureaucracy over the interpretation of the regulations governing promotions. At the beginning of the twentieth century, the career path in the Royal Navy led through the battleship fleet. More fundamentally, the rules for promotion worked against those men who chose to remain in submarines. Even when men were happy to remain in submarines the best (usually the most ambitious) were compelled after only a short period to leave the service in order to advance their careers. To qualify for promotion, both officers and men were obliged to serve minimum periods of service in seagoing warships. Service on board warships in reserve did not count towards sea time. Furthermore, promotion to highest grades depended upon experience in the larger types of warships and completion of qualification courses at the appropriate shore establishment. According to the regulations, none of these conditions could be met by service in submarines. The only solutions, advised Captain Bacon, were to modify the application of the rules, or change them, or allow exceptions to be made.

In August 1904, the Admiralty appointed a special committee of experts to consider possible solutions to the Submarine Service's recruitment and retention problems. The committee was compelled reluctantly to endorse all of Bacon's recommendations. Subsequently, the rules of promotion were modified so as to allow service in submarines to count as experience in a seagoing fleet, and the Inspecting Captain of Submarines was empowered to promote ratings to acting rank (with full pay) without their first having to attend a training school. Finally, and most significantly, the Admiralty decreed that the Inspecting Captain could retain all the personnel presently serving in submarines for another two years. Thereafter, officers and men who had served in submarines for five years would be rotated back to general service. After serving two years in a big ship, these men would be allowed to return to the Submarine Service for a period of no more than three years. The idea behind this 'general service' rule was to prevent submariners from becoming a service apart from the Royal Navy, qualified and available only for service in submarines. But the huge expansion in the numbers of submarines in commission after 1905, and the consequent need to form more crews, compelled the Admiralty to waive this rule in the case of key enlisted personnel.

Between 1906 and 1910, officers and men serving in submarines increasingly regarded themselves as belonging to the Submarine Service. The physical hardships endured by all, the high levels of skill and competence demanded, and the unique relationship (at that time) between officers and men all helped to forge this identity. But perhaps

even more important was the exclusiveness of the group. In most warships, an average of 20 per cent of the crew was changed each year. In
submarines, by contrast, the turnover in personnel was almost non-
existent. The officers and the men knew each other; they worked side
by side for literally years. To all intents and purposes, in other words,
the Submarine Service was a 'closed shop' – almost a separate branch
of the Royal Navy. While Fisher remained First Sea Lord, this notion of
'a service within a service' was tolerated. Not even 'Radical Jack', however, would endorse the issuing of a special badge – such as a pair of
dolphins – to denote those qualified for service in submarines. Nor did
Fisher's administration approve repeated requests from Inspecting
Captains of Submarines that officers qualified to command boats be
distinguished in the Navy List with a special mark next to their name
like Navigating or Gunnery officers. Many senior officers at this time –
probably the majority – distrusted the emergence of specialist branches
within the Royal Navy in much the same way as they disapproved of the
staff course at the Naval War College. Both were resented as elitist and
seen as threatening to undermine the homogeneous character of the
Royal Navy officer corps.

When Sir Arthur Wilson became First Sea Lord in January 1910, he
at once took steps to 'reunify' the naval service. He first tried to end the
payment of hard lying money, but the old problem of recruitment made
this impossible. And his attempts to end the 'volunteers only' policy
proved no more successful. In August 1910, however, Wilson
succeeded in appointing his nominee to the post of Inspecting Captain
of Submarines and charged him to break the closed shop of the
Submarine Service. Until then it had been customary for the incumbent
to choose his own successor. Bacon had chosen Edgar Lees, Lees had
chosen Sydney Hall, and Hall had Frank Brandt in mind to be the next
Inspecting Captain of Submarines.[1] (All four officers, incidentally, were
torpedo specialists and qualified to command submarines.) Wilson's
choice, by contrast, Captain Roger Keyes, was an officer with no previous experience of either torpedoes or submarines. He was, in his own
words, a mere 'Salt Horse'. Once installed in office, however, Keyes
very quickly recognised the merits of encouraging the identity of the
Submarine Service and keeping it an all-volunteer branch of the service. He also exercised the prerogative of the Inspecting Captain to
retain key personnel scheduled to be rotated back to general service
thereby reinforcing the exclusiveness of the service. In short, Keyes

[1] Capt. Frank Brandt was killed in action at the Battle of Coronel (1914) while
commanding the armoured cruiser HMS *Monmouth*.

made no changes to the schemes of training and organisation established by his predecessors.

Submarine Development

So long as the submarine was slow with limited endurance, the opinion of the majority of naval officers continued to regard it as an essentially defensive weapon and thus of limited use to the Royal Navy. In 1905, however, the Admiralty Submarine Committee completed the plans for a submarine capable of sustained patrol on a distant European coast, transforming it into an offensive instrument. The D-type submarine marked a departure from previous designs in two important respects. First, the ballast tanks were moved outside the pressure hull, thus leaving room inside for more crew, fuel and torpedoes. The second important improvement was the fitting of diesel engines. These were not only safer to operate than the gasoline engines used previously, they were also far more fuel efficient. For a given volume of fuel, a submarine propelled by diesels could proceed twice as far as a vessel driven by gasoline engines. Yet though the Admiralty approved the plans for the D-type in 1905, there was a twelve months' delay in laying down the prototype. And another three years were to pass before D-type submarines were built in any numbers. During the interim, the Royal Navy continued to acquire more vessels of the superseded C class.

Initially, the Admiralty's hesitation in commencing the project was caused by difficulties in adapting the diesel for use in submarines. The high-power, lightweight engines available in 1905–06 were simply not reliable enough for naval use. But this was not the sole reason for delay. During 1906, the Admiralty came under intense pressure from the new Liberal Government to reduce the construction budget. At the same time there was a widespread feeling inside Whitehall that Vickers was exploiting the Navy. In 1902, the Admiralty had awarded the large armaments firm the exclusive rights to supply the Royal Navy with submarines. The so-called 'monopoly contract' was to last seven years and in return Vickers promised to expand their building capacity sufficiently to allow up to 25 new submarines to be laid down in any one year, and agreed to build only for the Royal Navy. Ever since, however, Vickers had raised their prices at every opportunity. Their initial tender for building D1, for instance, was a third more than the Admiralty had been expecting to pay. In response, the Admiralty refused to order the prototype D-class submarine until Vickers agreed to vary the terms of the 'monopoly contract' and to license the Navy to build submarines in the Royal Dockyards. The Admiralty's objective here was not to compete with Vickers or to expand submarine building capacity in the country, but to monitor and keep down prices.

The first to see the potential of the patrol submarine was Admiral Sir John Fisher. When he had first conceived his flotilla defence strategy, France had been the most likely enemy and the narrow waters of the English Channel were seen as the main theatre of operations. But once Whitehall's strategic attention shifted towards Germany, the strategy of flotilla defence appeared less practical. Although the B and C classes could operate up to the German coast they could not do so for long: but the D-type (and the projected E-type) were estimated to be capable of remaining inside the Heligoland Bight for up to a week. In late 1908, Fisher drafted what was perhaps his most prescient memorandum on submarine warfare – 'The Submarine Question'. In this paper he predicted that the submarine would dominate the war inside the North Sea, to the extent that there would be no role for the surface battle fleet. Admittedly Fisher qualified this assertion by pointing out that it would be some years before patrol submarines would be available in sufficient numbers to 'saturate' the North Sea; though at the same time he worked to minimise this period by securing additional money in 1909, to fund an increase in the production of D-class submarines from six to 20 vessels a year. But in January 1910 he was forced to quit the office of First Sea Lord and his successor, Admiral of the Fleet Sir Arthur Wilson, promptly reallocated the extra money for submarines to the battleship fleet.

Fisher received limited support from other Admiralty officials for his prediction that the German naval threat could be contained with a flotilla defence strategy in the North Sea. Even his closest supporters, among them Rear Admiral Sir John Jellicoe, the flag officer destined to command the fleet for most of the First World War, remained a proponent of the continued viability of the surface battle fleet. Jellicoe did agree, however, that 'oversea' submarines could play a vital role in the next war. But his vision differed greatly from that held by his mentor; Jellicoe wanted to see the development of a submarine with high surface speed capable of working with the battle fleet. Moreover, he was not alone. Vice-Admiral Sir Francis Bridgeman (C-in-C Home Fleet, 1906–08) and Admiral Sir William May (C-in-C Home Fleet and Channel Squadron, 1909–11) as well as Rear Admiral Alexander Bethell (DNI, 1909–12) amongst others, were keen to see the development of the fleet submarine. Against them stood Sydney Hall, the Inspecting Captain of Submarines 1906–10. Hall, a partisan for the patrol type, opposed the fleet-submarine concept and argued his position vigorously to prevent his limited construction budget being squandered (in his opinion) on their development. High surface speed submarines, he warned, although technically possible to build, would be highly unstable when running on the surface and possess almost no underwater endurance. Until 1910, Hall's views prevailed but after Jellicoe was appointed Controller and Fisher was replaced by Wilson, the fleet-submarine lobby became too strong to resist.

At the end of 1910, Hall was dismissed as Inspecting Captain of Submarines.[1] His successor, Roger Keyes, immediately endorsed the development of fleet submarines. The pressure for the Royal Navy to build fast submarines had been given renewed impetus earlier that year by intelligence reports that suggested at least two European rivals had made a start in this direction. According to the Director of Naval Construction, the DNI's information indicated that both France and Italy were better placed than Britain in the race to build an efficient fleet submarine. One report claimed that a French diesel manufacturer had achieved a technological breakthrough and was now capable of building engines three times more powerful than British-built units. Another stated that the Italian firm of Fiat had invented a more sophisticated hull-form that was admirably suited for surface speed. It was the latter which excited most attention at Whitehall. What Fiat had done was to develop a pressure hull that was heart-shaped rather than circular in cross-section, which allowed more machinery and equipment to be carried, and to encase the pressure hull in an outer shell that was shaped to maximise surface speed. The design and hull forms of British submarines, in contrast, favoured underwater performance. Supported by Keyes, in 1911 the Admiralty cancelled the next generation of patrol submarines (a 1000-ton design that was revived in 1916 and built as the L-class) and instead arranged for a British firm to build a Fiat-designed experimental submarine for the Royal Navy. The Italians refused to sell just one boat (correctly guessing that the British merely wished to copy their design features) and insisted on a contract for six. The Admiralty was compelled to agree. In February 1912, Keyes submitted a report to the new First Lord of the Admiralty, Winston Churchill, that called for the Navy to abandon the production of patrol submarines in order to develop the fast submarine as quickly as possible. Churchill agreed that

---

[1] Hall was dismissed for two reasons: first his continued opposition to the fleet submarine programme; second, Sir Arthur Wilson discovered Hall had been negotiating with Alfred Yarrow to head Yarrow Shipbuilding's efforts to break into the submarine building industry.

henceforth the fleet submarines should be given priority, but directed that patrol submarines would continue to be built – albeit in much smaller numbers and with no improvements.

The Royal Navy's decision to shift from the production of patrol submarines to the development of fleet-boats was, in light of subsequent events, most unfortunate. As a direct result, at the beginning of the First World War the Navy found itself chronically short of modern patrol submarines capable of sustained operations in the North Sea. In the interim, moreover, the submarine manufacturing industry in Britain was seriously dislocated. Arguably, the most damaging consequence was the ending of the special relationship between Messrs. Vickers and the Admiralty. When Vickers learned that the Admiralty was trying to buy Italian submarines and French engines their lawyers immediately protested at this violation of the monopoly agreement. In March 1911, the Admiralty accordingly notified the firm that they intended to terminate the contract. This decision was confirmed in October, although a notification clause kept both parties bound together for another two years. After 1913, Vickers were free to build submarines for lucrative export markets. When, therefore, the Admiralty tried to revise their construction policy and buy more patrol submarines after being disappointed by the performance of the foreign engines and hulls they had purchased, they found the Vickers building facilities almost fully occupied.

*   *   *

After Fisher's retirement in early 1910, the Board of Admiralty abandoned the concept of flotilla defence and reverted to a more orthodox operational strategy that relied upon an overwhelming fleet of battleships. Between 1910 and 1913, accordingly, the war strength of the Home Fleets was increased by 50 per cent – from 22 battleships to 33 battleships. Additionally, the Commander-in-Chief demanded and was given large numbers of smaller craft – mainly the new-model light cruisers and big destroyers – with which to screen the battle fleet from hostile torpedo craft. Attaching support craft directly to the battle fleet was a new and controversial development in naval tactics. Difficulties experienced in handling such large formations of warships during the 1912 and 1913 manoeuvres, prompted officers such as Admiral Prince Louis of Battenberg to question the practicality of the new 'Grand Fleet of Battle' tactical system. He and others argued that there were now too many ships for the fleet admiral to control effectively using existing methods of communication.

There were other reasons to question the viability of the 'Grand Fleet of Battle' strategy. Driven by large battleship programmes, spending on warship construction appeared to be spiralling out of control. In 1910, battleships were priced at roughly £1.8 million; the average cost of the four *Queen Elizabeth*-class ordered under the 1912 programme was £2.7 million. In addition, the burden of maintaining the additional capital ships in commission was hardly less onerous than that of building them. Each super-dreadnought required a crew of 1000 trained seamen. Moreover, whereas battleships could be built in two or three years, it took at least six years to train recruits to operate the highly sophisticated machinery with which they were fitted. As the Grand Fleet of Battle grew in numbers, as Treasury protests grew louder, and as the strain on the Royal Navy's personnel resources increased, Fisher's strategy of flotilla defence appeared increasingly attractive. For the price of one battleship the Navy could buy 20 submarines, and 20 submarines absorbed fewer men than a battleship. Finally, the annual maintenance cost of the submarines was considerably less. In July 1912, Fisher tried to persuade the Committee of Imperial Defence to overrule the Board of Admiralty's resistance to his plan for the battle squadron in the Mediterranean to be replaced with one or two flotillas of submarines.

In June 1913, the First Lord of the Admiralty, Winston Churchill, ordered a comprehensive review of the Navy's submarine policy in the light of immediate operational requirements. Over the previous twelve months, a growing number of officers at Whitehall, such as Captain George Ballard – the Director of the Naval War Staff Operations Division and a long-time disciple of Jacky Fisher – concluded that 20 submarines in European waters might possess a greater deterrence value and prove far more useful than one more battleship. In July, Churchill circulated a paper written by Ballard arguing that the proper response to further dreadnought construction by the central powers was to build more submarines. They cost less to build than battleships, could be built more quickly and were cheaper to run. Ballard wanted the Royal Navy to develop the capability to impose close blockade of the entire German and especially Austro-Hungarian coastlines using submarines. To blockade Germany alone, he estimated, 36 patrol submarines would be required. The problem, he complained, was that the Navy was no longer building craft that were suitable for this mission. A second paper, by the Chief of the War Staff, Vice-Admiral Henry Jackson, echoed Ballard's protest and asked the Commodore of Submarines to explain his construction policy. Roger Keyes responded by reminding those serving at Whitehall that he had been asked to develop the fleet submarine. He further reminded them that while this project had been made top priority, the Admiralty had not given him sufficient additional resources. The result, Keyes explained, had been a cut in the construction of patrol submarines in order to build experimental fleet-boats.

Churchill's response to these papers was ambivalent. On the one hand he accepted the War Staff's argument for the need to acquire more patrol submarines; on the other his sympathies lay with developing the fleet submarine as quickly as possible. At the end of August 1913, for example, the First Lord approved the purchase of another highly experimental underwater craft powered by steam turbines. The only practical solution, reasoned the First Lord, was to find sufficient funds to pay for the construction of both types in adequate numbers. This was easier said than done, however. Churchill knew the Treasury would not sanction a further increase in the naval estimates, which meant the money would have to be found by cutting the production of destroyers, cruisers or possibly battleships. Churchill concluded that substituting battleships for submarines could be countenanced only when a working fleet submarine had been developed. Until then, increased submarine production would have to be funded by cutting the number of new destroyers. The rest of the Board, however, was unhappy with this proposal.

In December 1913, the Admiralty was prompted to reconsider its submarine policy afresh after Admiral of the Fleet Lord Fisher of Kilverstone presented Winston Churchill with a paper containing his views on the importance of the submarine in future naval wars. Since the beginning of the year, Fisher had been growing increasingly disturbed at the magnitude of the Navy's effort to develop the fleet submarine, which he regarded as a serious misallocation of resources. He was also afraid that the current First Sea Lord, Admiral Battenberg, did not appreciate the extent to which the submarine had changed the conditions of war in the narrow seas around the British Isles. Fisher's paper contained three main themes: first, that the submarine had supplanted the battleship as the decisive naval weapon – at least in European waters; second, that the proper role for the submarine was to blockade and deny the seas to potential enemies; and third, that as a consequence of the fleet-submarine development programme, the Royal Navy was woefully short of modern long-range patrol types. The paper also contained a number of subsidiary themes, the most important of which was his analysis that submarines would inevitably be used to attack maritime commerce. Although historians have been much impressed by Fisher's prescience here (in light of the events of the First World War) this observation was neither original nor particularly controversial.[1] What really excited Fisher's readers was his insistence that submarines would be compelled to sink their prey without warning. But to reiterate, this was not the central message of the paper.

On 9 December, Winston Churchill presented copies of Fisher's paper to his senior advisers. After much discussion, in January 1914, the Sea Lords nervously approved Churchill's new idea that two of the four battleships scheduled to be laid down under the 1914–15 programme should be secretly cancelled and the money reallocated to boosting the construction of patrol submarines, light cruisers and other torpedo craft. Dropping these two battleships from the programme meant that for the first time in 25 years, the Board of Admiralty was content to maintain a smaller battle fleet than the combined strength of the next two strongest naval powers. This change amounted to a fundamental departure in British naval policy and a renunciation of the battleship as the measure of relative naval strength. Lingering uncertainty at the wisdom of taking such a drastic step induced the Sea Lords to postpone giving their formal approval to the substitution policy – as it was referred to – until the last possible moment. The Board's reticence notwithstanding, warning was given to the submarine construction industry to expect large orders. The six-month interval also allowed Churchill (with Fisher's help) to bolster the Admiralty's resolve and recruit more allies. In May 1914, Admiral Frederick Tower Hamilton was appointed Second Sea Lord on the condition that he endorsed the substitution of submarines for battleships. Hamilton did so willingly. In July 1914, Churchill submitted the plan to the Board for final approval. Before anything more was achieved, however, the Admiralty was overtaken by events. On 4 August 1914, Britain went to war with Germany.

Submarines at War

At the beginning of the First World War, the personnel of the Submarine Service consisted of 168 officers and 1250 ratings. There were in addition 20–30 qualified officers and approximately 300 trained seamen serving in the main fleet. At the head of the service stood Roger Keyes, who was ordered by the Admiralty to remain in charge instead of the Commodore-designate Captain William 'Blinker' Hall. Of the 62 completed submarine-boats under Keyes's command, 15 were classified as oversea boats capable of sustained operations on the

---

[1] See the series of articles entitled 'The Influence of the Submarine Upon Naval Policy', in *The Naval Review*, vol. 1 (1913), pp. 256–61, 396–402; vol. 2 (1914), pp. 47–52. The anonymous author of these articles was Capt. Sydney Hall.

German coast. Most of the remainder were coastal submarines of the B and C types; although quite capable of crossing the North Sea, their poor endurance and questionable habitability meant they were incapable of patrolling the Heligoland Bight for more than a day or two and even then only in fair weather. In August 1914, the 15 available D- and E-class patrol submarines were grouped into the Eighth Submarine Flotilla alongside HMS *Maidstone* and based at Harwich. When hostilities commenced, despite an objection by Keyes, the submarines of the Eighth Flotilla were deployed to patrol the Heligoland Bight. On 6 August, HM Submarines E6 and E8 returned from a reconnaissance of the German Coast to complete the first-ever war patrols.

The first month of the war contained no real surprises for the officers of the Submarine Service. The hazards of operating close to the enemy coast in the face of nimble patrol craft and mines had been anticipated, as had the difficulty in finding targets. This is not to say that all went as expected. The shortage of oversea submarines meant that the available boats were worked much harder than had been anticipated and as a result their mechanical reliability suffered. It was found necessary to strip and rebuild the diesel engines each time a boat returned from patrol. Assistance from local civilian engineering firms allowed the work to be completed within three days – a period which allowed the boat crews sufficient time to rest and recuperate. A more worrying problem emerged with the torpedoes. On 23 August, Lieutenant Commander Godfrey Herbert commanding HMS/m D5 fired two heater torpedoes at point blank range towards a small and slow-moving German cruiser and watched both pass under. After other frustrated submarine officers complained they too had apparently missed easy targets, an investigation was made and a design flaw discovered. Basically, the torpedo depth-keeping apparatus (which had been designed for relatively slow 30-knot weapons) was too sensitive for the latest generation of torpedoes that could be set for speeds up to 45 knots, and caused them to undulate through the water. The same mechanism was also responsible for most torpedoes not picking up their set depth after launching until they had advanced at least 500 yards. Not until the very end of the war was this problem rectified to the satisfaction of submarine officers. During the interim, captains were advised not to shoot at small, light-draught vessels at close range, and also not to use the high speed setting.

By the end of the second month of war, September 1914, it became apparent that large-scale submarine operations in the Heligoland Bight were both dangerous and unproductive. There were too many anti-submarine craft (including submarines), extensive minefields laid by both sides, and too few targets. British submarines had made just 11 attacks and scored only one success: the light cruiser *Hela* was sunk on 13 September by Lieutenant Commander Max Horton. After the loss of HMS/m E3, the victim of a torpedo from U-27, Keyes directed that regular patrols inside the North Sea should be avoided and that submarines should remain submerged during daylight hours. The question of how best to exploit the Royal Navy's handful of oversea submarines was placed high on the agenda at a conference of senior fleet and Admiralty officers held on board the fleet flagship, HMS *Iron Duke*, on 17 September. During the meeting, Winston Churchill asked Keyes if it would be practical to move several to a base in the Baltic Sea. The idea was an old one and had been conceived by Admiral Fisher at least three years before. Despite concerns voiced at the difficulties of navigating submerged through waters suspected of being mined, and the legality of passing submarines through Danish territorial waters, the meeting nevertheless agreed that two boats might be sent on a 'raid' into the Baltic to attack German battleships known to be conducting gunnery practice off the eastern entrance to the Kiel Canal. On 10 October, Keyes counter-proposed that two boats might be sent on a less ambitious foray to attack the German cruisers guarding the entrance to the Kattegat. The suggestion was rejected.

On 15 October, amidst much confusion, three submarines were dispatched to the Baltic. They were: HM Submarines E1 (Lieutenant Commander Noel Lawrence); E9, (Lieutenant Commander Max Horton DSO); and E11 (Lieutenant Commander Martin Nasmith). Their orders were straightforward: pass into the Baltic, seek out the German Fleet at exercise, sink the battleships, proceed to the Russian port of Libau for refuelling, then return to the UK. The mission was expected to last approximately two weeks. Lawrence and Horton successfully penetrated the Baltic, but Nasmith, having been delayed with engine trouble, was prevented from following them in by a swarm of German anti-submarine forces that had been alerted by an unsuccessful attack on a light cruiser by Lawrence. E11 was obliged return home. In the meantime, E1 and E9 failed to locate the German battleships and running low on fuel proceeded to the Russian port of Libau. Shortly after they were greeted by an astonished Russian Admiral, the Admiralty decreed they would remain in the Baltic under the orders of the Russian fleet commander – Admiral von Essen – and only informed the Commodore of Submarines afterwards of their decision. Ice prevented the submarines from mounting any further operations until after the New Year. Not until April 1915 did operations resume.

The next important event was the Emergency Construction Programme. Since the beginning of the war, the Admiralty had been desperate to acquire more submarines. A brief survey by the Controller of available shipbuilding capacity in the country, however, convinced the Board that no more than eight additional craft could be laid down. Although the Submarine Service tried to increase the aggregate number of North Sea patrols by employing coastal units, as expected they were quickly found to be unequal to the task during the winter months. Only patrol submarines were really suitable. It seemed that nothing more could be done to increase the available force. Then on 31 October 1914, Admiral Lord Fisher returned to the post of First Sea Lord. Rejecting the findings of the Controller's department, Fisher informed Churchill that his contacts in the industry assured him that at least 20 more submarines could be laid down at once and completed within twelve months. Three days later, Fisher convened a special meeting of naval administrators and shipbuilding executives to discuss exactly how many could be ordered and to apportion contracts. Fisher informed the assembly that in order to speed delivery of the submarines, all parties were authorised to dispense with normal bureaucratic procedures and even the paperwork. He told them: the Navy wanted submarines – as soon as possible – and regardless of cost. Fisher directed the shipbuilding representatives that if they encountered any obstruction or problem they were to ignore the usual chain of command and phone his special assistant – former Inspecting Captain of Submarines Sydney Hall. Turning next to the subject of manning, Fisher ordered the Second Sea Lord and N (manning) Branch to ensure that trained crews would be ready for the new submarines as soon as they were completed.

Alas for the historian, the Whitehall bureaucrats apparently took Fisher at his word. The Admiralty archives contain only a handful of documents on the design and building of submarines during the First World War, and almost none on the wartime expansion and administration of the Submarine Service. Similarly, the surviving files created by the Commodore of Submarines and his staff hold few clues as to how they achieved a fourfold increase in submarine personnel without compromising the standards of crew efficiency that before the war were held to be essential to the efficient and safe operation of submarine boats. It would be interesting to learn, for instance, why and how at the beginning of the war large numbers of untrained Royal Naval Reserve officers were drafted into the service, later supplemented with volunteers from the Royal Canadian Navy, and even hostilities-only Royal Naval Volunteer Reservists. In short, there is an almost complete set of war patrol reports in the archives but little else.

To resume: after Fisher adjourned the meeting on 3 November 1914, he contacted the American financier and industrialist Charles Schwab and asked him to supply the Royal Navy with submarines to be built in the United States.[1] Schwab agreed and promised to deliver within eight months 20 craft of a type approved by the American Navy. Eventually the US Navy's 'H' design of 1911 was selected, not because it was the best available, but because the Navy Department objected to their more modern designs being given to the British. In any case, this brought the total number of submarines ordered by the Royal Navy since the beginning of the war up to 63. In December, preparations were made to build 42 more boats in the state-owned Royal Dockyards. This number was curtailed, however, after Churchill questioned whether the Navy really needed so many. On reflection, Fisher agreed it would be better to rely upon the private sector to supply the Navy's immediate requirements. The Dockyards would be better employed developing and building new experimental types, beginning with the J class.

The year 1914 closed with a spectacular success for the Submarine Service. Since the entry of Turkey into the war on the side of the central powers, the British and French navies had maintained a flotilla of submarines off the entrance to the Dardanelles. On 13 December, Lieutenant Norman Holbrook navigated his primitive (1904 vintage) coastal submarine HMS/m B11 through the enemy minefields guarding the straits and attacked several large warships known to be lying in a bay used by the Turkish Navy as a forward anchorage. Despite encountering far more mines than expected, vicious cross currents, and patches of fresh water that plunged the submarine to the limit of its safe diving depth, he successfully torpedoed the 10 000 ton battleship *Messudiah* and returned.[2] For this action Norman Holbrook was awarded the Victoria Cross.[3]

The year 1915 began slowly for the Submarine Service. The vessels of the Eighth Flotilla kept up the systematic and increasingly monotonous patrol of the Heligoland Bight. Few submarines were rewarded with a fleeting glimpse of the enemy and fewer still found themselves in a position to attack. After March 1915, the odds against making a successful torpedo attack on an enemy ship were considerably lengthened after the Prime Minister issued directions that extreme care must be exercised when attacking merchant ships. The new 'rules of

---

[1] Charles Michael Schwab (1862–1939): President, US Steel, 1901–03; Chairman, Bethlehem Steel, 1904–39; Director-General, Emergency Fleet Corporation, 1917–18.
[2] *Messudiah*: classified by Jane's *Fighting Ships* 1914 as battleship. Laid down 1874 but reconstructed at Genoa in 1902. Two 9.2-in. and twelve 6-in. guns. 16 knots.
[3] Gazetted 22 December 1914.

engagement' were so strict as to make attacks on blockade runners – such as freighters carrying iron ore from Norway to Germany – almost impossible. Life in the coastal patrol was even more tedious. After the Scarborough raid, the coastal submarine flotillas were broken up and the boats formed into groups of three and scattered along the east coast to guard against further bombardments of coastal towns by the High Sea Fleet. Although their primary role remained coastal defence, they were also used to train and sift new officers and crewmen. Those who graduated were then posted to a patrol submarine to gain extra experience before being transferred to man one of the submarines under construction.

The two submarines in the Baltic could not recommence patrols until late April owing to danger from ice. Once at sea, they began to find ample targets, but owing to unreliable torpedoes scored few hits. Not until the autumn, after the Admiralty had sent five more E-class boats and a consignment of new torpedoes, did the British submarines make their presence felt in the Baltic. In August, a torpedo hit on the battle cruiser *Moltke* by Noel Lawrence in HMS/m E1 persuaded the German navy to withdraw its support for the army's attack on the town of Riga. And in October, Lieutenant Commander Francis Cromie in E19 sank eight merchant ships in one patrol – all according to the letter of prize regulations. The following month the charismatic Max Horton found his eye and together with Cromie (E19), Robert Halahan (E18), and Charles Goodhart (E8) they began sinking merchant ships in large numbers, stemming the flow of Norwegian iron ore to German steel-works and compelling the German navy to reallocate warships for escort duties. Max Horton, the darling of the British press, quickly became dubbed 'Emperor of the Baltic' and the Baltic renamed 'Horton's Sea', but it was Francis Cromie who deserved most of the credit. Lawrence and Horton were recalled in 1916, leaving Cromie in command of the flotilla until he was murdered in 1918 by Russian revolutionaries.

In the Mediterranean, meanwhile, the Turkish reply to the sinking of the *Messudiah* was to sow more mines in the Dardanelles Straits and withdraw their remaining heavy units to Constantinople. This placed them well beyond the reach of the B-class submarines patrolling off-shore. At the end of January 1915, after the Cabinet War Council voted to dispatch an expeditionary force to capture the Straits, the Admiralty sent four E-class patrol submarines as reinforcements. This addition to the east Mediterranean flotilla left England on 27 March and arrived at Malta on 5 April 1915. While the Army made their ill-fated preparations for landing on the Gallipoli peninsula, the Navy attempted to pass the oversea submarines up the heavily defended Straits and into the Sea of Marmora where they would be in a position to interdict the Turkish army's supply lines. On 17 April, Lieutenant Commander Theodore S. Brodie in E15 made the first attempt to run the gauntlet but he fell victim to the unpredictable cross-currents; E15 grounded in front of a fort and was destroyed. The second attempt was made by Lieutenant Commander Henry G. Stoker, commanding the Australian submarine AE2. Although Stoker managed to negotiate the Straits and reach the Marmora, ultimately he was no more successful. None of AE2's six torpedoes found their mark, and during the last attack mechanical problems forced AE2 to the surface under the guns of an enemy escort and she was promptly sunk.[1] On 27 April, Lieutenant Commander Edward C. Boyle in E14 made the third attempt. He too reached the Sea of Marmora, and, after sinking a Turkish gunboat and damaging a transport, rejoined the fleet.[2] Boyle was awarded the Victoria Cross.[3]

On 19 May 1915, HMS/m E14 was joined in the Marmora by HMS/m E11 under the command of Lieutenant Commander Martin E. Nasmith. For two weeks Nasmith and E11 played havoc with the Turkish supply lines, returning on 7 June from one of the most successful war patrols ever completed by a British submarine. The most graphic account of events is found in the draft patrol report (published for the first time in this volume) which was heavily edited before submission to the Admiralty. Undoubtedly, the highlight of the patrol was Nasmith's daring attack up the Bosphorus into the harbour of Constantinople where he torpedoed a large merchantman moored alongside the arsenal. To prove that E11 actually accomplished this unlikely feat he took two photographs of the Grand Mosque through his periscope. Nasmith certainly rode his fortune that day: the first torpedo he fired during the attack ran wild and circled back narrowly missing the submarine; the second missed its intended target by 15 feet and hit a much larger ship moored nearby – the good fortune was not that the torpedo struck a more valuable ship but that the intended target was in fact an American naval vessel, the USS *Scorpion*! The remainder of the patrol was hardly less eventful. Only after one of the two main engines failed did Nasmith decide to return down the Dardanelles – but not before turning back up the narrows, when half-way home, to sink a liner

[1] A narrative of events written by Capt. Henry Stoker after his release from POW camp in 1919 can be found at f.418, ADM 137/2077.
[2] Sunk gunboat *Nuakibahri*, 198 tons; SS *Gulcemal*, 5071 tons.
[3] Gazetted 21 May 1915.

with his last torpedo. This act earned him the double reward of a Victoria Cross and an immediate promotion to the rank of Commander.[1]

E11's second and equally successful patrol of the Marmora was in many ways much more interesting than the first. The patrol lasted almost two months – an unprecedented length of time. This was made possible by plundering all captured vessels for food and water, and most importantly by careful nursing of the diesel engines. Every day, one of the twelve cylinders on each engine was dismantled, overhauled, and replaced. During this second patrol, Nasmith accounted for 35 000 tons of enemy shipping including a full-sized battleship (and one merchant ship he managed to sink twice). The First Lieutenant, Guy d'Oyly-Hughes, conceived and executed the first commando raid launched from a submarine. He was assisted by the third officer, Lieutenant Robert Brown RNR.[2] Equally remarkable, given the state of technology at that time, was the Royal Naval Air Service's ability to supply E11 throughout the patrol with up-to-date intelligence on enemy ship movements gathered by aircraft fitted with wireless equipment. Another reason why E11 accounted for so much tonnage during her second patrol was that she had been fitted with a 3-inch gun during a refit at Malta, allowing the torpedoes to be conserved for the larger targets. Any torpedoes that missed, moreover, were recovered and reused after Nasmith modified them to float on reaching the end of their runs.

In November 1915, E11 departed for a third patrol in the Sea of Marmora. Again, Nasmith was finding and sinking Turkish supply ships with almost embarrassing ease, until E11 was recalled early after the army decision to evacuate Gallipoli. After the safe return of HMS/m E2 on 3 January 1916, no more submarines attempted the passage of the Dardanelles. The crews of the remaining boats were sent home, and the submarines moved to reinforce the Franco-Italian blockade of the Adriatic. Despite some spectacular successes, the British submarines that operated in the Sea of Marmora never accomplished their mission of cutting the Turkish Army maritime supply lines from Constantinople to the front at Gallipoli. This was because the Turkish navy very quickly introduced a highly efficient convoy system. And rather than transport the munitions to the front in large, highly visible transports, they loaded them instead into light-draught barges pulled by tugs which were escorted along the coast by two or more gunboats. Although

---

[1] Gazetted 24 June 1915. During the summer, E11 and E14 were reinforced by HMS/m E2 (Lt Cmdr David Stocks), E7 (Lt Cmdr Archibald Cochrane), E12 (Lt Cmdr Edward Bruce), E20 (Lt Cmdr David Warren) and H1 (Lt William Pirie).

[2] Lt Robert Brown RNR. Officer in merchant marine with Blue Funnel Line.

British submarines did engage some of these convoys, their significance was never appreciated and they were usually too well protected. The failure to achieve the strategic objective notwithstanding, the patrols of the Marmora were the most spectacular and certainly the most successful carried out by the British Submarine Service during the First World War.

Until the beginning of 1916, the Royal Navy remained chronically short of patrol submarines. The available craft, moreover, were distributed between three separate theatres of operation. From the middle of 1916 until the end of the war, by contrast, the Navy found itself with a surplus of oversea submarines of which the overwhelming majority was based in the North Sea. There were at last sufficient craft available to maintain a permanent blockade of the Heligoland Bight. And the Admiralty could even meet the demands from the Commander-in-Chief, Admiral Sir John Jellicoe, to attach one flotilla of patrol submarines to the Grand Fleet of Battle. But the Royal Navy now faced a different kind of materiel problem. The large number of E-type patrol submarines in hand were found to be unsuitable for many of the roles they were now called on to perform. Before the war, all British submarines had been designed primarily for anti-shipping missions.

Furthermore, the pre-war tactical scenarios had envisaged the submarine being able to approach its target to within point blank range (500 yards or less) before firing its torpedoes. Based upon this assumption, E-class vessels had been provided with only one bow torpedo tube (later increased to two). War experience had taught, however, that submarines were generally forced to shoot at ranges of over 1 000 yards. To have a reasonable chance of hitting a target at this range, moreover, they required as large a bow salvo as possible. In addition, as the war progressed and as fewer and fewer German ships ventured into the North Sea, British patrol submarines were increasingly employed in alternative roles: as minelayers, shore-bombardment vessels, fleet-submarines, seaplane carriers, anti-submarine craft (some were fitted with depth-charges) and some even as anti-aircraft platforms. As the E-class submarines ordered in 1914 were completed, therefore, new types of submarines purpose-built for these 'alternative' missions were laid down. In April 1915, for instance, Winston Churchill had authorised the building of 20 K-class submarines – originally designed in 1913 – propelled by steam turbines and capable of speeds up to 24 knots on the surface. In 1916, the Admiralty dusted off another old design and placed a large order for improved (1000-ton) patrol submarines with four bow torpedo tubes (the L class). Also laid down that year were submarine cruisers designed to carry two 5.5-inch guns (L50 class); big-gun anti-submarine submarines fitted with 12-inch guns (the M class); and hunter-killer submarines provided with six bow tubes and capable of underwater speeds over 15 knots (the R class). But due to the shortage of skilled shipbuilding labour after the passing of the Conscription Act in the summer of 1916, only a handful of the new model craft were completed before the end of the war.

From the middle of 1916, many senior fleet officers began to feel that the submarine force was not being properly utilised. At the same time, there were symptoms that the routine of constant North Sea patrols and the lack of action was beginning to damage morale. In October 1916, Admiral Jellicoe addressed a memorandum to the Admiralty predicting that Germany would resume unrestricted submarine warfare in the new year and warning that the U-boat posed the most serious threat to British naval supremacy. His suggestion was to withdraw most of the submarines allocated for patrol duties in the southern part of the North Sea and along the east coast of Britain, and instead redeploy them on anti-submarine missions in the Channel, off the Scottish coast, and the west coast of Ireland. To support his recommendations, Jellicoe combed his so-called 'Grand Fleet' for acknowledged experts on submarine warfare and grouped them into a committee under the chairmanship of Roger Keyes. While Jellicoe's proposal does at face value seem logical – even with hindsight – it is possible that he may also have had an ulterior motive. During this period he been under pressure from Whitehall to release some of the destroyers attached to the Grand Fleet at Scapa Flow for reallocation to anti-submarine duties. Jellicoe was an ardent believer in the 'Grand Fleet of Battle' concept and was dismayed at the thought of weakening the force he used to screen the battle fleet during its infrequent excursions into the North Sea. In other words, Jellicoe may have been trying to shift attention away from 'his' destroyers and on to the submarine force.

In December 1916, Jellicoe relinquished command of the Home Fleets to become First Sea Lord. Command of the battle fleets passed to Admiral Sir David Beatty, who soon began echoing his predecessor's demands for submarines to be redeployed from the North Sea to guard the trade routes. By this time, however, Jellicoe had learned that the U-boat menace was far more serious than he had thought, that the available submarines really were not suitable for anti-submarine work, and finally that destroyers were the most effective warships for combating this threat. Jellicoe thus found himself in the position of the poacher turned gamekeeper. Nevertheless, the Admiralty did make some effort to hunt U-boats with submarines. In 1917, the submarine depot ship HMS *Ambrose*, under the command of Captain Martin Nasmith VC, and a number of D- and E-class vessels were sent to the west coast of Ireland. The *Ambrose* flotilla achieved some notable successes. On one patrol HMS/m E54 attacked three U-boats on the same day and sank one. But for the most part, and as predicted, submarines that sighted U-boats were compelled to shoot at long range and invariably missed. In 1918, the task became slightly easier after Nasmith perfected a gadget he had invented to assist captains compute the torpedo-hitting solution for small, distant targets. Known as the IS-WAS, it was first successfully employed by HMS/m D4 against the German UB-72.[1] After the war it was adopted by all major navies and was not superseded until the invention of torpedo data computers ('fruit machines') during the late 1930s. But the most obvious drawback to using submarines to hunt enemy submarines was the danger from allied surface ships. Captains of merchantmen, warships and airships tended to regard all underwater craft as hostile and attack on sight. British submarines were frequent and occasionally fatal victims of 'friendly fire'.

* * *

The early history of the submarine in the Royal Navy has been fundamentally misunderstood for two main reasons. First, naval historians have incorrectly believed that the Admiralty was a techno-logically conservative institution that hated the idea of the Royal Navy developing the submarine. The documents clearly show that this was not the case and even those officers who did oppose its development, moreover, did so from a rational perspective. Second, historians have been guilty of looking at pre-First World War submarine policy in the light of wartime events and of having judged – and invariably condemned – pre-war policy-makers for failing to anticipate the effectiveness of the submarine as a commerce destroyer. As a corollary to this, they failed to recognise that before 1914, British naval policy-makers had not only conceived but even adopted a new strategic policy that reflected their belief that the submarine would play a central role in future wars. The Royal Navy developed their submarines with 'flotilla defence' – a sea denial strategy – in mind. A change in leadership in 1910 did result in a change of direction in British submarine policy. Although the Royal Navy's efforts to develop fleet submarines did have

---

[1] Patrol report (17 May 1918) by Lt Claude Barry, (later RA (S) during World War 2) f.692, ADM 137/2076.

significant negative consequences for the Submarine Service, it should not be overlooked that the new policy still reflected the Navy's confidence in the submarine as a weapon of war. The fleet-submarine concept, however, was just an aberration and in 1913 the Admiralty returned to the sea-denial strategy and made every effort to make up the ground lost. During the First World War, it was the personnel of the Royal Navy Submarine Service that manned the front line in the war at sea.

Selected Bibliography

For survey of British submarine policy based upon in-depth archival research see:

Nicholas Lambert, *Sir John Fisher's Naval Revolution*, (University of South Carolina Press: Columbia, 1999).
Michael Dash, 'British Submarine Policy, 1853–1918', unpublished Ph.D. dissertation (London University, 1990)

Also see:

Nicholas Lambert, 'British Naval Policy 1913/14: Financial Limitation and Strategic Revolution', *The Journal of Modern History*, 67:3 (Sept. 1995) for a more detailed account and analysis of Churchill's 'substitution' policy.
Alex Rowland, *Underwater Warfare in the Age of Sail*, (Indiana University Press: Bloomington, 1978) for an introduction to the history of early submarines.
Gaddis Smith, *Britain's Clandestine Submarines*, (Yale University Press: New Haven, 1964) recounts the story of Fisher's negotiations with Charles Schwab over the building of the American H class submarines for the RN.

Technical histories of early submarines:

Norman Friedman, *U.S. Submarines Through 1945: an Illustrated Design History*, (Naval Institute Press: Annapolis, 1995) provides invaluable detail on the Electric Boat (Holland) designs built for the US and Royal navies.
Murray F. Sueter, *The Evolution of the Submarine*, (J. Griffin & Co.: Portsmouth, 1907) written by one of the first officers to captain a Royal Navy submarine.

Narrative histories of British submarines during the First World War:

Don Everitt, *The K boats: the Amazing Story of Britain's Steam Submarines*, (Harrap: London, 1963).

Bernd Langenseipen and Ahmet Guleryuz, *The Ottoman Steam Navy 1828–1923*, (Conway Maritime Press: London, 1995).

Anthony Shankland and Peter Hunter, *Dardanelles Patrol: the Incredible Story of the E11*, (Collins: London, 1964).

General surveys of British defence and naval policy before the First World War:

Nicholas d'Ombrain, *War Machinery and High Policy: Defence Administration in Peace-time Britain, 1902–1914*, (Oxford University Press: Oxford, 1973).

Nicholas Lambert, *Sir John Fisher's Naval Revolution*, op. cit.

Nicholas Lambert, 'Admiral Sir John Fisher and the Concept of Flotilla Defence, 1904–1910', *The Journal of Military History* 59 (October, 1995): pp. 639–60.

Keith Neilson, *Britain and the Last Tsar: British Policy and Russia, 1894–1917*, (Oxford University Press: Oxford, 1996).

Jon T. Sumida, *In Defence of Naval Supremacy; Finance, Technology and Naval Policy, 1889–1914*, (Unwin Hyman: London, 1989).

Jon Sumida, 'Sir John Fisher and the Dreadnought: the Sources of Naval Mythology', *The Journal of Military History* 59 (October, 1995): 619–38.

Jon Sumida, 'British Naval Administration and Policy in the Age of Fisher', *The Journal of Military History*, 54, (January 1990) 1–26.

Jon Sumida and David Rosenberg, 'Machines, Men, Manufacturing, Management and Money: The Study of Navies as complex Organisations and the Transformation of Twentieth Century Naval History', John Hattendorf ed., *Doing Naval History: Essays Towards Improvement*, (Naval War College: Newport, 1995).

Rhodri Williams, *Defending the Empire: The Conservative Party and British Defence Policy, 1899–1915*, (Yale University Press: New Haven, 1991).

For still useful though now outdated accounts of British naval policy during this period, see:

Julian Corbett and Henry Newbolt (eds.), *History of the Great War – Naval Operations*, 5 volumes (Longmans: London, 1920–31).

Arthur J. Marder, *From the Dreadnought to Scapa Flow*, 5 vols. (Oxford University Press: Oxford, 1961–70).

Idem, *A History of British Naval Policy in the pre-Dreadnought Era, 1880–1905* also published under the title of *The Anatomy of British Seapower, 1885–1905*, (Alfred Knopf: New York, 1940).

Autobiographies and biographies of key personnel:

Malcolm H. Murfett (ed.), *The First Sea Lords: From Fisher to Mountbatten* (Praeger: Westport CT, 1995) provides useful career summaries for Admirals Sir Arthur Wilson, Sir Francis Bridgeman, Prince Louis of Battenberg, Sir Henry Jackson and Sir John Jellicoe.
Admiral Reginald H. Bacon, *From 1900 Onwards*, (Hutchinson: London, 1940) contains important material on the early history of the Submarine Service.
Paul Halpern (ed.) *The Keyes Papers: Volume 1, 1914–1918,* (Allen and Unwin for Navy Records Society: London, 1979).
Roger J. Keyes, *The Naval Memoirs of Sir Roger Keyes*, 2 volumes (Thonton Butterworth: London, 1934) gives one perspective of submarine policy before the war, though the draft manuscript for the first volume, which was censored by the Admiralty, is very much more revealing. The drafts are kept in the Keyes Papers held by the British Library, Keyes Mss. 18/1.
Ruddock F. Mackay, *Fisher of Kilverstone*, (Oxford University Press: Oxford, 1971) provides the best analysis.
Jan Morris, *Fisher's Face*, (Viking-Penguin Press: London, 1996) is the most insightful.
Arthur J. Marder, *Fear God and Dread Nought: The Correspondence of Admiral of the Fleet Lord Fisher of Kilverstone*, 3 vols. (Harvard University Press & Jonathan Cape: London, 1952–59).

APPENDIX 1: FIRST APPOINTMENTS TO THE SERVICE

The following were the first officers and men appointed to the Submarine Service in September 1901:[1]

Lieutenant F.D. Arnold-Forster
Lieutenant S. Bowle-Evans
Lieutenant J.B. Moreton
Engineer Robert Spence
William R. Waller, PO, 1st class
F.C. Knight, PO, 1st class
Joseph B. Rees, PO, 1st class
Ernest E. Neville, PO, 1st class
William J. Robinson, ERA, 3rd class
William Muirhead, ERA, 3rd class.

[1] Taken from Appendix 1, Reginald Bacon, *From 1900 Onwards*, p. 377.

APPENDIX 2: COMPARATIVE STRENGTH OF SUBMARINE SERVICE, 1914–1918[1]

(i) *Number of Submarines in commission*

Class	4 Aug. 1914	11 Nov. 1918	Net increase or decrease
Coastal	42	20	−22
Patrol	20	86	+66
Fleet	0	14	+14
Monitor	0	1	+1
Anti-submarine	0	6	+6
Minelayer	0	6	+6
Totals	62	133	+71

(ii) *Numbers of Submarine Officers and Ratings*

	4 Aug. 1914	11 Nov. 1918	Increase
Officers	168	612	444
Ratings	1250	5446	4196
Totals	1418	6058	4640

[1] Half-yearly Report on the work of the Submarine Service by Commodore (S) Sydney S. Hall, ADM 137/2077.

PART I

THE DEVELOPMENT OF THE SUBMARINE

[ADM 1/7422A]

Paris
22 January 1899

In transmitting to your Lordship the enclosed confidential despatch which has been addressed to me by Captain Jackson, naval attaché to HM Embassy, reporting on the successful trials recently made with a submarine torpedo boat, I have to state that the very interesting account given by him in writing, and the verbal opinion which he has communicated to me of the value of the invention, induce me to call the serious attention of HM Government to the subject of submarine warfare as likely to be developed by the employment of such craft in the French Navy.

As a professional man, absolutely without technical knowledge with regard to it, I should expose myself to ridicule if I did more than this; and I need only remind your Lordship that this subject is at present occupying the attention of the French Public to a considerable extent in consequence of the appeal made by the [newspaper] *Matin* for subscriptions for the construction of a submarine vessel; and that the belief in the success of the invention is very likely to encourage Frenchmen to regard their naval inferiority to England as by no means so great as it is considered to be in the latter country.

[Attached extracts from Captain Henry Jackson][2]

22 January 1899

France
Submarine Torpedo boats

*   *   *

The *Gustave-Zédé* proceeded out to sea, unaccompanied by any vessel, till well out of sight of the Fleet. She then turned and steamed towards the fleet well out of the water at 10 knots speed, with her bridge raised and 4 men on it; she was observed from the [battleship] *Magenta*, at a distance of 3000 metres, who hoisted a distinguishing signal. The men on the bridge instantly went below and the bridge was lowered; the *Magenta* dipped the flag. The boat was submerged till the conning

---

[1] Sir Edmond Monson, British Ambassador to France. Marquis of Salisbury, Prime Minister of Great Britain, 1885–86, 1886–92, 1895–1902.

[2] Capt. Henry Jackson: naval attaché in Paris 1896–99.

tower only was awash, its top only 20-inches above the mean water line.

When at 1500 metres distance from the *Magenta*, the wash of the boat's screw, but not the conning tower, was observed; the flag was rehoisted, and this was observed in the boat, which was at once totally submerged to a mean depth of 3 metres. The flag was dipped as she did so.

At a distance of 400 metres from the *Magenta*, the boat was, purposely, brought to the surface momentarily, for a time estimated at 3 seconds, during which her conning tower was visible. The Captain of the boat judged his distance and observed his course was correct during this rise, and at 250 yards distance he fired his torpedo from the stem tube, which struck the *Magenta* fairly amidships. The boat proceeded straight on and dived and passed directly under the keel of the *Magenta*, coming to the surface about 200 yards on her opposite beam, the trial being then completed.

*   *   *

I have been unable to obtain actual details of her night trials, but understand they have been equally successful, and the general results shew that these submarine vessels have now realised a practical stage in modern warfare, and will have to be reckoned with, and met, in a future European war.

[Extract from attached minute (16 March 1899) by Director of Naval Ordnance][1]

As regards action against our Blockading Squadrons I think that the Submarine boats would not be a great danger to a fleet or ships under weigh but if anchorages were occupied close to an enemy's base, no doubt the use of nets *while at anchor* would be necessary.

The question remains whether such boats if their development continues might not be of great value for offensive purposes against an enemy's fleet in their ports. (French.)

As we could convoy or tow them across to within a short distance I am of the opinion that they might be used most effectively.

[Attached minute (16 March 1899) by Controller][2]
Noted. No action seems necessary at present.

---

[1] Capt. Edmond Jeffreys: DNO 1897–99.

[2] Rear Adm. Sir Arthur Knyvet Wilson: Controller 1897–1901. The Controller of the Navy, responsible for naval materiel and management of the Royal Dockyards, was sometimes referred to as the Third Naval Lord. In 1912 the title of Controller was officially abolished (although it continued to be used on many official documents) and instead the title Third Sea Lord was adopted.

[2] *Statement by First Lord of the Admiralty in
the House of Commons*[1]
[Parliamentary Debates]

6th April 1900

Mr Goschen: Close attention has been given by the Admiralty to the subject of submarine boats. The submarine boat, even if the practical difficulties attending its use can be overcome would seem, so far as the immediate future is concerned, to be essentially a weapon for maritime powers on the defensive, and it is natural that the nations which anticipate holding that position should endeavour to develop it. The question of the best way of meeting its attack is receiving much consideration and it is in this direction that practical suggestions would be valuable. It is certain that the reply to this weapon must be looked for in other directions than in building submarine boats ourselves, for it is clear that one submarine boat cannot fight another.

[3] *Discussion on the Use of Contact Mines for Defence Against
Submarines*
[ADM 256/39]

*Extract from Report by Captain of HMS Vulcan, dated 5th February
1900*[2]

(5) The question of submarine boats may shortly become a very serious one, even in harbours far removed from the enemy's bases, and the question of their destruction should be carefully considered. The use of blockade mines by our Fleet has been negatived [*sic*] by the Admiralty, but I submit the question of using a mine of this type might with advantage be reopened. It is an offensive weapon, in my opinion, and great importance is attached to its use by foreign European navies, who are introducing designs in their construction, and building special vessels for its use, and considering the impossibility of foreseeing all the phases of a future naval war, and the fact that several efficient patterns of this mine have been tried in the *Vernon*,[3] and the unsuitability

[1] George V. Goschen: First Lord of the Admiralty 1871–74 and 1895–1900.
[2] Capt. Henry Jackson: captain of HMS *Vulcan* (torpedo and electrical school at the Nore) 1899–1901. A fuller (albeit still edited) version of this report can be found in 'The Annual Report of the Torpedo School 1900', pp. 23–4.
[3] HMS *Vernon*: RN Torpedo School at Portsmouth. Hulk used to train officers and ratings in torpedo. Also employed by the Admiralty as the RN's principal torpedo research and development establishment.

of our E.M. mines for the purpose, I submit it would be of advantage if some of the best known forms of this type of mine were made and issued to the *Vulcan* for practical trial in the fleet, so that at least we could be ready with a pattern mine, and our men instructed in its use, if it should be ever considered advisable to re-introduce them into the Service.

[Extract from Attached minute (24 March 1900) by Captain of HMS *Vernon*][1]
Experiments for blockade mines were discontinued by A.L.G. 6577/848/94 of 1 February 1895, but if it is desired to reopen the question I am prepared to submit a firing gear from which 12 sets might be made for trial, six in *Vulcan*, three for *Vernon*, and three for *Defiance*,[2] I think this would be the best way of determining the value of this form of mine.

[Attached minute (14 April 1900) by Director of Naval Ordnance]
In 1894 (see marked part of G. 6577/94), [not reproduced] Assistant-Director of Torpedoes and Director of Naval Ordnance considered it to be doubtful whether we should adopt blockade mines. Director of Naval Intelligence was also doubtful mainly on the ground that our adoption would justify and encourage other nations in doing the same.

Sir J[ohn] Fisher, then Controller, concurred. Sir G[erald] Noel thought that some should be provided and kept in depots.[3] Lord W[alter] Kerr did not recommend adoption,[4] and First Naval Lord decided not to adopt.

It is now submitted for decision whether, as recommended by Sir J. Fisher [now C-in-C Mediterranean], the above is to be reconsidered. The question may be said to be somewhat changed since 1894 by two facts. Firstly, that foreign nations, especially France and Russia, have not waited for our justifying and encouraging them, but have adopted the system on, I believe, an extensive scale. Secondly, the submarine boat appears to be rapidly approaching a defined position as a new instrument of warfare. See copy of Captain [Douglas] Gamble's letter attached.[5] The only practical way to stop these boats, or frighten them

---

[1] Capt. Charles G. Robinson: Captain of HMS *Vernon* 1899-1901.
[2] Torpedo training schools at Medway, Portsmouth and Devonport respectively.
[3] Capt. Gerald Noel: Junior Naval Lord 1893-97.
[4] Rear Adm. Lord Walter Kerr: Second Naval Lord 1893-95.
[5] Capt. Douglas Gamble succeeded Capt. Jackson as naval attaché in Paris at the end of 1899.

so much as to keep them at home, seems to be by blockade mines.

[Attached minute (18 April 1900) by Controller]
Propose to reopen the question of blockade mines, taking action as in Captain of *Vernon*'s minute.

[Attached minute (23 April 1900) by Director of Naval Intelligence Division (DNI)][1]
The countries which have already adopted blockade mines are –
France, Russia, Germany, Austria, Italy
It is submitted that it seems to be unwise to be behind other nations in this respect. It can hardly be accepted that the blockade mine is the only practical way to meet the submerged boat.

[Attached minute (24 April 1900) by Senior Naval Lord][2]
As to the general principle of adopting blockade mines under conditions that have arisen since 1894. I shall be much obliged to Admirals Moore and Douglas if they would give me their views.[3]

[Attached minute (26 April 1900) by Second Naval Lord]
I am of opinion that it is very desirable to adopt the blockade mine, believing that occasions might arise in war time when it could be used with advantage.

[Attached minute (30 April 1900) by Junior Naval Lord]
With regard to the general principle of adopting blockade mines, I am of opinion that they form one of the best defences against underwater boats, and also would be most useful in keeping the enemy out of our ports, and out of their own. A certain number should be supplied to every battleship. The repairing ship and water ship should carry them; these ships being specially fitted for their discharge.

[Attached minute (30 April 1900) by Senior Naval Lord]
I concur that it is desirable to re-open the question of blockade mines. The march of events now calls for some response on our part to the action taken by foreign Powers in their construction of submarine boats, and an organised system for laying blockade mines. I do not think these mines

---

[1] Capt. (later Rear Adm.) Reginald Custance: DNI 1899–1902.
[2] Adm. Lord Walter Kerr: Senior Naval Lord 1899–1904.
[3] Vice-Adm. Archibald Douglas: Second Naval Lord 1899–1903. Rear Adm. Arthur Moore: Junior Naval Lord 1897–1901.

should be carried in the ships beyond what is necessary for instruction, but we should have the material ready for placing in special ships.

In the first place the *Vernon* should be instructed to carry out the proposal of the Captain of Torpedo School in his submission herewith. Orders accordingly.

[Attached minute (4 May 1900) by Senior Naval Lord]

The success of the French submarine boats appears to be sufficiently assured to make it necessary to consider how to meet them.

Blockade mines will have to be introduced and any other steps taken that are likely to be effective.

The Harvey towing torpedo was not a success, but the proposed weapon submitted by the *Defiance* may be of use and worth continuing to experiment.

With submarine boats there are two points to consider, viz.:–

1. How to find them.
2. How to destroy them.

I concur with the Controller, and propose a draft in the sense of his minute be prepared.

[Attached minute (6 May 1900) by First Lord]

This is very interesting. Let the experiments proceed and every encouragement be given. Concur with Controller and Senior Naval Lord.

[Attached memorandum (17 May 1900), Secretary of Admiralty to Commander-in-Chief, Devonport][1]

Sir,

I am commanded by my Lords Commissioners of the Admiralty to acquaint you that they are pleased to see that the question of the best means of dealing with submarine boats, and destroying them when discovered, is receiving attention in the Torpedo School at Devonport.

Any experiments necessary for that object should be continued as far as the resources of the Torpedo School permit.

With regard to the particular plan proposed by the Captain of the *Defiance*, it would appear that even if the depth-keeping was satisfactory, and the exact position of the submarine boat was known by the optic tube, or some part of her being above water, there would still be considerable difficulty in judging when the towing torpedo, which cannot be seen, is sufficiently close to ensure her destruction when fired, and consequently the limits of accuracy to be expected in this

---

[1] Sir Evan McGregor: Permanent Secretary at the Admiralty 1894–1907.

respect require to be determined by experiment, as well as the accuracy in depth-keeping.

Up to the present, the most promising suggestions that have been made for dealing with submarine boats have been –

(1) The use of blockade mines at the entrance of the ports where they are known, or suspected to be, to prevent their issuing, and

(2) Hunting them when seen on the surface by destroyers, torpedo boats, or ordinary steam pinnaces.

As regards (2) the vessels of the *Narval* class if caught under steam can be destroyed by gun fire, and when in this condition they require at present, as far as is known, a considerable time to dive, though it is expected that this time may be reduced when further experience is gained.[1]

With the other descriptions of boats, and the *Narvals*, when working electrically, much depends on the distance they can go under water without showing on the surface, and on this point there is very little reliable information.

It is stated that even when the conning tower is above water and opened for observation, the distance at which these boats can be seen is very small. There will therefore be great difficulty in discovering them in the first place, and in following them when discovered, if the distance they can travel under water is considerable.

The best organisation for the destroyers and steam boats for keeping touch with submarine boats after they are discovered, or failing this, of waylaying them on their return to port, in positions where they will be compelled to come to the surface for the purpose of navigation, is a matter that should be strictly confined to officers and men in HM Service.

The latest information in the possession of their Lordships as regards the different patterns of submarine boats now under trial abroad will shortly be issued in N.I.D. Report No. 577.

[4] *Submarine Boats in the United States*
[ADM 1/7462]

[Minute (18 May 1900) by assistant DNI][2]
Submitted for information a Report of the evidence given by Admiral

---

[1] The *Narval*: First purpose-built submersible. Designed for French Navy in 1896 by Eng.-Cmdr Maxime Laubeuf. Redesigned on orders from Conseil des Travaux in 1897. Laid down 1898. Began builders' trials October 1899. Commissioned summer 1900. Reported (accurately) to require 30 minutes to shut down steam power plant and dive.
[2] Commander Frederick Doveton Sturdee: a/DNI 1900–1902.

Dewey U.S.N. before the United States House Committee on Naval Affairs while the said committee was considering a bill providing for twenty submarine boats.[1]

[Attached minute (22 May 1900) by Senior Naval Lord]
Seen. The matter of submarine boats cannot be ignored and will have to be taken up by us – our first want is a design.

[Attached minute (not dated) by First Lord of the Admiralty]
I have read the whole of these papers very carefully, they are not pleasant reading for clearly great progress is gradually being made with submarine boats. I have read them as well as Capt. [Charles] Ottley's report,[2] the report on submarine boats compiled in the department of N[aval] I[ntelligence],[3] and it appears that there are many uses to which we could put submarine-boats, if they do what is claimed.

The question was discussed between myself and some of my colleagues a short time ago, when objection to obtaining plans from British firms – was more or less put forward, and admitted to have some weight: but I feel we ought to be in a position to act if necessary and I feel the force of the SNL's minute.

[5] *Extract from Rear Admiral Lord Charles Beresford to Vice Admiral Sir John Fisher*

[Add Mss 49713]

12 June 1900

25. Submarine boats may or may not be successful in warfare, but it would be [as] unwise to under-rate their capabilities as to overrate them. When a common-sense level-headed nation like that of the United

---

[1] In April 1900, the US Congress instructed Secretary of the Navy to purchase the submarine *Holland* from the Electric Boat Company, which the previous year had purchased from the near bankrupt inventor John Holland all of his patents and designs as well as his prototype vessel. Later that month, Representative Amos Cummings (Democrat – New York) proposed a bill calling on the US government to buy 20 more submarines (Electric Boat's head office was located in Cummings' constituency). Fleet Adm. George Dewey, whose professional opinion carried great weight in Congress after the Spanish–American War, testified before the US House Naval Committee in favour of the bill. In June, Congress provided an appropriation for $850,000 requiring the Navy to buy five submarines. These were laid down as the *Adder* class.

[2] Ottley, US Submarine Boat Holland, 18 December 1899, enclosed in FO 3 January 1900, ADM 1/7471.

[3] N.I.D. Report 577, Submarine Boats, printed May 1900, in Proposal to Print a Report on Submarine Boats, NID 577, ADM 1/7461B.

States, has tried and adopted submarine boats, it would appear probable that such craft must have some value in warlike operations, and it would be wiser to practically prove their utility than to rest satisfied with assertions based upon theory.

[6] *Statement by First Lord of the Admiralty to House of Commons*
[*Parliamentary Debates*]

17th July 1900

Mr. Goschen: ... I am afraid that I cannot gratify the natural curiosity that is felt in regard to that matter. The hon. Member said that we ought to make experiments, and at the same time he pointed out the enormous importance of submarine boats. If we are to make experiments we are not going to disclose the results, which we believe might rebound more to the advantage of our competitors than ourselves. If we are to induce shipbuilders to put their mind into the building of submarine boats, we must not make known what has been done to nations which might have the greatest use for these boats. I do not propose publicly to declare whether the Admiralty believes in submarine boats or not. I must ask the House to excuse me. Of course, we do not wish to encourage or discourage other nations by stating, as hon. Members wish us to state, how great would be the danger of these submarine boats to ourselves. The House will allow me to be extremely reticent on the subject. ...

[7] *Lord Nathaniel Rothschild to the First Lord of the Admiralty*
[ADM 1/7515]

New Court
23 July 1900

I enclose a copy of a letter I have received from Belmont. At present I have not seen Mr. Rice; but I hope you will kindly let me know *if I am to give him a letter of introduction* to the Admiralty. Excuse my dictating these few lines.

[Attached: August Belmont to Messrs N.M. Rothschild and Sons of London][1]

---

[1] August Belmont, New York financier and head of August Belmont & Co.

August Belmont & Co.,
New York
13th July 1900

Gentlemen,

We have today given a letter of introduction to Mr. Isaac L. Rice, President of the Electric Boat Company and of the Consolidated Railway Electric Lighting and Equipment Company. He was at one time largely interested in the Electric Storage Battery Co., and is still interested in many industrial enterprises.

The object of Mr. Rice's visit to Europe, aside from recreation, is to exploit, if possible, the patents for the Holland Submarine Torpedo Boat and for lighting trains from the car axle, the former, however, being of the greatest importance. The Electric Boat Co. owns all the patents and has acquired all the rights of the Holland Torpedo Boat Co., which, as you are probably aware built the Torpedo boat Holland, which after most exhaustive and thorough tests by our experts, proved highly successful and was acquired by our Government, and contracts have now been signed for six more of similar boats and for one which has already been under construction for some time past, making in all eight submarine boats.

The Company expects to make contracts with other Governments, but believes the best way to accomplish this would be to organise separate companies in the various countries in Europe and elsewhere and transfer the patent rights to them either for a consideration of cash or stock in the companies so to be organised. The successful trials of the first Holland boat and the decision of our Government to acquire eight of them will no doubt induce other governments to take up the construction of these boats, and the matter may consequently become of considerable importance, on account of which we have thought it might be agreeable to you to take the matter up and interest yourselves in the organisation of such companies as Mr. Rice contemplates.

Should this business appeal to you, we shall be glad to have you take it up with Mr. Rice, but at all events, if you are not inclined to interest yourselves, we shall be greatly obliged to you if you will kindly furnish Mr. Rice such information and advice as you may be able to or deem proper under the circumstances.

*   *   *

[Attached minute (26 July 1900) by assistant secretary to First Lord][1]

[1] Oswyn Murray, assistant secretary to the Admiralty.

Mr. Brown: Would you kindly show this to the Controller and find out what he thinks the reply should be.

[8] *Submarine Boats Considered by USA House Committee*
[ADM 1/7462]

[Attached minute (3 August 1900) by Controller]
I have discussed the best means of destroying submarine boats with the Captain of the *Vernon* who is carrying out certain experiments, but it seems advisable that we should if possible obtain one submarine boat of a type used by foreign nations for the purpose of ascertaining for ourselves the limits of the power of these vessels and the best means of avoiding and destroying them.

Propose in the first place to ask the Holland Company whether they are in a position to supply one boat or to furnish us with drawings and specifications to enable us to construct one in the dockyard, and if so on what terms.

[Attached minute (3 August 1900) by Senior Naval Lord]
Concur to ask as proposed but if the Holland boat patents have become the property of the U.S. Government as I gather from the enclosed letter then, we may have more difficulty in getting a satisfactory answer.

[9] *Isaac Rice to Admiralty Secretary*[1]
[ADM 1/7515]

Claridges Hotel
London W.
17th September 1900

In compliance with the desire of the First Lord, when I had the honor of an interview at the Admiralty a few days since, I have formulated a proposal in reference to the Submarine Torpedo Boats which we then discussed. He asked me to communicate with you as soon as I had done so in order that another interview might be granted at which I could submit the same. May I, therefore, request you to be good enough to ascertain when it would be convenient that I should attend.

[Attached minute (19 September 1900) by DNC][2]

[1] Isaac Rice, President of Electric Boat Company, 1899–1915.
[2] Sir William White: DNC 1887–1901.

Our principal object is to obtain a successful type of submarine boat for the purpose of trial. The Holland type seems to afford the best opening.

Mr. Rice's proposal is made naturally from a commercial stand-point: he wishes to secure a certain profit if he sells the Admiralty one vessel. He is content to obtain this either by building other vessels at a relatively high price (par. 2): or by getting a large royalty on other types if the Admiralty prefer them to the Holland type (par. 3).

It is noted that the price named for the first boat (£34,000 about) is high in relation to the dimensions. The larger French boats are said to cost about £24,000 to £26,000. No doubt the cost of production is greater in America than in this country: but it may be assumed that a very handsome profit is intended, as is natural considering the large preliminary expenditure that has been incurred, before present success has been obtained.

* * *

In all probability the proprietors of the Holland type will not agree to sell us a boat for trial, unless they can enounce a return for their preliminary expenditure.

My suggestion is that Mr. Rice should be asked to state a lump sum for which he would agree to build and deliver the vessel described in Par. 1 of his letter, apart from any conditions of further orders being given by the Admiralty, or royalties being payable by the Admiralty on other submarine boats which may be ordered. Further that Mr. Rice be required to state specifically what guarantees of speed (at surface or submerged), power of covering distance, time vessel can remain below the surface, ... Also whether his co. will accept the condition of the trials being made in England, under their direction and at their risk; and how they would propose to deal with the provision of a trained crew and the expenses attending the trial.

[Attached minute (8 October 1901) by Controller]

Concur generally with the remarks of the D.N.C. attached, but on further consideration I think we require more than one boat, and under these circumstances the terms offered would with some modification and with the proviso that the boats are to be delivered in England be, on the whole, more favourable to us than an arrangement by which we paid a lump sum.

Our primary object is to test the value of the Submarine boat as a weapon in the hands of our enemies and to study the best way of meeting its attacks. For this purpose I think we should obtain five boats as soon as possible, one to be attached to the *Vernon*, one to *Defiance* and the other three to be allocated one to each port to be used in connection with the Destroyer Flotillas in practising methods of meeting their attacks. I do not think a less number of boats will suffice as the two attached to the Torpedo Schools will be fully occupied with Instructional and Experimental work, and it is very important that as large a number as possible of officers, especially those who command Destroyers should be made familiar with the real extent of the danger to be apprehended from submarine boats, and the best methods of dealing with them.

As our main object is to keep in touch with improvements that are made in these vessels abroad, it will almost certainly be necessary to purchase more boats from the Company after 2 or 3 years' experience so that the balance to be ordered elsewhere on which we shall have to pay the £10,000 royalties are not likely to be large.

Propose to inform Mr. Rice that it is desired to obtain five submarine Torpedo boats of type No.7, but that it is essential that the boats should be delivered in England and that the trials should take place in an English port. He is requested to state whether he can undertake to do this and what increase in the price will be involved. ... He should also state the conditions which he is prepared to undertake that the boats shall fulfil on their trials, namely: –

Speed on the surface and radius of action with oil motor.
Speed when submerged and radius of action with accumulator.
Distance that the vessel can go submerged and time for which she can remain closed up without inconvenience to the crew.
Limits within which course and depth can be maintained.
Time required to pass from working on the surface with oil motor to the submerged condition.

A crew should be provided by the Company for carrying out the trials and also to instruct a Naval crew in the management of the boat. The trials should include working the boat with a naval crew under all conditions. As regards orders for subsequent boats after the first five, the company to undertake to give the Admiralty the benefit of *all improvements* that may have been made by them in later boats without additional royalty, charging only the actual additional cost of the modifications plus 10% for profit. Any improvements required by the Admiralty to be also made on the same terms.

It is expected that the negotiations may be treated as confidential.

[Attached minute (8 October 1900) by Senior Naval Lord]

Concur generally with the Controller, but I am not clear how we stand with regard to the Company if after getting the five boats, or while they are in course of delivery, we happen to hear of something we like better. ...

[Attached minute (19 October 1900) by DNC]

Mr. Rice called today with Lieut. Dawson[1] (representing Messrs Vickers) and saw the Controller and myself.

Mr. Rice stated and Lieut. Dawson agreed:

1. That Messrs Vickers had made an arrangement with him to become sole licensees for Europe of the patents of the Holland Torpedo Boat Co.

2. That Messrs Vickers would be fully informed as to the inventions owned by the Holland Company and of any improvement made from time to time.

3. That expert assistance would be given to Messrs Vickers by the Company in carrying out the construction of submarine boats.

4. That Messrs Vickers (acting as licensees of the Holland Co.) would be prepared to continue the correspondence with the Admiralty as to the construction of the five boats contemplated to be built: and to answer all questions raised by the Admiralty letter of 13th inst.

5. The Holland Co., if as deemed, would assume joint responsibility with Messrs Vickers for the performance of the boats ordered and the fulfilment of the contract. Or they would leave the responsibility for the contract entirely to Messrs Vickers, who would be covered by their agreement with the Company.

6. Mr. Rice stated that, after consideration, he was prepared in view of the contemplated order for five boats, to make an offer for them at the same price as is to be paid by the U.S. Navy for similar boats (viz. $170,000 per boat): and that no conditions as to royalties etc. on any future submarine boats ordered by the Admiralty would be insisted on by the company in connection with that offer.

It was understood that a further communication would be made and that meantime no reply need by sent to the enclosed letter.

---

[1] Arthur Trevor Dawson: Managing Director of Messrs Vickers, Son & Maxim; former Lieutenant RN.

[10] *Minute by Controller on Offer by Holland Torpedo Boat Co. to build Submarines for the Royal Navy*

[ADM 1/7515]

23 October 1900

Draft letter to the Treasury herewith for approval. It would be perhaps advisable not actually to send it until Messrs Vickers proposal has been received.

I am commanded by my Lords Commissioners of the Admiralty to acquaint you for the information of the Lords Commissioners of the Treasury, that they have had under consideration for some time the best way of meeting the attacks of submarine boats which are now building in considerable numbers in France and of which successful trials have recently been made in the United States.

This weapon will probably be used by the French principally to attack vessels attempting to blockade their ports, and unless suitable means are devised for meeting their attacks and destroying them they will form a very serious danger to our blockading squadrons. The French also contemplate crossing the Channel with these vessels and attacking our ships in our harbours.

This question of meeting these attacks had been carefully studied, and some progress has been made, but it is evident that no satisfactory method of defence can be worked out without actual experience of the vessels themselves, and the difficulties and limitations associated with their use. The methods must be not only studied theoretically but men and officers must be practised in carrying them out.

For this reason My Lords have been anxious for some time to obtain specimens of the submarine boats in use in Foreign Countries. Those built in France being entirely under the control of the French Government, it being impossible to obtain any of these vessels from that Country, but very successful trials have been carried out in the United States with the submarine boat, and negotiations were opened with the Holland company with a view to purchasing a vessel for trial.

Serious difficulties however, arose in the endeavour to purchase a single vessel, as the company were unwilling to sell a single vessel without a guarantee that the Admiralty would pledge themselves to purchase 10 from them in the course of five years or pay a Royalty of £10,000 on each of 20 boats constructed or purchased elsewhere.

After carefully considering what would be the least number of boats that would enable experiments, instruction and practice in meeting the attacks of these boats to be efficiently carried out, My Lords came to the conclusion that at least five would be necessary, one to be attached to each of the two torpedo schools for experiment and instruction, and one to each of the three principal ports to enable exercises in their discovery and destruction to be carried out.

After further negotiations the company have expressed their willingness to make Messrs Vickers, Sons & Maxim construct five boats for us for $170,000 each, which is the same price for which six boats have been ordered by the United States Government. In consideration of an order being given for five boats the company will agree to waive any further conditions as to Royalty on the purchase or construction of other submarine boats.

My Lords consider that these conditions are very favourable, and [as] it is very important that no time should be lost in obtaining these boats, they request the sanction of Their Lordships of the Treasury to complete the negotiations on these terms.

The service cannot be postponed without serious detriment to the public service. Until the whole of the details have been discussed with Messrs Vickers, Sons & Maxim and a representative of the Company, it will not be possible to estimate what proportion of the cost is likely to fall on this financial year but the amount is not likely to be large.

[Attached minute (24 October 1900) by First Lord]

I do not think we should confine ourselves so absolutely to the doctrine that it is only in order to ascertain the best means of meeting foreign submarine boats that we wish to buy the 5 boats from the United States. They may be useful to us in many places, like our torpedo boats, e.g. Hong Kong, and other ports which we may wish to defend in the absence of our own men of war.

[Additional attached minute (25 October 1900) by First Lord]

At all events, I cannot commit myself to the opposite doctrine. I think members of the Board have somewhat modified their opinions. As a question of policy is involved, I think the Senior Naval Lord should glance at these papers.

[Attached minute (26 October 1900) by Senior Naval Lord]

I fully concur in the employment of Submarines for any purpose to which they can be adapted. In fact their employment against other Submarines in my opinion affords a very limited sphere of usefulness. If they proved to be of value, it is as an intimidation to large vessels menacing our Ports. One of the principal uses of the Submarine Boats at the present stage is to work out if possible, some plan for meeting hostile Submarines, but it is not proposed to meet Submarine by

Submarine as at present advised. These are details which need not be included in the Treasury letter, however. It is desirable to word the letter to give the impression that the sphere of usefulness of these vessels may be very wide if found to be a success.

[11] *Extract from Memorandum to Cabinet by Lord Selborne*[1]
[CAB 37/56/8]

17 January 1901

Submarine Boats:

In respect of these boats the French claim to have passed beyond the experimental stage. They claim to have perfected a type which will be capable of steering along the surface of the water for a distance at least sufficient to cross the Channel, and then of submerging itself and acting as a submarine boat. Experience can only show whether the danger from this invention is as great as it appears to be. It is quite certain that if all that is claimed for it should turn out to be true, there is no defence yet known against a submerged boat except to steam away.

The submarine boat has also been perfected in the United States by a Mr. Holland, and adopted already for the United States Navy. My predecessor felt, in common with the whole board, that it was no longer safe to remain in complete ignorance of the real value of this new invention to which the French are attributing so much importance and from which they expect such great results. Five of these boats have been accordingly ordered from Mr. Holland, the first of which it is hoped will be delivered not later than 1st November 1901.

We shall then begin to know something of a subject on which we at present know nothing and I do not think the Cabinet will consider that the step has been taken a day too soon.

[12] *Memorandum by Financial Secretary to First Lord*[2]
[Add Mss 50294]

10 January 1901

Submarine Boats – Premiums to Inventors

In reply to your memo of yesterday's date I have to say that I do not think the plan suggested, viz., that of offering premiums to new

---

[1] Lord Selborne: First Lord of the Admiralty, November 1900 to March 1905.

[2] H. Oakley Arnold-Forster, Parliamentary and Financial Secretary to the Admiralty. From December 1900 to March 1905, the First Lord of the Admiralty was William Palmer, Second Earl of Selborne.

inventors in this country, would enable us to obtain workable boats at an earlier date than that now anticipated. In the case of British builders we should have to allow for the preliminary and experimental stages which, it is suggested, have already been satisfactorily passed through by other designers.

On the other hand, I am strongly of opinion that if the policy of building these boats is decided on, *it is advisable to encourage British Constructors to design and produce them.* Personally, I think this end would be most easily achieved by offering premiums to well known firms, allowing them to conduct the somewhat difficult and not always satisfactory negotiations with the inventors. But this is a matter which I should like to have time to consider in consultation with others. I shall be glad to do so on learning that you wish to receive a report on the matter.

[13] *Memoranda and Minute by Controller*
[ADM 1/7515]
21st January 1901

Submarine Boats
Ordered to be Circulated for the Consideration of the Board.

I think there is no doubt that the responsible authorities in France take a perfectly just view of the value of the submarine boat to them, and they are probably fully aware of both its powers and its limitations.

Their policy in trying to develop it is perfectly sound, but that does not imply that our best policy would be to meet it by submarine boats of our own as suggested by Mr. Brennan and the First Lord.[1]

It is perfectly certain that one submarine boat cannot chase and destroy another.

It may be thought that if the French submarine boats are a danger to our ships our boats would be an equal danger to theirs, but this would only come to be the case if our Fleet was so weakened that the French were able to attempt a blockade of our ports

As far as one can see at present the principal use of the submarine boat will be to attack ships blockading a port, although efforts are being made to extend their action.

The *Narval* Class are designed to cross the Channel on the surface with liquid fuel, and may, if successful, compel us to add somewhat to the passive and active submarine defences of the ports on our

---

[1] Louis Brennan: Australian inventor of wire-guided torpedo adopted by the Army Royal Engineers Corps of Submarine Miners for port defence.

South Coast. It would be comparatively easy to make our ports safe in this way against the attacks of these vessels, and still easier for the French to render their Ports safe from the attacks of ours, as it is not so important for them to maintain free access for their own ships.

The Holland boats are practically on the same principle as the *Narval* and will give us definite information as to the risks to be apprehended from vessels of that kind, and as to the best means of dealing with them.

The development of submarine warfare must be detrimental to a nation depending on navigation at the surface for its supplies of food and the necessaries of life. We cannot stop invention in this direction, but we can avoid doing anything to encourage it. Our Naval policy has been consistent in this matter since Lord St. Vincent made his often quoted remark with reference to Fulton's torpedo, namely: that Pitt was the greatest fool that ever lived to encourage a system of warfare that those who command the seas don't want and which if successful would deprive them of it. That remark and the spirit which inspired it delayed the introduction of submarine mines for half a century, and after the experience of the American Civil War had made their general introduction inevitable, the attention of the Naval Torpedo School was mainly devoted to the methods of attacking them which are now practised by our Fleets.

The question of submarine boats is taking a very similar course. A very well thought out design for a submarine boat was brought to my notice while Commander of the *Vernon* about 1879, which only required one small addition which any torpedo Officer could have supplied to make it efficient. Experiments were carried out which proved the practicability of the one point in this invention which was novel, and the inventor was given no further encouragement. A very similar course has been adopted with all the various submarine boats that have been brought forward since. Each design has been carefully examined and sufficient experiment has been made in each case to ascertain its probable value. It has then been quietly dropped with the result of delaying the development of the submarine boat for about 20 years.

Now we cannot delay its introduction any longer, but we should still avoid doing anything to assist in its improvement in order that our means of trapping and destroying it may develop at a greater rate than the submarine boats themselves.

Politicians should take all favourable opportunities of enlisting the moral sense of nations against this method of warfare, and above all avoid saying anything to prevent the sternest measures being adopted in war against the crews of submarine boats when caught in the act of using them.

Naval Officers should devote their attention to the best means of trapping and destroying them. This necessarily requires as much secrecy as can be maintained without loss of efficiency.

In purchasing the Holland boats and directing the attention of the Torpedo Schools to the subject, we have I think done all that is possible at present.

Mr Brennan has no title to be consulted in this matter. His Torpedo is an ingenious piece of mechanism, but it has much less in common with the submarine boat than a Whitehead Torpedo has. His principal title to fame is that he obtained the largest reward ever paid to an inventor for a weapon of very limited application.

As a reference to submarine boats will have to be made in the First Lord's statement explanatory of the Naval Estimates, I should propose some such statement as the following:

"Certain Foreign Nations having devoted considerable sums to the construction of submarine boats, and having shown their intention to make use of this underhand method of attack in future wars, it has become necessary to provide the means of training a sufficient number of Officers and men in the best methods of trapping and destroying these vessels, if they put to sea with hostile intent."

"Five Submarine Boats have therefore been commenced with that object in view. It is obviously not advisable to make any public statement as to the methods to be employed."

At a later stage I think it would be advisable to make a public statement on the part of the Government on some favourable opportunity to the following effect, provided it is not at variance with the instructions that were given to our delegates at the Hague Conference:

"While this country cannot afford to deprive itself of the right to employ any weapon which is liable to be used against it, the British Government considers that it would be to the advantage of all the Maritime nations of the world if the use of submarine boats for attack could be prohibited."

"It goes much further in the direction of secret attack than any other recognised method of warfare hitherto permissible, and it is peculiarly liable to abuse by being used for unlawful or piratical purposes such as destroying harmless merchant ships or neutral vessels, owing to the impossibility of detection or identification of the perpetrators. If, however, submarine boats are used against us, the Government will have to make use of every available means for their destruction."

[Attached minute (30 January 1901) by Senior Naval Lord]
Submarine Boats were introduced by France in the first instance as a means of defence and protection to their harbours, by keeping off an attack of ships on them and to prevent a close Blockade of their Ports. In this they seem to have attained considerable success and a blockade must in consequence be maintained at a greater distance from their Ports than formerly, thus affording greater facilities for their ships to evade an enemy.

So long as the matter rested there we were not greatly concerned, the weapon was purely defensive and as such not of the same value to us. With the increased radius of action however, that these boats now claim to possess, the position changes, and they can assume the offensive, and as such would have their uses for us, and we could no longer afford to disregard the enlarged uses to which they can be put.

It was recognition of this that led to orders being placed for the supply of five of the Holland boats, a type which after years of trial had emerged from the stage of experiment and had become such a success that the United States Government felt justified in largely adopting it. In doing this I think that we have not only adopted the best course that was open to us, but also all that we can prudently do for the moment.

I do not consider it advisable to go into the market for designs until we have reason to suppose that the Holland boats are not satisfactory nor can I advise calling in the aid of Mr. Brennan who after all would be only an experiment and would have to begin from the beginning. I am confident that when we have the Holland boats to work upon, we shall, without outside aid, develop and improve them where they are found to be wanting. If not, outside assistance can be sought. We have no experts in this class of work in the country – it is necessary therefore to avail ourselves at the outset with the experience of others to save long and tedious delays. While the Controller's proposed remarks for the First Lord's statement are perhaps too forcible for that purpose I concur in the arguments he brings forward, as I do also in the views of Admirals Moore and Douglas.

While we are bound to follow up the development of the submarine boats and thus to have at our disposal whatever advantages they may prove to possess, it is not desirable to plunge too heavily as it must be at first in the dark nor until experience points to the direction in which we should work.

I do not think that we can prudently go further than has been arranged for.

[Attached minute (13 March 1901) by Financial and Parliamentary Secretary][1]

The policy which has now been adopted by the Board appears to me that which the circumstances demand. The view that the Submarine being undesirable is also negligible has been abandoned, and a useful and instructive experiment is about to be made. The examination and manipulation of the Holland boats will give our Officers and Designers a far better idea of the value and possible development of the Submarine, than any number of reports.

It seems clear at present that the Sub-marine cannot be regarded as thoroughly efficient even in France. But it is important to bear in mind that the problem of submarine navigation is by no means incapable of solution, and that the distance which separates the present admittedly incomplete boats from a thoroughly successful type, is very small. There is no warrant for assuming that this distance will not be traversed. At the present moment the principal difficulty to be overcome is the want of a motor sufficiently powerful to drive the boats at high speed. There are other difficulties, but this is the principal one. It would be unwise in view of the progress which has recently been made in increasing the efficiency of the electrical accumulator, and of the development of highly efficient engines of very small weight, to assume that the required motive power will not be forthcoming. When it is applied, the Submarine will become very formidable.

The view taken by the Controller seems to me somewhat dangerous. Our moral objections to any particular weapon will not prevent a foreign power using it against us, if it can be used to our injury. Other forms of protection seem to me more reasonable, and likely to prove more effective. Whether it be desirable for us to build additional Submarines, is a question which may be open to doubt, but that if we do build them, we should have the very best type, and should have at our disposal the latest scientific knowledge with respect to them, seems to me quite clear. I therefore hope that when the Holland boat is introduced, every effort will be made to perfect it.

[1] H.O. Arnold-Forster.

With regard to the whole question, I think it is well to remember that our position is peculiar. The United States, like ourselves, naturally dislike the whole system. They are in a position to indulge their dislike, but we are not. If the Submarine became a practical success tomorrow, not only would the United States be no more threatened than today, but the American harbours would be more easily protected than they are now. On the other hand, if the French were by this time next year to have a squadron of twenty perfected Submarines, it is impossible to doubt that our shipping in the narrow waters of the Channel would be exposed to serious danger. In fact we are more vulnerable to the attack of Submarines than any other nation. For this reason it seems to me desirable that we should lose no opportunity of learning practically all that is being done, and can be done in the matter of submarine navigation. To rely upon the French not being able to perfect their designs, does not seem to me wise. French Constructors and French Artillerists have on many occasions proved themselves fully up to, and sometimes in advance of our own.

[Attached minute (19 February 1901) by Admiralty Secretary]
I concur with the Naval Lords that the Controller's policy was certainly the right one so long as it was possible to retard the evolution of the Submarine. But as he himself says that is no longer possible and the history of inventions proves that when once the utility of a general principle is recognised and it comes into practical use, its scope and value will increase rapidly. This stage has now unfortunately been reached in the case of submarines and this seems to me to compel us however unwillingly to abandon our policy of discouragement and to adopt one of unostentatious progress both in the direction of using and meeting these new engines of war. It is so evident that we are individually interested in vetoing anything which might tend to reduce our present Naval superiority that I fear it would only excite ridicule if we were now to attempt to put down submarines as underhand.

We have got to face them not only as they are, but as what they are likely to develop into, and I cannot see much difference between them and a torpedo from a moral standpoint except that they involve a much greater risk to the user of them.

I believe the pluck and resource of the British Sailor will give him an even greater advantage in such warfare than he now possesses and if submarines can be towed or carried by war ships they might prove a very valuable offensive weapon to a blockading fleet. We are certainly to all appearances behindhand now, but that is only natural in view of the policy we have hitherto rightly followed, and it is not too late to follow up the step already taken in ordering the 5 Holland Boats.

I fear that an announcement of policy in Parliament as proposed by Controller would subject the Admiralty to severe criticism and I should prefer to say that we quite recognise that submarines have become a serious factor in war, that we have ordered 5, and as soon as we obtain them we propose to apply the experience gained in their use to ordering as many more and of such designs as may seem wisest. Also that we shall fully investigate any inventions in this direction which are submitted to us which seem to be of value, and this is the course which I think we must adopt.

[14] *H. Oakley Arnold-Forster to Selborne*
[Add Mss 50294]

8 August 1901

In returning this interesting paper, I ask leave to point out that it confirms in a remarkable way various contentions with regard to the question of the submarine which I have made on many occasions during the last few years viz.:

1. That the submarine cannot be correctly called the weapon of the weaker power, because the power that possesses it, necessarily becomes the stronger power.

2. That the submarine is, in fact, the true reply to the submarine, and that any other view is erroneous.

3. That by far the best protection for our mercantile shipping – and indeed our men-of-war – against submarines, is to keep them as far as possible out of the effective range of action of these vessels and that, consequently, it is most desirable to divert our shipping from the Channel to the North Atlantic.

4. That provided we are as well equipped in the matter of submarines as our neighbours, the introduction of this new weapon, so far from being a disadvantage to us, will strengthen our position. We have no desire to invade any other country; it is important that we ourselves should not be invaded. If the submarine proves as formidable as some authorities think is likely to be the case, the bombardment of our ports, and the landing of troops on our shores will become absolutely impossible.

The same reasoning applies to every part of our empire which is approachable by water only.

[15] *Extract from Memorandum to Cabinet by Lord Selborne*
[CAB 37/59/118]

16 November 1901

* * *

Submarines and Destroyers

I regret to have to record my conviction that the submarine is a vessel to be seriously reckoned with. The true answer to the submarine is the submarine. Not that one submarine is of any use for hunting or destroying another; that work must be left to the destroyer, and we are working strenuously to devise the best method of dealing with the submarine boat when found. Submarine is the answer to the submarine in order that whatever value the submarine may prove to have in war in the future it may be an asset on our side as well as to our opponents, and that whatever damage they may be able to work upon us as its means, we may be able to retaliate upon them. Additionally it adds, undoubtedly, to our difficulties and anxieties, on the other hand, I take it, that the possession by us of submarines would make it even more difficult and dangerous than it is at present the task of invading this country.

While, however, we must continue to increase the number and improve the quality of our submarines, it is none-the-less necessary to increase and improve the quality of our *destroyers*. The invention of the destroyer was a great service to the navy. I cannot exaggerate their value for the protection of our Battleships and Cruisers in narrow waters from the Torpedo-boats and submarines of the enemy and for attacking the Battleships and Cruisers when the opportunity offers.

The Origins of the Submarine Service

[16] *Lieutenant F. D. Arnold-Forster to Captain Charles G. Robinson*[1]
[ADM 1/7522]

HMS *Vernon*,
Portsmouth,
7 May 1901

In the event of the delivery of one of our submarines boats by Messrs Vickers Maxim in the autumn, I have the honour to submit my name for recommendation to the Admiralty for service in the same, with a view to going to Barrow and making myself acquainted with her mechanism[s] so as to be able to take charge of her during the preliminary experiments.

I believe that many officers have applied already, but suggest that a torpedo officer is better qualified for this duty than any other, in which a knowledge of Whiteheads [torpedoes], torpedo boats, dynamos, motors, secondary cells, oil engines, and diving would be essential.

[Attached: Captain C.G. Robinson to Captain Reginald Bacon]
23 July 1901

Will you ask for a Lieut[enant] T for submarine boats? I have Lt. Arnold-Forster ready after the manoeuvres for your service. I have mentioned it to Admiral [Charles] Douglas and he approved so I don't think there will be any difficulty but will *you* start it.[2]

P.S. You will find Arnold-Forster a keen, intelligent and pleasant little man to work with you – a keen mechanic and I quite recommend him to you.

[17] *Memorandum by Inspecting Captain of Submarines*
Addressed to Controller[3]
[Ships' Covers 185]

3 July 1902

Naming of Submarine Boats

No. 6 submarine will be ready for launching on 9th inst. Submit that

[1] Capt. C.G. Robinson: Captain of HMS *Vernon*, 1900–1903.
[2] Adm. Archibald Lucius Douglas: Second Naval Lord, 1901–1903 C-in-C Portsmouth 1904–1906.
[3] Capt., later Rear Adm. Sir, William May: Controller March 1901 to March 1905.

it would be advisable to name this and future boats with names distinctive to each class as they may be built.

The names of pre-historic reptiles appear suitable and distinctive. The name Ichthyosaurus is particularly applicable to this boat fitted with an optical tube corresponding to the marvellous eye of the reptile which was two feet in diameter. Some names of the Saurans are appended.

Ichthyosaurus
Somosaurus
Plesiosaurus
Discosaurus
Pistosaurus
Nothosaurus.

[Attached minute (5 July 1902) by Controller on S15336/02][1]

Captain Bacon has proposed some names for submarines but I consider on the whole it will be more convenient to retain the numbers, prefixing a letter to show the type that the boat belongs to. Thus I propose to call No. 6 of the A class and as she is the first of the class to call her A1.

[Attached minute (7 July 1902) by Senior Naval Lord]

Concur with Controller. I think it preferable not to give names to these submarines. In any case those proposed by Captain Bacon are rather formidable.

[Attached minute (7 July 1902) by First Lord]

I agree!

[18] *Bacon to Rear Admiral William May: Hulk for Crews of Submarine Boats*

[ADM 1/7605]

16 August 1902

Now that the submarine boats are beginning to assemble at Portsmouth some provision for accommodation of the officers and crews is necessary as well as dynamo and compressed air machinery to keep the accumulators and reservoirs charged.

The most convenient depot would be a 2nd class Cruiser preferably the *Latona* which is available, and since no alterations are necessary would still be ready for instant mobilisation if required.

[1] Rear Adm. William May.

The only men required for the cruiser would be a certain number of stokers and engine room Ratings and sufficient seamen to keep the ship clean and efficient. *These can all be supplied by HMS Hazard* assuming as most probable that *Hazard* will never be required to steam more than 10 knots.[1] If therefore the loan of this cruiser is approved, she will merely be transferred from the basin to the stream with the officers present appointed to her. Her cabins will save compensation being paid to the officers of the submarines and the moderate use of her boilers and auxiliary machinery will in all probability keep her more efficient than lying in the Basin.

The accumulators of these boats are worth alone between two and four thousand pounds apiece requiring daily inspection and weekly charging; and without some sort of depot as that suggested it is difficult to see how they can be kept from rapid deterioration.

[19] *Minute by Inspecting Captain of Submarines on Proposal to Appoint a Commander for Service with Submarines*
[ADM 1/7605]

20 December 1902

Submit that it is very desirable that a commander may be appointed for service with submarine boats. Shortly there will be five boats at Portsmouth each a tender to *Latona* and all commanded by Lieutenants. I have to be frequently away from that Port on matters connected with the design and manufacture of new boats and also trials and experimental work at Barrow. During my absence there is no officer at Portsmouth senior enough to take charge of the whole establishment and supervise the routine and running. Since sound judgement as well as mechanical knowledge is required for such work, I would suggest that Commander Edgar Lees would be a very suitable officer for the appointment if approved.

[Attached minute (22 December 1902) by Controller]
Concur with Captain Bacon. I consider he requires extra assistance as the work is increasing. I propose that Commander Lees be appointed in command of the *Hazard* and that Capt. Bacon be appointed to the *Latona*.

---

[1] HMS *Hazard*. Torpedo gun-boat of the 'Dryad' class (1,070 tons) launched 1894. Employed as tender for submarines, 1901–14.

[20] *Minute by Inspecting Captain of Submarines on Convoy of three*
Submarine Boats from Barrow
[ADM 1/7605]

10 January 1903

Nos. 1 – 4 – 5 submarines will be ready to leave Barrow on 18th instant. *Hazard* will therefore require to leave Portsmouth on 15th.

Further at this time of year with the probability of bad weather at short notice and also with long hours of darkness, it will be desirable to provide for towing each boat separately in case of necessity. The most convenient form of towage is with destroyers as being of ample power and yet handy for picking up the boats in tow.

Submit therefore if above is approved

(1) That C in C at Portsmouth be directed to order *Hazard* to leave Portsmouth on 15th and to catch the midday tide at Barrow on 17th.

(2) That two destroyers belonging to the Home Ports may be ordered to be at Holyhead on 17th inst. And to report their arrival to me on board *Hazard* at Barrow by telephone. I can then rendezvous them off the entrance to Piel as weather may allow of the boats starting. Holyhead is the nearest convenient port for the boats to lie. The anchorage at Piel being unsafe for destroyers.

[21] *Inspecting Captain of Submarines to Commander-in-Chief at*
Portsmouth[1]
[ADM 1/7725]

HMS *Latona*
Portsmouth
31 May 1903

I have the honour to forward herewith for the information of their Lordships a report on the running of the submarine boats in the vicinity of Portsmouth up to the above date.

SUBMARINE BOATS

Sufficient experience has been obtained with these boats to assign to them a definite role in the armaments of the Navy, and to make the question of the number of boats required, and their disposition, one that may now be considered.

At present the boats have been always worked from a permanent

---

[1] Adm. Sir Charles Hotham: C-in-C Portsmouth 1901–1903.

base, and have shewn that when employed in this manner they limit the operations of ships in two ways.

(1) That it is almost impossible for a ship to remain near that base.

(2) That it is very hazardous for ships to pass within a distance of about 25 miles.

To thoroughly appreciate the value of these boats it is necessary to place oneself in the position of the Captain of a ship in the vicinity of a port known to contain boats. My experience at Portsmouth after many attacks, leads me to the statement, that, on starting to pass near that port I am always confident that one boat at least will successfully approach the ship near enough to attack. However good a lookout may be kept, however practised and keen the observers, a well handled boat, even in calm weather, will press her attack home without being seen before the attack can be avoided.

The risks of allowing a large ship to approach such a port are so great that I unhesitatingly affirm that in war time it should never be allowed.

But even supposing the optical tube [periscope] of a boat is sighted at sufficient distance for the ship to avoid her attack – what should the Captain do? What course should he steer? This is a most difficult question; but to my mind admits of one answer only, namely, to turn 18 points and steam straight ahead at maximum speed. The reason for this course of action is, that, even though one [optical] tube is seen, those of other boats need not be. The sighting of one boat argues the presence of others. If the boat is merely evaded, in avoiding Scylla, Charybdis, in the shape of a second boat is probably encountered, and the ship sunk. To return by the course of approach is probably the safest course.

One other course of action is open, especially if the boat is no great distance off. Namely to steer straight for her, so presenting the smallest target for her fire and, by steaming hard at her, to disconcert her Captain. This may probably be successful with one boat, but how about others near? Who are probably hovering about the infected area. Such a position is one of very great danger to a ship. If no boat is sighted, the terrible danger exists of being attacked by an unseen enemy. If one boat is sighted, it is merely an assurance that others are hovering near. No ship will, in Naval wars of the future, be at sea without some definite purpose in view. It is inconceivable that a ship will be near a Port except to observe attack on that port, or (in narrow waters) pass that port going to a definite objective. If she has to turn and run at the sight of an optical tube is it worth sending her to be certainly forced into retreat?

If therefore, as is most assuredly the case, boats can prevent enemies' ships approaching a harbour, what is the use of laying down mines? By laying mines, and trusting to them for defence, money is being merely locked up in fixed defences which have absolutely no mobility. Mines have to be laid sufficiently near guns to be protected by them. Ships must know the rough position of all our heavy guns, and the approximate extent of our mine fields. Both are fixed, both can only defend a limited area, and neither would prevent an enemy observing the harbour, or attempting to land men under cover of their large ships, in places out of range of the guns and mine fields. Such a defence can merely be a spotty defence, and can never provide a protected belt round our island or other shores. If boats of fair speed were worked from suitable small harbours, a complete protection would be provided, which could attack and ward off the enemy even when out of sight of land.

* * *

As regards the comparison between the defensive properties of guns in fixed batteries, compared with submarine boats for harbours or arsenals, the question becomes more complicated by the consideration of the weather, and sea experienced in the offing, and whether it is such that boats can work with certainty. In fine weather, and moderately fine weather, boats have the enormous advantage of mobility and invisibility, and in moderate weather they would form a more serious defence than fixed gunfire. But in heavy weather, during which the boats could not work with certainty, the value of the gun increases enormously since its platform is unaffected.

* * *

Having therefore shewn the use of the submarine even in the form of the small Holland Boat, we will next consider the organisation and use of these craft. Submarine boats are daylight craft only. At night time owing to the loss of light, their one great attribute "invisibility due to submersion" vanishes; the necessity for diving vanishes, and the more efficient destroyer under this protective cloak of darkness takes their place. This is the keynote in the use of submarine boats.

Submarines by day, Destroyers by night.

Of course in fine weather a submarine may be used at night but she becomes merely a third class torpedo boat; she wastes attributes useful by day by being employed under uncongenial conditions at night.

* * *

Now the submarine is in daytime, what the Destroyer at night time is to the defences of a port.

It has functions absolutely similar to those of the Destroyer. Its invisibility is ensured by submergence, and not darkness, and it possesses the great advantage of being invisible and yet able to see. Its chief inferiority to the Destroyer lies in comparatively slow speed and uncomfortable accommodation.

These two craft, the Destroyer and submarine, should be considered complementary to each other. The Destroyer working by night, the submarine by day.

This conclusion definitely argues that both these craft should be under one organisation and one head; and that the organisation and distribution that experience shews is best suited for destroyers, should be applied to submarine boats.

* * *

The Type of Submarine for defence

Submarine Boats have one peculiarity which is inherent in them only, and does not apply to any other type of vessel, namely, that the production of a superior type of submarine by a foreign nation does not lessen the value of an existing though inferior type for defensive purposes. The reason for this seeming paradox is, that one submarine cannot normally be used to fight another, and therefore a larger, faster, or better equipped boat cannot crush a weaker submarine. Of course with all above water ships, inclusive of Destroyers, a more powerful vessel can be used to crush a less powerful, and therefore the construction of improved types reduces considerably the effective value of weaker ones. The invisibility and invulnerability, of submarines prevent this in their case. The value of a submarine is an assessment directly between the boat and the ship that may be its objective, and is uninfluenced by rises in value of boats of similar nature.

The type of boat required for Defence

* * *

Numbers required for Home Coast Defence

* * *

Submarines for Foreign Service

The two places where submarines would be most eminently useful, even above all others, would be Gibraltar and Malta. At the former they would be of great use in controlling the Straits, and at the latter they would be most useful for local defence during enforced absence of the Fleet from Mediterranean Waters. The same applies to Alexandria, where a considerable portion of the coast line of Egypt would be guarded by them. In fact most of our isolated coaling stations and foreign arsenals would be considerably strengthened by their presence. Exact numbers for these purposes are difficult to fix, but 12 at Gibraltar and 6 at Malta and Alexandria, or 24 for the Mediterranean cannot be considered an excessive number to work up to.

Other uses of Submarine boats

Although I have only dealt with the uses of boats for Coast Defence during the absence of the Fleet, there are other uses which have to be considered – a brief summary will not be out of place. Considerable prejudice has always existed against England developing torpedo craft chiefly on account of a seductive formula stating that torpedo craft were the arm of the weaker Power. Such a statement is pure nonsense. A sea keeping torpedo craft is essentially an offensive vessel, but who dare prophesy that the strongest Power may not temporarily have to act on the defensive? Taking our numerous possessions and Fleets all over the Globe, it is inconceivable that some will not have to act at times defensively. Naval History continually affords such examples. Again, who can prophesy that an action may not leave us with a shattered fleet, or the fortune of war make us temporarily inferior either in the Mediterranean or Channel? When for a few months strong local defence may mean salvation.

It is unwise to assume that the strongest power will at all times be able to assume the offensive in all the different theatres of war. Hence torpedo craft for local defence become a wise insurance. But beyond this the strategic position of England, thrown as a barrier across the sea exit of all Northern Europe, gives us two small guts to hold, to prevent the egress of their fleets. Namely the Dover Straits, Channel and the sea between Scotland and Norway. The former might, and should be easily held and controlled by torpedo craft without risking large ships at sea, wasting coal and exposed to attack in such narrow waters. Then the only exit for the enemy's fleet will be the more Northern and very circuitous route. In time boats may be built which may control the Northern passage also, but at present a sufficiency of boats should effectually block the Dover passage. The same applies to Gibraltar, where with our Fleet close at hand but in security the passage of a fleet or ship should be closely disputed.

As regards action further afield we have no experience except of the great facility that the boats can be towed, which admits of a deceptive and bewildering mobility for using boats on a definite raid or purpose. Used in conjunction with a Fleet in presence of another Fleet in narrow waters, possibilities exist by skilful manoeuvring of drawing an opponent on to boats left in the track of the fleet, and so precipitating a submarine attack before the action commences. This class of use has yet to be tried; but the fact of the possibility existing has to be reckoned with, and though perhaps only a possibility, will tend to drive fleets from narrow waters to the open sea.

The one use for which boats are eminently *unsuited* is for entering a fortified harbour. No fear need be felt of any boat forcing an entrance to any defended port, if moderate precautions and a decent look out are provided.

Submarine Depot at Portsmouth

* * *

The following broad principles are therefore submitted for approval.

(1) To build 42 A2 class boats or improved type by 10 yearly.
That is at present 13 building 1903

10	1904
10	1905
10	1906

Total   43

(2) To affiliate these when passed into the Service to the Destroyer Depots, Gibraltar and Malta.
(3) H.M.S. *Thames* to remain experimental and instructional ship. To pass all boats and train all officers and men.

GENERAL REMARKS

In this period of the work with the submarine boats, the absolutely initial period, the main underlying feature has been to instil care of handling in the officers of the boats. No hurry, and caution, have been the watchwords. To have in any way hurried the boats, to have attempted to run before they could thoroughly walk would merely have resulted in carelessness. If the results obtained are neither dramatic or great the teaching has been sound, the riper fruit will be gathered later;

but to have hurried would merely have been to court disaster. To have lost a boat through 10 seconds flurry would have been a blow to an experimental service which it would have been criminal to have incurred.

I am in no way ashamed to say that the Captains of boats have themselves protested at times of the limitations I have imposed on them, but I have always endeavoured to instil into them that risks that are legitimate in war; or rapidity of action that is warranted by large experience are at present out of place and that knowledge and confidence are more useful equipment on active service than premature quickness even in manoeuvres.

We have had to test the boats in varying weather and sea, as well as the reliability of the methods and fittings under more or less prolonged conditions of use, and in looking back I do not regret a day of the quiet practice or more or less infantile manoeuvres that we have carried out.

The improvement in reliability of the boats and their handling has been most marked and I am quite satisfied with all the Captains of the boats. Some naturally have proved themselves more qualified than others for the particular work, but taken as they were merely from volunteers of whom I had no previous knowledge, representative of the Torpedo, Navigating and general service branches it is extremely satisfactory to note that they have all done well and that in no sense has any been said to have failed.

The only fear as regards the safety of the boats is that familiarity may breed over confidence and that some day an officer in taking an off chance may come to grief. Provided certain general rules are adhered to the boats are safer than surface boats but if over confidence breeds carelessness accidents will follow. But I hope and believe that the conditions are so simple [and?] that care is so ingrained that the boats will be safely worked and accidents forestalled.

The boats can work roughly speaking in any weather up to a sea usually raised by a wind of 6 in open water. Wind below force of 2–8 makes them visible some distance off, but as soon as the weather breaks the optical tube becomes very invisible. Dull heavy weather makes it difficult for them to see their enemy especially if painted lead colour.

The optical tubes do not mist in thick weather provided the boats dive and wash them.

The torpedo practice from the boat's tube is excellent, but of course estimation of the enemy's speed is quite as difficult as in a torpedo boat, and therefore the chances of getting in a shot are about the same.

Even these little boats would be a terror to any ship attempting to remain, or pass, near a harbour holding them.

The larger boats building should be very much more formidable and at the same time more invisible.

Finally, I have been frequently obliged to be away at Barrow on matters connected with new boats building. During my absence the duties of supervising the running and maintenance of the boats has devolved on Commander Lees and I feel obliged to call to notice the very thorough and able way he has carried out this none too easy work.

[22] *Inspecting Captain of Submarines to Commander-in-Chief at Portsmouth*

[ADM 1/7644]

HMS *Hazard*
3rd August 1903

I have the honour to forward the following report on the passage of this ship convoying A1 submarine from Barrow to Portsmouth.

This submarine is the first of the new type, which differ considerably from the Holland type, but more particularly as regards size, and (by having a high conning tower) are intended to keep the sea in all weather, a matter which is impossible in the Holland Boat.

The main features I was anxious to gain information on were therefore:

Behaviour of the Boat in a seaway more especially as regards any effect the high conning tower might have on her rolling or heaving.

The working of the oil engine.

Reliability of the propeller with adjustable pitch.

We left Piel roads on Thursday 23 July at 11 AM and arrived at Holy head at 9 PM the same day. The weather was fine and sea smooth. I took passage in the submarine to generally observe behaviour. The oil engine worked well except for defects in the electrical ignition but otherwise for the eleven hours run was quite satisfactory. The Boat was quite clear and free from exhaust fumes, being in fact better in general comfort than many engine rooms.

The next day was spent at Holy head examining the engine and charging batteries.

Saturday 25th we left at 8.45 AM; at 10 o'Clock stopped and took A1 in tow as the breeze was freshening from the SE. The force of wind increased to 6 so I ran for the Duilleyn Road for a lee. This necessitated turning beam on to the existing sea and I was able to observe that the behaviour of the boat was excellent.

Sunday 26th left at 5.30 AM; took A1 in tow as ignition was giving trouble and steered for Fishguard to overhaul the igniters, anchored the same evening. Ran the engine during the night with good results. Remained during Monday as it was blowing fresh from SE with a falling Barometer.

Tuesday 28th left at 4.10 AM and found considerable swell outside. Took A1 in tow. The swell was considerable but the wind light and variable with a steady barometer and having satisfied myself that the boat was thoroughly comfortable I continued towards the Lordships. At 6.30 I got out a second towing hawser; swell had increased considerably but still no wind. At 8 PM wind sprung up from the westward and by 10 o'Clock was blowing 6–7 with a very heavy SW swell and a rising cross sea from WNW.

As it was dark and the actual behaviour of the boat was difficult to see even with a search light, I lay to head to wind to keep boat astern and the swell on the Port bow – going dead slow.

At daylight the motion of the boat not exceeding 15° roll I bore up again for the Lordships in a really very heavy swell and a nasty breaking cross sea. *Hazard* rolled at times as much as 25° to 30° and pitched very heavily. The submarine pitched considerably and rolled up to a maximum of about 25° with a pitch sharp. The conning tower in no way appeared to affect this although seas were constantly breaking against it.

At 5.30 Submarine semaphored that they were experiencing fumes from the Battery which made the Boat difficult to ventilate. A battery in good condition when not charging never gives off fumes, hence it was evident some damage had occurred and although I had intended laying to again and riding out the gale, I determined it was better to run for shelter and find out exactly the cause of the damage.

It was now that the tremendous superiority between the boat and the Holland type became apparent. The conning tower being 10 feet above the water could be opened for a man to come out and semaphore and the crew as they suffered from the pungent acid fumes were able to come out in pairs for an airing. While the ventilators extending 8 feet higher allowed fresh air to be drawn into the boat.

The crew had a very uncomfortable time, the pungent acid fumes irritating the eyes and nose and throat considerably but air still could be obtained and they were in no danger. Had however a Holland Boat been overtaken in a similar sea with a like mishap to her batteries, to have opened the conning tower would have meant almost instant foundering – to have kept it closed, suffocation.

I estimated some of the seas by careful observation to be between 16 and 20 feet high which for these latitudes is very large and ordinarily speaking this is the largest sea a submarine will probably even encounter. But in every way she proved herself a most excellent sea boat.

At 10.20 I anchored in St. Ives under a poor lee and examined the batteries. I found the pitching had caused considerable damage to the plates, many being broken away from their bridges, the ebonite separators washed from their places and the plates and cells shortcutting, the boat was full of hot damp pungent Hydrogen fumes. The condition of the Battery was such as to require considerable work to restore and rebuild the plates but the plates themselves are in excellent order.

I cannot be too glad that the boat did meet this sea and have this experience, for I should never have anticipated any motion producing the results that were produced. It is no difficult matter to obviate this occurring again now that we know the weakness. Thorough welding of the plates will entirely prevent it and this can easily be done in all the boats. The present system of wedging is useless against the tremendous forces brought into play in weather such as we experienced.

I immediately undertook such temporary repairs that I could effect, to prevent further deterioration, but I deemed it advisable to wait for more moderate weather even though the condition of the cells urgently required experienced lead burners.

Thursday 29th. I picked up the moorings I had laid down for the submarine and lay prepared to run as it was blowing a gale from the Northward and the shift of a couple of points to the eastwards would have necessitated instantly putting to sea.

Friday 30th left at 5AM for Portsmouth and met with a considerable confused sea off the Lands End. The boat pitched and rolled normally nearly the same as previously but the wedging of the plates and other temporary repairs to the battery prevented any further giving off of fumes.

Saturday 1st August – arrived at Portsmouth

One word about the crew of the submarine. These men are representative of the several branches in the service. Here they were boxed up in a confined space, practically cut off from outside help, rolling and pitching sharply and considerably, with the incessant roar of the breaking seas all round the hull, suddenly finding the appliances they trust to, and whose scientific action they only partially understand, evidently going wrong. Pungent and irritating fumes the exact nature of which they are ignorant are given off and affect their nose eyes and throats – naturally talks of explosions and poisoning in submarine boats, so sedulously propagated by our sensational press must have occurred to their minds. Yet through all this unknown they kept their heads and preserved excellent discipline. Surely it is occasions such as this that throw a prophetic light on what the behaviour of our personnel will be in time or war!

The pioneers of experimental work of an entirely new departure must be prepared for experiences such as these – experiences, which owing to correction and improvement will in the future be totally unknown.

[23] *Extract from Medical Report by Surgeon Captain Stewart* [ADM 1/7725]

The Determination of Carbon Monoxide in the Air of Submarine Boats
A number of cases of illness having occurred amongst the crews of the submarine boats, the symptoms of those affected resembling closely those of CO poisoning, it was necessary to further investigate the subject with the view of arriving at a definite conclusion as to the presence of this dangerous gas.

In order to describe the method adopted for the detection of CO gas it is necessary to consider shortly the nature of this gas.

* * *

In the month of July 1903, each submarine boat was supplied with a mouse in a wire cage which was suspended in the vicinity of the gasoline engine. Observation of condition of the mice was made at regular intervals during the time the gasoline engine was running. It was noticed that when the boats were running with the conning tower open and the ventilation was good, no effect was produced on the mice. During rough weather however when the conning tower was necessarily closed down, the ventilation being less perfect, the mice became uneasy, and were evidently affected by the vitiated air. The state of the mice was coincident with certain symptoms in the crew such as headache &ct. On the 6th July the mouse in No.3 Submarine was suspended in a cage in the vicinity of the engine from 9am to 5pm. The boat was manoeuvring off Portland, the weather at the time being very rough, a SW gale blowing and the conning tower was closed down for $4^1/2$ hours, the engine running all the time. The mouse became very uneasy, panting, and resting on its belly and later on appeared more or less helpless and lay on its side. It was then taken into the fresh air where it recovered.

On 8th July, Submarine No.4 was out at sea for $8^1/2$ hours with the gasoline engine running the greater part of the time. The mouse after some time showed signs of distress, panting etc. It lay down on its side, became more and more helpless and died just before the boat arrived in harbour.

Examination of the blood in dilute solution gave a decided pink tint and was estimated to be about 30% saturated with CO. A number of the crew suffered this day from very severe headaches but recovered shortly after leaving the boat.

This was the first and only occasion on which we had definite proof of the presence of CO in the air of the Submarine boats, but I think there can be no doubt that its presence in small quantities accounted for those cases of illness which I attributed as due to CO poisoning.

Mice are now regularly carried in the submarine boats, but since improvements have been made in the ventilation arrangements, they do not appear to suffer from any ill-effects.

A Role in Imperial Defence: Part 1

[24] *Minute by Director of Naval Intelligence discussing the Role of*
Submarine Mines in Naval Warfare[1]
[ADM 1/7717]

26 February 1903

1. This is a letter from the War Office asking their Lordships to favour Mr. Brodrick with an expression of opinion on the functions of submarine mines in future Naval Warfare.[2]

2. There can be no doubt that the time is ripe for revising the question of submarine mines in connection with fixed defences, owing to the progress of science as represented by
   (a) Increased gun range,
   (b) The Submarine.

3. As regards (a): It is perfectly obvious that if a ship can lie outside the minefield and yet reach her objective by gun-fire, the minefield is useless. And if local conditions make it impossible to advance the minefield sufficiently to keep attacking ships out of gun range, then the mine field must be abolished.

4. It is therefore necessary to review the position of every existing minefield by this standard.

5. As regards (b): It is probably quite accurate, to say that the submarine could in the near future be relied upon to do all that a minefield does now and probably a good deal more. It does not however follow that submarines in sufficient numbers should therefore be allotted to each defended port as part of its defences.

6. The arrangement by which the War Office defends our ports leaving us free to do our duty at sea, is the basis of our War Policy. It is not a question as some Naval Officers contend, that we could do it better than the Army. Probably we could. The point is that if we were to undertake it, a portion of the strength which we are now able to develop at sea, would be absorbed by local defences.

7. It may however be urged that the Navy should work the submarines (taking the place of minefields), the Army to look after the rest. Such duality of command and responsibility would be fatal, quite apart from the question of general policy.

8. As regards Home waters it is thought that the submarine may still take the place of the R[oyal] E[ngineers] Mines and yet not be tied

[1] Capt. Prince Louis of Battenberg: DNI 1902–1905.
[2] St John Brodrick. Secretary of State for War, 1901–1903.

down to a particular port, any more than the torpedo boats operating from certain points on our coasts and intended to patrol certain coast districts.

9. There is an important point as regards the nature of the mines provided by War Office. It is submitted that no electro-contact mines should be permitted in any portion of a mine-field which may have to be traversed by any of our submarines.

10. From the above it will be seen that if a joint Naval and Military Committee were now appointed to carefully consider the general question of the future functions of sub-marine mines in Naval Warfare (to quote Mr Brodrick's words) there would be ample material to work upon.

11. It is therefore submitted to reply to the War Office in the sense that their Lordships gladly avail themselves of the opportunity presented by Mr Brodrick's request to suggest a small committee of Naval and Military Officers being appointed forthwith to consider this important subject by the light of recent developments of War Material afloat.

[25] *Secretary of State for War to Lord Selborne*[1]
[Selborne Mss 34]

2 November 1903

I am very anxious to get the opinion of the Admiralty with regard to a question which gives me some concern. I write to you unofficially because I believe that is probably the best way of starting the matter, but if you agree with me in thinking that the question is one which can with advantage be thoroughly investigated I will bring it before you formally.

1. The point is this: we are spending annually £556,000 upon the maintenance of 5,802 officers and men who are engaged in submarine mining. The mining is undertaken with the object of protecting maritime ports against attack from the sea; in other words, with the object of denying access to foreign men-of-war. I have frequently heard it said that in the opinion of Naval officers, much of the work done by these submarine miners is useless, or superfluous, so far as the Navy is concerned. I remember that there have frequently been complaints during the manoeuvres on the difficulties caused by the want of harmony between land and sea forces, respectively.

---

[1] In October 1903, H. Oakley Arnold-Forster was promoted from Parliamentary and Financial Secretary at the Admiralty to become Secretary of State for War.

2. Now if it be the fact that the Navy does not desire to have the ports protected in this way, I am naturally led to question the advisability of continuing to spend this large sum of money upon a service which has so little value. If the Navy can defend the ports and prevent landing without the aid of submarine appliances, then, obviously, there is no Military need for the maintenance of this aquatic corps, and the correct thing to do would be to abolish it. If, on the other hand, the Navy thinks that submarine miners are necessary from the naval point of view, but that their being controlled by land forces leads to confusion, then the reasonable conclusion would be that the Navy itself should undertake a service they are particularly qualified to perform. Of course it would be a great mistake to act hastily in this, or in any other matter, but I should like to ask you to consider the following proposal ...

* * *

6. Will you consider the whole question? The more I think about it the less do I like this expenditure on military aquatics and I would gladly see it ended. I think it would be a good thing if we could have from the Admiralty a distinct statement that it is the opinion of the Board the maintenance of this force is not necessary for the defence of Naval Ports and for the prevention of invasion.

7. However, I do not propose at present to ask you for any such cut and dried statement, but merely to bring this matter before you.

[26] Lord Walter Kerr to Lord Selborne
[Selborne Mss 34]

4 November 1903

From our point of view the end of submarine mining is well in sight. In fact I mentioned this to Arnold-Forster only a few days ago.

Not only are submarine boats more effective in themselves, but owing to increased range of artillery, hostile ships could in many cases be outside the mines and shell the dockyards or harbours they were originally placed to protect.

I rather think that the subject was referred to in a paper on submarine boats which I sent you a few days ago. We may very much want at Portsmouth and Devonport the ground now occupied by the submarine miners, for the Boats and their plant, gasoline tanks etc., and I am very glad to see that the Secretary of State for War so cordially shares our views.

I suppose that it would hardly be advisable to actually abolish the mines, until we have the submarines for the ports, but this is well in sight for the principal ports. I had a long conversation with Bacon on the subject not long ago.

I think that we may well accept in principle, that wherever we have submarine boats the mines may go – with regard to other places we should have to consider each port on its merits. The question of how far we can take charge of the local miners and work them is a bigger question and I am inclined to think they should remain with the army wherever it is decided that it is an advantage to still retain them.

We should have to add to our present personnel a good deal *especially* in officers – but this would have to be worked out. Our RN volunteers[1] are hardly formed enough [*sic*] yet to express an opinion.

I will talk the matter over with the D.N.I. in the light of Arnold-Forster's letter, but in the general policy of doing away with submarine miners you will find both of us in full accord.

We shall be quite ready to talk it over next week.

[27] *Lord Selborne to H.O. Arnold-Forster*
[Selborne Mss 34]

14 November 1903

I have carefully considered your letter of the 2nd November with the Senior Naval Lord and the D.N.I., and I think the following answers will show clearly the position of the Admiralty.

1. The Admiralty are not in favour of the system of submarine mines now existing. Whatever may have been its past raison d'être, circumstances have now changed. [deleted text reads: They were so far as I can judge inaugurated by the War Office on their sole responsibility, and their continued existence was only admitted by the Admiralty in the year 1893, under protest, and recognising the difficulty of the War Office then withdrawing from a service in which so much capital had been involved. If you turn to the Instructions on Defence Matters, 1901, p.22, you will see clearly the Admiralty view of the matter. The Board resigned themselves to a position they were not responsible for and disliked after securing regulations which left the real power in their hands when the moment of crisis came.]

2. In considering the question of the work of the military submarine miners, you must, however, bear in mind that besides dealing with the

[1] Royal Naval Volunteer Reserve. Established, 1903.

mines, they work electric search lights, portions of which are a necessary adjunct of the gun defence and which the Admiralty regard of course in a different light from that in which they regard the mines.

3. I find that at home and abroad there are 37 ports to which this system of submarine mines has been applied. Of these, 19 may be called naval ports: the rest are purely mercantile ports. If the War Office applied to the Admiralty for an opinion as to the policy of submarine miners, that opinion would be frankly expressed. If the War Office ask the Admiralty to relieve them of the responsibility for submarine mines, the Admiralty will reply that so far as the Naval Ports are concerned they are willing to have that responsibility transferred to them as submarines become available. We could I think begin with the main home ports at once. But in respect of the 18 ports in which there is now submarine mining organisation but which are not naval ports, the Admiralty would not be prepared to accept the responsibility. In the future, when our number of submarines has multiplied and our experience of them is greater, I can conceive it possible that submarines might be stationed at these non-naval ports in the charge of the Naval Volunteer Reserve [RNVR], if that reserve developed into the efficiency for which its best friends hope. But it is too early to speak definitely on that subject, and therefore the Board are not prepared now to express readiness to assume responsibility for the non-naval ports.

* * *

[28] *H.O. Arnold-Forster to Lord Selborne*
[Selborne Mss 34]

16 November 1903

I am greatly obliged to you for your letter. I will take care that a communication is sent to the Admiralty without delay in the sense you suggest.

[29] *Private Diary of H.O. Arnold Forster*
[Add Mss 50335]

22 November 1903

Saw Sir F[rederick] Brackenbury and Sir W[illiam] Nicholson with respect to Selborne's letter re aquatics. In deference to their views I agreed to postpone sending a reply to the Admiralty asking their views as to the value of the submarine business until the committee now sitting has reported.

[30] *Minute by DNI on Acquisition of Fort Blockhouse for Use as Submarine Base*

[ADM 1/7717]

14th December 1903

The Inspecting Captain of Submarines was provided, at Their Lordships' request, with a War Office pass to visit the Submarine Mining establishments at Portsmouth, Devonport and Sheerness with a view to seeing how far these would be suitable as Depots for submarines whenever it may be decided by agreement with the War Office to substitute submarines for mines at these three ports.

Captain Bacon's report, enclosed herewith, shows that these establishments would be eminently suitable.

The following is therefore submitted:

A letter to be sent to War Office to say

(1) that the Admiralty is prepared to substitute submarines for existing minefields at the following places and dates.

    A. At Portsmouth, 1st February 1904.

    B. At Devonport, 1st October 1904.

    C. At Sheerness, 1st October 1904.

(2) If Mr. Arnold-Forster agrees it is proposed that the Royal Engineer mining establishments at

Block House Fort (Portsmouth)

Cattewater (Plymouth)

Sheerness be handed over to the Admiralty on the dates named.

(3) that the establishment in Stokes Bay be retained by W.O.

(4) that the submarine boats at Portsmouth would take the place of the mine-fields both at Spithead and at the Needles.

(5) that if this be agreed to, the Inspector of Submarine Defences and the Inspecting Captain of Submarine Boats be directed to confer and settle the details.

[Attached minute (16 December 1903) by Senior Naval Lord]

Admiral Durnford[1]

---

[1] Rear Adm. Sir John Durnford: Capt. HMS *Vernon* 1896–98; Junior Naval Lord 1901–1903.

Admiral Drury[1]

Will you consider this question?

The immediate proposal, and beyond which I do not think we need enter, is that we should offer to replace submarine boats [for] the present mine field defences at Portsmouth, including the Needles channel, Devonport and Sheerness. The former on February 1st, the two latter in the following autumn.

Commercial and other naval ports in the United Kingdom will have to be considered in the future but the commercial ports in any case must be left until our foreign naval bases have been provided. ...

The first point to be settled is as to the principle of taking over the responsibility and replacing the Royal Engineer mine fields with naval submarine boats.

When it is decided by the Board that the principle be accepted, the first steps can be taken, this will however leave much detail to be filled in later.

[Attached minute (24 December 1903) by Junior Naval Lord]

I consider that before deciding to substitute submarine boats for submarine mines at the principal ports, it is necessary to ascertain how far the boats are capable of the service proposed. It may turn out in some instances that they can replace mines, in others mines will be more effective, and that under some circumstances both mines and submarine boats are needed.

As far as I know, no *practical* experiment has been made by us in this direction. Our submarines have never run a torpedo at a ship underway or at anchor for that matter, and I strongly urge that more practical experiments be undertaken, as for instance in attempting to prevent ships of the Home Fleet entering the Solent.

Has it been definitely ascertained that the explosion of 200lbs of wet guncotton, the Whitehead charge, will not injuriously affect the submarine boat or crew, at say 50, 100, or 200 yards?

Again, have the submarine boats gained experience of the Needles waters and tides, and can they stem the tide at the Needles when submerged? I know something of the Needles waters, and at times the tide will turn a Torpedo Boat round.

It is absolutely essential that the boats should live in those waters a month or so and find out whether they can maintain themselves and handle their torpedoes &c.

If either a submarine defence or submarine boats are necessary for a

[1] Vice-Adm. Sir Charles Drury: Second Sea Lord 1903–1907.

proper defence, it will I imagine be agreed that it must be done properly whichever it is. As to submarine boats, it is proposed to allot 3 for Spithead and the Needles. This is surely not a wise course to adopt, and one unsuited to the consequences. I need scarcely point out that at night or in a fog submarines are of little or no use: also that whilst the net is an efficient protection again to the Whitehead, no defence is possible against the submarine mine. The mines are there, the submarine boats may not be.

Let anyone suppose war to be declared against one or possibly two Powers with strong navies on the 1st April next: Is Captain Bacon seriously prepared to undertake the responsibilities of this situation with 3 submarine boats at each port? What arrangement or agreement has been come to with the artillery defences? I regret that as at present advised I am unable to agree to this far-reaching proposal, as we are in no sense ready for the transfer. Captain Bacon, with his eyes fixed on the success of submarines has become an enthusiast, and is carried away with the one idea, viz. – *to stamp and seal the principle.*

I would urge the Board to take further opinion in this matter before committing themselves to such a serious change of established principle in the defence of our principal dockyard ports, and I suggest experiments, such as I have alluded to, under the Admiral of the Home Fleet.

As regards the ultimate question – if the principle is, after exhaustive inquiry and examination, definitely accepted, well and good, but surely we should wait until we are prepared. It is a great and additional burden to the Navy in men and material, the Naval Estimates must bear it: these are and must be limited, and do what you will Vote 8 is the loser. A larger and well trained personnel will be required sooner or later. It is more than probable if submarine mines are now abolished, and war declared, you would be compelled to re-institute the defences in many instances, at a considerable cost, whereas now the stores exist and the cost of maintenance is small.

I think the acceptation of the principle as regards Home ports will in the end involve taking over a great deal, including probably the coaling stations abroad, a proposition that has been always strongly resisted, as involving the Navy in local defence and making the Commander in Chief of the Station responsible for the safety of localities, thus hampering his liberty and his freedom of action with the Fleet at sea.

[Attached minute (29 December 1903) by Second Naval Lord]
I welcome with delight any system of defence that will efficiently take the place of a submarine mine defence and I think there is every

reason to assume that Submarine Boats can in the near future perform this duty and can at the same time defend a much greater area than submarine mines.

I note that Captain Bacon states in his remarks:

The principle involved, i.e. that the Navy are going to take over now the depots of the R.E. submarine mines wants definitely nailing down and fixing so that we may know exactly what we are looking for.

This is a principle of defence that their Lordships have up to the present time never admitted as part of the duties of the Royal Navy. It has been stated frequently that the forces of the Navy must be free to move in whatever direction their Lordships or the Commander in Chief consider desirable for the general defence of the Empire. If this principle is now adopted the Admiralty must be prepared to appropriate a large number of Submarine boats and personnel as *fixed defences* which, outside a limited area cannot be controlled by them or the Commander in Chief of the Port.

This appears to me to be the first question to be decided, and a very large and important one it is. It involves creating an entirely new and separate department of the Service for which an additional vote must be added to the Naval Estimates.

Presuming the principle to be adopted: is the Navy now in a position to take over the defence of the three great military ports as proposed, in 1904? I am disposed to think there are several problems to be worked out before this can be done and am of opinion that to abandon the Submarine defences without a practical trial of the Submarine boats to prevent the passage of a Fleet into say Spithead is not wise. I would propose that the Submarine boats for the defence of Spithead be turned over to the Commander in Chief Home Fleet to work out under his directions what they can do early next year and they should be supplied with collision heads.

The experiments might take the following lines:

1. The submarine boats might be directed to prevent any Ships or Destroyers of the Home Fleet from entering the Solent between certain dates.

2. To get an idea of how far they are capable of maintaining the necessary condition of readiness for Action night and day in all weathers.

3. What effect a charge of gun cotton of from 10 to 100 lbs. exploding near the submarine has on the boat and crew.

4. The Officers of the Home Fleet would get idea of the nature of the

risks to be insured, the kind of look out required, and generally to set their minds to work on the problem.

With regard to 3. I understand experiments have been carried out in this direction.

[Attached minute (5 January 1904) by Controller]

I am afraid that neither the Second nor Junior Naval Lords has had the benefit of seeing the reports of tactical exercises that have already been carried out by the Submarines and which in my opinion make it certain that Warships will not approach within about 10 miles of any Harbour where it is known Submarines exist, unless they are provided with some means which at present do not exist of destroying the submarine. The Torpedo has certainly not been fired against the *Hazard*, the vessel that was used during the trials, but the Submarines got within striking distance and torpedoes have been fired at targets from the Submarines with satisfactory accuracy. I may mention that the Whitehead was in the Service for some time before the introduction of collapsible heads and it is only quite recently that we have had them for the 18 [inch?] torpedoes.

Trials have also been carried out with explosive charges, leading to the conclusion that at not more than 80 yards the submarine would suffer no inconvenience from the explosion of 200 lbs. of Gun Cotton, and furthermore it was found that the effect of the explosion was the same whether the boat was floating on the surface or totally submerged. The ordinary distances of injury from charges which apply to ships also therefore apply to a Submarine Boat.

I hardly think any modern Fleet would attempt to come into Spithead and certainly not by the Needles unless it had previously silenced the guns, but I can quite understand a Fleet endeavouring to throw shell into the Dockyard from some distance outside Spithead, say five or six miles, and the Submarines should prevent this being done whereas the mines will not. I don't think three Boats are sufficient and have already recommended six boats as we must allow for some being under repair.

The Admiralty have always refused to take over the Submarine Mining and I certainly know of two occasions when the War Office wished us to do so but Their Lordships wisely declined to have anything to do with fixed defences. I also remember when the Submarine Miners wanted to protect Harbours with the Brennan Torpedo discharged from a moving vessel and then Their Lordships declined to allow them to have anything to do with mobile defence.

The conditions of the Defence are now undergoing a change and we wish to adopt a mobile defence which should prevent our Base Ports being bombarded at long ranges. Such being the case the Navy should work them; if it is necessary we must have Submarines that are attached to the Ports and work under local control and others that would be free to move to any other port.

If the Navy take over the Submarine Defence it will naturally mean an addition to Navy Votes and it is to be hoped and expected that the Army Vote shows a corresponding diminution. The Navy have already incurred liabilities up to a million on Submarines and this has been or will be paid for by Vote 8 and I can see nothing against the principle.

I cannot agree with the Junior Lord in his concluding remarks. I think we are a long way off taking over the defence of the Coaling Stations and even if we did the Commander-in-Chief would still be quite free as the Coaling Station would be commanded by another officer as it is now.

I am fully in accord with the proposal to carry out further experiments with Submarines against Fleets but we must be careful not to have accidents, for if one of the Submarines is run down it will destroy the confidence of Officers and men.

[Attached minute (6 January 1904) by Senior Naval Lord]

The Junior and Second Naval Lords see difficulties in adopting the proposal to substitute submarine boats for submarine mines at Portsmouth, Devonport and Sheerness, which do not present themselves to me – at any rate in an equal degree, and I concur with the Controller that they can hardly be aware of the extent of the experience already gained in them.

In no case can Submarine Boats, in my opinion, be classified as fixed defences. They are free to move up to the extent of their limitations, as the Service requires, and as the Commander in Chief of the port may direct. We shall have to maintain submarines at our base ports, whether submarine mines are laid or not.

That we want more experience in working the boats is unquestionable, and this steps are being taken to obtain; but such experience as we have so far is very satisfactory. I do not think sufficient importance has been given to the moral effect of Submarine Boats, as a deterrent to attack on a port possessing them.

I cannot see the connection between superseding Submarine Mines at our principal naval Ports and our coaling stations elsewhere, nor can I see that any principle is conceded by so doing.

I concur in the remarks of the Controller.

[31] *Private Letter from Kerr to Selborne*

[Selborne Ms 41]

6 January 1904

As there is a difference of opinion somewhat between the Naval Lords, we may like to discuss the subject at a meeting of the Board. So doing would I think lead to a rapprochement.

PS. I have sent for Bacon and I am going to talk over with him, Controller, + D.N.I. how we can best extend our experience in the competition with the Home Fleet.

[32] *Meeting of the Board of Admiralty. Minute by First Lord*

[ADM 1/7717]

13 January 1904

This question was discussed at a Board Meeting held today at which all the Members of the Board were present except the Civil Lord, who has started for Malta. The D.N.I. and Captain Bacon, in command of the submarine boats, were present in attendance.

It was decided:

1. that as they become available a certain number of submarine boats will be added to the present torpedo boats and placed under the orders of the Naval Commanders in Chief at the three Home ports. These boats will be used by the Commanders in Chief at their discretion either to assist in the defence of the port or otherwise for the general defence of the United Kingdom, the principal object always being to destroy the ships of the enemy.

2. that if the Admiralty are asked by the War Office whether in their opinion the continuance of the present system of submarine mines is essential for the defence of Portsmouth, Devonport, and the Medway, the Board will reply in the negative.

3. that as the sole responsibility for the defence of Portsmouth, Devonport, and the Medway, will henceforward as heretofore rest with the War Office, it is the War Office which must eventually decide what methods of defence they intend to adopt.

The Junior Naval Lord was unable to concur in No. 2. on the grounds that he doubted whether submarine mines were a form of defence which could ever be safely neglected, and that at all events sufficient experience had not yet been gained with submarine boats to know how far they will prove effective aids in the defence of the ports.

It follows from the above decision that, if the War Office are prepared to abandon the existing mine fields at the three home ports, the Admiralty will be prepared to take over the R.E. mining establishments at Blockhouse Fort, Portsmouth, at Cattewater, Plymouth, and at Sheerness, at dates to be arranged by Captain Bacon with the approval of the Senior Naval Lord. These mining establishments will then become available as depots for the submarine boats. It is not proposed that the War Office should relinquish its establishment in Stokes Bay.

I shall be glad if the members of the Board present will initial this minute, if they approve of it as correct.

PART II

AT PORTSMOUTH, 1903–1905

[33] *Extract from Comments written by Admiral Sir John Fisher on a Memorandum by the Prime Minister (Arthur James Balfour) circulated to the Cabinet Defence Committee in November 1903 entitled: The Possibility of Serious Invasion*[1]

[Add Mss 49710]

c. November 1903

... Serious Invasion (as defined in this paper) is absolutely now beyond the conception of pessimists however extreme because as stated (though in hardly forcible enough terms) in this paper the development of the submarine boat has absolutely precluded the idea of a mass of transports approaching any position where the landing of troops is feasible. Only those who have seen a flotilla of submarine boats (as at Portsmouth) working out in the open sea can form the right conception of the revolution they have caused.

[34] *Fisher to Jack Sanders*[2]

[Add Mss 49710]

Admiralty House,
Portsmouth
5 December 1903

I have just had a letter from Lord Esher saying he thinks the Prime Minister would like to come and stay at Admiralty House some day and see submarines gambolling about![3] I really think he would be greatly interested. It is only by seeing them disporting themselves about that any proper apprehension of the immense revolution they have effected can be obtained, so if you see fit will you kindly convey to him that eight bedrooms in this house are at his service. Unless he comes this week before Friday December 11th, it would be better for him to postpone his visit till the middle of January as we shall have most of the submarines laid up between these two dates.

*   *   *

[1] From September 1903 to September 1904 Adm. Sir John Fisher was C-in-C at Portsmouth. Arthur James Balfour, Prime Minister 1901–1905.
[2] Jack Sanders, Private Secretary, to Prime Minister, Arthur Balfour 1892–1911.
[3] Reginald, Viscount Esher, chairman of special War Office Reconstitution Committee, 1903–1904.

[35] *Fisher to Jack Sanders*

[Add Mss 49710]

Admiralty House,
Portsmouth
29 December 1903

I enclose a very secret print for your edification on Invasion and Submarines and another print not so private very nicely written by our most able naval attaché in Paris.[1] I got out the invasion print from our War Office Committee to show the futility of invasion and the six Army Corps[2] and the mismanagement of Woolwich Arsenal.[3] Sir Evan McGregor (Secretary of the Admiralty) a devoted friend of mine was staying here when I wrote it and he was simply aghast at the thought of Lord Selborne or any of my late colleagues hearing of it! Well it's all quite true – Magna est veritas et piovalebit! but I quite see of the wisdom of not kicking the shins of the Admiralty so I am working subterraneously [*sic*] and with much effect to get matters done. My metier is that of the mole! You know of me by upheavals. I believe someone said the other day Whenever you see the Admiralty, depend upon it, it's that d——d fellow Jack Fisher who is taking a rise out of them! I have spun all this long yarn to impress on you the necessity of keeping enclosures private.

*   *   *

[36] *Memorandum by Admiral Sir John Fisher*

[ADM 116/942.]

late November 1903

INVASION AND SUBMARINES

*   *   *

[1] Captain Charles Ottley, 'A Voice from the French Naval War College', printed and circulated from Admiralty House, Portsmouth *c.* 1903.

[2] In early 1903, the Secretary of State for War, St John Brodrick, proposed a reorganisation and expansion of the British Army into six army corps, three of which would comprise reservists and reserved for home defence, leaving the other three available for service overseas. The scheme was rejected by the Cabinet as too expensive.

[3] The Royal Gun Factory at Woolwich Arsenal, maintained by the War Office, was responsible for supplying the Royal Navy with most of its torpedoes.

EXPLANATORY STATEMENT

The primary object of the enclosed remarks is to make clear that the Submarine Boat has made Invasion impracticable, and this being so, that it follows the Army requires to be reconstituted because Invasion has apparently been hitherto a governing condition in arranging its strength, and this reconstituted Army necessitates a different reconstitution of the War Office than would be the case were the six Army Corps system and the present large Regular Army to be maintained.

The subsidiary object desired to be brought into prominence as affecting the War Office (Reconstitution) Committee is:

That somewhere between the War Office and the Admiralty there has been a lamentable failure in regard to the development of the Whitehead torpedo in that we have dropped behind foreign speed and range to a most serious extent, (Russian torpedo 3,000 yards at 24 knots – English 2,000 yards at 18 knots), and this points either to some grave defect in the manufacturing organisation of Woolwich Arsenal in failing to keep pace with foreign improvements or else to Admiralty inability to recognise our inferiority in sufficient time to bring pressure to bear to remedy this state of things.

The War Commission Report has a pungent paragraph alluding to some discreditable deficiency which seems applicable here – it is as follows:–

It may be acknowledged that to have dealt promptly and effectually with the matter in the midst of a great war reflects credit on those concerned. What is not so satisfactory is that so far as any cause is assigned for the occurrence of so serious a scandal, no sufficient safeguard is suggested to prevent its recurrence.

Note: From a purely Naval point of view the marvellous development of the Submarine Boat and of the Automobile Torpedo will have momentous consequences in the near future which has compelled some of the enclosed remarks, as the facts indirectly bear on the work of our Committee.

Mr Jones, of Fiume, is just now the central figure in Ocean warfare!

THE EFFECT OF SUBMARINE BOATS.

These remarks can only be fully appreciated by those who have witnessed the Flotilla of Submarine Boats now at Portsmouth practising out in the open sea.

It is an historical fact that the British Navy stubbornly resists change. For instance, masts and sails were obsolete 40 years ago, and they haven't even yet quite left us. I remember when I was a young

Lieutenant the First Sea Lord of the Admiralty telling me that he never washed when he came to sea and he didn't see why the devil the Midshipmen should want to wash now! This was apropos of an application for a Midshipmen's wash place in a large new ship then building, where there was ample room for it.

Another First Sea Lord also told me on another and later occasion that there were no torpedoes when he came to sea, and he didn't see why the devil there should be any of the beastly things now! This was apropos of my attracting the attention of his serene and contented mind to the fact that we hadn't got any torpedoes at that time in the British Navy, and that a certain Mr Whitehead (with whom I was acquainted), had devised an automobile torpedo costing only £500, that would make a hole as big as His Lordship's carriage (then standing at the door), in the bottom of the strongest and biggest ship in the world, and she would go to the bottom in about five minutes.

Thirty-five years after this last interview, on September 4th, 1903, at 11am, the ironclad *Belleisle* having had several extra bottoms put on her and strengthened in every conceivable manner that science could suggest or money accomplish was sent to the bottom of Portsmouth Harbour by this very Whitehead automobile torpedo in seven minutes.

This Whitehead torpedo can be carried with facility in Submarine Boats, and it has now attained such a range and such accuracy (due to the marvellous adaptation of the gyroscope), that even at two miles range it possesses a greater ratio of vitally injuring a ship in the line of battle than does the most accurate gun. This is capable of easy demonstration (if any one doubts it).

There is this immense fundamental difference between the automobile torpedo and the gun – the torpedo has no trajectory, it travels horizontally and hits below water, so all its hits are vital hits – but, not so the gun – only in a few places are gun hits vital, and those places are armoured. It is not feasible to armour the bottoms of ships even if it were effectual – which it is not.

During last October, (1903), our representatives at Whitehead's Torpedo Factory at Fiume in Austria, saw some foreign specimens, (notably a Russian torpedo) run accurately for 3,000 yards at $24^{1}/_{4}$ knots, and we are on the eve of getting greater results than these and we may rely on soon having accurate running at over two miles range.

But the whole pith and marrow of the whole matter lies in the fact that the Submarine Boat which carries this automobile torpedo is up to the present date absolutely unattackable. When you see battleships or cruisers, or destroyers, or torpedo boats on the horizon, you can send others after them to attack them or drive them away! You see them –

you can fire at them – you can avoid them – you can chase them – but with the Submarine Boat you can do nothing! You can't fight them with other Submarine Boats – they can't see each other!

Now, for the practical bearing of all this and the special manner it affects the Submarine Boat and the Army and the Navy – for they are all inextricably mixed up together in this matter.

As regards the Navy it must revolutionise Naval Tactics for this simple reason – that the present battle formation of ships in a single line presents a target of such a length that the chances are altogether in favour of the Whitehead torpedo hitting some ship in the line even when projected from a distance of two miles. This applies specially to its use by the Submarine Boat, but in addition, these boats can in operating defensively come with absolute invisibility within a few hundred yards to discharge its projectile not at random amongst the crowd of vessels but with certainty at the Admiral's ship for instance, or at any other specific vessel desired to be sent to the bottom.

It affects the Army, because, imagine, even one Submarine Boat with a flock of transports in sight loaded each with some two or three thousand troops. Imagine the effect of one such transport going to the bottom in a few seconds with its living freight.

Even the bare thought makes invasion impossible! Fancy, 100 000 helpless, huddled up troops afloat in frightened transports with these invisible demons known to be near. Death near – momentarily – sudden – awful – invisible – unavoidable! Nothing conceivable more demoralising!

It affects the Army and Navy conjointly because how could there possibly be any bombardment of any place (fortified or not) with Submarine Boats present, or even, if suspected of being present? It would be quite sufficient for one Submarine Boat to discover its optical tube above water for a few seconds to cause the bombarding fleet to flee for their lives! They would say, Here is a decoy! This brute has shewn itself here to draw off our attention from its colleagues approaching from other quarters! and it would be Sauve qui peut!

It affects the Chancellor of the Exchequer because over half a million sterling a year is now being thrown in the gutter by the upkeep of stationary mines in our military and mercantile ports which can under no modern circumstances of war be of any earthly avail. The brass buttons were retained on the sleeves of the Midshipmen's jackets long after they had taken to pocket handkerchiefs and had ceased to wipe their mouths and noses on the sleeves of their coats!

It is the same with the costly Brennan torpedo which can only be used where no hostile ship will ever come and which can be avoided by the biggest fool in the British Navy with the aid of a shark hook and a grass hawser![1]

It affects the existence of the Empire because just as we were in peril by the non-adoption of the breech-loading gun until after every Foreign nation had it, and just as we were in peril when Napoleon the Third built *La Gloire* and other French ironclads, while we were still stubbornly building wooden three-deckers, and just as we were in peril when before the Boer war we were waiting to perfect our ammunition and in consequence had practically no ammunition at all, so are we in peril now by only having 20 per cent of our very minimum requirements in Submarine Boats because we are waiting for perfection! We forget that half a loaf is better than no bread – We strain at the gnat of perfection and swallow the camel of unreadiness! We shall be found unready once too often!

Note: It may possibly be said in reply that we are building Submarines to the utmost extent of our existing manufacturing capabilities – but it only requires a sufficiently large order to be given to make it worth while to set up fresh plant – an order for 25 more Submarines would cost less than one Battleship. Which is the more pressing? Especially since the splendid feat of buying the two Chilean battleships counting four on a division and saving us £5,000,000 – £1,800,000 = £3,200,000.[2]

Spend this saving on Submarines and longer range, faster, automobile torpedoes.

The development of Submarine Boats has now reached such a stage of perfection that renders it imperatively necessary that this country should take some decided and prompt action to ensure the necessary provision of them being made to meet war requirements. It is now universally admitted (for technical reasons unnecessary to introduce here) that the era of stationary mines for the defence of fortified ports and mercantile harbours is past and gone. Their present up-keep involves an enormous useless expenditure annually, and they lock up a very large and expensive body of Officers and men of the Corps of Royal Engineers in their care and maintenance, and whose entire

[1] The Brennan Torpedo (after its Australian inventor Louis Brennan) was a wire-guided torpedo used by the Army for port defences.
[2] In early 1904, the British Government purchased from Chile two battleships under construction in British yards to prevent them from being sold to Russia on the eve of the Russo-Japanese War. They were commissioned into the Royal Navy as HMS *Triumph* and HMS *Swiftsure*. Although generally regarded by naval historians as second-class warships, their fighting value in 1904 was greater than it appeared. These two battleships were the first in the world to be outfitted with capped armour-piercing shells – capable of penetrating any armour at then anticipated fighting ranges.

absence from military duties in sea work is a great anomaly.

Quite apart from the enormous capital invested in the mine defence of our harbours, the yearly expenditure is at least half a million sterling, and it is money utterly thrown away, because later developments have rendered these stationery mines futile and obsolete.

Two Submarine Boats would be of infinitely more value than the whole present stationary mine defence of Portsmouth (our principal naval arsenal). The Submarine Boat would seek out the approaching enemy but the mines are on the principle of catching a bird by putting salt on its tail. No rational sea Officer of any Navy in the world is ever coming where those mines are now laid because the mines are and must be placed under the protection of gun fire, and the last thing any sane Admiral would do is to attack a fort.

Now, as regards Invasion. Destroyers by night and Submarine Boats by day are the absolute preventive.

What does Invasion mean?

Masses of transports to be prepared for the large bodies of troops which Invasion implies. In these days the concentration of such a number of transports must be known. With all our immense mercantile resources it took nearly three months to get our first 50,000 troops out to South Africa.

The landing places for an Invading Army are few.

No rational Commander would rely on landing on an open beach. Hence, some sort of an harbour must be used. All such suitable places on the Coasts of the United Kingdom can be counted on the fingers of one hand, and if provided with three Submarine Boats such would absolutely intimidate any transports from using them.

The word *intimidate* is used, since the history of the world points to intimidation being the greatest safeguard against warlike operations.

A rash man may neglect this provided he deals only with unencumbered ships; but with transports full of troops no outside risk can be taken, because they of themselves are defenceless and slow.

Gibraltar provided with Submarine Boats would give us back the command of the Straits, which has lately only been a plausible fable.

Malta with Submarine Boats would be independent of the Fleet, even if the Fleet were temporarily obliged to vacate the Mediterranean.

We must always allow for temporary reverses in different parts of the globe; hence the value of having such a defence as Submarine Boats which will prevent temporary raids.

Our great weakness is in not allowing for such temporary reverses.

The great advantage of Submarine Boats is that, although of great defensive value, they can through their large radius of action become offensive. Thus, the Malta Submarine Boats could be off Toulon towed there by armoured cruisers in $2^1/2$ days and if the French were unprepared they would be put into the harbour like ferrets, and out would have to come the French Fleet like rabbits (to be fought by our Fleet) or be sunk in their own harbour!

A Submarine Boat of a certain fighting value – say of the value of the present boats – retains that value, however other nations or ourselves may improve boats. This is because one Submarine Boat cannot fight another, and therefore the progress of the type does not reduce the value of the use of another against ships.

Other boats may be of more value, but the intrinsic value of a type remains, because improvement cannot destroy the weaker type. This is the only class of vessel or ship to which this applies.

This is a most important consideration and gets over our predilection of waiting for perfection before we order anything.

So that however many boats of an immature type are built, their value remains constant, and equal to that they had at the time of building, irrespective of future improvement in type.

Although the construction of these Submarine Boats is at the present time proceeding at the full extent of the manufacturing capabilities of the one firm employed, it is only a question of giving a sufficiently large order, such as to justify the extension of the manufacturing plant to get any further required number built.

We have at present built or building only about 20 per cent of the total number imperatively needed.

(APPENDIX B)
THE AUTO-MOBILE TORPEDO AND ITS RELATION TO THE SUBMARINE BOAT

In these days of close formations of ships in line, the space between the ships is practically equal to the length of ships themselves. If any Whitehead or Auto-mobile Torpedo be aimed at the centre of such a line, it is even chances whether that torpedo strikes a space between the ships, or one of the ships themselves. If two torpedoes are fired the chances are that one must hit a ship. If therefore we have torpedoes which can maintain a good speed for three or four thousand yards, one of every two torpedoes when fired at a line, say of twelve ships (or in other words a *target of two-and-a-half miles long*), should without fail sink a ship. The line is so long (namely $2^1/2$ miles) that it is impossible for the torpedo to miss this line, and therefore the chances of hitting a ship become merely the even chance of striking ships, or the spaces between them. The importance of this cannot be exaggerated when we come to compare the damage accruing to the ship when struck by a shell or by a torpedo. In the case of the shell, damage would undoubtedly be done. In the case of the torpedo, the ship would be absolutely incapacitated.[1]

Hitherto the small damage done by a shell compared to a torpedo has been justified by the longer range at which good accuracy with the shell could be attained compared with the range and accuracy of the torpedo.

One very vital consideration affecting the accuracy of striking of these two projectiles, the shell and the torpedo, has largely been over-looked. Missing with a shell is chiefly due to the trajectory of the shell, which renders an exact knowledge of range all-important for good shooting to be made, and which very largely decreases the probability of hitting a ship, as the range increases over three and four thousand yards. A torpedo has no trajectory, and therefore a knowledge of the range is absolutely unimportant.

The errors which cause missing with a torpedo are, small variations to the right or left of its set course, or estimating wrongly the speed at which the enemy is travelling. In these days, the former source of error has been almost entirely overcome, and the latter cause of error becomes largely minimised by increasing the speed of the torpedo compared to that of the enemy's fleet.

Both these are of vast importance when firing at long range at a single ship, but they disappear when a target of such magnitude as a line of twelve ships is presented as an objective.

The importance to us of these considerations is overwhelming.

At the present time our manoeuvring distance from the enemy is usually accepted to be about 3,000 yards. A few seconds want of appreciation on the part of an admiral might reduce this considerably.

Our length of line in our first fleet action would probably be not less than twelve ships. Our close order formation in line causes our ships and the intervals between them to be equal. We have therefore in our present system of fighting, the whole of the necessary factors to enable an enemy's fleet to bring irretrievable disaster on us, if that enemy happened, unknown or unappreciated by us, to have torpedoes capable of running 3,000 yards at a good speed. It would indeed be a day of awakening!

To obtain ranges of 4,000 or even 5,000 yards means only substituting a longer air chamber for the present one, it is evidently a

---

[1] In September 1903, the Royal Navy concluded its attempts to make battleships invulnerable against torpedoes after the target ship *Belleisle*, which had been fitted with every conceivable form of protection, sank inside Portsmouth Harbour after being hit by a single torpedo.

matter that could be done almost secretly. The lengthening of the torpedo means the lengthening of the tubes. This (without entering into technicalities) can easily be done. It is therefore not impossible to imagine our first fleet action in a big war, fought against a fleet fully appreciating and being provided with weapons of this sort, and this without our previous knowledge. At all events the possibility is one which demands our gravest attention. (The trials at Fiume in October last (1903) accentuate the deep significance of these remarks.)

The easiest work that a Submarine can perform is the defence of a harbour. Since its object is achieved, whether it frightens away or whether it sinks the enemy's ship, it is therefore not a matter of such great importance whether Submarine Boat in this case remains absolutely invisible or not during its attack. If a ship is ever rash enough to approach a harbour she suspects of being defended by Submarine Boats, the sight of a foot of the optical tube of the Submarine Boats above water would send her steaming away for all she is worth.

The sight of one boat argues the presence of others, most probably invisible, and it is but the commonest form of trap to lead a ship by the sight of an optical tube of a boat unfavourably placed for attack, into the arms of other boats more favourably situated.

Conclusions such as these all point to the fact that ships will not risk themselves in narrow waters known to contain Submarine Boats. The risk is out of all proportion to the gain.

[37] *Arthur Balfour to Fisher*

[Add Mss 49710]

Chatsworth
3 January 1904

I have read with the deepest interest your private and secret notes on submarines.

Some of the things you recommend have, I think, been already practically agreed upon by the Defence Committee and the Cabinet, e.g., The substitution of submarines for mines, and the defence of places like Malta, Gibraltar and Bermuda, by submarines.[1]

It is unnecessary to tell you how heartily I am in sympathy with your observations on the relation between submarines and invasion: indeed, my paper on Home Defence, which I think was shewn you, is largely based upon the considerations to which you refer.

[1] See minutes of 64th meeting of the CID, November 1903, CAB 2/1.

The aspects of the torpedo question, however, on which you dwell, are new to me. I was not aware of the extraordinary efficiency of the modern Whitehead as demonstrated in appendix B of your paper. It is very disquieting, and positively alarming when supplemented by your observations on the superiority of foreign torpedoes. ...

I shall not, of course, use your name, but I must be permitted (as from myself) to raise in Defence Committee or otherwise, some of the points to which you draw attention.

I am very little consoled by an observation which occurs on p.3. of Appendix A, where you point out that the submarine may be used for offensive, as well as for defensive, purposes. On the whole, this seems to me to be greatly to our disadvantage. I take it that Portsmouth for instance, is more accessible than either Brest or Toulon, and the game you propose to play at the latter [Toulon] could be played by the French even more effectively at the former [Portsmouth].

Forgive these hasty notes,

P.S. Your observation on the *permanent efficiency* of submarines, even though of antiquated type, is most acute, and seems to me, at least, perfectly sound.

[38] *Balfour to Lord Selborne*
[Selborne Mss 39]

Chatsworth,
7 January 1904

I am anxious to get on with my draft report on Smaller Invasions:

* * *

Supposing the enemy were, by a small expedition, able to take Portland or Dover from the land side by a *coup de main*, would there be any possibility of their accumulating a large invading force on our side of the Channel by ferrying over in fast transports successive instalments of troops, which could, of course, be safely and rapidly landed at such places, so long as they were held by the enemy?

This is a somewhat different problem from the one attacked in my paper on Home Defence; and it seems to me the only alternative not there dealt with.

I wish we had more submarines. Would it not be possible to induce some new firm to build us a few? They are, after all, cheap, and their peculiarity is that, inasmuch as they cannot be attacked by other submarines, the type does not become antiquated:– in other words however much submarines may be improved in the future, existing submarines will never become obsolete as against the types of vessels with which they are intended to deal.

[39] *Fisher to Balfour*

[Add Mss 49710]

5 January 1904

I have written confidentially about it to Prince Louis of Battenberg (*who is out and away the best man inside the Admiralty building*) and to Admiral May the *Controller* who is the only progressive member of the Board (but not too much so, alas!) and I enclose his reply. He doesn't realise that half a loaf is better than no bread! See the extract I enclose from the French naval estimates as marked in red ink! As I have written in red it is the old old story – we strain at the gnat of perfection and swallow the camel of unreadiness! Why I don't send him the reasoned statement is that even Satan disguised as the Angel of Light wouldn't persuade my late colleagues at the Admiralty that in the course of a few years no fleet will be able to remain in the Mediterranean or the English Channel! But at the same time submarines at Malta, Gibraltar, Port Said, Alexandria, Suez and Lemnos will make us more powerful than ever. (The Russians are welcome to Constantinople if we bag Lemnos and infest the Dardanelles there from with Submarines!)

Submarine Development

[40] *Memorandum for the Controller by Inspecting Captain of*
Submarines on New B type Submarine
[Ships' Covers 185]

S.30250/03.
7th November 1903

Attached are proposals for an experimental submarine. If you approve the design can be quickly got out as we possess all requisite data. I have attached reasons dealing fully with the question of not largely increasing tonnage.

Type of Submarine Boat for 1904 – B type.

The A type of boat was designed as a more seagoing class than the Holland. A1, the first boat built was hurried on to try whether a boat of 100 feet length could be easily handled below water, whether generally this size of boat was seaworthy, whether light petroleum engines of suitable weight and dimensions could be built; and, what is equally important, installed in a submarine preserving the boat cool, ventilated and habitable.

As soon as A1's diving trials shewed the type to be an improvement, even on the extreme handiness of the H boats below water, A2 A3 A4 were laid down, the lines being suggested by Mr. [Edward] Froude to give increased speed at economical powers.

A1's engine meanwhile gave promise of success but was below the HP anticipated. A more powerful engine was therefore designed which on trial has developed 750 HP but which at the same time has taken a longer time to develop than was anticipated, the number of practical and unforeseen difficulties had been very large but one by one they are being overcome, with a result that we have not only a light oil engine of as a large a power as we are ever likely to employ with light oil, but a fund of practical experience in the design of engines which is invaluable.

As soon as it was seen that engines of this type presented no fundamental objections the hulls of A5–13 were proceeded with. At this time the Engineer in Chief who has been studying the heavy oil engines undertook to install one of these in A13. This engine if successful, and there is every reason to suppose that it will be so, will be a very useful type for future boats on account of the cheaper oil that can be used.

The question therefore of a B type of boat is ripe for consideration, that is in what directions should the type of submarine boats be improved. Unhesitatingly the answer is in seakeeping qualities.

The A2 class boat is primarily useful for work off harbours and coastlines. Broadly their qualifications should prove as follows:

Surface Speed – Maximum 11–12 knots; Cruising half power – 10 knots.
Submerged Speed – Maximum 8–8¹/₂ knots for 4 hours; ordinary – 6 knots for 8–9 hours.
Seaworthiness – Able to remain 3 days out at a pinch to ride any ordinary bad weather.
Radius of Action – About 400 miles.

Now for a more seaworthy craft evidently the two most important improvements would be increased radius of action and increased habitability. These can both be arrived at by increasing the tonnage of the boat, so enabling more fuel to be carried, and a more suitable superstructure added to add to the comfort and freedom of the crew. But this increase in displacement will affect the speed both above and below water, and it is well for this reason, as well as tactical and strategical considerations to examine carefully what speeds are essential to a submarine boat.

The surface speed of a submarine is of solely strategical, and not tactical value. When a submarine sights a ship it is an axiom of her tactical rules to instantly submerge and steer by compass at right angles to the course of the ship to cut her off. Surface speed therefore ceases to exist tactically. The risk of detection from breaking water, or from the high magnification on calm days of long distance telescopes, forbids her remaining on the surface.

The use of surface speed is therefore entirely strategical, and need only be of such a value as to take her conveniently from place to place. This I think we may safely assess at 10–12 knots. At all events it is not worth sacrificing either radius of action or any other quality, to exceed this rate of speed. We must in considering this point divest our minds absolutely of the governing principles of action of destroyers and torpedo-boats to whom high speed is absolute necessity because to them it has *tactical* importance, both in making an attack, and also in escaping from pursuing enemies. To a submarine, attack is made submerged, invisibility allowing of close approach and also of escape from the close attentions of pursuers.

Submerged speed is solely of tactical and not strategical value. Submerged speed is of course the exact converse of surface speed, and only of use when in touch with an enemy, therefore normally the greater the submerged speed the better; but the attendant difficulties of attaining high submerged speed are so great that we will find it necessary to fix some rate, less than a theoretical maximum, which will not rob the boat of equally important attributes.

A few figures will easily settle this.

The submerged power necessarily to drive a boat at a given speed varies approximately as the displacement of the boat. That is if a 200-ton boat requires 150 HP to get a speed of 8 knots for 4 hours then a 300-ton boat will approximately require 225 HP to get the same speed for 4 hours. But by increasing the tonnage of a boat the weight of hull is increased in about the proportion of 7/20; the weight of the batteries carried are also about 7/20 of the displacement. Therefore in an increase of say from 200-tons to 300-tons *to preserve the same speed* submerged, 70 tons out of the extra 100 tons are absorbed by hull and batteries leaving 30 tons. These 30 tons are required for many purposes or at all events the greater part of it is, so that little if any of the extra displacement is available for increasing submerged speed.

Again, the increase of batteries means complication, increase in original expense, and also in upkeep, so that it is desirable to keep these batteries as few as possible. It will therefore be seen that only a necessary submerged speed should be provided for.

Now let us turn to actual attack. The obvious rule for a submarine is (since her submerged speed is always less than that of a ship) to steer at right angles to the course of a ship until ahead of her. If a submarine bears 10° on the bow of a ship going 15 knots the speed of the submarine must be 2.5 to get ahead of her. If the bearing is 20° the speed of the boat must be 5.4 knots.

If 30° speed must be 8.5 knots.

If 40° speed must be 12.4 knots.

If 45° speed must be 15 knots.

So the difference in angle of bearing between 6 and 8 knots is only 22° to 28° and since the total angle of sighting is only 90° (see figure 1) the advantage of 8 knots over 6 knots is only as 28:22 or 4:3.

[figure omitted]

The gain in advantage is hardly commensurate with the sacrifices involved in increasing speed especially since boats working in groups are sure to have one of their numbers in a favourable position for attack. At all events the tactical gain is not so great in a knot's increase of speed.

There is a way however of getting higher speed for a short time, and that is by discharging the batteries at a high rate, this though uneconomical would on occasions allow of one or two knots increase in speed for a short time, and since an attack is not likely to last over half an hour, there is not much objection to this method.

I would therefore prefer, instead of putting in battery power to drive the boat at 8 knots for 4 hours, to increase the weight of motors and enable her to go at 8 knots for 2 hours, keeping her normal 4 hours submerged speed at 6 knots.

The best captain of a submarine boat that we have prefers if possible to manoeuvre below at 4 knots in an Holland boat, and his attacks are by far the most successful, which is additional evidence that a high submerged speed is not always desirable. I would therefore propose to have a normal submerged speed of 6 knots for 4 hours but to be capable of attaining 8 knots for 2 hours.

Radius of Action above water is a matter of importance far more so than actual speed above water. *Radius of Action below water* is unimportant but *time* that a boat can be kept down is a serious matter, since at times a boat will have to trust to remain below water to escape from pursuit by a fast light craft. Eight hours is easily attained and should prove sufficient.

We must now consider whether submarines cannot be given methods of defence. Submarines at present have only an offensive armament. Two loaded torpedo tubes should be sufficient for practical purposes offensively. This coincides with a destroyer's torpedo armament, and so far as I know, no torpedo-boat or destroyer has ever practically in manoeuvres found more than two torpedoes a necessity.

Defensive Armament.

There can be no doubt that some form of defence would be very valuable to a boat. At present the knowledge that your sole defence is to skulk below water is not inspiring and for destroyers to know that a submarine will probably not shed their teeth in firing torpedoes at them, and that beyond this that they have no other means of retaliation, is decidedly unnerving. I therefore unhesitatingly advocate trying in our experimental boat providing one 12lb. Such a gun loaded from the conning tower can be easily arranged.

The knowledge to a destroyer that a submarine could approach unseen, rise and fire a point blank shot of a calibre sufficient to sink them will destroy the present feeling of security they possess, and make them far more careful how they not only dog a submarine, but how they loiter near our ports. You will introduce a feeling of unrest to the destroyers, something like the ships feel, which will be a great advantage.

The extra weight and complication will be small and before anything else this should be tried. A tracing shewing the broad principles only is attached.

The experimental boat therefore for B type I suggest is as follows:–

Length	135 feet
Displacement	300 tons
The same engine as A2 (improved) to give 12 knots.	
One sixth more battery power ...	
Heavier motors ...	
Radius of Action on surface	800 miles
Additional superstructure for crew to use	
Sleeping accommodation	

The extra 100 tons of displacement would be roughly devoted as follows:–

Hull Increase	35
Extra oil	10
Extra on motors	3
Extra water ballast	18
Extra batteries	10
Gun	1.5
	77.5

leaving 22.5 tons for ballasting purposes and increasing metacentric height.

* * *

The cost of the boat is fairly easily computed ... £47,100 + cost of gun.

[Attached minute (14 December 1903) by Controller]

Concur with Captain Bacon that our principal object in a new design of submarine should be to improve sea-keeping qualities and this should be done by increasing the radius of action and providing greater comfort for the crew.

The relative merits as to the value of the surface and submerged speeds is well presented and I propose to have the normal submerged speed at 6 knots for 4 hours but to be able to attain 8 knots for 2 hours.

Concur in providing two loaded torpedo tubes which should be made large enough to take our most modern 18-inch torpedoes. The proposal to work a gun from a submarine is certainly a novelty. I can see no real objection to it and consider it is worth a trial for the reasons given by Captain Bacon.

I propose to approve generally the dimensions etc suggested and to order this experimental submarine type B on the tenth boat of this year's order.

[Attached minute (15 December 1903) by Senior Naval Lord]

I concur in the proposals except as regards the gun on which point I think that some further consideration is necessary. It is as the Controller says a novelty to introduce a gun armament into a submarine, and it is a question of policy whether the additional weight and obvious complication on the possible chance of using a submarine against a torpedo boat destroyer is worth, what carrying a gun involves.

No account appears to have been taken for weight of ammunition. I am a little sceptical about having cordite among such inflammable materials as a submarine carries. As at present advised I do not think the game is worth the candle, but I am open to conviction, after a fair discussion.

I should like a meeting of the Naval Lords to discuss the matter and refer the paper to the Junior and Second Naval Lords to read before we meet.

[Attached minute (22 December 1903) by Senior Naval Lord]

The result of the discussion of the Naval Lords was that while concurring in the new type (B) submarines it was considered undesirable to introduce a gun armament into it.

[41] *Memorandum by Captain Reginald Bacon and Subsequent Correspondence relating to the Appointment of a Naval Constructor to Assist the Inspecting Captain of Submarines in the Design of Submarine Boats*

[ADM 1/7745]

19 December 1903

I submit the time has arrived to place the design of Submarine Boats on a more permanent footing – at present I have assistance from one constructor and one Engineer Officer at the Admiralty, both of whom however have nearly the whole of their time employed on other matters.

The rapid advance in demand for these boats, and the necessity for adapting every commercial, and scientific improvement to obtain the most advanced type of Boat, absolutely require the entire time of two such officers.

It is not an exaggeration to say that up to the present all suggestions for improvement in design, other than outline for speed which is entirely due to Mr. [Edward] Froude,[1] have lost considerably in value from the want of digestion and the undivided attention of such specialised officers. It may be argued that employment would not be found for them for eight hours a day, for six days in the week – with this I do not agree.

There are many questions waiting solution. There are many trials to witness and to be further initiated, construction has to be watched – and above all I desire officers with sufficient leisure from routine work to apply fresh and unweakened brains to development of type. I need not instance [sic] France who has three of their greatest constructors devoting their time to this question.

Rapidity of evolution of type in this class of weapon is a national necessity. Up to date we have roughed through difficulties and obtained a good working type – ahead there still lie vast possibilities, in the realisation of which we must not be behind hand. Now is the time that we require specialised and undivided attention.

It is because we cannot afford at this present junction to lose any time in the study of this ever developing branch of construction that I press the need for this assistance for your consideration.

[Attached minute (5 January 1904) by Director of Naval Construction]

The necessity for making every possible improvement in submarine boats as rapidly as possible is fully recognised. In accordance with the agreement between the Admiralty and Messrs Vickers, these boats have up to the present been designed by the Firm named, who have a special staff engaged both on the preparation of the outline design, and the subsequent preparation of drawings of individual portions of the work, and the firm has undertaken entire responsibility for the realisation of the contract conditions as to speed, radius of action, power of propelling, apparatus, &c, as well as for the provision of proper strength and stability in the boats.

Any improvement in the design as regards speed, radius of action, seaworthiness, &c, is dependent on the maximum dimensions which can be accepted, and the introduction of some lighter form of propelling apparatus in relation to power than is now available.

Improvements as regards individual parts of the boats – and it is presumed Captain Bacon refers more particularly to these – would not, it is considered, require the undivided attention of a constructor who

[1] Edward Froude: Superintendent of Research, Admiralty Testing Tank, Haslar.

would initiate improvements and superintend the draughtsman preparing the drawing.

The constructive officer who has been directed to work in association with Captain Bacon is available, as pointed out on paper, either to examine a new design for submarine boats while in course of preparation by contractors, or on its receipt in office. The latter course is preferable unless urgency is of primary importance.

With regard to details of individual parts of the boat, all proposals received by DNC have been at once examined and reported upon.

With regard to Captain Bacon's specific instances of work to be done, the present constructive officer could attend all trials affecting hull work, and an Overseer could be appointed to watch construction.

As recently reported, the existing staff of Constructors and Assistant Constructors is not now sufficient to deal satisfactorily with the large and constantly increasing amount of work in office. The constructor selected to work in association with Captain Bacon, has also charge of all Scouts, Destroyers, and 1st Class Torpedo Boats, and neither this officer nor any other could conveniently be detached for work on submarine vessels alone.

[Attached Minute (15 January 1904) by Engineer in Chief of the
Navy][1]

Though the orders for submarine boats are for the present given to Messrs Vickers, Sons & Maxim, in accordance with an agreement made with that Firm, it is probable that when that agreement expires these boats will have to be designed by the Admiralty.

It appears desirable that a small staff of professional officers be detailed to devote more study than at present to this class of vessel which has many special features, the information being obtained and recorded to provide reliable data with which to work out future designs. The air compressors, bilge pumps, propelling machinery, torpedo fittings, &c, are all specialities and require separate and special study. In the Engineer-in-Chief's Branch much information has been obtained concerning oil fuels and internal combustion engines and this information represents so much advance made towards the ability to design a more satisfactory engine than the present main engine of the boats now being constructed at Barrow.

It appears that for the present it would be sufficient as regards machinery to appoint a Senior Engineer Officer as an additional Engineer Inspector on the Engineer-in-Chief's staff, this officer to

---

[1] Rear Adm. A. John Durston: Engineer in Chief of the Navy.

devote all his time to studying the particular type of machinery, main and auxiliary, best suited to the requirements of the submarine. He would be assisted by the information already in Office before-mentioned as regards the internal combustion engine and by the present staff detailed to supervise torpedo fittings. We would work in conjunction with the Inspecting Captain of Submarines and give him all possible assistance in making improvements in the engine now being built, &c, as well as working out any suggestions for future designs which the Inspecting Captain may make from time to time. By this means it is considered that the Engineer-in-Chief's Branch should be in a better position when the agreement with Vickers expires, to work in conjunction with the Director of Naval Construction and design the machinery for future boats at the Admiralty if this course should be decided on.

[Minute (16 January 1904) by Controller]
Captain Bacon – any remarks?

[Minute (1 February 1904) by Inspecting Captain of Submarines]
Lognote the first and last remarks of DNC — *The necessity for making every possible improvement in submarine boats as rapidly as possible is fully recognised and the constructor selected to work in association with Captain Bacon has also Charge of all Scouts, Destroyers and 1st Class Torpedo Boats* — I fail to see how these two can be reconciled. To shew [*sic*] how little the difficulties and extent of my work in connection with the design of submarine boats is appreciated in the above remarks, I would point out that out of the fine elements of design connected with construction attributed to Messrs Vickers only one is dealt with by them viz. – the preparation of drawings of individual portions of the work. In all the remainder – preparation of outline design, speed, and radius of action – the firm gave no guarantee of performance and left it to our responsibility. And as regards stability – no one has any idea of the best metacentre helpful for these boats.

Again the statement that any improvements in design as regards speed, radius of action and seaworthyness are dependent on maximum dimension and lightness of available power, totally ignores the difficulty of the problem since there are two speeds, not one speed, two radii of action, not one radius of action, two separate motive powers of different ratios of weight per HP, not one motive power each of these being co-related and dependent on the other.

To be perfectly frank, all improvements in type of these boats have been introduced by myself – and not by Messrs Vickers – who have no man of sufficient practical experience in the boats to initiate a design. It is not the examination of these designs in office that I attach the slightest value – But what I *do* want is the undivided help of a constructor for six months whose technical knowledge will greatly assist my practical experience – To deprive me of such assistance is neither fair nor wise – I do not know what the salary of a constructor may be – but putting it at £500 a year – such assistance for six months would represent only a one half percent charge on our annual order of Submarine Boats.

As regards remarks of Engineer-in-Chief – I am glad to note that much information has been obtained concerning internal combustion engines by his department and that ability to design better engines than those now being built at Barrow, and (I presume also than one being constructed by Messrs Hornsby Ackroyd) may ultimately be looked for – But the whole burden of my request is for a practical education of my engineer assistant not accumulation of information. I venture to think that had my present able assistant been absolutely free to attend the experiments during the last year at Barrow, *knowledge of* would have been added to *information on* the subject.

I recognise with pleasure the cordiality of the EinC's desire to supply an engineer officer to assist one untrammelled by other duties – The appointment of this officer as an additional inspector at the Admiralty seems excellent provided it is recognised that he should be absolutely free to work with me as my assistant to experience the practical difficulties of our necessities as well as absorbing all information available in office.

[Minute (2 February 1904) by Controller]

I concur with Captain Bacon. An Officer having charge of all Scouts, Destroyers and 1st Class Torpedo Boats cannot have much time left to study submarines and help in the initiation of improvements. It is of the highest importance not to fall behind other nations in the design of this type of vessel and I consider that a Constructor and an Engineer Inspector should therefore be told off entirely for work in connection with the Submarines. As the DNC and E-in-C respectively for a period of 6 months. They should be appointed as soon as possible.

[Minute by Accountant General, 15 February 1904][1]

If, as is understood, a Constructor is intended to be lent from one of

---

[13] N.W. Awdry: accountant-general.

the Home Dockyards and the post of Engineer Inspector to be filled by a senior Engineer Lieutenant RN, the approximate cost for a period of 6 months would be as follows:

* * *

Total. £469

The retention of the Officers for any period in excess of 6 months will require Treasury sanction.

[Minute (9 March 1904) by Director of Naval Construction]

It is proposed to detail *Mr. H.G. Williams*, Constructor on the Admiralty Staff, to perform under the Director of Naval Construction the duties connected with the design and construction of Submarine Boats. Mr. Williams will devote his entire time to these duties and will work in close association with Captain Bacon.

It is submitted that while Mr. Williams is employed on this duty Mr. A.G. Fox, Constructor, Portsmouth, be transferred to the Admiralty Staff if Director of Dockyards has no objection. Mr. Watts has been communicated with and concurs in these proposals.

Submarines versus Battleships: the 1904 manoeuvres at Portsmouth

[42] *Vice Admiral Sir Arthur Wilson to Lord Selborne*[1]
[Selborne Mss 21]

24 February 1904

* * *

We had a preliminary look at the sm. boats off the Nab yesterday, we actually begin operations on the 8th March.

You know I attach great importance to developing the means of destroying submarine boats, while all efforts hitherto have been made on the side of ~~developing~~* improving them. I am putting all the brains of the Home Fleet to work on the problem and I hope we shall be able to make at least a beginning in attacking it.

Even if we do not succeed to any extent the operations will be of great use in letting us know what the risks really are. I think Bacon is probably quite ahead of the French in managing the boats so we shall have a good taste of what is likely to happen.

[43] *Telegram from Commander in Chief at Portsmouth (Admiral Sir John Fisher) to Admiralty*
[ADM 1/7718]

9.40 pm
18 March 1904

Regret to report loss with all hands of A1 submarine boat which was run down by a Castle Line steamer off the Nab about three o'clock this afternoon. Lieutenant [Loftus] Mansergh and Sub-Lieutenant [John] Churchill were on board. Names of men will follow when verified.

[44] *Telegram from Commander in Chief at Portsmouth to Admiralty*
[ADM 1/7718]

19 March 1904

Begins. The circumstances leading up to the sinking of the

---

[1] Vice Adm. Sir Arthur Wilson, C-in-C Channel Squadron 1904–07.
*Words scored through are crossed out in the original document.

Submarine appear to be as follows but will require to be verified. The Cruiser *Juno* of the Home Fleet had been successfully attacked South West of Nab by Submarine No. 3 about 2 p.m. the Submarine having got unobserved within four hundred yards of *Juno* and hit her with her torpedo.[1] Captain Bacon had also ordered Submarine A1 to proceed to attack of Cruiser *Juno* of Home Fleet. Submarine A1 was not then submerged and proceeded on this duty which accounts for [S.S.] *Berwick Castle* reporting seeing her four points on her Port bow quarter of an hour before she struck her. She could not at that distance have seen her if only periscope was above water. Submarine A1 was steering South and *Berwick Castle* about S.E. by E. and *Berwick Castle* must have struck the starboard side of the Submarine which is the side now uppermost of the Submarine and apparently hit her near the stern. The *Berwick Castle* was observed from the *Hazard* to go full speed astern with her helm hard a starboard about the time of striking Submarine. All the above will require verification. I only send it as the best information available at the moment of my sending in this message. We hope to have Submarine A1 slung for towing by midnight as divers are now making good progress. Ends.

[45] *Kerr to Lord Selborne*

[Selborne Mss 41]

Admiralty
19 March 1904

This is a great misfortune and it makes me very sad.

I had at AM time [*sic*] decided to forgo my visit to Portsmouth in case of anything being wanted at the Admiralty, but there is nothing that we can do at the moment in London, so I have decided to go down and ascertain what one can do on the spot.

The only gleam of satisfaction is, that if it had to be, the accident was not caused by one of our own ships during the manoeuvres. We know no particulars yet, these I will endeavour to find out.

I shall be back this evening,

PS. I hope to find out what chances there are of recovering the boat.

---

[1] HMS *Juno*: 'Eclipse' class 3rd class cruiser (5600 tons). Eleven 6-in. guns. 19 knots.

[46] *Telegram from C-in-C, Portsmouth to Admiralty*
[ADM 1/7718]

8.57am
29 March 1904

Bad weather prevents any material progress in salvage operations yesterday worse weather this morning will I fear stop work altogether.

[47] *Fisher to Lord Selborne*
[Selborne Mss 24]

Portsmouth House,
31st March 1904

It is kind of you to have written as it has done Bacon good. He is much affected by it all. He is overworking himself and I don't know what to do with him. He says it would be no relief to him if he went away on leave nor do I believe it would.

He doesn't know that I've found out he is taking what they call brain tonics which means nature is not giving him the necessary sleep! I've asked him to dinner to meet you on April 7, so perhaps you'll kindly give him a lecture then!

What I fear from the delay is explosion of the air cylinders through acid eating away the iron.[1] There are 10 tons of acid loose in the boat. I've warned Capt. Elkind that every day's delay introduces a new danger.[2] Weymss hopes you'll go to Osborne April 8.

[48] *Extract from Umpires' Report on Manoeuvres Between Home Fleet and Submarines*
[ADM 1/7795]

March 1904

On the eighth day:–
The *Resolution*[3] on eight occasions was almost within torpedo range of submarine boats, who could not quite reach her, owing to her speed

---

[1] A reference to the danger of battery acid eating through the steel hull of HMS/m A1.
[2] HMS/m A1 was finally raised on 18 April 1904.
[3] HMS *Resolution*: Royal Sovereign Class (14,150 tons) battleship. Laid down Palmers January 1891 under 1889 Naval Defence Act. Four 13.5-in. muzzle-loading guns and ten 6-in. BL. 15 knots.

and constant alteration of course. No torpedoes were fired, though *Sprightly* and *Leven* were put out of action by gunfire.

On the ninth day:–

The *Juno* had three torpedoes fired at her, the last of which went home, *Juno* being at the time 3 miles S by W of the Nab, on her way in to make her second reconnaissance. *Juno* had no destroyers accompanying her except one (*Peterel*) for picking up.

It is therefore clear that on these days the attacking vessels ran great risks, at a time when they could devote the whole of their attention to submarines, without having to pay any attention to the gun defence of the port, within 7,000 to 8,000 yards of which they constantly approached. Speed on the part of the ships and constant alteration of course are the two principal methods by which to circumvent the submarine.

The risk from submarines seems to be undoubtedly very great to a force operating on an enemy's coast, or even within 100 miles of it or more. That the accepted functions were realised was proved without a doubt.

Submarines certainly assist the gunfire of the Defence. They extend very greatly the defence of a port beyond the limit of its gunfire, as instanced by the torpedoing of *Royal Oak* 6 miles from the Nab, the attack on the *Empress of India*[1] by a boat without a periscope 9 miles from the Nab, and the torpedoing of *Juno* 3 miles from the Nab.

The question as to whether submarines can provide the protection afforded by mines is more difficult to answer. Submarines can hardly claim to replace mines at night, or in difficult navigational waters even in daylight. On the other hand, it is most unlikely that battleships and cruisers will attempt to enter even the outer anchorages of an enemy's fortified port at night, and mines are, undoubtedly, a constant source of danger to the ships and submarines of a defence, and to the mercantile trade of a port.

In conclusion, we consider that the submarine, used as either an offensive or defensive weapon, has achieved a state of completion and perfection which must render it in naval warfare a continual danger and menace to an enemy in enclosed waters, or in any position within its radius of action. Its capabilities in the hands of well-trained and experienced officers are very great, and the fear of what it can do renders its strength still greater.

Every vessel within its radius, at sea or in harbour, is open to its attack, and it is very evident that some means of protecting battleships

[1] HMS *Empress of India*: Royal Sovereign Class battleship.

and cruisers must be devised, or some method of construction must be adopted which will render the attack of a modern torpedo less fatal than it now is.

Finally, it may be considered as most conclusively proved by these Manoeuvres that submarines are a powerful and deadly addition to the defence of any port, fortified or mercantile, and that submarines must be provided for the defence of all our important ports, if we are to effectively deny the waters of these ports to our future enemies, and, moreover, make invasion impossible.

(signed)

Captain Robert Arbuthnot[1]

Commander Herbert A. Fyler[2]

Commander Thomas Ogilvy[3]

[49] *Admiral Reginald Custance to Lord Selborne*[4]
[Selborne Mss 23]

31 August 1904

The report on the submarine manoeuvres which took place in March last has just reached me and it is a disturbing document not so much from the advance made by the sm. which it indicates, as from the attitude of mind assumed by the umpires. They appear to regard the sm. purely from the defensive point of view and sum up by recommending that submarines must be provided for the defence of all our important ports, if we are to effectively deny the waters off these ports to our future enemies, and moreover make invasion impossible.

I protest against this view, and feel sure that you will agree with me that the most effective method of defending our ports and preventing invasion is a rigorous offensive against the floating force of the enemy, and that the submarine should be developed with that in view – as an offensive and not defensive weapon. If the views of the umpires are to prevail the history of the mines will be repeated with the sm. and

---

[1] Capt. Sir (later Rear Adm.) Robert Arbuthnot Bt: Capt., 1902; Rear Adm., 1912. Flag-Capt. to C-in-C Portsmouth 1903–04, Commodore (T) 1910–12; Rear Adm. 2nd Battle Squadron 1913–14; 1st Armoured Cruiser Squadron; killed in action at the Battle of Jutland 1916.

[2] Cmdr (later Rear Adm.) Herbert Fyler.

[3] Cmdr (later Capt.) Thomas Ogilvy: Capt. HMS *Natal*, 1908–10. Leading RN gunnery expert until his death in 1910 of food-poisoning.

[4] From 1902 to 1905 Rear Adm. Reginald Custance held the post of Rear Adm. Mediterranean Fleet.

large sums will be diverted from the offensive to the defence.

* * *

The fact is that naval opinion is and has been for years saturated with the ideas of defence not withstanding the efforts of a small minority to counteract them. The cause is to my mind largely due to the narrow system of education and to men's minds being concentrated on materiel for too large an extent but this would require too much space to explain and would take up too much of your valuable time, so I will conclude with great respect from,

[50] *Fisher to Rear Admiral William May*
[ADM 116/942]

Admiralty House, Portsmouth
20th April 1904

I will begin with the last thing in your letter, which is far the most important, and that is our paucity of submarines. I consider it the most serious thing at present affecting the British Empire! That sounds big, but it's true! Had either the Russians or the Japanese had submarines the whole face of the war would have been changed for both sides. It really makes me laugh to read of Admiral Togo's EIGHTH attack on Port Arthur! Why! had he possessed submarines it would have been ONE attack and ONE attack only! It would have been all over with the whole Russian Fleet caught like rats in a trap! Similarly, the Japanese Admiral Togo outside would never have dared to let his transports full of troops pursue even the tenth of their way to Chemulpo and elsewhere!

It's astounding to me, *perfectly astounding,* how the very best amongst us absolutely fail to realise the vast impending revolution in naval warfare and naval strategy that the submarine will accomplish! (I have written a paper on this, but it's so violent I am keeping it!) Here, just to take a simple instance, is the battleship *Empress of India.* The Flagship of the Second Admiral of the Home Fleet nine miles beyond the Nab Light, (out in the open sea), so self-confident of safety and so oblivious of the possibilities of modern warfare that the Admiral is smoking his cigarette, the captain is calmly seeing defaulters down on the half-deck, no one caring an iota for what is going on, and suddenly they see a Whitehead torpedo miss their stern by a few feet![1] And how

[1] Attacked by No. 5 commanded by Lt J.B. Moreton.

fired? From a submarine of the pre-adamite period, small, slow, badly fitted, *with no periscope at all* – it had been carried away by a destroyer laying over her, fishing for her! And yet this submarine followed out that battleship for a solid two hours under water, coming up gingerly a mile off, every now and then, (like a beaver!) just to take a fresh compass bearing of her prey, and then down again!

Remember, that this is done, (and I want specially to emphasise the point), with the Lieutenant in command of the boat out in her for the first time in his life on his own account, and half the crew never out before either! Why, it's wonderful! And so what results may we expect with bigger and faster boats and periscopes more powerful than the naked eye, (such as the latest pattern one I saw the other day), and with experienced officers and crews, and with nests of these submarines acting together?

These last manoeuvres are the most misleading manoeuvres ever devised by the art of man! They really are the most misleading set of circumstances that the mind of man could have evolved! These six original first built inadequately fitted too slow submarine boats competing against a powerful fleet and three flotillas of destroyers all at their prime, and the paucity of the submarines, (we ought to have had at least 30 instead of 6!) rendering it impossible to make attacks as in actual war from a number of boats acting together, and then again there were the destroyers calmly laying over the submarines, (so utterly out of the question in actual war), fishing for them as if they were trying to catch whiting! The whole thing was ridiculous and misleading in the extreme!

However, YOU will be the person to be hung, and not I! As I have not disguised my opinion in season and out of season as to the essential, imperative, immediate, vital, pressing, urgent, (I can't think of any more adjectives!) necessity for more submarines at once, at the very least 25 in addition to those now ordered and building, and a hundred more as soon as practicable, or we shall be caught with our breeches down just as the Russians have been! I don't blackguard you personally, it's the d—d cautious old age spirit that actuates and always has actuated and always will actuate the Board of Admiralty!

*   *   *

However, I've got away rather from the submarines in this long digression, but in all seriousness I don't think it is even *faintly* realised the immense impending revolution which the submarines will effect as offensive weapons of war. When you calmly sit down and work out what will happen in the narrow waters of the Channel and the Mediterranean – how totally the submarines will alter the effect of Gibraltar, Port Said, Lemnos, and Malta, it makes one's hair stand on end! As I hear you are coming to stay with us at Admiralty House with Mrs May and Co. in a few days, I will leave the rest of your letter for personal reply.

I hope you don't think this letter too personal!

A Role in Imperial Defence: Part 2

[51] *Secretary of State for War to Army Chief of the General Staff*[1]
[Add Mss 50308]

War Office
19 May 1904

Aquatics:

I wish to call your attention to the accompanying correspondence between Lord Selborne and myself with regard to the subject of that part of our expenditure which appears in the estimates under the heading of aquatics. [See documents 24, 26, 27]

You will observe that the Admiralty are apparently not unfavourable to a change in the existing arrangements. I think, therefore, that the matter should not be allowed to drop.

The distinction made by Lord Selborne between the essentially naval and the non-naval ports appears to me reasonable, and I think we may content ourselves with asking the Admiralty to undertake the entire maritime defence of the former.

The principle that I have laid down in my letter as to the question of cost, seems to me sound. The Admiralty view is that our apparatus are not of use to them, at the same time, they undoubtedly depend upon our arrangements to a certain extent.

It will therefore be reasonable to hand over our apparatus, together with the cost of maintaining them.

This will ensure a reduction on our own Estimates, and at the same time will enable the Admiralty to carry on the system to a modified extent, until they can replace it by a proper installation of submarine boats. There is no objection to the Admiralty utilising the money for other naval purposes if they choose to do so.

I commend the whole subject to your attention, and shall be glad if you could see your way to dealing with it in a broad spirit, with the object of removing what I believe to be an anomaly to both services, and likely to lead to great confusion in war.

[1] General Sir Neville Lyttelton, Chief of General Staff (1904–07) and brother of Alfred Lyttelton, Colonial Secretary 1903–1905.

[52] *Extracts from the private diary of H.O. Arnold-Forster*
[Add Mss 50341 and Add Mss 50342]

22nd November 1904

Committee of Defence, 11:30 to 2:30. Subjects:–
1. The abandonment of submarine mining
An odd situation. I, who originally started the idea, in November 1903, and was rebuffed by the Admiralty, now appear as the councillor of moderation, begging the Admiralty representatives not to go too fast, even towards so desirable an end. They are going too fast, and Fisher made very exaggerated statements as to the dangers arising from the use of observation mines, which Austen,[1] who of course knows nothing about the matter, naturally took up in support of his purely financial plea for root and branch abolition. I fear the change may yet produce greater expenditure for new guns than economy due to the removal of the mines.

I pointed out that the position of the Military officer responsible for the defence of a port must be reviewed. Clearly he cannot be expected to do the same after half his weapons have been removed as he could do while he had them. However, I am quite content that the change should be made at once at the Naval Ports. I believe there will be a great fuss in the Mercantile towns if we made a change before we have anything to put in the place of the mines.

23 November 1904

Went to the *Admiralty* and saw *Prince Louis of Battenberg*. Spoke to him about the previous day's discussions at the CID. I told him that I thought that the meeting had been hasty in its conclusions; that there had been considerable exaggeration; and that it would be necessary for the War Office to get a clear pronouncement as to the future responsibility of the Army in connection with the defence of non-naval ports. ... I then saw Fisher, who was in the middle of what he calls a vivisection committee, i.e. A committee formed to investigate the whole of the Estimates, with the view of effecting reductions. ... I told Fisher that he had exaggerated grossly in his statement about the danger inseparable from submarine mines. Well, he said, one has sometimes to lay it on with a rather thick brush. I said that if that was his idea he had certainly lived up to it.

[1] Austen Chamberlain: Civil Lord at the Admiralty 1895–1900; Postmaster General 1902–1903; Chancellor of the Exchequer 1903–1905.

25 November 1904

Lunched at the Senior,[1] and thence to the Defence Committee, where we discussed the submarine mining question again. I think I have made the committee realise a little more fully the slap-dash character of last week's proceedings, and its disadvantages. I am persuaded that half the discussion last week was carried on by A.J.B.[alfour] and the Ch[ancellor] of [the] Ex[chequer] to say nothing of some other members of the Committee, under the firm impression that the mines concerned were floating contact mines, instead of observation mines controlled from the shore. I strongly criticised the view taken by Sir JF that submarine defences were a greater danger to friend than foe, and pointed out that in no single instance since the Blockade of Charleston has any incident occurred which could give the slightest colour to such a statement.[2] The Navy now seem inclined to substitute the modest word inconvenient for dangerous.

2 December 1904

To the Committee of Defence where we discussed submarine mines, as I think with much precipitation and very little knowledge. We finally came to the conclusions which I think will not do harm if we exercise a little judgement in carrying them out ... but there has been no discrimination, no consideration of local circumstances, and no examination of details.

* * *

I also strongly advised that we should clinch the bargain with the Admiralty by taking over their surplus guns, so as to get the whole of them under Army charge.[3] Fisher – bless him – is quite capable of offering the whole lot over again to the Home Office, or to the Colonial Office, or the Australians, or anybody else, if by doing so he can in the least assist any little plan on which he has set his heart. So a letter is to go accepting at once.

[1] The Carleton Club.

[2] Charleston, South Carolina. Principal port of the Confederate States of America during US Civil War (1861–65).

[3] In December 1904, the Admiralty announced a redistribution of the fleet. The station fleet system was abolished and the gunboats and 3rd-class cruisers that had been stationed overseas mainly for constabulary duties were recalled home and scrapped. The guns of these ships – mainly 12-pdr and BL 6-in. ordnance – were declared surplus to naval requirements and given to the Army.

[53] *Extract from 60th Meeting of Committee of Imperial Defence*
[CAB 37/6/117]

2nd December 1904

2. The question of the general policy in regard to submarine mines was again discussed.

* * *

Conclusions

The following Resolutions were adopted, vis:

a. The Admiralty must be the sole authority for advising as to what classes of hostile ships may reasonably be expected to attempt to enter certain waters, and whether the attempt to enter such waters would ever be made.

b. As it has already been decided that no submarine mine defences are to be laid out in any of the naval ports without Admiralty sanction, the whole installation of the submarine mine defences with the steam mine-laying vessels, and also the electric lights pertaining thereto, where not essential to the efficiency of the gun defences, should, at the above ports, be at once transferred to Admiralty charge.

c. As regards the commercial ports, two categories have to be considered –

(1) Ports which, for special reasons, such as the fact of their containing large factories of war material, e.g. [Messrs. Armstrong's] Elswick [ordnance factory] on the Tyne; shipbuilding centres, such as the Clyde, Tyne, and Mersey; and coal distributing localities, such as Barry and Cardiff, have special claims to protection on account of the broad national interests involved, and

(2) Admiralty decide that there is no reasonable probability of such attempts, the submarine mine defences should be removed. Each individual port, as to which the Admiralty decision is in the converse sense, should be made the subject of inquiry, with a view to determine whether any special measures of local defence are necessary, and, if so, what measures.

d. In all cases where, in accordance with (e) submarine mines are removed from commercial ports, the buildings and vessels involved shall be transferred to Admiralty charge, to be used in connection with submarine boat stations, if it should be decided to establish the latter at the ports in question. Minor ports, where only private mercantile and not national interests are involved.

e. The cases of the ports coming under the two categories (1) and (2) should be referred to the Admiralty to decide as to whether the channels of approach are such that vessels of the cruiser or larger classes could reasonably be expected to enter them for hostile purposes. If the Admiralty decide that there is no reasonable probability of such attempts, the submarine mine defence should be removed. Each individual port, as to which the Admiralty decision is in the converse sense, should be made the subject of inquiry, with a view to determine whether any special measures of local defence are necessary, and, if so, what measures.

The Personnel

[54] *Memorandum [probably Captain Bacon] on The Training of*
Officers and Men for Submarines
[*Naval Necessities*, vol. 2, pp.454–6]

April 1903

PART I. – OFFICERS.

As soon as sufficient boats are built they will be organised in flotillas at different ports both in England and also abroad.

These depôts will have a certain number of crews who will run all the reserve boats in turn, keeping them efficient.

A certain number of officers and men will be constantly employed in boats, and a certain number of spare officers and men will be required thoroughly trained and available to commission all the boats in time of war.

The officers required are –

1 lieutenant and 1 sub-lieutenant to each boat.

1 commander to each port.

1 captain in charge in England, or in each country where the number of boats makes this desirable.

The chief considerations that govern the selection of these officers:–

Captains and commanders must have a knowledge of electricity and general Whitehead work, and some mechanical knowledge, and, if possible, should have been captains of submarine boats themselves.

The captains of boats –

1) should be young,

2) be good rough navigators,

3) hard-headed and careful,

4) have a good general electric and Whitehead [torpedo] knowledge.

Sub-lieutenants should be promising officers who are merely borne to be sifted and give opportunity for selection of capable captains of boats.

Probably two years in submarine boats is as long as an officer should stay, on account of the strain both on mind and constitution.

It is proposed that an officer should only stay for two years in the submarine service. Very high qualities are necessary to handle submarine boats efficiently. The officers are incessantly under a certain mental tension; their vision is more limited than in a conning tower; they have to navigate by eye and rough methods, and to pay exclusive attention to the handling of their ship; and they must learn not to meddle with the business of subordinates but to mind their own business of the moment; they must learn to carry out the intention of their officer without signals or communications, exactly as may have to be done in modern fleet actions, and in this way they get excellent training for the command of ships thereafter.

A sub-lieutenant model for subsequent employment in a submarine boat will not require further training. As sub-lieutenant he will have to take to pieces and put together every portion of the fittings of the boat, pack joints, grind valves, drive an oil engine, and work practically with accumulators. A special artificer engineer is borne for the training of these officers.

For training purposes it is advisable to have sub-lieutenants to each boat; one can be trained as captain, the other in turn take every duty in the boat. On promotion to lieutenant, all those recommended will have become eligible for employment as captains of boats, and it is suggested they should have the letter (old English S) [sic] after their names in the Navy List.

PART II. – CREWS

It has been found that, in consequence of the strain involved, the crews of the submarine boats cannot (consistently with full efficiency) work in them continuously, and the following double crew is proposed for each A class boat, half running the boat daily, and the other half resting, but both being employed for overhaul and repairs:–

2 petty officers, 1st class – general service ratings – as coxswains.
2 leading torpedo men as electricians.
2 engine-room artificers.
2 stoker mechanics.
4 able seamen (seamen torpedo men).

This gives two crews of one of each the above ratings, and two able seamen. One engine-room artificer in each crew is a necessity with the large engines.

To train these men it is proposed to keep the present original boats' crews to form a backbone and training staff. It is proposed to train each crew for six months, which means that, with four boats (allowing one always laid up), it would be possible to train eight complete crews a year, and never have more than four crews locked up at a time under training. In case of mobilisation these double crews could split up into nucleus single crews, and train each another half crew in a very short time. It is proposed that four of the double crews as specified above be taken for training at once.

To avoid locking up more men than necessary, and also because of the very limited accommodation in *Latona*, ratings should be borne as follows:–

	Part Complement	Supernumerary
P.O., 1st class	2	6
L.T.O.	2	6
A.B.(S.T.)	4	12
E.R.A.	2	6
Leading stoker	2	6
Stoker mechanic	2	6

those shown as part complement being borne instead of ratings now on board *Latona* and *Hazard*.

[55] *Inspecting Captain of Submarines to C-in-C Portsmouth*
[ADM 1/7644]

HMS *Thames*
Portsmouth
8 May 1904

In accordance with ALM8965 of 29th July 1903, I have the honour to forward the following report in the training of crews for submarine boats, together with certain suggestions, the outcome of the experience gained.

On the whole the results of the training have been satisfactory, but in certain ratings the wastage has been greater than was anticipated, and several alterations in the numbers required for training are necessary. I propose to deal first with the officers and subsequently with the crews.

Training of Officers.

In originally putting forward proposals on this subject, I suggested training sub-Lieutenants so as to create a reserve for war time – as well as supplying Captains for the boats commissioned, rather than accepting the services of older men.

I am more than ever convinced that this is the right way of supplying Captains for the Boats; but at the same time I have had the conviction forced on me, that we cannot rely too much on the officers thus trained forming an efficient reserve – since I am convinced that the mental, and nervous strain, on the Captain of a Boat, tells on him in time, and that with increased service in the Boats the essentials of a good captain more often decrease than increase.

I do not say this is invariably the case, but it is true in the majority of cases. I therefore do not anticipate that captains of Boats who have been to sea, subsequent to their training, will return to the Boats and be as good in command as those who have lately been trained.

I must confess that the result is not astonishing, it is merely what we have always found with Torpedo Boats, that the younger man, whose mind has not been *biased* by experience, will regard the risks less, and the object to be gained more. In ordinary manoeuvres he comes more or less to grief, but generally gets his attack home. With a Captain of a Boat, whether torpedo boat or submarine, it is grasp of immediate initiative, and not the arguments of an experienced, and too evenly balanced mind, that stamps the man as a success. *(this is absolutely correct as I can vouch for from personal experience of the Destroyer and Torpedo boat flotillas in the Mediterranean JF)[1]

The rule is of course not invariable but it governs the majority. With the crews it is different. I have no reason to think that any amount of work below the water affects them in the slightest, either in health, or mind, and the same is the case with the torpedo boat's crew.

My opinion is therefore that with the Captain of the boat it is not a case of loss of nerve anymore than it is the case with any of the crew – but merely the constant strain and responsibility makes them less suited for the special work of commanding these boats.

With submarine boats alone of all other craft it is not the man who attacks, but the man who gets in who is the success. The practical outcome of this is that the majority of the captains of the boats should be young, but that each flotilla should be controlled by an older and more experienced officer, both to check rashness and also for disciplinary purposes.

I would particularly emphasise that I do not commend rashness, in fact my life is spent in preaching caution. But there is a wide gulf between the two, which perhaps may be defined in the main best, by saying that one generally seizes on an opportunity to press home, while the other has a tendency to wait for a better chance.

* * *

I have already stated my opinion that, after a certain age, officers as a rule are not so adapted to command boats as when younger, and I am confident in my previous opinion, that, as a rule, two years is a sufficient time for an officer to remain in command. Hence every two

[1] Marginal Comment by Adm. Sir John Fisher, C-in-C Portsmouth.

years, sufficient officers will have to be trained to supply captains for *all boats* in commission.

We must therefore be prepared, as additional boats are delivered, and depots formed, to increase the number of sub Lieutenants under training. This I submit should be commenced when the Devonport Depot is started.

Training of Men

The training of men presents at present even greater difficulties – since the numbers required are considerable, and in the case of special ratings such as LTOs, ERAs and Leading Stokers, unless those trained be permanently retained, volunteers will hardly suffice to maintain the numbers.

I have previously remarked that the work does not seem in any way to tell on the crews, and therefore I can see no objection to retaining the men trained as long as they feel themselves, or are considered, to be fit to stop.

* * *

If volunteers still come forward, sufficient should be trained, allowing for wastage, by the end of the financial year. But it is hardly to be expected that volunteers will come so freely as hitherto, since all those who have volunteered have been taken on and therefore none of these initially keen remain. It will be impossible to keep the numbers required unless all men volunteering be trained, and *kept* as long as they are fit.

If men are to be encouraged to remain, each ERA selected to have charge of an A class or larger boat should (if he has passed) be rated CERA, and be given charge pay, otherwise he is at a disadvantage compared to the general service ratings. Six more ERA or CERA ratings should be called for and trained at once to make up for wastage. As regards Leading and chief Stokers, a definite proportion of chief rates, say one to every four boats, should be allowed. So that every leading stoker may stand ultimately a fair chance of a chief rate.

* * *

Recent experience in manoeuvres has shown the necessity of providing double crews for each boat in war time.[1] At present we are

---

[1] The proposed system of double crews was approved by the 1904 committee, but never implemented because the Admiralty deemed it to be too expensive in manpower. In 1905, a compromise was reached. Thereafter, four crews were provided for every three submarines.

only training sufficient of the ERA and LTO ratings to provide single crews. As soon as the Devonport Depot is started additional training of those ratings should be commenced.

In conclusion, I would ask for their Lordships' approval, for reasons explained, of the following definite proposals:

To enter on board *Thames* and train at once 6 additional ERAs.

For the artificer in charge of an A class boat to be given the rate of Chief Engine Room Artificer provided he has passed the necessary qualifications.

The artificer in charge of an A class boat's engines to be given charge pay as in a Torpedo boat.

That authority be given to carry one chief stoker rating to each four boats.

That LTOs found suitable may be advanced to the rating of PO 1st class, and sent to *Vernon* to qualify for TI. The number of TI's borne not to exceed one for every three boats. 6 additional LTOs to be taken at once.

That in future the Leading Stoker ratings to be filled from stoker ratings trained, as far as is possible.

That Coxswain ratings be filled up from AB ratings already trained.

And finally, that, after volunteering for sm. Boats, every man should remain in that service as long as he is fit, taking his turn of foreign service only in submarine boats at foreign depots.

[Attached minute by Assistant Secretary to the Board of Admiralty][1]

28 May 1904

Captain Bacon's proposals in regard to the men will, if approved, lead to the following results on the basis of the numbers approved for the 33 boats calculated to be in wartime on 31st December 1906, viz.:

ERAs, out of a total of 66, 28 will be Chief ERAs, almost 1 to 2. The normal proportion of the Chief to the other rating in this class is 1 to 3.

The qualifications for promotion are 6 years service of which 3 must have been actually afloat and they must have a certificate from the Captain and Engineer officer of the last ship they served in that they are considered fit for advancement. It must also be remembered that these men are eligible for an advancement (after examination) when they have completed 8 years' service from date of entry of which 4 years must have been afloat. It is presumed service in the submarines will count as service afloat and the question will therefore require consideration. Possibly the grant of Charge Pay alone – if fixed at a

---

[1] Grahame Greene: principal clerk at the Admiralty.

suitable rate – might operate in the direction Captain Bacon desires.

As regards Stokers the number of Chief Ratings would be in very close accord with the proportion on force for the Service generally.

The proposals for Crews of the Submarines approved on M0277 included 6 TI's for the base. Captain Bacon now wishes to have one for every three boats making 11 in all. Presumably these will be in addition to the 6 for the base. Present regulations require these men to be selected by the Captain of the Torpedo School. The proposal that these LTOs who may be recommended on account of the Submarine Service would be rated PO 1st class serves rather more than the occasion warrants considering that even when he passes for TI a man does not necessarily receive such a rating but only obtains one step e.g. from AB to Leading Seaman.

It is recognised that special arrangements are necessary for the submarine service but the points raised as to ERAs and TI's require consideration.

[Extract from attached minute (4 July 1904) by DNI]

It is submitted that a decision be now given as to whether double crews are to be provided for all Submarines in war. This appears desirable, and if approved would help to remove many of the difficulties referred to by Captain Bacon in regard to the extra ratings required, as the additional numbers would come eventually on the Estimates and thus afford more men for Peace training. The additions to war requirements 1909–10 would be 440 of all ratings.

The proposal that men in the Submarine Service should be divorced from the General Service until no longer fit for submarines offers many objections, and should not, it is submitted, be finally adopted until other means have failed. In the present initial stage of this service no doubt every man trained is badly wanted for training others to meet the increasing number of these craft being delivered by Contractors, and for a time it may be necessary to confine men to this branch of the service for longer periods than is generally desirable, but as soon as practicable they should take their share of service afloat.

Men permanently employed in submarines, when discharged to the General Service, from age or other cause, would in many cases be out of touch with the latter and might clog the list of higher ratings for promotion. Want of experience would result in their being unfit for the responsibilities of the rating to which they had risen to in the submarine service. [The] E[ngineer] in C[hief] points out ... that it is necessary for Chief Stokers to have considerable E[ngine] R[oom] and Stokehold experience, and similarly seamen ratings require sea experience. The proposal would also render men in the Submarine Service unavailable for Foreign Stations except on those where submarines are kept, and this would throw an undue share of such service on other men. It is therefore considered that ultimately sufficient men should be trained in submarines to permit of their serving afloat for periods equivalent to a ship's commission.

It is considered that not more than one step in rank should be given to a man in the Submarine Service unless a period in another ship intervenes. Thus a man might put in, say, 3 years with submarines, receive a step in rank, followed by a commission afloat, during which he would be eligible for another step, and subsequently return to the submarine service. This would prevent men being rated up without the requisite experience.

It will be necessary to offer inducements to attract men below water, and it is thought this could be done by giving them non-substantive ratings for submarines qualification, accompanied by extra pay when employed in such ratings, this extra pay being so adjusted as to attract the class of men required.

As regards the manning of submarines in reserve, and the provision for wastage, a great deal depends on the length of training required. Captain Bacon does not say in his report what length of training is necessary. If it is only a question of six months or less, a reserve might be created by passing men from the Submarine Service into harbour posts at ports with Submarine Depots, to complete their Home Service, on the lines proposed for officers. It is submitted that Captain Bacon be called upon to report as to the length of training necessary for each rank and rating to qualify for Submarine Service.

[Attached]

[At a meeting at the Admiralty on 29 August 1904, it was agreed that the Inspecting Captain of Submarines be empowered to promote ratings on his own authority. It was also resolved that:] ... men who volunteer for submarine boat service should for the present remain in the special service as long as they are fit, taking their turn of foreign service at depots abroad. It was agreed that while the submarine requirements are growing it would be undesirable to draft to general sea service men who have been trained in submarine work; and until a number have been trained equivalent to at least double crews, it would be a waste of energy to send men away after short periods of service with submarine boats, when those men could be utilised for training others.

Instructions should therefore be given that during the next 3 years, men told off to the submarine service should, if possible, not be drafted away to general service, but their service at home and abroad should be arranged principally from the point of view of the requirements of the submarine service. At the end of this period [1907], the question of service in submarine boats in relation to other branches of the general service to be reviewed.

(signed)

Captain [Charles] Briggs [Captain of Torpedo School]

Captain [Reginald] Bacon [Inspecting Captain of Submarines]

Captain Hon [Alexander] Bethell [assistant Director of Naval Ordnance]

Engineer Rear Admiral [Henry] Oram. [for Engineer-in-Chief]

Mr. Grahame Greene [Assistant Secretary to the Admiralty]

Mr. Butler. [representing Head of N Branch]

[56] *Inspecting Captain of Submarines to Admiralty via C-in-C, Portsmouth*[1]

[ADM 1/7795]

HM Ship *THAMES* at Portsmouth

2 August 1905

I have the honour to submit that the continuous increase of the Submarine Flotilla makes it necessary to review and modify the existing system of obtaining Officers for it.

It has been approved to obtain every six months, a number of Sub-Lieutenants who have volunteered for service in Submarines and who have also obtained a 1st class certificate in Torpedo; these Officers are trained for six months and at the end of that time, if found suitable, are sent as second in command of Submarines, with a view to ultimately succeeding in command those officers who have either served the period of about 2 years in command, or who for any other reason are appointed away.

It will be seen that not only must officers be trained in sufficient numbers to provide for new boats, which are being delivered at the rate of one a month, making for that purpose alone 24 officers a year, but also a sufficient number to replace all officers in command once every two years or less, roughly about another 24 officers or 48 annually in all.

This number is sufficiently serious in itself, exceeding as it does the

[1] From 1905 to 1906 the post of Inspecting Captain of Submarines (ICS) was held by Capt. Edgar Lees.

usual number trained annually for either Torpedo or Gunnery, but a still more serious consideration is the fact that the best Sub-Lieutenants are those who join the Submarines, it is from amongst them that the best applicants for Torpedo come, in fact although these officers would prefer to remain in Submarine Boats, if it were possible to do so and the service was considered good service, yet nearly all apply to qualify as either Torpedo or Gunnery Officers, principally Torpedo, believing such qualifications to be the best means for promotion.

Although the regulations require a Lieutenant to serve for one year at sea before being allowed to qualify for Torpedo or Gunnery, and although service in Submarines is the necessary sea time, yet it is I consider highly desirable for the good of the service that this sea time should be actually in a *ship* of war as distinct from Torpedo craft or Submarines if this interpretation of the Admiralty order is the accepted one, then all these officers in submarines, just as they are specially trained for extremely responsible and difficult duties, have to go to sea and *leave the submarines* on the *chance* of being selected for Torpedo or Gunnery.

Consequently in addition to the 48 officers required annually we shall have to train a further number to make up for this wastage, this under present circumstances is obviously impossible.

After due consideration I am forced to the conclusion that the best, in fact the only, solution lies in making the submarine service a special service, from which the officers best fitted for the command of submarines shall not be taken except to serve for a minimum of 3 years in a ship at sea to obtain the necessary watch-keeping and disciplinary experience to qualify them for promotion to commander, and that this 3 years service at sea may be at any time during their Lieutenants service, as suits the efficient officering of the Submarines, that being the primary consideration.

It is submitted further that two of the most experienced officers in command of Submarines, both at Portsmouth and Devonport, shall be appointed in command of Submarines and to the staff (of [depot ships] *Thames* and *Forth*) for instruction of Officers and Men, that these appointments be made by the Admiralty on the recommendation of the Inspecting Captain of Submarine Boats, shall be for two years and shall if the duties are well and ably carried out be considered good service.

In making this submission I am guided by the fact that our present submarines of the B class (vessels of over 300 tons) cannot be commanded and handled by Officers of only a few months experience, without loss of efficiency and running undue risks of accident. It is most important that those who command them shall be the very best and have great experience with them, and therefore it is that I have put forward this proposition, which briefly is:

a. To make, as regards the executive officers, the Submarine Service a special service in which they shall remain during their time as Lieutenants, subject to a minimum of 3 years served in an actual *Ship* of war at sea.

b. To have two of the most experienced officers who have commanded boats to form an instructional staff in both *Thames* and *Forth*, the appointments to last 2 years, these Officers to be appointed additional in command of boats and their duty being to instruct Officers and Men in the details of working Submarines.

[Attached minute (8 August 1905) by assistant Secretary to the Admiralty][1]

The main difficulty lies in the fact that both the Torpedo and the Submarine Service want the same officers. It is rather waste of efficiency to train an officer in submarines and, just when he is becoming efficient, send him to sea to get in sea time with a view to qualifying in torpedo. The proposal of the Inspecting Captain seems the only solution and will have the effect of reducing the number of officers required to be trained annually in the submarine service. This will set free the first class sub-lieutenants who would go in for Torpedo and would release more sub-lieutenants for the general service. Captain Lees mentions 48 sub-lieutenants as required annually. It is difficult to spare this number now when the sub-lieutenants list is abnormally large, but it will be quite impossible in a few years' time when the list has been reduced by nearly one hundred.

---

[1] Minute signed by Charles Walker, clerk at the Admiralty.

PART III

THE IMPACT OF THE SUBMARINE UPON NAVAL STRATEGIC THOUGHT

[57] *Fisher to Balfour*[1]

[Add Mss 49710]

24 January 1905

Dear Mr. Balfour,

These two papers will interest you. Please don't answer.

Yours,

JA Fisher

– This is written very roughly but I think sufficiently clear

*   *   *

Submarines used Defensively

A submarine boat, therefore, is a daylight torpedo boat of medium speed but considerable radius of action, which latter can be enormously increased should, under convenient conditions, towing be resorted to. Obviously one use these boats can be put to is to drive an additional nail into the coffin of invasion. The destroyer by night, and the submarine by day, should render it practically impossible for transports to remain in a locality sufficiently long to discharge troops. As a check, therefore, to destructive raids on any of our territories where such aggression might be conceived, these boats should be a valuable adjunct. I am not arguing the probabilities of invasion; but we must never totally leave out of account temporary embarrassments which may occur in large combinations against us. Submarine boats may in a broad sense be looked on as extending the defence of a port enormously beyond the range of gunfire, and as linking the defences of ports along ranges of coast now locally undefended. They therefore should relieve the anxieties of commanders-in-chief, should their fleets be pitted against combinations that tax their resources to the utmost.

The capabilities of these boats do not, however, end here; their use in expectant blockade cannot be denied, whether this watching is in the offing of an enemy's harbour or in confined waters within reach of the boats' bases. We must also not neglect the possibility of certain waters being denied to large ships, from the danger of being attacked in daylight by submarine boats, and at night by torpedo craft. The only way, at present, of meeting such an investment is by following suit, and denying the waters in turn to the enemy, thereby neutralising these areas for offensive operations. Such a case may be far, at present, from actual

[1] Adm. Sir John Fisher held the post of First Sea Lord from 20 October 1904 to 25 January 1910.

realisation; but affairs move quickly in these days, and we must be ready to forestall any dangerous contingencies.

Submarines used Offensively

Submarine boats can be used offensively within the limits of their radius of action,

Radius of action is limited by two factors –

(a) Fuel carried.

(b) Sea-keeping qualities of the craft.

As regards (a), sufficient fuel is carried by our later boats to ensure steaming 500 miles at economical speed. This, again, can be supplemented by towing. No form of craft tows better than submarine boats. They can, moreover, be towed when sunk to their low level, and are, therefore, practically invisible, and in this condition can slip the towing hawsers from inside the submarine, and so slip away to the attack unnoticed. These boats can, therefore, not only have their radius of action largely increased by towing, but they can be towed to the vicinity of an enemy, and almost up to striking distance, and be let go to fasten on their prey without any visible sign of so doing, even in broad daylight! As regards condition (b), each successive class are better sea boats. Being absolutely watertight and having ventilators that reach at least 16 feet above the water, they can ride out any weather they might reasonably be expected to encounter. So that in their employment at a distance from a base no great anxiety need be felt for their safety from the effects of bad weather.

How then, and for what purposes would this type of boat be used?

First of all, offensive strategy must be held to include the circumscription of the free movements of the enemy; any action that limits their free movements is action of offence. Under this head, closing the Straits of Dover is one of great importance. In a war with Germany, closing these Straits means forcing the German ships to steam at least 1,000 miles further than otherwise they need. The complementary action of submarine boats and destroyers (that is, submarines by day and destroyers by night) should practically ensure this being done. Again, take the Straits of Gibraltar. Here similar work can be done by the co-operation of the destroyer and submarine. All ships passing the Straits in the day time can be subjected to a close scrutiny, and, if enemies, can be attacked at night. A chain of destroyers from Gibraltar to Ceuta within almost touch of one another, and by day a chain of submarines similarly disposed make a stone wall against the passage of an enemy's fleet!

There is one other use of these boats offensively that merits attention, that is, their use in a fleet action in waters within reach of a base. An inferior squadron if accompanied by these boats, and especially if towing them, has always a chance of rendering subsequent events more even by working in co-operation with them.

It is not intended to advance the idea that normally fleets will tow boats into action; such a general use would only hamper the ships, but what is certain is that in future naval actions and warfare, great advantages will be gained by the unexpected use of vessels of all descriptions. The use of the armoured cruiser as a torpedo vessel in fleet actions is practised even now! The destroyer after the first stage of a fleet action is a trump card of the future! And the Admiral who lays himself out to use his subsidiary craft in a daring and unexpected way may bring off a successful coup (e.g., the Destroyers dashing out as we practised in the Mediterranean Fleet from the blind side of each ship of the Battle Fleet, and going for the enemy in a confused moment!). In peace time we are obliged to weigh too nicely the chances of the safety of the craft; no operation dare, rightly enough, be undertaken where the safety of vessels are risked: in war time it will be a totally different thing.* No longer will the question be, Is it certain that the boats will not be risked? But Is it probable that I shall gain material advantage, even if I lose all the boats? This restraining influence in the use of naval weapons is absolutely unavoidable in peace time, and, therefore, we are apt to fix peace values on our craft; but the very essence of the use of torpedo craft in war time is to incur their risk when legitimate chances of success exist, especially when such success means subsequent equality, instead of inferiority. We may, therefore, expect the weaker side to use their craft in a thoroughly bold manner, and, consequently, the co-operation of submarine boats at unexpected distances from land may be anticipated, since the more unexpected their presence the more probable their success. We must always remember, that while always hoping that we will be superior in strength to our opponents, we must never do what it is so tempting to do, namely, to consider the uses of vessels to us when superior, but keep the possibility of our being inferior to strong combinations out of our minds. It is in the latter case that the offensive use of our small craft will be most prominently brought out.

Now let us turn to the use of submarine boats against us.

The position in the Channel is the same to us and France when opposed to one another. The submarine is the only answer to the

---

* What is criminal to do in peace may be criminal not to do in war! What is criminal rashness in peace may be criminal prudence in war!

submarine! Since they should be able to elude all craft, and no one particular vessel can be built which can be relied on to destroy them. This being so, by the use of these craft it may be made impossible to keep large vessels in the Channel, or other confined waters. *If we cannot do, but the enemy can, then invasion is a certainty; hence the necessity for the provision of these craft on our sea frontiers.* But having them for this purpose they become instantly available for still further extended use both by us and our enemies! Take the Mediterranean and draw a line 100 miles from the coast of France and Spain, and see the little puddle left in the western basin of this sea! Anywhere in this 100 mile riband [*sic*] submarine boats can operate; anywhere are our ships liable to attack both by day and by night. Before many years, navigation in the western basin of the Mediterranean in war time, equally with the English Channel will be a very dangerous undertaking, owing to the offensive action of this class of boat. The fact of the boats being conveniently towed, makes their offensive action much greater. Once a fleet is located, boats can be towed to their vicinity, and perhaps the fleet taken wholly by surprise. With no class of weapon will audacity and offensive action be repaid so well as with submarines.

[58] *Memorandum by the Earl of Cawdor, circulated to Selected Members of the Cabinet*[1]
[CAB 37/75/57]

March 1905

Confidential.

Submarine Boats

The policy of the Admiralty as regards these boats has been definite and progressive. Prior to 1900 the progress in the development of this form of vessel had been carefully watched, and as soon as it became apparent that submarine boats were likely to develop into practical factors in naval warfare, immediate steps were taken to provide the nation with them, both to assess their value in offence, and also to investigate the most likely methods of overcoming their attack. Obviously the practical way of making a start was to purchase boats that were known to have accomplished work under water, so that working on a type of accepted success, it could be improved and modified to suit

[1] Cawdor, third earl: Chairman Great Western Railway 1895–1905; First Lord of the Admiralty March–December 1905.

our ideas and requirements. The Holland boats offered the best prospects. Five were ordered and constructed by the firm of Vickers, Sons and Maxim.

As it was highly desirable that no time should be lost to improve the type up to the latest scientific developments, the improvement, design, and trials were placed in the hands of one officer in direct communication with the Admiralty, so that rapidity of development was assured. Towards the end of 1901, before a single Holland type had been completed, a close study of the question placed us in a position to lay down a very much improved type of boat, No. A1; her building was hurried on, and directly her hull was finished, and her electric batteries installed, without even waiting for her surface propelling machinery, she was tried under water. These trials being eminently satisfactory, three more of a still further improved type, A2, A3, A4, were immediately commenced. Difficulties in the development of the petrol engines were now experienced, but the moment ultimate success in these was assured, nine more A class, A5 to A13, were laid down, making a total of 13.

To jump from 150 to 600 hp at a single step, and then on to 850 hp in the petrol engines, will be acknowledged by engineers as a successful feat: this was one of the details in the progress of the boats, where the development of every detail required a vast amount of skill, forethought, and care. As soon as the first of the A class was thoroughly tried, a still larger type was laid down called the B type of 300 tons, 13 knots surface speed, nine knots below water speed, a surface distance capacity of 500 miles, and a below-water endurance of 10 hours, and moreover a good sea boat. This is the type we are now building, and propose to build in the immediate future. It will therefore be conceded that the Admiralty have not wasted time in this matter. In four years we have placed 13 large boats on the list of the Navy, and have a further ten well on towards completion; besides these we have improved the type from $7^{1}/_{2}$ knots and 120 tons displacement to 13 knots and 300 tons displacement with enormous gain in their sea-going capacity. These boats have been constantly, at work during the last two years, and have been subjected to manoeuvres of great severity, but on all occasions they have proved themselves thoroughly reliable.

The submarine boat of our Navy is a boat of small buoyancy, which is propelled on the surface by a petrol engine, and can in a very short space of time disappear and navigate below the surface. This she does by admitting water into certain tanks till she has almost completely lost her buoyancy; then, by moving ahead, she can, by means of horizontal rudders, steer herself down and maintain any depth she wishes, much in the same way that a ship can alter course and steer any direction on the surface of the water. The motive power below water is obtained from electricity stored in accumulators. The reason for using electricity below water, and petrol above, is that when below water air in the boat is a valuable asset and cannot be wasted in the petrol engine, but at the same time the method of storing electricity necessitates so great an expenditure of weight that it is uneconomical to use it on the surface where air is available; hence the two methods of propulsion are used, each suited to the particular condition of the boat. The supply of electricity can be renewed by a dynamo worked by the petrol engine when on the surface. Below water vision is obtained by a device called an optical tube, which is a peculiar telescope arrangement so that the horizon can be swept and objects seen as distinctly as with the naked eye.

The time necessary to dive from a position on the surface is about three minutes. No difficulties are experienced in the provision of fresh air below, in being able to see objects on the surface, or in steering an absolutely correct course. No fundamental difficulties in the development of submarine boats now exist; the main direction in which improvements will take place in the future is in increase of seaworthiness in bad weather. Improvement in this direction is only to be obtained by great practical experience.

A distinction has been drawn, especially abroad, between two different classes of submarine boats, namely submarine and submersible; the latter really only differ in the amount of buoyancy they possess for surface cruising. A submarine has usually a buoyancy of about 10 per cent to 12 per cent, and a submersible of about 30 per cent to 40 per cent; even the latter falls far short of that of ordinary surface craft. The disadvantage of the submersible is that she takes longer to disappear, and, for equal motive power, is slower when below. We do not consider that the small increase of buoyancy in a perfectly watertight craft counterbalances these disadvantages. Developments, however, in this direction are being carefully studied.

Submarine Boat Stations

We propose to establish and equip submarine boat stations at the more important of our large naval bases. Money for three such stations has been allowed for in the Estimates. It is the intention to send submarine boats to at least one foreign base during the present year.

Submarine Boats in War Time

I have no intention of in any way entering upon the manner of use we intend to make of submarine boats in war time, or of our intentions as regards their allocation; to do so would be neither a wise nor proper precedent. I will merely indicate some of the general uses to which these vessels may be put in war time by nations possessing them. Generally speaking, submarine boats are complementary to destroyers. By Destroyers I mean large sea-going torpedo boats. They can in certain waters, in daytime, accomplish what the destroyer can only do at night. Their main attribute is invisibility, which both aids them to approach a ship unseen, and also provides for their safety of escape; moreover it invests them with a subtle power of producing great uncertainty and apprehension in the minds of officers and crews of vessels working in certain waters. We have only to recognise the disturbing effect produced by the presence of fixed blockade mines during the present war, to foreshadow the increased mental strain that would be produced by mobile submarines. Invisibility confers the power of attack on the submarine in the same way that darkness and high speed do on the destroyer.

The destroyer has greater speed and a larger radius of action than the submarine, both on account of the fuel carried and also because of their greater habitability in bad weather; but it must at the same time be remembered that a watertight boat like a submarine is safe in practically all weathers, and therefore bad weather is not a fundamental deterrent to their use. In one respect the submarine has the advantage, namely, that she can perfectly well see the details of the ship she is attacking in daytime, whereas it is often difficult for a destroyer to determine the nationality of a ship at night.

A submarine boat, therefore, is a daylight torpedo boat of medium speed but considerable radius of action, which latter can be enormously increased should, under convenient conditions, towing be resorted to. Obviously one use these boats can be put to is to drive an additional nail into the coffin of invasion. The destroyer by night, and the submarine by day, should render it practically impossible for transports to remain in a locality sufficiently long to discharge troops. As a check, therefore, to destructive raids on any of our territories where such aggression might be conceived, these boats should be a valuable adjunct. I am not arguing the probabilities of invasion; but we must never totally leave out of account temporary embarrassments which may occur in large combinations against us. Submarine boats may in a broad sense be looked on as extending the defence of a port enormously beyond the range of gunfire, and as linking the defences of ports along ranges of coast now locally undefended. They therefore should relieve the anxieties of commanders-in-chief, should their fleets be pitted against combinations that tax their resources to the utmost.

The capabilities of these boats do not, however, end here; their use in expectant blockade cannot be denied, whether this watching is in the offing of an enemy's harbour or in confined waters within reach of the boats' bases. We must also not neglect the possibility of certain waters being denied to large ships, from the danger of being attacked in daylight by submarine boats, and at night by torpedo craft. The only way, at present, of meeting such an investment is by following suit, and denying the waters in turn to the enemy, thereby neutralising these areas for offensive operations. Such a case may be far, at present, from actual realisation; but affairs move quickly in these days, and we must be ready to forestall any dangerous contingencies.

There are other uses of great importance to which these vessels may be put; but, as these will form the subject of future manoeuvres, it is premature to further remark on them. It is sufficient to add that the constant manoeuvres carried out with these boats during the past year have been convincing in showing the importance of these vessels as adjuncts to our Navy, and towards preserving the sea frontier of the Empire and our free sea communication.

[59] *Fisher to the Earl of Cromer*[1]
[Fisher Papers, FISR1/4]

22nd April 1905

You will get letters at same time as this from Sir E. Gorst[2] about dredging [a] new passage into Alexandria, but I want to add a few words for your very own self to emphasise to you the coming importance of Alexandria in naval strategy.[3] The Prime Minister fully concurs with me. No foreign nation has yet given a sign of realising what the impending immense development of submarines involves. The reason is that their submarines are as yet miles behind ours (years, I ought to say!). I won't weary you with technicalities, but suffice it to say that within three or four years of this date (and you might keep this letter for curiosity!) the English Channel and the western basin of the Mediterranean will not be habitable by a Fleet or Squadron in war time. Malta will lose its significance as the base of the Mediterranean Fleet, but it will retain its importance, as absolutely locking up by means of

[1] Earl of Cromer: Consul-General in Egypt 1883–1907; President of Dardanelles Commission 1916.
[2] Sir Eldon Gorst: Assistant Under-Secretary of State for Foreign Affairs, 1904–1907.
[3] The work of dredging Alexandria Harbour was quietly commenced in 1906.

the mass of submarines we shall station there, the passages from the western to the eastern basin of the Mediterranean. There will only be a small puddle in the middle of the western basin of the Mediterranean that will not be dominated by the French submarines on the French Algerian and Corsican coasts! Our Mediterranean Fleet, therefore, will have its new base at Alexandria, and this is as it should be, if the Suez Canal is to remain neutralised. Also, further, I personally (though yet in a minority of perhaps one) am absolutely convinced that our fighting policy is to have free access to the Black Sea for warships of all nations, and for that reason we want Alexandria, not Malta, as our chief naval base.

Time presses, as Sir E. Grant wants this at once to go by mail this afternoon. I haven't studied my language, but it's all true.

The D type Oversea or Patrol Submarine

[60] *Minutes taken at Meeting of Submarine Boat Design Committee
on 23 June 1905*
[Ships' Covers 290]

Present:
Controller of the Navy [Captain Henry Jackson],
Director of Naval Construction, [Mr. Philip Watts],
Engineer in Chief, [Admiral Sir A. John Durston],
Captain [Reginald] Bacon, [Naval Assistant to First Sea Lord]
Captain [Edgar] Lees [Inspecting Captain of Submarines]
The question of design of hull was first discussed, the two new
designs C2 and D being produced for examination.

It was explained that in the case of both designs the main departures
from the existing B type were provision of a greater reserve of
buoyancy, this being added in C2 by tanks on the top and in D by tanks
to the side, and the fitting of side rudders.

Captain Lees stated that the displacement of the new design was
about 414-tons, that the battery power was increased from 159 to 212
cells and the cost was estimated at roughly £10,000 per boat more than
type B. The main advantages claimed are the greater safety owing to the
provision of extra buoyancy, the greater economy when proceeding at
slow speeds when submerged, double the armament of torpedoes,
double the storage of petrol, twin screws and better accommodation for
the complement, enough to provide reliefs, thus enabling the vessels to
remain longer away from their base. The vessels though largely
increased in size over B type will still be of somewhat smaller
displacement than some of the French boats which reached 450-tons
displacement. Hydroplanes were very desirable in boats of the size
proposed.

Controller and Captain Bacon pointed out that the extra expense was
a serious consideration in the case of vessels which must be built in
numbers, and that the largely increased battery power involved
continual heavy expense in renewals; and the latter [Bacon] stated it
was doubtful whether the carrying of additional men for reliefs would
enable the vessels to remain longer away from their base, as the crew
could not well remain more than about three days in the boats in fine
weather and less in bad weather. Hydroplanes had been tried
successfully in B type, but were fitted on the conning tower where they
were much less subject to injury than at the ends or side.

It might be possible to modify B type to take 3 torpedoes.

The new design would require examination in greater detail before a final opinion could be expressed, but the main point for discussion was whether the increase in size was necessary. After further discussion the Controller said that the matter was much too important to be settled off hand and suggested that the first step was to try the effect of the side rudders proposed. Captain Lees said that these could be fitted in the last vessel of the B type building at Vickers without heavy expense, and it was agreed that this experiment should be carried out and the question of increasing the displacement and reserve of buoyancy deferred for further consideration.[1]

Some discussion however took place on the relative merits of designs C2 and D, the DNC pointing out that C2 gave increased freeboard and greater comfort for the crew in smooth water, with increased surface speed. Captain Bacon and Captain Lees however were of the opinion that the increased freeboard was not of much advantage and that D was on the whole more suitable than C2, principally on account of the protection afforded by the side tanks; the D design also required less depth of water and was of somewhat better shape for diving and for steering steadily on a horizontal plane when submerged than C2. It was finally agreed that C2 should be set aside, D on the whole being more suitable, and that the DNC should see in what way this type could be still further improved.

* * *

It was also agreed that heavy oil should be adopted as soon as a suitable engine working with it is available, and that experiments in this direction should be pushed on.

[61] *Further remarks on Meeting of Submarine Boat Design Committee on 23 June 1905*
[Ships' Covers 212]

[Attached minute (4 July 1905) by Engineer in Chief]
(1) Submitted for existing boats the question of using a heavier oil than petrol is being considered.
(2) For new boats it is desirable to consider whether a diesel engine which is about twice the weight and one and a half times the volume of a petrol engine for the same power, but which only uses about

---

[1] HMS/m B7 was completed with hydroplanes fitted to the sides of the conning tower.

half the weight and less than half the volume of an oil of 200°F flash point and less than half the value per gallon could not be adopted without a reduction in speed.

[Attached minute (4 July) 1905 by Captain Bacon]
The question of using heavy oil engines has been under consideration for sometime but hitherto a satisfactory engine has not been produced – until an engine has been made and tried, no boat should be designed for oil unless A13 is taken for the purpose.[1]

Makers are so apt to take a rosy view of the difficulties attending producing an engine varying perhaps only slightly from their standard types that nothing short of the exact engine at work should be taken for granted.

A flash point of 200°F is unnecessarily high, and a reduction of 50% in the HP of the engines too great; moreover the great compression of the diesel is to be avoided if possible. Other types would probably give better results – the question of air economy should be considered with the engine design, as it may have an important bearing later on submerged running.

Barrow is I believe well on with a paraffin engine – I will be interested to see how this turns out.

(signed) Reginald Bacon.

[Attached minute (19 July 1905) by Controller][2]
The sub-committee desires an expression of policy on the question of cost of these vessels, to enable them to regulate the design accordingly. Propose to approve building the B type for the present.

[Attached minute (10 August 1905) by First Sea Lord]
£60,000 should be the limit at present.

[62] *Memorandum by Bacon discussing Validity of the Holland Company Patents, and Renewal of Monopoly Agreement with Vickers*
[Ships' Covers 290]

26 August 1905

I have frequently expressed the opinion that none of the Holland

---

[1] HMS/m A13 was modified on the stocks to take a Hornsby-Ackroyd heavy oil engine. For further details see: Norman Friedman, *US Submarines Through 1945* (USNIP: Annapolis, 1995), Appendix A, Propulsion.
[2] Capt. (later Rear Adm.) Henry Jackson: Controller 1905–1908.

patents are of the slightest use except the one which deals with the disposition and shape of the tanks. Further, I told the late Controller that I was quite prepared to design a submarine boat which would in no way infringe the Holland patents. It was with this point in view that I started the designs of the C and D types, so that when the consideration of the renewal of the agreement with Messrs Vickers came up for review the Admiralty would be in a position to say if you do not fall in with the terms we consider just, and you cannot satisfy us that you can build on the terms we propose, then we will build for ourselves independent of the Holland patents.

I have further always insisted that the agreement of the Admiralty with Messrs Vickers bound them, for the term of years specified, not to build, or cause to be built other than by that firm, any boats which were known as Holland boats, or which were built on the general lines of these boats; because at the time of the agreement the Admiralty accepted the validity of the contention that the boats were covered by patents, and such acceptance was the basis of the agreement then made. For the Admiralty to have suddenly repudiated the validity of the patents afterwards would have been a very unfair proceeding. It must be remembered that by accepting the patents, we received, not merely the patents now under review, but the whole of the accumulated experience of the American experimenters, which was more valuable than any printed or accepted patents. It was this that the Admiralty really bargained for. This was the sole reason for the Admiralty, approaching the Holland Co, namely to get a working concern. Reference to the papers on the question of building the boats will amply prove this. For this reason I have always maintained that while the old agreement lasted with Messrs Vickers, the Admiralty had no right to fight the patents or to encourage other firms to do so. But when the agreement expired then the whole case was changed; and I have always strongly urged, though not always successfully, that in the new agreement Messrs Vickers should be looked on as a manufacturer rather than a patentee; that the new agreement should be a manufacturing agreement, and that the principal feature in it should be the regulation of price by a schedule of cost details to be corrected as necessary by experience of building in our own yards.

There is no reason for us now to repudiate the patents. If any other firm like to build boats on the Holland lines and choose to fight a patents action – let them do so, not us. We cannot do better than co-operate with Messrs. Vickers in building the numbers we want. They have experience which it will take three years for any other firm or the [Royal] Dockyards to acquire. We will have to pay for this experience in the case of the yards, but there is no reason that we should do so in the case of private firms. The division of the work between Messrs. Vickers and ourselves will provide just sufficient for both. There is no reason to increase the number of builders, in fact there is every reason against it.

* * *

[Attached minute (28 August 1905) by Controller addressed to the Financial Secretary]

I consider Captain Bacon's views thoroughly sound and good to act upon. The question of the new agreement will be up shortly for consideration and you may like to see these papers before we again discuss the matter.

[63] *Extract from Minute by Captain Reginald Bacon on Memorandum by Captain Edgar Lees dated 16 November urging building of D class* [Ships' Covers 212]

17 November 1905

… we should not begin this class at Barrow before the new agreement is ratified.[1]

[64] *Minute by Controller Detailing Reasons for Further Delay in the Adoption of the D-type Submarine*[2] [Ships' Covers 290]

18 December 1908

After careful consideration of all the circumstances, I propose that tenders for four more submarines of the class C22–30 should be called for from Vickers, and, separately, tenders for one D class with the modifications proposed by DNC at M of his minute of 30 November.[3] We are not likely to have the reports of D1 much before March, and to await reports before proceeding with any more orders will result in a very considerable delay to the programme. As pointed out by DNC in his minute of 30th November there are many experimental features in the D class of boats, and all Admiralty experience goes to show that an order placed for a gun, ship or mounting that has not been thoroughly

---

[1] The new agreement was signed on 17 May 1906.
[2] From 1908 to December 1910, Rear Adm. John Jellicoe held the post of Controller.
[3] Laid down as HMS/m D2.

tried, leads to endless delays. In spite therefore of the possible or even probable advantages of the D type I am much averse to holding up our orders any longer. The first high price of the D class (£75,000 to 80,000) is a serious matter also, and although the armament is greater, there is a very considerable argument in favour of numbers in the case of submarines which applies to this class of vessel more than to any other.

[65] *Fisher to Reginald McKenna*[1]
[Fisher Papers, FISR 1/8]

24th September 1909

Dear First Lord,
You will think my letters are falling on you now as thick as the leaves in Vallambrossa! (where I am going to tomorrow morning so it happens!) But I would like you to read all enclosed and kindly return to me direct without any action – I think these papers should be kept private. My only object in sending them is to let you see clearly where we are in the submarine business. After analysing with Bridgeman and Jellicoe on my return I will put forward for your consideration what is suggested should be done as regards Captain Hall's recommendations.[2]

[66] *Draft Memorandum by Fisher*[3]
[Fisher Papers, FISR 5/13]

[n/d, November 1908]

THE SUBMARINE QUESTION

Until a few years ago we had left the submarine severely alone, the idea prompting this action having been the same as that held by St. Vincent in the days when Fulton came to this country with his Torpedo designs.[4]

---

[1] Reginald McKenna: First Lord of the Admiralty, April 1908 to October 1911.

[2] At that time, Francis Bridgeman was Second Sea Lord, John Jellicoe was Controller, and Sydney Hall the ICS.

[3] A later version of this paper was enclosed with above letter, Fisher to McKenna, 24 September 1909.

[4] On 20 July 1804, the Prime Minister William Pitt signed a contract with the American submarine pioneer Robert Fulton whereby the British government promised to contribute £7000 towards the costs of developing a submarine boat capable of penetrating a French harbour. Fulton was also given a monthly stipend of £200. In addition, Pitt promised to give Fulton a prize of £40,000. for sinking his first French warship inside the harbour of Boulogne or Brest. See: 20 July 1804 Pitt/Melville/Fulton, ADM 1/5121/22. (I am indebted to Captain Peter Hore for this reference.)

Our latest submarines, as a result of the embodiment of our own ideas and improvements over 5 years, are now 5 times the displacement of the original type, and hardly recognisable even as a development.

To the completion of this latest type of submarine is due the following two conclusions, which have forced themselves to the front during the last year:

(1) *The latest type of submarine has the power of remaining autonomous for two months or more*, a characteristic that does not apply to any other type of war vessel from destroyer to battleship, on account of the necessity for the renewal of their fuel, etc., etc.

(2) *No practical means at present exist or appear to be feasible for effecting the destruction of the latest type of submarine*, or of being even warned of her approach, since she requires no attendant surface vessel to assist her, that may betray her presence.

The question arises, what should be done in view of these two definite facts? Three conclusions offer themselves:

(1) Continuous effort must be directed towards elaborating a submarine destroyer, just as the advent of the Torpedo Boat produced the entirely British antidote, the Torpedo Boat Destroyer.

(2) The submarine of the latest type is bound in time to supplant the present Torpedo Boat Destroyer in so far as the latter's functions as a torpedo vessel are concerned, for the reason that the submarine's fighting capability by night is becoming in excess of that of a destroyer, whilst she retains her capacity for day fighting unimpaired.

(3) It is inevitable that when the Germans fully realise the capability of this type of submarine – they probably do not do so yet, on account of having had small experience with them at sea (they have but 3 to our 60) – the North Sea and all its ports will be rendered uninhabitable by our big ships – until we have cleaned out their submarines.

The first practical necessity that arises from a consideration of the above facts is that – in view of the Germans having, this year, for the first time, devoted a large sum of money ($^1/_2$ a million) to the construction of modern submarines – this country must produce more than the six a year which our present vote provides.

One of our Officers has been enabled, unknown, to go on board and study the latest development of the German submarines.[1] He has satisfied himself that the Germans possess a class of vessel which though not yet equal to ours, is equally capable of development, *and of maintaining itself at sea, unaided, for long periods*, which is the main point to which this paper calls attention.

[1] Austrian 'U-3', report by Lt Algernon Boyle.

The vessel thus surreptitiously visited has made the voyage successfully to Pola in the Mediterranean from a German port, via Bay of Biscay, with a convoy. Our latest submarine will not require such convoy, being quite capable of making such a voyage as this by herself.

To sum up –

The arguments in this brief record in no way attempt to lessen the influence and necessity of big armoured ships – the latter will after all govern the final conflict for command of the sea on the ocean lines of communication.

They do however point to a complete approaching revolution in the type of our war with *any* power, particularly with any European power, on account of the narrow waters of the North Sea and Baltic, English Channel and Mediterranean, being denied to large ships of war until the submarine is cleared out.

A collateral issue which flows from all this is the absolute death blow to fears of Invasion.

[67] *Views of Rear Admiral Sir John Jellicoe. Controller to First Sea Lord*

[Fisher Papers, FISR 1/8]

18th April 1909

I send you a few notes on the paper you sent me yesterday, in case you discuss the submarine question with Mr McKenna to-night. My fear is that this submarine question may be made an excuse to avoid spending, – what appears to me to be essential money – on dock accommodation on the East Coast.[1] I feel that our present situation in this matter is one of the utmost gravity and open to much criticism, and I hope you will agree with me that nothing that can occur in the next 8–10 years should lead us to abandon the provision of necessary docks on this coast. Even if Germany spends a million a year on submarines, it will be 8 years before the submarine menace in the North Sea is really bad, and I don't imagine we shall wait eight years for the war. [I agree. JF]

I entirely agree in the conclusions that we must spend more money on submarines, and that we must devise something in the shape of a submarine destroyer. The sooner we get an air ship the better since we may find the solution here, for day work at any rate.

[1] The construction of Rosyth naval base was authorised in 1902, but up to 1909 only token sums had been allocated towards its development.

[Attached Notes]

1. It seems to be going rather too far to say that the German submarine development must render the North Sea and all its ports uninhabitable by big ships and that this fact inevitably points to big ship battles being fought in more open waters.

My reasoning is as follows:

In the early stages of a war with Germany it will no doubt be the case, when the German submarines become very numerous. At this stage it would seem that the command of the narrow waters will be fought for by small craft and submarines, the big ships being kept in safety. But a time will come when the submarines will have been so reduced in numbers by this fighting that present conditions will be reproduced, the big ships will get into the North Sea and the decisive action may well be fought in those waters. I can hardly conceive that Germany is likely to send her main Battle Fleet far afield so long as we are in any great superiority, and therefore the time must come when our own Battle Fleet will be forced into the North Sea to endeavour to bring the German Fleet to action. [I don't agree. JF]

2. It therefore seems to me that the harbours and docks on the East Coast are still required.

3. Even were the effect of the advent of submarines in large numbers to be as stated, this period is so far distant – some 8–12 years in all probability – that it does not seem at all desirable to relax our efforts to get proper dock accommodation on the East Coast in the near future. [Agree. JF]

4. It should be noted, regarding the Forth and Clyde ship canal, that there are no docks at Glasgow capable of taking a Dreadnought except in a very light condition.[1]

5. The destroyer is of course a necessity so long as other nations possess vessels of this or of the Torpedo Boat class since the submarine cannot catch them to destroy them, and cannot therefore act as an inshore squadron of observation at present. No doubt she will be able to do so before very long. [Yes this is true. JF]

---

[1] A reference to the proposed trans-Scotland ship canal.

[68] *Inspecting Captain of Submarines to Commander-in-Chief,*
Home Fleet[1]

[ADM 1/8128]

HMS *Mercury* at Portsmouth
5 August 1910

In accordance with Home Fleet Memo. No. 76 of 11 February 1910, I have the honour to report upon the exercises carried out by Submarine Flotillas attached to Home Fleet for month of July.

Bonaventure, Forth, Hazard and 25 Submarines were employed in the Main Fleet Manoeuvres on the Red Side. All except D.1 were stationed at various places for the defence of the Red Coast assisted by 24 Torpedo Boats (Ex Coastals).[2]

D.1 was sent to act offensively on Blue Coast; considering that she was one blade short on port propeller and her heavy oil engines hardly out of experimental stage, her performance was considered satisfactory.

There is no doubt that when these engines become as reliable as the petrol engines the superiority of them over steam is very marked under war conditions. For example the surface capacity of D.1 is on paper about the same as the T.B's (ex coastals), about 2–3000 miles at ten knots. No doubt both would do it if kept running, but when lying about waiting but ready to go full speed, which is what happens practically the whole of the time, the T.B's seem to burn more oil than if they were underway at 10 knots, whereas D.1 ran upon none at all. If the T.B.'s are suddenly wanted for a burst they are therefore on an average about half out of oil.

D.1 this manoeuvres went from Portsmouth to Milford, did 800 miles before returning there and then returned to Portsmouth via Mounts Bay and Torquay, the crew having lived on board continuously for 30 days, on her return she had still 2400 gallons of oil left or enough for 400 miles. During this 30 days, she charged her own batteries for auxiliary purposes including all the cooking, a total of 60 hours charging.

Vulcan's Submarines have been employed by Admiral [Cecil]

---

[1] From 1907 to 1910, Captain Sydney Hall held the post of Inspecting Captain of Submarines. The post of C-in-C, Home Fleet was held by Adm. Sir William May (March 1909 to February 1911).

[2] These torpedo boats (ex-coastal destroyers) were built under the 1906, 1907, and 1908 programmes. They were designed primarily for operations in the Channel. They were fitted with turbines and designed to burn only fuel oil.

Burney's Committee to test their navigational capabilities,[1] they appear to have made two runs of 260–270 miles into the North Sea, on the second occasion the Submarines found unassisted and successfully attacked the *Seagull* representing an enemy's fleet 270 miles out from Dundee towards Norway and then returned to Dundee. A more detailed report is attached.

The Harwich Submarines have also been cruising on the East Coast.

No defects were developed except D.1's propeller (there were no blades left on the port one when she arrived at Portsmouth) and a bearing became hot in B.3 on her way to Milford before Manoeuvres began.

It is submitted that *Vulcan's* report may be returned to me.

---

[1] The Admiralty's Secret Anti-Submarine Committee was established by Sir John Fisher in late 1909. The first president was Rear Adm. Cecil Burney who was succeeded in 1910 by Vice-Adm. Frederick Sturdee, who was himself succeeded in 1911 by Rear Adm. Bernard Currey and Rear Adm. Reginald Tupper.

Development of Training, Recruitment and Administrative Organisation

[69] *Inspecting Captain of Submarines to Commander-in-Chief Portsmouth*

[ADM 1/7921]

HMS *Mercury* at Portsmouth,
5th February 1907

Sir,

I have the honour to bring forward for consideration the following in regard to the accommodation of Submarine crews at Haslar Submarine Depot.

In April last HMS *Mercury* was sent temporarily to form living quarters pending decision to build barracks at Haslar.

I understand it has now been decided not [to] build the barracks, so it is necessary to decide on some alternative. There are two solutions:–

1. Retain *Mercury*
2. Provide hulks.

1) is neither economical nor convenient, as it involves a double staff and in many cases double plant. All the plant required for maintenance and nearly all the staff, are already provided for at Fort Blockhouse: the only thing wanting is a place for the staff to live in, it is obviously unsound to keep *Mercury* for this purpose as she requires another staff to keep her efficient.

The best alternative I submit is (2) and the ships suggested for the service are *Wanderer* and *Dolphin* now on the sale list and moored on the Mother Bank.¹ These vessels are small enough to lie alongside the jetties without overcrowding Haslar Creek, and having no engines or boilers will not require a staff for upkeep. The lighting can be run from Fort Blockhouse Power Station. This will free *Mercury* for a fixed Depot Ship at Plymouth or Dover, which will be required at about the time that *Wanderer* and *Dolphin* are completed.

The points then, I submit for consideration and decision are:–

1. May *Wanderer* and *Dolphin* be turned over to Submarine Service as living quarters to replace *Mercury*.

2. If this is approved may they be turned over to me for fitting out, the necessary materials being provided by the Dockyard and assistance being given by carpenter ratings lent from the General Depot.

---

¹ Mother bank: term applied to warships in the reserve fleet marked for disposal.

[Attached minute (7 March 1907) by M Branch][1]
Controller,
As the *Wanderer* has been sold, will you please say what other vessel
to be used as a hulk at Portsmouth is suggested. The Dir[ector] of
Contracts on M1968 attached has been asked to suspend the sale of
Dolphin.
Referred also for any remarks generally

[Attached minute (23 March 1907) by Controller][2]
Propose *Dolphin* for Portsmouth and *Onyx* for Devonport as
submitted by I.C.S. ...

[Attached minute (23 March 1907) by M Branch]
As regards the disposition of submarines and their bases, submitted
to approve the proposal on sheet I as modified by the Controller's
proposals: the *Dolphin* and *Onyx* to be prepared for service at
Portsmouth and Devonport on the lines suggested by the I.C.S.

[Attached minute (25 March 1907) by First Sea Lord]
Approve

[70] *Secretary of the Admiralty to Commander Sydney S Hall*[3]
[ADM 1/7880]

6 November 1906

A committee consisting [of]: The Second Sea Lord,[4] Captain
Reginald HS Bacon, Captain Edgar Lees, Captain F. Haworth-Booth,[5]
Captain WR Hall[6] and Mr. Evans[7] (Naval Branch, Admiralty) discussed
the accompanying memorandum on 28th September, and it was
arranged that the remarks of the members should be attached thereto.
The Second Sea Lord has now directed me to forward to you a copy

[1] Minute signed by Alex Flint, deputy head of M (manning) Branch, Admiralty civil
service.
[2] Minute signed by Capt. Henry Jackson.
[3] In November 1906, Cmdr Sydney Hall was designated to succeed Capt. Edgar Lees
as ICS and assumed office in January 1907.
[4] Vice-Adm. Sir Charles Drury: Second Sea Lord 1903–1907.
[5] Capt. (later Rear Adm.) Francis Haworth-Booth: a/DNI 1905–1908; Naval
Representative Commonwealth of Australia 1911–20.
[6] Capt. W.R. Hall: Inspecting Captain of Mechanical Training Establishments,
1906–07; CO HMS *Natal*, 1910–11; naval assistant to the Controller, 1911–13.
[7] Mr Evans: principal clerk at the Admiralty.

of the memorandum with a request that you will add any remarks you may wish.

Memoranda Relative to Service in Submarines and the Future Allocation of Submarines

1. The present inducements offered to ratings to enter Submarine Service are considered to be sufficient.

2. Service in Submarines, as heretofore, should continue to be voluntary, and as far as practicable, the personnel required should be drawn from each of the three Port Divisions equally. By return of numbers now serving in Submarines it is found that the personnel has been supplied principally from Portsmouth.

3. This unequal distribution is attributable to the following causes:–

(a) Establishment of Submarine Head-Quarters at Portsmouth

(b) Convenience and facilities for exploiting the resources of the port in which the Head-Quarters is situated.

(c) Volunteers are more readily forthcoming for any special service from the port in which the Head-Quarters of such special service is located.

(d) Indefinite allocation of Home bases and Submarine vessels, and the omission to establish a definite system of appropriation of ratings belonging to a Port Division to the Submarines employed in the vicinity of that division; this has involved a disproportionate drain on the Portsmouth resources and a congestion of Submarines at Portsmouth.

(e) Centralisation of training of volunteers at the Portsmouth Submarine Head-Quarters.

4. To remove the above-mentioned objections to the present system it is proposed to –

(a) Establish a Home base at Devonport and at Chatham (or at Dover) and to allocate the Dover base to Chatham.

(b) Establish a Submarine Roster at each port by which men of the Port Division will be employed as far as possible only in the Submarine vessels attached to their respective Port Divisions.

(c) Exploit Devonport and Chatham Port Divisions to a greater extent.

(d) Allocate definitely Submarines to each Port Division.

(e) Establish a system by which each Port Division will train its own men for Submarine Service in Home and Sea-going bases, instead of only at Portsmouth.

5. The special nature of service in Submarines renders it desirable that such service should be a closed service for a definite period. It is considered that the maximum period in Submarine Service at one spell, including training, should not exceed five years, but exceptions may be made in special cases, which should be referred to Admiralty for approval.

Concur, except as regards Stokers. See later remarks.
(Captain Hall.)

6. Volunteers should be nominally entered, in the first instance for five years, but such period should not be considered as arbitrary, and if it is found that any rating by serving the full period would suffer as regards advancement, when compared with similar ratings in the general service, such cases to be judged on their merits and the men permitted to revert to general service.

As regards Seamen ratings, it would appear that –
(a) All men who joined the Submarine Service as Leading Seamen will get P.O. ratings in place of P.O.'s whose term of service has expired.
(b) All except a small percentage of A.B.'s should get rates (during their term of service) to fill vacancies.
(Captain Hall.)

7. Any rating who has served five years in Submarine Service, unless specially permitted to remain, must revert to general service, and if subsequently desirous of returning to Submarine Service, after a commission at sea or absence from Submarines of two years, may re-volunteer, and if accepted may serve for a further period of three years, making in all a maximum possible service in Submarines of eight years. If any rating serves for two years or

If the conjectures in (b), above, are correct, the ratings who re-volunteer for Submarine Service will nearly all be Leading Seamen and P.O.'s, while the volunteers required will be A.B.'s, thus re-volunteering may be entirely stopped owing to the fact that lower ratings are required.
(Captain Hall.)
(With reference to Captain Hall's Note) –
If the re-entry is found to

more but less than five, and then for purposes of advancement or other legitimate reason desires and is permitted to return to general service, such rating may, after two years' absence or such time as is decided on, re-volunteer for Submarine Service and, if accepted, may continue for a further period provided that the combined service in Submarines does not exceed eight years in all. In no case can a rating serve for more than five consecutive years in Submarine Service, except such as have been specially approved.

8. Service in Submarine depots, Home and Sea-going bases (Parent ships) should count as Home Service, but Submarine Service. Service in Foreign sea bases should count as Sea Service, but not as Submarine Service.

9. Advancements in Submarine Service should only be made to fill vacancies in that service.

block advancement it can always be stopped.
(Captain Hall.)

Lines 3–6, in lieu of words and if subsequently … re-volunteer, and, if, insert, and should not be allowed to return to Submarine Service until after two years or serving a commission at sea. If then.
(Mr. Evans.)

This must be considered with 6 and 7. As regards the Stoker branch, the new system of advancement depends on whether an Acting Leading Stoker successfully passes the examination, after a three months' course in the Mechanical Training Establishment. Thus, any Stoker who wishes to get on must first qualify as Leading Stoker in one of the schools. Again, Stoker P.O.'s desirous of qualifying as Mechanician, must be recommended from a seagoing ship, after doing a course in that ship of auxiliary watchkeeping. Two points therefore arise:–

(a) Whether Stokers in Submarine Service are to come under the same regulations as those in the Sea Service; if so, no Stoker can be advanced beyond Acting Leading Stoker, and on attaining that rating he should, within two years, go to one of the schools?

(b) Whether an Acting Stoker P.O., who is specially noted in the schools as likely to make a Mechanician, ie to be sent to the Service at all?

(Captain Hall.)
The answer to (a) of Captain Hall's note is, **Yes**: the answer to (b) is, No.
(Commander Hall.)

10. It is understood that the only rating there is difficulty in obtaining is the E.R.A. Apparently a feeling exists among E.R.A.'s that the additional pay allowed to all ratings in Submarine Service should be made proportionate to the pay of the rating. They argue if a rating whose pay is 4s. a day receives 2s. 6d. additional pay, a rating whose pay is 8s. a day should receive more than 2s. 6d. a day additional.

It is for consideration whether it will be necessary in the future to include an E.R.A. in Submarine complements, and having regard to the policy in connection with Mechanicians and E.R.A. ratings it would seem that the future Mechanician should be substituted for E.R.A.'s, if not entirely, at all events proportionately, in the larger types of Submarines.

If this can be done without losing efficiency it is obvious the E.R.A. difficulty will be removed.

Suggest this portion be deleted and para. 10 be allowed to read: It is for consideration whether . . .
(Captain Lees.)
This is, of course, inadmissible, for it would involve settling a special rate of pay for each class of rating.
(Mr Evans)
Concur with Captain Lees, to delete this first paragraph. It is very inadvisable to raise this question.
(Commander Hall.)
This should most certainly be done.
(Captain Bacon.)

The Mechanician will have a good knowledge of engine-driving and of their adjustments. Provided that men are carefully selected, I see no reason why they should not prove to be exceedingly reliable.
It should be decided whether, in order to get these men in Submarine Service as soon as possible, they can be sent there as Acting Mechanicians, and receive confirmation in due course in the Submarine Service.
(Captain Hall.)
The difficulty in obtaining sufficient E.R.A. Volunteers will probably disappear if the proposal in para. 2 is carried out, and the personnel drawn from each port division equally.
(Engineer-Captain Lane.)
Even from the point of view of efficiency, the E.R.A., if available, is preferable to the Mechanician.
(Engineer-Captain Lane.)

11. The following complements for each existing type of Submarine are therefore proposed:–

	Holland	A.	B.	C.
Officer	2	2	2	2
C.P.O or P.O.1/e(Coxswain)	1	1	1	1
Leading Seamen	1	1	2	2
Able Seamen	2	3	5	5
Chief E.R.A. or E.R.A. or Mechanician.	1	2	2	2
Stoker P.O.	–	–	1	1
Leading Stoker	1	1	–	–
Stoker	–	–	2	3
Total	8	10	15	16

Included in foregoing:– One L.T.O. in Hollands and A type, and one L.T.O. or Torpedo Gunner's Mate 2nd Cl. in B and C types.

The complements proposed above are considered to be the minimum necessary to work the vessels efficiently, and it is essential that the Submarines should at all times be fully manned, i.e., kept on a war footing in peace time.

12. The nature of Submarine Service is stated to be such that, although the vessel may be capable of continuing cruising, the crew will require to be relieved periodically; consequently a considerable number of spares crews should be available for this purpose.

13. The Inspecting Captain considers there should be a fully-trained complete spare crew for every three commissioned Submarines. Thus, if there are 90 Submarines there should be 120 crews. This proportion seems to be very large, and it is very necessary to determine this point. The decision would seem to be dependent on the actual probabilities as regards the time a Submarine can be continuously employed without requiring to re-charge, &c.;

Except, the Holland boats, which should be struck off the War list.

(Captain Bacon.)

Concur, and concur with Captain Bacon to strike Hollands off the War List.

(Commander Hall.)

This is somewhat misleading; it is rather dependent on the time the boat can be running as compared with the time she is necessarily not employing the crew. Experience shows that the boat, although only attacking by day, uses much of the night in getting to and from the place of attack.

(Captain Lees.)

I am in agreement with my predecessor in that it is desirable to have one spare crew for every three boats. These spare crews to form the nucleus of the crew of sea-going bases being relieved only on mobilisation.

The ideal number to have would be a spare crew for every boat, and after a long passage (in average weather, two days) they would be required if the submarines

also what is the maximum continuous service a crew, under ordinary conditions, can undertake, bearing in mind that a Submarine is generally employed only by day, and taking into consideration the locality where employed.

14. Since the initiation of the Submarine Service the only established Home base or depot is at Portsmouth, where Fort Blockhouse, with workshops, &c. and a floating dock have been appropriated.

It is understood that it was at first contemplated to spend a considerable sum on Blockhouse to make it capable of accommodating the staff of the Submarine School, and all personnel attached to the Portsmouth flotilla, as also all under training. This decision was, for financial reasons, altered, and the *Mercury*, which had been appropriated as the living quarters pending the completion of Blockhouse, is now necessarily retained.

15. It has been decided to establish two Home bases, viz., at Portsmouth and Devonport, each with a definite local flotilla, consisting respectively of 11 and 7 Submarines.

The increase in numbers and size of Submarines has now raised the question of utilising them over sea, and three Sea-going bases are also to be established, based respectively on Portsmouth, Devonport, and Dover, each consisting of one Parent vessel or Sea-going base and 9 Submarines.

It is herein proposed that the Sea-going use at Dover should be allocated to the Chatham Division for manning, and that a definite local Submarine Flotilla should also be allocated to Chatham, based on some place to be decided on, to consist of six vessels.

16. It is approved that the crews of each sea-going flotilla are to be borne in a Parent vessel. Three of these Parent vessels are selected – *Forth*, *Thames*, and *Bonaventure*. The two former are already fitted and in commission and

had proceeded under their own motive power, and were required to operate at once. But it is possible some of the boats could be towed, and when operating from their base it is a fair assumption that six of the nine would be out and three in reserve. Three of these six could be relieved the first day, and the second three of the six the second day, and so on, giving each crew two days out and one in.

(Commander Hall.)

Blockhouse living quarters not yet finally abandoned. The Estimate is again included for consideration – for 1907–08, and it is hoped will be approved.

(Captain Lees.)

It is to be hoped that the living quarters will be built at Blockhouse, thus liberating *Mercury* for a fixed base at Plymouth or Dover when required.

(Commander Hall.)

It is possible that the lack of volunteers for Submarine Service from Chatham, is due to the fact that there is no flotilla near their own port.

(Captain Hall.)

Concur, but to read as follows:–

It has been decided to establish three Home bases, at Portsmouth, Devonport, and Dover, with twelve, six and six submarines respectively.

(The numbers are altered because of spare crews being one in three.)

(Commander Hall.)

are allocated – *Forth* to Devonport and *Thames* to Portsmouth.

It is also approved that the Dover sea-going flotilla shall be borne in *Thames*, consequently it is herein proposed to transfer *Thames* as Dover base to Chatham. When completed it is proposed to allocate *Bonaventure* as sea-going flotilla base to Portsmouth.

By the above arrangement the three sea-going flotillas will be provided for, but the Home bases, including Portsmouth, will still have to be considered. From the Submarine point of view, the present arrangement is not entirely satisfactory, nor from a general point of view does it seem to be economical.

17. Fort Blockhouse as now constituted requires a definite complement for its care and upkeep and the working of plant fitted for service of Submarines, but cannot accommodate the personnel required. This necessitates *Mercury* as living quarters. *Mercury* is not fitted with necessary plant, and therefore without Blockhouse and its workshops, &c. is valueless except as living quarters. Until Blockhouse is completed *Mercury* or some other vessel is absolutely essential simply as living quarters for the Portsmouth Submarine personnel.

Thus we have two partial complements for really one duty, neither of which is satisfactory or can exist without the other, and the combined total of which is greater than one whole complement.

It is very questionable whether *Mercury*, even as living quarters, is a suitable vessel. She requires a considerable complement solely for care and upkeep of ship. It is understood that if Blockhouse is not fitted as living quarters, that a serviceable hulk with sufficient accommodation could better replace *Mercury*. Manifestly from the Submarine point of view, the best arrangement would be to complete Blockhouse.

If Blockhouse cannot be completed, it would be more economical to reduce *Mercury* to the status of a hulk. If the only thing required at Blockhouse is a ship in which the crews can be accommodated, the *Emerald* from Queenstown would probably meet all requirements for many years.
(Captain Hall.)

Mercury should be reduced to a hulk pending building of living quarters at Blockhouse.
(Commander Hall.)

I do not advocate this, but, as pointed out, it would certainly reduce Vote A, if that is desired.
(Captain Lees.)

And Vote 14, Pensions.
(Captain Brown)

Should be Local Flotilla – 12 Submarines.
(Commander Hall.)

Mercury could then, as regards Portsmouth, be dispensed with. Failing the completion of Blockhouse or the substitution of another vessel for *Mercury*, it would seem feasible to effect a considerable saving in personnel if *Mercury* was reduced to the status of a hulk.

It is also for consideration whether many of the duties in connection with the working of Blockhouse now performed by Active Service ratings could not equally well be performed by Civilians in the same manner as obtains at the Dockyards and Torpedo Sub-Depots. If this is practicable, Vote A could be considerably reduced.

It will be seen that everything points to the necessity for determining the future of Blockhouse, and that if practicable it would be of the utmost advantage if the Portsmouth Division bases could be determined as follows:–

Permanent base – Blockhouse, completed
Sea-going base – *Bonaventure*.
Tenders – As at present
Local flotilla – 11 Submarines
Sea-going flotilla – 9 Submarines

18. The only Submarine base at Devonport is *Forth*, which vessel now acts in the dual capacity of a permanent and sea-going base. It is therefore for decision whether the existing resources of the port can provide (without considerable additional cost) a definite permanent base capable of accommodating the crews of the local flotilla, staff, &c., workshops, and necessary electrical plant. Although it is understood that the local Submarine Flotilla could be berthed alongside the North Wall of the yard, and their crews could be accommodated in the Barracks, and that electrical plant is available in yard and possibly also in *Defence*, workshops are apparently not available. This would not be so satisfactory, from the Submarine point of view,

Whatever the type of vessel is selected, she must be fitted up as a large workshop, and as the numbers to be accommodated will be large, it would seem desirable to take a bigger ship than a *Bonaventure* class. If it could be spared, a vessel such as the *Agincourt* (*Boscawen*) would appear to be admirably adapted. Failing this, the *Iron Duke*. The sale of guns, mountings, and racers would produce a fair sum, which could be expended in preparing her for the service required. The *Forth* could then continue as seagoing base.

(Captain Hall.)

I am of opinion that *Forth* (in view of number of Submarines available) can do as the provision of a definite vessel as the Devonport Home base. It would seem that the best arrangement would be to provide another vessel of *Bonaventure* class specially fitted to accommodate staff and crew of Submarines and with necessary electrical plant and workshops. The provision of such a vessel would also have the advantage of enabling the vessel to be employed, if required, as an additional sea-going vessel, although normally the permanent base.

If, therefore, this could be arranged the Devonport branch of the Submarine Service would be as follows:–

Permanent base – Shore establishment, hulk, or *Forth*

Sea-going base – A *Bonaventure* class

Tenders – As at present

Local flotilla – 7 Submarines

Sea-going flotilla – 9 Submarines

19. Chatham division has hitherto only supplied a small part of the personnel to Submarine Service. It is now, however, proposed to establish a local flotilla at Dover or some other convenient place, and it has been approved to establish a sea-going base and flotilla at Dover, both of which it is proposed should be allocated to Chatham.

If these proposals are approved, it will be necessary, in the first place, to provide a permanent or Home base at whichever port it is decided to establish the local flotilla.

It is understood that, generally speaking, the existing facilities for Submarines at Dover are good, and with a moderate outlay a shore base could be established. Alternatively a hulk could be appropriated as living quarters and fitted with small workshops, the electrical plant, &c. being available in the port.

If these arrangements can be made the Chatham branch of the Submarine Service would be as follows:–

this for the present, but that it is desirable to establish a fixed base as at Portsmouth and Dover. The best solution seems to be to build living quarters at Blockhouse and send *Mercury* to Devonport.
(Commander Hall.)

The permanent base for Chatham flotilla requires the same treatment as that for Devonport, as quarters are not provided on shore.

If it be decided to have a ship as the permanent base, one of sufficient size should be selected.
(Captain Hall.)

Permanent base – Either on shore or hulk fitted as necessary.

Sea-going base – *Thames* at Dover

Tenders – To be determined

Local flotilla – 6 Submarines at port to be decided on

Sea-going flotilla – 9 Submarines at Dover.

20. It will be seen that the main present difficulty is the definite provision of permanent Home bases for each of the three Port Divisions. Possibly the cheapest and best method would be:–

(1) Complete Blockhouse

(2) Fit *Mercury* and transfer her to Devonport, or Dover if shore base is not available at that port.

(3) Fit another vessel of *Bonaventure* class to release *Forth* for Home base.

By this means the Submarine Service would be provided with 3 Home bases and 3 Over-sea bases, which will meet all requirements until 1907–08, after which only Foreign bases will have to be provided unless additional Home bases are required at any other Home port.

In lieu of this proposal, suggest –
(1) Complete Blockhouse. (Sale of *Mercury* covers cost);
(2) Fit *Emerald* as base at Devonport:
(3) Fit another vessel (*Agincourt*) as base at Dover if suitable accommodation cannot be provided on shore.
It should be accepted in principle that Permanent bases do not move.
The Sea-going bases would then be –
Portsmouth – *Bonaventure*
Devonport – *Forth*
Dover – *Thames*
(Captain Hall.)

Under these circumstances there need be no additional bases (apart from living quarters at Blockhouse) considered until 1st January 1908, the matter standing thus on 31st March 1908:–

	Portsmouth	Devonport	Dover
Home Base and Submarines	Fort Blockhouse 7 A class 3 B class 2 C class	*Mercury* 6 A class	– –
Sea-going Base and Submarines	*Bonaventure* 6 C class	*Forth* 4 B class 5 C class	*Thames* 4 B class 5 C class

At this time a hulk or living quarters will be required at Dover to accommodate Submarines built during 1908–09, observing that *Bonaventure* has still only six.
(Commander Hall.)

21. The allocation proposed above provides for Submarines up to 1907–08; it is therefore essential to decide at what other ports Submarines, as they become available, will in future be based, and in what numbers.

It would seem there must be some limitations as to numbers required to protect any base adequately, and upon this limitation the future policy as regards distribution of Submarines and their allocation to Home ports for manning seems to depend.

Assuming any of the following ports are suitable for the employment of Submarines, which should be first so provided? – and how many Submarines are necessary for each?–

Grimsby, Gibraltar, Rosyth, Malta, Pembroke, Alexandria, Queenstown, Hong Kong, Liverpool, Singapore, Clyde, Colombo.

If these points can be decided, the allocation of future Submarines can readily be regulated, but so long as they are undetermined the definite appropriation of Submarines is impracticable, and congestion of the Home bases must result.

22. The definite classification of the functions of Submarine bases, particularly the sea-going bases, distinguishing the peace and war functions is most important. From a manning point of view this classification is absolutely essential, for without it the necessary complements cannot be satisfactorily settled.

Functions of Home Bases in Peace and War.

23. PEACE:–

(1) Head-Quarters of each Port Division's branch.

(2) General charge and management of local flotilla.

(3) Accommodation of personnel of Head-Quarters, crews of local flotilla, spare crews,

Submarines being of little use without the base, the question of what to utilise as bases must be considered before the boats can be allocated to bases.

(Captain Hall.)

Future policy, after 1909:–

It would not seem necessary to distribute Submarines along the coast in peace time; and I suggest that for Home Ports the best policy will be to provide a sea-going base with nine Submarines in the following order:–

Pembroke,
Rosyth,
Grimsby

These facilities can be moved according to the strategical requirements of the case.

(Commander Hall.)

Add to Peace Functions of House or Permanent Base: Upkeep and repair of Submarines in local Flotilla.

If this view is incorrect in the absence of the sea-going flotilla, the local flotilla must be entirely dependent on the Dockyard for repairs. That this is not intended is evident

and entries.

(4) Portion of training of new entries.

(5) Collection of and distribution of Submarine personnel.

WAR:–

(1) As in peace and the local defence of base.

Functions of Sea-going Bases in Peace and War

24. (1) Head-Quarters of sea-going flotilla.

(2) General charge and management of sea-going flotilla.

(3) Accommodation of personnel of staff, sea-going flotilla's crews, spare crews, personnel under training.

(4) Completion of training of new entries.

(5) Upkeep and repair of Submarines forming sea-going flotilla.

(6) Capacity to shift base at any time without additional personnel, to steam from one port to another by day at easy speed, and convoy seagoing flotilla.

25. With regard to (6) the definition of easy steaming may be considered to be at a speed of from 10 to 12 knots. Under favourable conditions a Submarine can do 12 knots on the surface, and as a flotilla will consist of nine boats, it is probable the flotilla will not be able to approach such a speed for any length of time. Taking average conditions, it may be calculated a flotilla will not be able to accomplish a passage at a higher rate than 10 knots. The Parent vessel will, therefore, not be required to steam at a higher rate than 12 knots in peace, and will usually only require a speed of 10 knots in peace.

Again, in peace, the passages are, as a rule, to be undertaken in day time only. Thus, in the summer, a passage is limited to a maximum of 18 hours steaming by daylight, and at other seasons very much less. It is therefore,

from the fitting up of Blockhouse with workshops.
(Captain Hall.)

The distance apart of ports renders steaming by day alone not always possible.
(Captain Lees.)

reasonable to suppose the probable peace passages will not exceed 12 hours steaming at 10 knots, giving a distance of, approximately, 120 miles from base to base.

Such passages being undertaken each month, therefore, a sea-going base, apart from short trips in and out of harbour, will not cruise for more than 240 miles per month at a speed of 10 knots.

26. (1) To convoy flotilla to a distant base, possibly on an enemy's coast, at a maximum speed of 10 to 12 knots.

Para. (2) to apply only to armed parent ship.
(Commander Hall.)

(2) To be able to protect flotilla by gunfire against Destroyer attack (?).

(3) To steam day and night as necessary, and take entire charge of flotilla.

(4) That the command of utmost speed is necessary in case the Parent vessel is attacked by superior force, and her safety is dependent on her speed in flight.

If (4) is concurred in, the sea-going bases should have a speed of at least 20 knots.
(Captain Hall.)
Suggest deleting para. (4).
(Commander Hall.)

(5) That it is probable a Submarine Flotilla would be convoyed while on passage by a fleet of some sort.

27. The complements of these vessels is entirely dependent on their functions and therefore it is at once evident it is most desirable to distinguish in the cases of armed sea-going Parent ships, such as *Bonaventure*, between Peace and War complements. For Peace it is considered that a two-fifths or Nucleus Crew is ample for the work of the ship. This Nucleus Crew should be augmented by special ranks and ratings for working of plant requisite for Submarines, and for training the new entries in the Submarine Service. When the ratio of spare crews for each flotilla is decided upon, the lower ratings of the spare crews can, be absorbed in the War Crew of the Parent vessel. By the utilisation, if necessary, of spare crews and ratings under training, when making passages in Peace time, *no addition whatever* will be necessary to crews of the sea-going

Nucleus Crew is probably sufficient in Peace time for sea-going base.
(Captain Hall.)

In peace time crew of sea-going parent ships should be up to Nucleus Crew strength (2/5), augmented by special ranks and ratings for working of plant requisite for submarines and for training new entries. In the case of Bonaventure an increase will be required in war to enable her to fight her guns and steam full speed.
(Commander Hall.)

bases at such times; the work in connection with general repairs and charging Submarines, &c. being undertaken at other times, if necessary, than when cruising, or immediately after arrival at a new base. *Scheme of Complement attached.* (Appendix I.)

28. In War it is possible that no ratings under-going training will be embarked, and in view of all the important ratings being borne in Peace complement, it would seem that the only additions necessary will be a moderate increase in the numbers of lower ratings in armed sea-going Parent vessels such as *Bonaventure* sufficient to steam full speed and to fight armament. These additions would be embarked on receipt of Warning Telegram in the same manner as obtains in Destroyer and T.B. Flotillas, &c.

The *Bonaventure* class with proposed War complement, and the crews of Submarines who live on board, would seem to be rather over-crowded. *(Captain Hall.)*

Scheme of Complement attached. (Appendix I.)

[omitted]

[71] *Minute by Assistant Director of Mobilisation Division on Recruiting for Service in Submarines*
[ADM 116/1122]

[not dated]

In the attached papers the Treasury were informed, by Admiralty letter N.2665 of 3rd June 1910, in reply to an inquiry as to whether the experience gained since 1901 justified the continuance of the rates of extra pay then approved for the Submarine Service, that the question was engaging their Lordships' attention and a reply would be returned when their investigations of the varying conditions of the Submarine Service had enabled them to arrive at a definite conclusion on the point.

A detailed report was called for from the Inspecting Captain of Submarines (then Captain Sydney S Hall), as to how far in his opinion service in Submarines involved risk of life, discomfort, injury to health &c beyond what may be regarded as incidental to the ordinary course of the Naval Service. The report, however, (dated 19th May 1910) did not show what the Board wished most to learn, viz – to what extent the risks in Submarines were reduced in the then newest type, the D Class, as compared with the earlier classes.

The following decision was accordingly come to:

(1) When the D Class had been employed with Fleets at sea, to call on ICS for a further report of the comparative safety of the types C and D, particularly as regards control in a vertical plane.

(2) To defer any action as regards revision of pay until the risk of liability to collision due to method of discharge had disappeared with the advent of the larger Submarines, carrying broadside Torpedo tubes and provided with water-tight bulkheads.

The decision at (2) practically amounts to a postponement of the question of pay indefinitely, and it therefore hardly seems worth while to take any action on (1). It is pointed out, moreover, that unless a sliding scale of extra pay is introduced for the varying types of submarines there is little object in making the inquiry at (1).

Apart from the question of satisfying the Treasury enquiry, the matter of pay has acquired fresh importance in view of the ICS's proposal that the Submarine Service shall be made a closed service, in so far that men should be retained in the Submarine Service so long as they continue to give satisfaction.

At present men can do only two periods of service in Submarines, the first for 5 years, the second for 3 years, and a period of at least 2 years' general service must intervene between the two terms of Submarine service.

The question of making the Submarine service a closed service must be considered from the following points of view:–

(a) Effect on manning and drafting.
(b) Effect on pay and prospects of men.

As regards (a) it is not seen that there is any serious objection to extending the period of service in Submarines to cover a man's whole career, apart from the fact that the division of the personnel into two Services would add a fresh complication to drafting and necessitate two margins for sickness reliefs &c with a consequent possible increase in numbers over the present system. The D[irector of] M[obilisation] D[ivision] can say more as to this aspect of the question. As regards (b) the scale of extra pay for Submarines is now as follows:–

	a day (s. d.)
Chief Petty Officers, Petty Officers and Leading Seamen)	2/6
Others	2/0

If these rates are to be regarded solely as risk pay, or compensation for discomfort, there is no ground for making any change in them simply because of an extension of the period of service. During their term of service in Submarines, however, under existing conditions most Seamen are prevented from obtaining any advance in non-substantive rating and the extra pay may be regarded as covering not only risk and discomfort but as compensation for any possible loss of prospects. If a man is kept permanently in the Submarine Service this loss of advancement will be perpetuated, and constitutes a further argument against any reduction of the existing rates of Submarine Pay. It is possible also that permanent employment in Submarines might militate against a man's qualification and selection for Warrant rank.

If therefore anything in the nature of a closed service is adopted the pay of men retained permanently in the Submarines should not be reduced on that account. A more logical arrangement would be to reduce the pay of the men during their first 5 years and to restore it to its present level in the case of those permanently retained.

The chief argument used in favour of such retention, however, is the suggestion that sufficient volunteers cannot be obtained under the existing system. If this fear should prove unfounded there is hardly any justification for making any change. If the argument should be substantiated men might be given the option of entering the Submarine Service under existing conditions, or for retention so long as efficient under conditions such as those suggested in the preceding paragraph.

[72] *Report by Inspecting Captain of Submarines on the Pay and Conditions of Submarine Personnel*

[ADM 116/1122]

HMS *Mercury* at Portsmouth
19th May 1910

I have the honour to forward the detailed report called for by their Lordships in Admiralty Letter N.2665 of 12th May 1910, on the present pay and conditions of service in and recruiting for Submarines – under the following headings:–

    (1) RISK OF LIFE
    (2) DISCOMFORT
    (3) INJURY TO HEALTH
    (4) GENERAL COMPARISONS WITH CONDITIONS IN DESTROYERS.
    (5) RECRUITING.

I have the honour to be Sir, Your obedient Servant
(signed) SS Hall

1. RISK OF LIFE

When a new service at its outset causes considerable loss of life and then settles down until this loss is no greater than in other somewhat dangerous services it may be assumed that the word risky no longer applies to it.

I submit this depends entirely upon what is meant by the expression risk of life.

The risk of life in Submarines arising from accidents beyond the control of those whose business it is to manage them may now be said to have disappeared – if in fact it ever existed. If it is held that immunity from accident entails absence of risk it may also be said that there is no risk of life in Submarines for there has been no serious loss of life for 5 years with the exception of the 13 lost in C11 due to a surface collision and this might have happened to any other vessel.[1] The expression risk of life, however, is taken to be meant in its broadest sense and to include that arising from accidents due to the human element. The risk diminishes in direct proportion to the care in selection, efficient training and supervision of the personnel. With the limitations referred to later, when Submarines are submerged, it may be said that the risk of life is dependent entirely on the efficiency of the personnel. With proper precautions the various explosive agents with which the vessels are charged can be safely handled, but the term proper precautions includes not only the ordinary care of the vessel common to all ships, but an incessant attention to detail, on the part of all concerned, with petrol service, electrical storage which is always explosive on charge, and the trimming of the vessels, particularly when handling large quantities of water in a very short time. If the selection or training is slackened to any extent by lowering the standard of entry, or other cause, the riskiness will very shortly re-appear, for the dangerous elements remain, as they always were, ready to assert themselves with far reaching consequences in response to any carelessness or oversight. It is in this respect that the risk of life may most certainly be said to be far greater in Submarines than in any other branch of the Naval Service, the results of accidents are more serious and the contributory causes much more numerous.

---

[1] HMS/m C11. Rammed by merchant vessel while running on the surface and sunk in 1908.

In the case of a surface collision due to the absence of W[ater] T[ight] compartments, it is doubtful if many can escape; if any man falls overboard there is small chance of picking him up; if any explosion occurs it is almost certainly serious because it is confined. Taking the comparison of a destroyer:–

If navigational and collision risks are excluded (they are common to Submarines) and night manoeuvres without lights (dealt with later) the risk of life is practically confined to the bursting of steam pipes or accident to a boiler and when the vessel is in harbour these disappear. In a Submarine, however, the chances of accident are always present and at no time is it possible to relax the care so necessary, the risk of life or if preferred the chances of accident are as great in harbour, though from different causes, as they are when at sea either on the surface or when submerged.

The foregoing applies to Submarines on the surface and to all classes except the D class. In this class, one of the chances of accident, the petrol service, is entirely removed: in the case of surface collision also, due to a greater reserve of buoyancy, the results though probably the same will take longer and give more chance of escape to those inside – but not very much in view of the numbers concerned.

Directly Submarines become submerged different classes of risks are introduced, those are as follows:–

(a) IMPERFECT LOOK OUT AND RESULTING RISK OF COLLISION.

(b) CONTROL IN VERTICAL PLANE.

(c) LIABILITY TO COLLISION DUE TO METHOD OF DISCHARGE.

Taking these in order–

(a) The look out from a Submarine may for practical purposes be compared to an invisible vessel being worked by a one-eyed man in rather a bad light with an horizon of about 1.5 miles, and a field of only 40° at any one time, at intervals even this must be given up to render her attack possible, and is at all times liable to interruption from small errors in depth keeping. This is the greatest disability from which Submarines suffer, it entails a great deal of judgement on the part of the Captain for he cannot be assisted and must judge his movement in two planes, gauge the deflection for his torpedoes and fire them at the right moment, usually with helm on, it entails also no small amount of endurance on the part of the remainder of the crew to always have to place their lives in one man's hands, knowing the difficult conditions under which he is working. It might be concluded from this that the Submarine is but a poorly equipped fighting machine and little to be feared; it is sometimes forgotten that collision is her only foe, at any rate at present. It is the equivalent of the enemy's gun fire to a surface ship which has no terrors for a Submarine and the latter's war achievements are more likely to approach these attained in peace than in any other vessel for the reason that she is almost constantly exercising under as nearly war conditions as it is possible to get.

It is the reality of these conditions which entails the risk to life in Submarines when submerged. The risk varies with the number of vessels employed on both sides but it is always present, and is common to all classes of Submarines including the D class; in the latter the vessels are much longer and their tactical diameter [i.e. turning circle] submerged exactly double that of the C class so that the chances of collision will be greater. The only parallel in the case of destroyers is on those occasions when night exercises are carried out on very dark nights without lights – in this case the risks to the ship are approaching those to a Submarine, but the results of collision to a Submarine are likely to be more serious.

(b) CONTROL IN VERTICAL PLANE

The principal risk of life in this connection lies in the danger of the vessel sinking so rapidly that the pressure of the outside water rises more rapidly than the air pressure admitted to the ballast tanks to blow it out. It may be caused by an error on the part of the diving coxswains, or through undetected leaks in the hull causing the vessel to lose buoyancy whilst diving. It sounds a simple enough matter but it is one of the most surprising matters in under water work how very rapidly a Submarine sinks and how difficult she is to check once she gains any downward momentum. The net result is usually to take the vessel to the bottom; it is fortunate that up to date this has always happened in fairly shallow water; recently the limit was very nearly reached when [HMS] A8 took the bottom in 28 fathoms, she took 45 minutes to get up and fairly desperate measures had to be adopted.

(c) LIABILITY TO COLLISION DUE TO METHOD OF DISCHARGE

This is largely involved in (a) but is treated separately because it is a risk which shows signs of being a good deal minimised. There is no doubt that particularly with Submarines the size of the D class it is an unpleasant and dangerous business to have to place one's vessel at right angles to the path of an advancing ship or fleet; it is inherent with the right ahead discharge, when the beam discharge is adopted this will be a great deal less. The present effect is such that 99 out of 100 Submarines will say that the fleet formation they most dislike is line abreast. It is not considered that the risk of life is appreciably increased by the fact of Submarines operating against fleets at a distance. The usual rate for insurance in Submarines is 10% extra to ordinary risks. Army and Naval General Assurance Company will not accept them at all.

2. DISCOMFORT

The discomforts in submarines cannot be exaggerated; in my own experience I have found the old Yarrow Torpedo Boats entail a certain amount of discomfort unless the weather was fine, but compared with a submarine it is luxurious. Clothes cannot be dried, fires are not permissible, in cold weather it is difficult to keep reasonably warm, the amount of fresh water precludes any attempt at personal cleanliness and the roar of the Engines is all over the boat and though the Officers and men are nominally in watch and watch there is no certainty in the watch off. To many, the smell inside a submarine after she has been a short time at sea, which is absolutely peculiar to itself, is most revolting, All food tastes of it, all clothes reek of it, it is quite impossible to wear any clothes again after they have been used in it. It is considered that the conditions in this respect are undoubtedly improved in the D class, there is more room and being double the tonnage she is less affected by bad weather. D1 is only just completed and she has only been for one cruise of two weeks. During this time she was entirely self-supporting and the crew lived in her, she did 670 miles on the surface, 300 being a non stop run, dived at intervals on 7 occasions for 20 miles and fired 6 torpedoes. This is with a new vessel, there is no doubt that the time spent on board these submarines in the future will be much greater than before.

3. INJURY TO HEALTH

All Officers and men are carefully examined before entry, no one is sent out in a doubtful state of health, under these conditions no injury to health is experienced or expected.

4. RELATION OF PAY TO RESPONSIBILITIES IN SUBMARINES AND DESTROYERS

A good deal of this ground has already been covered. It seems to me that the responsibilities of the Officer in a Submarine are much greater than those in a destroyer, alone, without lookouts, glasses or signalmen, and with an inferior substitute for a pair of eyes he has, whilst conducting his attack in war, or his exercises in peace, to manage his vessel in two planes, to aim and fire his torpedoes, and keep his vessel clear of disaster. He has no Engineer or Warrant Officer to assist him and the responsibility for his engines and torpedoes with two kinds of motive power and all the auxiliary services such as blowing and pumping arrangements in addition is upon him. It is true he has always a second Officer to help him, but failure in any case is usually associated with the probable loss of the vessel.

In the case of a D class submarine I maintain the responsibility is out of all proportion to that of a destroyer and I have had considerable experience of both. This class of submarine is such a huge machine that only the very best class of all round Officer can be expected to command her successfully. With regard to the pay being in proportion to the responsibilities I would submit that it is, and that in view of the discomforts being undoubtedly much greater in the submarine than in the destroyer the proportion is reasonable. The hypothetical case quoted in the Admiralty Letter is not a real one at present and does not accurately represent the Conditions in the two services as they stand. At present Officers entering the submarine service remain in it as Lieutenants, but at least 3 years of the time is spent in big ships where no extra pay is drawn at all. Officers in Destroyers and in other specialised branches, remain in them all their time and therefore draw the special allowances continuously.

5. RECRUITING

It is at present difficult to get the stamp of Officer required in sufficient numbers. There is certainly an impression amongst younger Officers that once they come into Submarines they give up all chance of the higher ranks of the service even if they ever get promoted at all. There have I known [sic] many cases where Captains have told young Officers wishing to volunteer that they were making a great mistake and jeopardising their career. I think this is due to a misunderstanding of the work in Submarines, it is after all a seaman's work, the amount done under water is comparatively small and the training in giving Officers early responsibility is all good, the mere fact of having successfully conned a Submarine must be good for them and their nerves and general capacities under trying conditions improved. I hope as Submarines become better known and as the Submarine Officers go to sea in big ships, as they now are, in increasing numbers, that this may wear off. Certainly at the present moment I should not expect vacancies to be filled if the pay were reduced. The time when it is submitted this might be done and still obtain sufficient volunteers will be when the Submarine Officers reach the promotion area. If a definite number of promotions were given for a batch or two to Submarine Officers. I mean those who have specialised in it, the volunteering would probably improve. This cannot be for 3 or 4 years. Then the pay could quite well be reduced, but at present there does not seem anything to offer. The only reduction I would suggest at present is the command money allowed for the Holland and A class Submarines. These are practically harbour service tenders and the command money might be reduced to 2/6. This will necessitate the Submarine Officers attaining at least 4 years seniority before getting the full allowance as they command A boats before being allowed to take sea-going Submarines.

ERA's also present difficulties and should attractions be reduced it is extremely improbable that vacancies could be filled. There are at present 81 employed at Portsmouth and 9 on the roster. Seamen and Petty Officers up to the present have not presented any difficulties; the total from Portsmouth employed is 339, number on the roster 26.

Stoker Petty Officers and Stokers: there are 181 employed and 54 on the roster. The above numbers on the rosters of volunteers are the totals, they are not of course all available and it generally takes about 3 months to obtain necessary stokers.

I have as requested dealt with the risks and discomforts in submarines in detail. In doing so I feel that the impression may be left that there is a discrepancy between the alleged risks and the resulting accidents. The only reason that I can give for the number of accidents being so few is that, just because the risks are so real and the results so disastrous, the amount of care and attention to detail exercised is very great. There is no doubt that on every occasion of doing *anything* the crew of a submarine are well aware that they are undertaking a risky operation and that any failure on their part will result in serious accident. Though I do not attribute any slackness in the management of vessels such as destroyers I do not consider that the personnel are worked up to the same pitch of close attention to detail and realisation of definite risk as are the crew of a Submarine. Each man must and does feel that his own personal safety is concerned, and though familiarity may take the edge off this it does I contend remain more or less a constant strain on the Officers and men which will have to be well rewarded to be undertaken.

In conclusion I would respectfully submit that the comparisons of pay for responsibility, discomforts &c in Submarines and Destroyers could best be judged by an independent witness going for a cruise in both for a few days. Though I have had considerable experience in both it may be that the longer time in submarines has magnified their dangers and discomforts.

The following is a summary of some facts in connection with the numbers of Officers, serving and wastage &c.

Number of Officers serving (including 12 at sea in big ships)   145
Number killed on duty   6
Number incapacitated from accidents   2
Number married   28
Number discharged unsuitable or at own request   29

[73] *Letter by Inspecting Captain of Submarines on the Conditions of Service of Submarine Personnel*[1]
[ADM 116/1122]

HMS *Dolphin* at Gosport,
7th February 1913

With reference to my remarks on Admiralty paper AWS, MD18/1913, and in view of the present serious shortage of ratings available for entry into the Submarine Service, I have the honour to submit that the existing system of discharging ratings to the general service on the completion of 5 years in the Submarine Service and of re-entering them 2 years later for a further period of 3 years may be abolished, and that in future ratings may be allowed to remain in the Submarine service so long as they continue to give satisfaction.

2. The reasons for making this submission are as follows:–

i. When a man is discharged to the General service all his training and experience in Submarine work is entirely wasted.

ii. There are several men who are now about to be discharged to the General Service on the completion of their 8 years and who according to the present system will not be available for further service in Submarines at any future date. The great majority of these ratings are still in the prime of life and in every way admirably suited for this service, with 8 years of valuable experience behind them.

iii. If those men were allowed to continue in this service it would hold out a great inducement for them to re-engage at the termination of their first period, instead of taking their discharge as the greater number do at present.

iv. It is considered that in the event of this submission being approved, a considerable number of ST's might be replaced by young Able Seamen having no Torpedo Qualification, without impairing the efficiency of the Submarine service. These men would be thoroughly trained in Submarine and Torpedo work on entering their respective

[1] From September 1910 to February 1915, Capt. (later Commodore 2nd Class) Roger Keyes held the post of Inspecting Captain (later Commodore) of Submarines.

Depots, and I would submit that on passing a successful examination in this work, they should be allowed to hold the Non-substantive rating of Seaman Submarine (SS). In this connection it would be necessary to have a TGM borne in each of the three Instructional Depots for the purpose of training these ratings.

3. I would submit that this suggestion may be very seriously considered. It is realised that it possesses some disadvantages, but the military value of a Submarine depends entirely on its personnel, and the efficient manning of this rapidly expanding service is becoming increasingly difficult under the existing regulations.

4. It may be said that a man entering the Submarine service under the proposed conditions would have a poor prospect of advancement, but it is considered that the prospects will be at least as good as those in the General service for the wastage in a Service where such a high standard is demanded must necessarily be considerable and there can be little doubt that the submarine service will continue to expand.

[2 tables omitted]

Enclosure No 3

Ratings		*A*		*B*		*C*
Number in submarines		913				
Spare crews		303				
composed of						
SEAMEN	*S/Ms*		*Spare*			
Chief and Petty Officers	80		27			12
Leading Seamen	119		39			8
Able Seamen	310		102			28
ENGINE-ROOM COMPLEMENT						
Chief and Engine-room Artificer	144		48			16
Stoker Petty Officer	63		21			8
Leading Stoker	64		21			4
Stoker	133		45			16
Including						
			S/Ms	*Spare*		
NON-SUBSTANTIVE RATINGS						
GL 3rd class	8.f		3.f	8.f	3.f	4
LTO	72.e		24.e	72.e	24.e	8.e
ST	–		–	366	120	28

A. Spare crews and in existing submarines as per Mobilisation Return No 1.
B. Non-substantive rating modifications concurred in by Commodore (S) on NMD 18/13.
C. Additions for every three E class commissioned, (i.e. four E class).
f. Except in D1.
e. In every fourth submarine may be replaced by a TGM.

[74] *Correspondence relating to the Eyesight of Submarine Officers.*
Commodore Roger Keyes to Secretary of the Admiralty[1]
[Keyes Mss 4/13]

HMS *Dolphin* at Gosport
20 February 1913

I have the honour to submit for the considerations of Their Lordships the following report regarding the eyesight of certain officers in the submarine service, and to request that a decision may be given as to whether the fact of wearing glasses for short-sight is to be considered as a disqualification for further service in submarines:–

2. It has been brought to my notice that Lieutenant Charles L. Kerr, commanding C8 has recently taken to wearing glasses and I therefore made a thorough enquiry into the condition of his eyesight. An examination of the detailed record of attacks kept by the commanding officer of his flotilla showed that his attacks had been consistently good and above the average, in fact, I was present in C8 during an attack on HMS *Hebe* and had an opportunity of observing his powers of vision, both on the surface and submerged, for about three hours. He informed me that he was rather short-sighted and had recently on the advice of an oculist, taken to wearing glasses while on the bridge of his vessel, but he did not use them at any other time as his vision was sufficiently good for ordinary purposes. He said that a periscope apparently had exactly the same effect on his vision as his glasses, as he was able to see perfectly through his periscope. This I corroborated with the assistance of Commander Willis, the commanding officer of his flotilla, after we returned to harbour, by observing objects on shore at various distances.

3. We are both satisfied that his vision through a periscope, without glasses, is quite normal and absolutely above suspicion. There is no doubt, however, that Lieutenant Kerr is otherwise short-sighted without his glasses, and I would recommend that his sight be tested at the Admiralty at an early date.

If considered sufficiently good for watch-keeping duties in a ship of war at sea, I have no hesitation in recommending that he be retained in the submarine service as he is an able submarine captain and we cannot afford to lose officers of his calibre. If, however, the medical authorities decide he is unfit to carry out the duties of an executive officer in a ship at sea, he must of course be relieved of his command.

4. A few days ago I received a similar report from the commanding

[1] Letter forwarded to the Admiralty via office of Admiral of Patrols, Rear Adm. John de Robeck.

officer of the Malta flotilla on the eyesight of Lieutenant Gill, commanding submarine B9. I have requested further information as to this officer's power of vision through a periscope and also details of his prescription for glasses.

5. A periscope is capable of being focussed and undoubtedly acts as a clearer and thus improves one's vision. It appears probable that a person with a tendency to short-sight and accustomed to the use of a periscope misses this aid to vision when he rises to the surface and in time finds it necessary to provide a substitute.

6. From a purely submarine point of view, vision such as Lieutenant Kerr's is absolutely normal while submerged. It is a question, however, to what extent glasses may be used by watch-keeping officers in command of a ship, particularly a small vessel such as a destroyer or submarine, whose bridge affords small protection against spray and rain. Personally I am of the opinion that an officer's services should be retained if his eyesight is fairly good and can be perfected by glasses, and provided he is under an obligation to carry at least two pairs on his person when on duty.

7. The two officers in question are thoroughly capable submarine captains who possess valuable experience and whose services can ill be spared.

[Attached minute by Winston S. Churchill][1]

8 February 1913

No action need be taken in view of report of Commodore S, and the whole matter is to be regarded as if it never occurred. ...

---

[1] Winston Churchill: First Lord of the Admiralty, October 1911 to May 1915.

PART IV

SUBMARINES AND FLEET SUBMARINES

[75] *Report On The Swedish Submarine* Hvalen, *and Discussion of its Merits in Comparison with British and French types of Submarines* [Keyes Papers, 4/22 (M01374/1909)]

Remarks of the Inspecting Captain of Submarines[1]

HMS *Mercury* at Portsmouth,
19 November 1909

In compliance with Admiralty letter M. 562/09 of 15th November 1909, and your Minute No. 562/09 of 16th November 1909, I have the honour to attach a report received from H.M. Ship *Vulcan* on the Swedish submarine *Hvalen* after the latter laid alongside her at Portsmouth.[2]

I concur generally with the report, which confirms the information we had previously about this type of submarine.

The principal difference between them and our C class (which are contemporary) lies in the two factors of surface buoyancy and speed – the surface horsepower is 50 per cent greater, and the surface buoyancy (including reserve of buoyancy) three times as great as in our C class, the result being that something very near a surface torpedo-boat is produced. The actual value to be given to surface buoyancy to obtain the best sea-going and sea-keeping results is a very old argument. The French have for years been carrying out comparative trials between vessels of small and large buoyancy, distinguished in their terms by the words Submarine and Submersible, this being the only practical difference between them. They have, it is well known, decided in favour of the latter type, and on this evidence one might therefore think that the Swedes' openly-expressed claim to have a superior vessel, in their *Hvalen*, to our C class, was justified.

On closer examination, however, the following considerations in my opinion absolutely reverse this verdict. They have never to my knowledge appeared in print and are worth mentioning at this stage, as I consider they account for the extraordinarily good sea-going qualities of our submarines, which have to be seen to be fully realised, and which are certainly not believed in by foreigners, with the exception of the Americans, who have a similar design.

The French decision in favour of a type with large surface buoyancy (called by them Submersibles) hinged upon competitive trials carried out between the Submarine class *Emeraude*, *Opale*, & c., and the Submersible type *Pluviôse*, *Ventôse*, & c. I attach photograph of each.

[1] Minute signed by Capt. Sydney Hall.
[2] *Hvalen*: built at Fiat works in La Spezia, Italy.

The difference in behaviour of the two was very marked, the submarine with only 5 per cent, never rising at all to the sea, and, directly the sea became any size at all, plunging considerably, the submersible with 30–40 per cent behaving more like a torpedo-boat and riding the sea. The Captain of the *Emeraude* told me, however, that his vessel was at all times steadier and therefore more comfortable inside; the only quality in his opinion that he wanted was twice as much surface buoyancy, i.e., 10 per cent. This was very interesting for he would by so doing have brought his vessel up to nearly the same standard as our C class, where the surface buoyancy is 12 per cent of submerged displacement.

I believe that if the French had had a properly conducted trial with their *Pluviôse* and an *Emeraude* of 12 per cent surface buoyancy, they would not have decided in favour of the former. Considering only vessels of not more than 300 to 400 tons displacement, I cannot see that their sea-going or sea-keeping qualities are increased by increasing their buoyancy beyond a certain amount. If, in addition to giving them buoyancy, plenty of hatches and direct communication to outside air could be provided for the whole of the interior, as in the case of a destroyer, it might be so, but remembering that, however much you increase the buoyancy, the crew must live inside the pressure hull which is common to both types, the principal result of the extra buoyancy is only directed to throwing them about. The difference between the movement of a submarine and a torpedo boat of the same size is very marked and the limit of surface buoyancy which is advisable for vessels of 300 to 400 tons depends of course upon the size of the seas likely to be met; for North Sea and east end of English Channel, I am quite satisfied with 12 per cent.

There is a strong tendency to increase a vessel's surface qualities at the expense of the more important submerged ones; the former are more thoroughly realised and understood, and particularly in the case of a commercial undertaking (which these *Hvalen* class are), a surface speed of 15 knots makes a brave show, whilst a high efficiency battery and possibly considerable smoothing of the hull for submerged trials still enable her to make a fair show under water. The Captain of the *Hvalen* only, after dinner, claimed $6^1/2$ knots full speed for her under water. Fitted as she was, in Portsmouth, the hull was covered in obstructions which would take some time to remove, yet they were apparently necessary to get the full benefit of her claim for superiority on the surface, and they would be fatal to her underwater speed. Our C class, on the other hand, are always in a condition to dive and get their trial speeds, the hulls being kept smooth; and no extra obstruction is required to enable them to make a passage. Their endurance at 5 knots is about 20 hours, a result the *Hvalen* cannot approach. I attach photos of the *Hvalen* taken on her diving trials, which make one think there is something unusual about the wave thrown; in the case of the one marked attacking, the wave, due either to shape of hull or superstructure or perhaps shortness of periscope, is prohibitive.

Since the employment of submarines is still to a great extent speculative, it is easy to find arguments in favour of *any* type. The best position to take up, and at any rate the safest, is that which we took under Admiral Bacon's direction, and which has been adhered to ever since, namely, to make sure of a sound reliable vessel with no one quality exaggerated at the expense of any other. The overpowering and all-deciding element is the human one narrowed down practically to the capabilities of the captain. As I have so often pointed out, this is so large a factor that a gain in speed of a knot or so, on the surface or submerged, sinks into insignificance compared with many qualities that do not appear in contract trials. Where such gain is obtained at the expense of other qualities, as in the case of F.I.A.T. submarines, where undoubtedly submerged qualities suffer for exaggerated surface performances, I do not consider they are at all desirable and I can see no reason to justify the claims of these F.I.A.T. submarines to superiority over other designs of equal displacement.

Remarks of the Director of Naval Intelligence[1]

23 December 1909

With reference to the report of the Inspecting Captain of Submarines, particularly as regards the French portion, the buoyancy of the *Emeraude* class is officially recognised as being just over 7 per cent. The submarine proper had practically been abandoned in the French Navy before the comparative trials between the *Emeraude* and *Pluviôse* types, as about 33 *Pluviôses* and improved *Pluviôses* had been ordered before they took place, against one experimental submarine with 15 per cent buoyancy. The trials were carried out to make assurance doubly sure.

The statement made by so high an authority, that increased buoyancy does not add to the sea-going or sea-keeping qualities of vessels, is surely open to question, and it must be recognised that the French have had at least as much experience as we have in submarine navigation, while the results they have actually obtained compare most favourably with those obtained in the British Navy.

---

[1] Minute signed by Capt. Thomas Jackson (assistant DNI) for Rear Adm. Alexander Bethell, Director of Naval Intelligence, 1909–11.

As an example of the sea-keeping qualities of the *Pluviôse* type, in October 1909 the *Papin* went from Rochefort to Oran, a distance of 1,200 miles, in less than five days, without a stop; during part of the voyage bad weather was experienced. This constitutes a world's record, which has not been approached by any British submarine. Although it is not possible to open hatches along the whole body of a submarine, as in a destroyer, it may be borne in mind that in bad weather the destroyer's hatches are closed, and in addition to making her knock about more, her increased buoyancy enables her to keep a portion of the forecastle hatch open except in the worst weather, an advantage also obtained in the sea-going submarine with good buoyancy, which is able to keep its conning tower open except in very bad weather.

With reference to the remarks of the Inspecting Captain of Submarines on Page 3, it appears to me that seaworthiness and surface speed are all-important in submarines. The first consideration is that they should be able with certainty and rapidity to reach their scene of action, and that must be done on the surface. A great radius of action when submerged is not essential, nor, until the submerged speed more nearly approaches that of surface vessels, is it of great consequence to obtain a knot or two more speed when submerged, nor is it desirable that any seaworthiness or surface speed should be sacrificed to obtain this. The *Pluviôse* type have a submerged speed of 8 knots at full speed, and the *Emeraude* 9 knots, but this speed can only be maintained for one hour. A constant speed of 6 knots can be kept up for as long as it would be necessary. This may fairly be considered efficient, and shows that in the French submersible the submerged qualities are not unduly sacrificed in order to obtain an increase of buoyancy. This result compares well with those obtained in British boats.

As the Inspecting Captain of Submarines has confined his comparisons chiefly to the French and British boats, the Swedish *Hvalen* has not been criticised, but there is no doubt that the Italian type presents a submersible torpedo boat capable, in most circumstances, of rendering valuable services.

Remarks of the Director of Naval Construction[1]

21 January 1910

The following comparison of the principal qualities of the later C class submarines and of the *Hvalen* has been prepared from the figures given in the enclosed report, supplemented by information obtained

[1] Minute signed by Sir Philip Watts, Director of Naval Construction, 1901–12.

from other sources, which are in general agreement with the report, as stated by the Inspecting Captain of Submarines.

	C.22–38	*Hvalen*
Length of hull	132 feet	139 feet
Submerged displacement	320 tons	300 tons
Surface displacement	291 tons	185 tons
Reserve of buoyancy in surface condition	29 tons	115 tons
Reserve of buoyancy as a percentage of surface displacement	10 per cent	62 per cent
Maximum shop trial power of petrol engines	600 B.H.P.	1050 B.H.P.
Maximum surface speed	$12^1/2$ knots	15 knots
Amount of petrol carried	14 tons	6 tons
Endurance at maximum speed	75 hours	28 hours
Estimated speed at 600 B.H.P (on basis of 1050 B.H.P. for 15 knots)		$12^1/2$ knots
Endurance at $12^1/2$ knots	75 hours	50 hours
Endurance at 10 knots	120 hours	96 hours
Maximum B.H.P. of electric motors for submerged propulsion	230	200
Maximum submerged speed	8.6 knots	6.5 knots
B.H.P. at 5 knots submerged	70	100
Number of cells in battery	166	100
Endurance at 5 knots submerged	12 hours	8 hours

The main qualities which distinguish the *Hvalen* and the similar Italian boats from our C.22 class, so far as they can be expressed in figures which have a direct relevance to the fighting value of the boat, are, therefore, the superiority in maximum smooth water surface speed, and the inferiority in submerged speed and in both surface and submerged endurance.

The figures for submerged endurance are based on new batteries. The cell used in the *Hvalen* is of a light type, having 45 per cent greater capacity than that used in C.22, and under the conditions of use in a submarine boat would no doubt show a faster rate of deterioration in capacity, so that the comparison is really less favourable to the *Hvalen* than the figures above would show.

From the technical point of view the remarkable feature of the *Hvalen* is the small displacement on which her actual qualities are obtained, quite apart from the question whether these qualities are combined in the best proportions to produce the most effective fighting vessel. The hull of a C class boat weighs about 125 tons; the engine, propelling motors and battery together about 100 tons; while the remaining weight making up the 291 tons surface displacement is absorbed in armament, petrol, auxiliary machinery, crew and equipment. The *Hvalen* is of non-circular section, and, therefore, liable to larger forces tending to produce rupture for a given external pressure than our circular section boats, and is longer and broader, and has been tested at a depth of 40 metres. Making every possible allowance for a low factor of safety and absence of provision for corrosion it does not seem possible that the hull could weigh less than 90 tons, which leaves only 95 tons for everything else, an amount insufficient to cover the weight of the propelling machinery and battery in our boat, although less powerful than in the *Hvalen*, without any provision at all for auxiliary services and equipment.

Lightness in construction and in machinery is very desirable in all classes of vessels, and, so far as it is obtained without sacrifice of durability and reliability, is a measure of the skill of the designers. Whether durability and reliability have been sacrificed in the *Hvalen* could only be determined by an extended and intimate experience of her working; but the considerable periods of remaining in port during the passage from Spezia to Stockholm are somewhat significant.

It is the extreme lightness of construction and of machinery which enables the high surface reserve of buoyancy to be obtained, for reserve of buoyancy in the surface condition represents a weight of water carried in the submerged condition and expelled to bring the boat to the surface. This should be remembered in any comparison made between a submarine and a destroyer as regards habitability. The reserve of buoyancy of the latter would be about 150 per cent of the displacement, and is available as accessible space inside the hull. If, however, it were merely tank space, as it would be in a submarine, it would considerably curtail the habitability of the destroyer, quite apart from any question of freeboard or behaviour in a sea way. Comparing the C class and the *Hvalen*, of not very different submerged displacement, the high reserve of buoyancy of the latter means that it can have only about 6,500 cubic feet of space in which to provide living space for the crew, and to stow fuel, compensating water, armament and machinery, and provide reasonable access to them, while the corresponding figure for the C boats is about 10,000 cubic feet.

Another point which should be taken into account in any attempt to compare the sea-going qualities of a destroyer is that for practical purposes the reserve of buoyancy in the two cases cannot be on the same scale. The *Hvalen* with 62 per cent reserve of buoyancy is considered to approach the extreme high limit of reserve of buoyancy which under practical conditions can be given to a submersible boat, while a destroyer has 150 per cent and upwards.

There is not, and never has been, any difficulty, except the laboriousness of the detailed work, in calculating the effect of varying proportions of reserve of buoyancy in a given design of submarine, the problem being the same in kind as in the case of a surface ship. The difficulty is that conditions such as the average state of the sea, the average risk of particular accidents, & c., cannot be definitely formulated, so that nothing but prolonged experience and careful observation can really show whether a high or low reserve is the better for practical purposes.

A high reserve is an element of safety in case a boat springs a leak, e.g. C.11 would have taken four times as long to founder if she had had the reserve of buoyancy of the *Hvalen*, a difference which might conceivably have allowed effective steps to have been taken to save the boat. It also prevents all danger of a boat diving or dipping spontaneously from the surface condition, as in the case of A8. Although on trial the C class would not do this in comparatively smooth water with much less than their full reserve of buoyancy, owing to the propeller coming out of the water, there is no doubt that they would be safer with more reserve in meeting all states of the sea.

High reserve of buoyancy, from the same cause that renders the boat safe against diving, also renders the pitching and rolling periods shorter, other things being equal, so that a moderate sea which simply washes over the boat with low reserve, and, if not too rough, leaves the bridge dry, may cause a degree of motion in the boat with high reserve which prevents the realisation of her smooth water speeds, is not good for the battery, and renders her a wetter boat to navigate from any possible bridge which can be fitted to a submarine, though a high reserve generally means a somewhat higher bridge than in the case of low reserve. In a heavy ocean swell of long period, on the other hand, it is possible that the boat with high reserve would ride over it, while the boat with low reserve would be practically submerged for half the time.

The general shape of the above-water part of the submarine in the surface condition will greatly affect the behaviour of the vessel in a sea way, apart from its absolute volume, which measures the reserve of buoyancy, and it is considered impossible to lay down any rule as to what the reserve of buoyancy of the submarine boat in general ought to be. The reserve of buoyancy is only a particular feature of each definite design and must be considered strictly in its relation to other features, which necessarily vary as reserve of buoyancy varies.

For example, taking the submerged speed figures for the *Pluviôse* and *Emeraude* quoted by the Director of Naval Intelligence, the endurance of the former at 6 knots would be about three hours, and of the latter 5 hours. If the former duration is as long as would be necessary, as stated by the Director of Naval Intelligence, two-fifths of the battery of the *Emeraude* might be removed and an equivalent weight of water-ballast carried to increase her reserve of buoyancy in the surface condition. This might very possibly add 5 per cent to 10 per cent to the reserve of buoyancy and give some colour to the opinion of the Captain of the *Emeraude* quoted by the Inspecting Captain of Submarines; though whether the *Emeraude* with 10 per cent to 15 per cent reserve of buoyancy would be as seaworthy as the *Pluviôse* would still be a matter of doubt without actual trial; there seems to have been no doubt as to her actual inferiority with only 7 per cent.

As pointed out by the Director of Naval Intelligence, the French practice is a valuable guide, being based on conditions resembling our own and on a long experience of a great variety of types of hull and machinery, with their corresponding differences in reserve of buoyancy. Until D1 was built with a reserve of buoyancy of about 25 per cent, corresponding fairly well with the latest French practice, our experience was limited to a single type of boat, having approximately a reserve of buoyancy of 10 per cent.

It may be observed that a submersible boat with a high reserve of buoyancy can reduce herself to any condition with a smaller reserve at will, to obtain, if desired, the sea-going qualities of a boat with low reserve, and on this ground it would be better to give a high than a low reserve, provided other desirable qualities are not sacrificed to attain that end.

Further Remarks of the Inspecting Captain of Submarines
2 February 1910

I would refer again to the last paragraph of my remarks with reference to the criticisms of the Director of Naval Intelligence. It is a comparatively easy matter to find arguments to support any type – he supports a general sacrifice to large reserve of buoyancy and surface speed. I would point out that there are very great dangers in exaggerating the surface qualities at the expense of those submerged. In the particular case in question –

The *Hvalen*'s full speed is 15 knots
The C class full speed is 12½ knots
    although –
The former's capacity at full speed is 420 miles

The latter's capacity at full speed is 937.5 miles

In order to obtain the exaggerated maximum surface speed, the *Hvalen* has only 100 small cells; with motors of a maximum of 200 H.P., and a hull requiring 30 per cent more power to drive it at 5 knots, than our C class, with 160 cells of a much larger size and 30 per cent lower power required to drive them, only get 12 hours at 5 knots. The question is does *Hvalen* get it? On a cold day? If the makers are allowed to charge the battery, and considerably raise its temperature thereby, just before the trials, they might put the capacity up 30 per cent and so get the result, but the vessel could not get it on service; the amount of endurance which the Director of Naval Intelligence advocates is, in my opinion, dangerously small, and no officer of experience in submarine attacks would be found to support it. A dive of 8 miles is very common in attacking a vessel under way in fine weather: if this is done at any speed, even if the battery is right up at the start, a submarine of *Hvalen*'s battery power will arrive very nearly exhausted; if another opportunity presents itself, or if she is harassed by any enemy, she will be captured. This is serious in itself, but what is far worse is the way the captain is tied and his action cramped; it must *all the time* be at the back of his head that his battery is running low and soon he will have to come to the surface. It is equivalent to sending a surface vessel into action short of coal, and I submit the principle of adding to surface speed at the expense of submerged qualities is unsound.

The Director of Naval Construction's remarks (*see end of sixth paragraph on page 5, and fourth paragraph on page 6*) explain more clearly why additional reserve of buoyancy is not comparable in submarines and destroyers; in the former only tank space is added. The cubic capacity of *Hvalen*, as the Director of Naval Construction shows, is about 6,500 cubic feet, that of our C class 10,000. I am told you cannot stand up in the former, and, in view of their length, this is probably correct.

Referring again to the remarks of the Director of Naval Intelligence:–

Par. 1. France is the only country I know of which has ever built submarines proper.

Par. 2. My statement was qualified, and expressly referred to vessels of 300–400 tons in the normal conditions in North Sea and Channel, and then only to submarines.

Par. 3. I do not think the run of a single vessel, such as *Papin*, for 1,200 miles can be taken as a record which has not been approached by any British submarine. Whole flotillas have run often 500, 600, and over 700 miles in station, and have worked at sea for over a week without the crews leaving them; besides it is impossible to know the conditions under which the vessel was run. She may have been making only a peace passage with her crew augmented (it is entirely a matter of personnel).

Par. 4. Already remarked upon.

Par. 5. I am under the impression that the French submersibles of *Pluviôse* class are much larger than *Hvalen*, and that their reserve of buoyancy is much less in percentage of displacement. I have never suggested that the *French* submersibles had unduly sacrificed submerged qualities for an increase of buoyancy. I still consider this has been done in *Hvalen*.

Par. 6. I do not understand what further criticism can be made of the *Hvalen*. The whole of my report, except pages 2, 3 and half of 4*, refers to her.

● i.e. from the fifth to the eleventh paragraph (inclusive) of Captain Hall's Remarks as printed *(see pages 2 and 3)*.

[76] *Captain Sydney Hall to Captain Roger Keyes*[1]
[Keyes Mss, 4/1]

[HMS] *Diana*
[undated *c.*11 Feb 1911]

Please see and keep Briggs' letter and my reply which I thought I should let you have – the *history* is as follows!:– McKenna stopped with Fisher for the latter's birthday [25th January] and told F[isher] that Briggs was to see me before I left. There is no sense in it and I told F[isher] that the business was in most excellent hands! Etc. But he would have it and so Briggs' letter is the result.

I hope you are well – we hope to sail on Friday

[Enclosure]

HMS *Diana* at Devonport
7 Feb 1911

Dear Admiral Briggs,[2]

I am sorry time does not permit of my coming to London before we sail on Friday. I told Captain Keyes my ideas about the new submarines.

I do not think the 800 ton design is large enough to give sufficient

[1] Capt. Roger Keyes: Inspecting Captain of Submarines, September 1910 to February 1915.
[2] Rear (later Vice-) Adm. Charles Briggs: Capt. HMS *Vernon* 1904–1906; Controller 1910–12; 4th Battle squadron 1912–14.

comfort for the vessel to fully realise the sea keeping qualities she otherwise possesses;[1] but the 1000 ton design should do so.[2] This vessel depends upon the engine but if she can be ordered, I think she would be better value. I suggest she should not have a bow tube, the space gained being given up to better accommodation for the crew. If there is not sufficient progress with the engines to warrant ordering the 1000 ton design, I suggest the 800 ton design should not have a stem *and* stern tube either, one or the other being given up to more accommodation for officers and men.

I do not know if it has been decided not to progress with one of the larger vessels; if not too late, I would like to see the policy of ordering one of the programme as an experimental ship reverted to, as in the case of B1 and D1. It seems to me a 1000 ton submarine with two good guns would form a most interesting comparison with a destroyer. Our knowledge of the handling of the water ballast and general management of the boat is sufficient to warrant such an advance, but all depends on the engine. I suppose ordering an engine from a continental firm is not to be thought of. At any rate, the quickest way of progressing seems to be to order the engine and then Vickers must advance. It seems that the French have a 1000 ton vessel afloat. I would like to see the vessel built at Chatham and the engine ordered from one of the good Diesel 2-cycle firms.

Now that the D class are coming along to replace a flotilla of C class as a sea-going flotilla, it does not seem necessary to order any smaller submarine yet. However, as the B class get older, I presume they will be replaced by a new class of about 3/400 tons, which is, I consider, the limit for the stem discharge. I suggest a design might be prepared for a twin screw type of 300–350 tons with a small turning circle underwater; ... it seems inevitable that we are at the parting of the ways in the design of submarines intended for defensive and offensive work.

I hope to sail with the submarines on Friday,

Yours sincerely,

(Signed) SS Hall

[1] Classified as D type Mod X – ordered under 1910 programme and laid down as E class.

[2] Classified as D type Mod Y – design amended in 1916, ordered and laid down as L class.

[77] *Memorandum by Constructor H. G. Williams to Controller*
[Ships' Covers 291]

1 September 1911
CN 02218/11

Programme 1911/12.

Submitted, the position as regards new designs is as follows:–

Three designs of a boat 230 feet long but of widely differing type have been prepared in detail. The first of these is an enlarged and modified E class which was originally submitted last year, but ordered to be brought up for reconsideration this year. Both the last year's and this year's modified version of it (the modifications being in the nature of a reduction of engines and battery power and increase in the reserve of buoyancy) are ready for consideration.

If either of these enlarged E class designs were approved to be laid down this year at Chatham, the question of getting the full information to the yard would be one of tracing drawing and typing specifications which would take about six weeks from the date of approval.

The other two designs have also been substantially completed, but recent reports of model experiments have been raised as to important improvements in their forms for surface propulsion which may require further model experiments for solution and the preparation of the drawings. This will probably take three months after the date of approval to build either of these boats at Chatham should it be so decided.

The approval of either of these three designs (or four designs including the two versions of the enlarged E class) involves an entirely new design of engine. The designs were originally made to suit an outline drawing of a Carrels engine of 2,400 HP (or 4,800 BHP on two shafts) attached to CN 0958/10 by Controller last year and understood to be under construction for a French submarine; but it is now understood that this engine is still in the experimental stage and that only 3,000 BHP can be got into the space and for the weight provided in our designs. The question of the provision of the engines for either of these three designs, appears therefore to require consideration before any one of them could be approved.

[78] *Note from Constructor Harris G. Williams to Keyes*
[Keyes Mss 4/4]

22 November 1911

Enclosed are some remarks on the drawings which you sent me of the big double bottomed boat, and of the small 33 ton boat. There is an article on the former in *Engineering* of the 17th inst. Which I have just seen.

In comparing the big designs with our own proposed big boats, the facts to be noted are that both the Electric Boat Co. and ourselves have to go to 230 feet length to get high surface speed. We, in addition, are forced to a much bigger midship section in order to get in the torpedo tubes. Consequently we shall be much bigger with heavier displacement; we are in fact heavier about in proportion to the square of the beam which is what is to be expected. With this bigger displacement we require more powerful machinery for propulsion and greater oil stowage, and as our propelling machinery is far heavier per unit [of] power than theirs, we have a less proportion of the submerged displacement available for water ballast and therefore a greater surface displacement in proportion to the submerged. This again, working round in a vicious circle, means still more power to get surface speed, and there is really no hope of competing with these foreign boats until we get the engines, batteries, and motors down to something like the figures which they use. That we shall gain some experience justifying advance along this line is the greatest argument in favour of buying a FIAT boat.

[79] *Hall to Keyes*

[Keyes Mss 4/22]

HMS *Diana*
Mediterranean
7 October 1911

It was good of you to write me at such length: but it was all of course most interesting. It is good news that you have succeeded in breaking the Vickers monopoly agreement or at any rate this is in sight and in so far as the Spezia visit helped I am in agreement, but you won't mind very much me saying, no in any other respect!

The question of buying or trying out the other designs has often been considered of course and I see no reason to change the line I still think the soundest. It is common training, interchangeability, stores etc etc. I always advised the Admiralty that simplicity and a homogenous lot was in my opinion worth more than any possible gain in material. – Of course the C design never attained its best results, but that was merely a question of money policy: [the] Admiralty said they preferred to have 12 single screw rather than 8 or 9 twin screw.[1] – I think you have now

---

[1] In 1908, Capt. Hall proposed the construction of a modified type C design fitted with diesel engines and two shafts, but it was rejected by the Admiralty as too expensive.

advertised to Europe that we are not satisfied with our own designs and have lowered the whole of our prestige in submarine work for we had taken a strong line and kept it.

I cannot understand [Commander Percy] Addison's change of front on the whole question![1] And I think some of his calculations are open to great question. He starts saying the boats are much safer and then cheerfully advocates abandoning the sluice valves and advises a quick closing rear door; also water under petrol etc. after saying that the engine was not very satisfactory; that the boat had had a battery explosion which caused no damage to any gear in the boat other than the container, although the commander stated three weeks was the least time she could be got ready in as a result of this explosion; on p.2. also he says it is impossible without actually diving in the boat to give an opinion of her diving capabilities yet at the end of [the] report cheerfully recommends buying one!

*   *   *

I am not clear if the FIAT design is any guide to you in the development of beam tubes in submarines? Surely not? We were, or so it seemed to me, most fortunately placed in that respect, and can they lead us in heavy oil engines even with all our delays regrettable as they have been? Of course the trial will be interesting but this seems so late to do it, certainly the only FIAT submarine I [have] ever seen was more or less a week coasting to England – surely it was [Engineer-Commander Hugh] Garwood who told me they were cut down to the last limit – she was in no condition to fight.

*   *   *

I hope you won't mind my frank opinions but I do feel we have abandoned our strong line for such a doubtful advantage: if it was really necessary to stump Vickers, of course, it's alright but I would have preferred to have seen a 350 ton twin screw C with a few improvements.

---

[1] Cmdr Percy Addison served as Roger Keyes' chief of staff from 1910–13.

[80] *Keyes to Hall*

[Keyes Mss 4/22]

HMS *Dolphin*
Gosport
19th October [1911][1]

I have been meaning to write to you for some time, to answer your criticism of our policy! As you know, one has not much time or inclination to write when one finishes one's daily job. You have given me your opinion pretty freely! Now I'll give you mine on your criticism! I think it is narrow-minded and rottenly unfair in that you quote extracts from Addison's report, to ridicule what we are doing, without taking any notice of statements which, if quoted, would qualify or alter the whole sense.

You seem to look upon what we're doing now as a reflection on your past policy, and to base your opinion of the present Fiat boats on one of their first, without giving them credit for any improvement or advance. The Swedish one certainly does not seem to have been an unqualified success; it would have been interesting to compare the running of that vessel with that of D1 – I am not sure it would be to D1's advantage.

I do think that if you and [Harris] Williams had had the opportunity of seeing and testing a Laubouf [*sic*] or Fiat before you were committed to the Holland type, you would have worked on different lines, and by now have evolved something better than the present D's & E's, I believe Williams is thoroughly ashamed of that ridiculous saddle tank. He accepted the principle worked on by Laubouf [*sic*] and Laurenti, but applied it in a grotesque way. He certainly had no intention of repeating it in the larger boats – but I'll refer to that later. At any rate, both he and Sir Philip Watts are most keen to have a Fiat or Laubouf [*sic*] boat, and admit that we have a lot to learn from them.

Your argument as to interchangeability of stores, etc., is really rather far-fetched when one compares our A, B and C with our D and E classes. What stores can be interchangeable? In what way are they homogeneous? You mention common training with a personnel like ours! What does it matter? Any trained crew from a C boat could have taken out a Fiat boat after an hour or two, and dived her just as well as an Italian crew. That is the opinion of Addison and Garwood, and I accept it. 'Simplicity' is another word you use – All three Officers came back very full of the ingenious way in which everything had been worked out and simplified to a fool-proof extent.

[1] Catalogued by the British Museum as dated 1912, but internal content indicates it more likely dated 1911.

You have a smack at Addison about the battery explosion – without, by the way, noticing the rest of his remarks. We have had similar but much more disastrous accidents. This one was due to an act of gross carelessness, and it speaks well for the design, that the damage was so localised. The three weeks delay was due to having to send to Germany for containers. You attack his cheerfully recommending the purchase without being able to give an opinion as to her diving capabilities – again without mentioning the rest of his remarks. You know there was no intention of ordering a boat until she had been thoroughly inspected diving, from inside and from the surface.

The same applies to the Engine; you scoff at the idea of recommending the purchase after saying the engine was not very satisfactory. You know that referred to the M.A.N. which we never contemplated buying; it was never considered satisfactory by the Fiat people, but was ordered by the Italian Government. You know that there was no question of ordering a boat until the Fiat engine, of which Garwood formed a very high opinion, had been actually seen running satisfactorily in the *Meduce*. Do you call that fair criticism?!

You know the delays in getting papers through the Admiralty; if we were to get a boat within a reasonable time of our deciding, it was necessary to get the preliminaries through as soon as possible. The whole thing was within the Admiralty, and the idea could have been dropped if further trial proved unsatisfactory.

Garwood came back a few days ago after seeing the Fiat engine running in the *Meduce*, and an 850 H.P. engine run a bench trial at Turin – the latter one of these for the latest German submarine. He thinks it is the best design of engine on the market. Addison came back some little time ago; I enclose a copy of his report which may interest you.

What is the good of making [breaking?] the Vickers contract, if we have no other firm in a position to build? What English firm would be in a position to compete for several years, unless they acquired the right to build a ready-made, well-tried foreign boat. I believe Yarrow has been sounding Laubouf; I hope he succeeds in getting him.

You say you don't see how this purchase is going to help in the design of the beam tube submarine – That we could not fit them in without the saddle tank design. You have struck the real reason for my keenness to get a Fiat. Prior to the visit, and before there was a question of it, the D.N.C., Williams, E-in-C, Garwood and I met in the Controller's room to discuss the designs of a new large boat. Williams produced three, each carrying 1 or 2 bow tubes, 1 stern tube and 4 beam tubes. One was an enlarged saddle-tanked E – a monstrous craft! One a Fiat, the other a Laubouf. The latter was cribbed from some drawings which got into

Sir Philip Watts' hands in an illicit way! The Fiat from their advertisements. The saddle-tanked atrocity was wiped out at once – the other two were much preferred, but the constructors rather funked them on the score of the difficulty to build. They said it was very doubtful whether they could build them satisfactorily in England without any experience, owing to the very confined spaces between the inner and outer plating. They could not understand how they built the smaller craft abroad – it would be difficult enough to build a craft of the size produced, i.e. over 1000 tons. Chiefly on the score that it was considered undesirable to continue the saddle-tank design in the larger craft, it was decided to abandon the idea of an enlarged E for the present.

This was naturally a disappointment. Then Boselli's offer occurred to me, and I wrote to ask him if he would allow expert Officers to inspect his latest boats, in view of the fact that there was not a 1000 to 1 chance of his getting an order. I said I did not want to send anyone there under false pretences, and I could not ask the Admiralty to send Officers unless he quite understood this. He replied that they were so satisfied with their boat that they would run the risk, as they had great hopes we would be so pleased that we would be tempted to buy.

In asking to send Williams, Garwood and Addison, I made this clear to the Admiralty and the three Officers, that they were going to pick up what information they could, without any sort of obligation to buy. They all three came back deeply impressed and unanimous in their recommendation to buy. I am not trying to shift the responsibility for our policy on to anyone else; it would not have got through if I had not been very pertinacious, for you can imagine the obstruction!

The policy is: To get one boat as they guarantee it, with all its qualities – good or otherwise, for the sake of experiment and comparison (one would think that you don't welcome the comparison). The recommendation to buy was based on the fact that Scott acted for the Fiat Co., and was prepared to guarantee certain performances of the boat, and to submit the boat and contents to tests much more severe than we impose on Vickers. If these guarantees are not fulfilled, we do not accept the boat – the absence of the sluice-door, which you criticise, was therefore accepted as a fact. There is a collision bulkhead, and the bow caps are under and abaft the stem, so the ramming of the stone wall, which you mention, would not have affected them in all probability.

I don't know where you got your figures from on which the D.N.C. based his opinion that the propulsion co-efficient of these boats was from 20% to 50% higher than ours under water; there is no truth in the statement as far as the boat we are considering is concerned. As regards the under water speed, the Fiat people offer to guarantee 8.5 knots – over double the speed of our boats submerged.

You say the question of bulkheads and safety is new; as we have had no accident that a bulkhead could possibly have helped, that you can see no case for them. I have used the arguments you gave me, to defend our past policy in this respect – I can't say I've ever believed them. I put my scepticism down to my ignorance, of which I am very conscious, but I believe I am right all the same; that our D's should be bulkhead-less, with the whole boat open to the battery, always strikes me as being criminal. The hatch at the base of the conning-tower – your one effort towards sub-division – would have saved A.1, and did save A.9. Has it ever struck you that if A.8 had been sub-divided as the E's are, the rush of water through the conning-tower would probably not have been sufficient to sink the boat. Williams tells me in the case of an E, she would remain afloat. It would at least have given the people in the other compartments a fighting chance! What do you gain in an open boat against this? Why abandon whatever you would have gained in the E, if it is of such value? C.11 might have been saved since she had only a comparatively small hole at one end. At any rate she *would* have remained afloat long enough for a few poor devils to escape. The bulkheads in [?], and the fact that the crew were able to get into a compartment free of the battery, and consequently of Chlorine gases, saved the majority of the crew. I am glad to think the E's have bulkheads; I would certainly have protested strongly, had they been omitted.

One argument you use is that, though the trial will be interesting, it is being made too late! How too late? You sent to inspect the Lake boat; presumably had the report been satisfactory you would have done something further. What are three or four years in the life of Submarine development. The fast Submarine Destroyer, of which Admiral Jellicoe dreams (and which will come), is not evolved yet. It will certainly never develop out of our heavily-built saddle-tank design – to quote Williams. There is really no hope of competing with these foreign boats until we get engine, batteries, and motors down to something like the figures they use. That we shall have some experience justifying an advance along these lines, is the great argument in favour of buying a Fiat boat.

You talk about our prestige being lowered – You say that we are advertising to the whole of Europe that we are not satisfied with our own design! If our prestige were based on our design, which is well known in Europe, it would not be worth much. Why have Whitehead and the Electric Boat Co. abandoned it, and why did not the Italians, Austrians and Germans follow it? I prefer to think that our Submarine prestige is based on our splendid personnel and training, and is so high in Europe on that account, in spite of the poor opinion they hold of our design. In that personnel I would include all those responsible for evolving such fine serviceable craft as our C class, out of such an indifferent beginning. The Austrians and Germans started later with much more experience to draw on, and so avoided our design (I am not pitting my opinion against yours, but merely stating foreign opinion). The Italians and French have grown out of it, and we alone have hammered on, developing a Holland boat on Holland lines; in a way, it is true, which has filled thinking foreigners with admiration for our pig-headed determination, but with no desire to copy us.

Now I think I have been almost as rude as you were!

In the *Engineering* of November 17th., you will see a description of the latest Electric Boat Company's boat designed by our originators. It doesn't *pretend* to be anything but a compromise between the Laubouf and Laurenti designs. I did not know of its existence when we started our new policy. It is curious that the same idea should have taken hold in America. The truth of the matter is that everyone has come to the same conclusion, and I am quite sure that if you were I.C.S. now, had seen Williams' beam tube Fiat and Laubouf designs, and could bring yourself to approach the subject with an open mind, you would thoroughly agree with what we're doing. We can't start a new type without much experiment. We have now the opportunity of acquiring the result of several years' experience, at small cost, so please don't look on this as any reflection on your past policy, for an entirely new situation has arisen. If Addison and Williams had come back from the United States, and told you that we had a lot to learn from Lake, surely you would have done likewise.

My friend, the Austrian I.C.S., did eventually answer my letter. They have tried German, Lake, and a boat which is practically our D. He says it simply beats him that we can continue on the lines of the latter. He naturally did not describe the compromise they have arrived at, but it is practically the craft described in the *Engineering* of 17th November. I enclose a lecture given by your friend Hagnusson – Read pages 34 and 35. It is the most complimentary opinion of our design I have ever had expressed by a foreigner – and I have talked 'Submarines' to several [foreigners].

Thank you for the excellent assistants you recommended, for of course I would never have had the nerve to embark on such an enterprise without their concurrence. Addison has read me a few extracts from your last letters. I see you still harp on prestige! How can prestige rest on a design which everyone else has either given up or avoided? As Hagnusson says, it is our well-trained personnel that gives us the lead. Nothing can ever deprive you of the credit of having developed our splendid submarine service, for the system of training on which its prestige (in my opinion) rests, was initiated by you, as all the Navy knows; I can buck about it, and do, since I found it and it is no credit to me. It is because I feel that we owe so much to you that I am at such pains to explain my motives. If you still condemn, I shall be sorry, but shall still think I am right.

[81] *Extract from Report by Submarine Committee on Future Material*
[ADM 1/8374/93]

His Majesty's Submarine Depot, Gosport,
29 February 1912

It is considered desirable to lay down, with as little delay as possible, a large oversea experimental submarine, which should be completed before any more vessels of the same displacement are laid down.

In order to replace the submarines which have become non-effective, viz, A.2, A.3, A.4, and also the remainder of the A class in the near future, it is considered that a class of submarines corresponding in surface displacement to our present C type, but of larger reserve of buoyancy, should be constructed.

Oversea Type – The following proposals for this submarine are submitted:–

1. This vessel should have large reserve of buoyancy.

2. Surface displacement about 1,000 tons.

3. Double hull (complete or partial).

4. Sub-division of hull into compartments, such as engine-room, torpedo tube spaces, living quarters, and, if possible, battery spaces. In addition to adding to the safety of the vessel the provision of these compartments will greatly improve her habitability.

5. Surface speed should be about 20 knots.

6. Submerged speed should be high for a short distance.

7. Large surface and submerged endurance at economical speeds.

8. The submarine must be capable of submerging in three minutes from surface condition.

9. Good accommodation for officers and men.

10. Armament: two right-ahead tubes, two beam tubes each side, stern tubes.

It is not considered that the best results will be obtained by increasing the displacement of the E class. In view of this it will be necessary to depart widely from this design, and therefore it is submitted that advantage should be taken of considering the designs of private submarine constructors in conjunction with Admiralty proposals.

The following types have been undoubtedly well tried, and their constructors have had much experience:–

Laubeuf

F.I.A.T. (Laurenti type)

Krupp

Electric Boat Company (closely allied, it is understood, to Messrs. Vickers and Messrs Whitehead, of Fiume)

It is noticeable that in the majority of these designs the question of habitability has been seriously considered, and apparently good results obtained; too much stress cannot be laid on its importance from the point of view of the health and endurance of the personnel. It is considered that the lack of habitability in our submarines places a limit on their range of action.

In order to obtain the speed mentioned (20 knots) it would appear that the horse-power of the heavy oil engines would have to be increased considerably above the present maximum – 850 horse-power per shaft in the E class – and there appears to be no reason why this should not be done.

(Here follow technical details regarding engines which are not relevant to the accompanying paper)

Coastal Type – The characteristics of this class should follow closely those of the oversea type:–

1. Larger reserve of buoyancy than the present C class possess, probably necessitating a watertight superstructure.

2. Surface displacement between 250 and 300 tons.

3. Double hull (partial or whole).

4. Sub-division into watertight compartments.

5. Twin-screw heavy oil engines.

6. Speed not under 14 knots; radius of action 1,200 miles.

7. Good accommodation for officers and men.

8. Two periscopes.

9. Lifting bolts built into the vessel to facilitate salvage.

10. Armament: two bow tubes and, if possible, one stern tube.

The remarks on engines for the oversea type also apply generally to the design of engine required for the coastal class.

TORPEDOES

1. Our submarine officers are trained to attack, at short range and at high speed; short-range torpedo is considered the most suitable for our tactics.

2. A special 18-inch heater, the Mark VIII, is being manufactured for the coastals and the broadside tubes of the overseas; speed 41 knots for 1,500 yards. The earlier vessels are provided with 18-inch cold torpedoes.

3. The want of a long-range torpedo for browning in cases when the submarine cannot by reason of her low speed get into close range, has been frequently felt in recent exercises, and long-range heater torpedoes are being supplied for the stem discharges of all D, E, and later oversea vessels.

4. The 21-inch torpedoes of the *Nautilus* and *Swordfish* will be of the latest type.

*   *   *

Alternative Views on the Use of Submarines

[82] *Memorandum by Inspecting Captain of Submarines*[1]
[Keyes Mss 4/13]

[Attached Note]
As there are no orders in existence as to the employment of submarines in time of war, I submitted the attached memorandum dated 3 June 1911 to the Vice Admiral Commanding 3rd and 4th Squadrons, Home Fleet, who transmitted it to the Admiralty. Admiralty letter M01082 of 30 August 1911 stated that my proposals were approved generally.

3 June 1911

1. Towards the end of the present year, when the organisation laid down in Admiralty letter M.01549 of 12th April 1911 is complete, the submarines in home waters will be allocated as follows:–
    12 C class with Headquarters at Dundee (Section VII)[2]
    12 C class with Headquarters at Harwich (Section III)
    15 submarines for the Straits of Dover, consisting of 10 C class (Section IV) and 5 B class (Section I). In peace time the former will have their Headquarters at Portsmouth until the new submarine harbour at Dover is ready to accommodate them. The 5 B class will be stationed at Devonport for recruiting and training purposes.
    8 D class (Section II) with Headquarters at Portsmouth in peace time, and Harwich in time of war.
    12 A class stationed as follows ... for local defence.
2. The duties of the 24 C class of Sections III and VII allocated to the East coast will, at any rate in the early stages of the war, be primarily of a coast defence nature. There will be no question of patrol in the sense of a continual watch at sea, but they will be stationed in one or more groups of three boats with a parent ship or tender at various strategic points on the coast ready at short notice to go anywhere they may be required, for instance, – to attack a raiding expedition or enemy's ships which may be cruising in the neighbourhood, or an oversea expedition etc. These groups will be in telegraphic (visual through a War Signal Station) communication or signal communication with, and will receive their orders direct from, the Admiralty.

---

[1] Signed Capt. Roger Keyes.
[2] Until 1912, submarines were grouped into sections rather than flotillas. This was perhaps more preferable than organising them into Shoals as Winston Churchill originally wished.

3. In order to get full value out of the submarines it is absolutely essential that they should dive before they are sighted by an enemy. In clear fine weather, provided a good look-out is kept, they should always be able to do so, and under such conditions it is preferable that submarines should not be accompanied by surface craft while lying waiting for an enemy or proceeding to attack some definite object, as they would be ready to dive at short notice and can attack unsuspected. In hazy weather, such as often prevails in the North Sea, however, they are certain to be seen and avoided by an enemy before they can get in a position to attack, and they also run great risks of coming under gun-fire of fast vessels before they can dive. Under such weather conditions, or, when making a long passage when there is a possibility of falling in with an enemy, they should be accompanied by fast surface craft to scout for them. Their parent ships and tenders, in addition to being very slow and having no military value, are invaluable to the submarines in that they carry their spare parts and torpedoes, besides charging and repair plant, consequently they should not be risked at sea and will not be available for scouting purposes. For this duty whenever possible, one or more destroyers from the destroyer flotilla operating in the same area will be attached to each group of submarines.

4. The 15 submarines stationed in wartime at Dover, will cooperate with the 4th Destroyer Flotilla employed in the examination service in the Straits, by lying a few miles (according to the degree of visibility) behind the latter's patrol line during daylight.

5. The 8 D class of Section II, with headquarters at Harwich in time of war, will be ready to go at short notice wherever they may be required. They are able to proceed under their own power on the surface about 2500 miles at ten knots; as they only consume fuel when actually underway, or charging batteries, they would be able to remain self-supporting on an enemy's coast for some days. It is considered that they would be most valuable a few miles behind an inshore blockading squadron ready to dive and attack any large vessels which might come out to drive it off.[1]

The B and C classes of submarines of Sections I, III, IV, and VII, are also of course quite capable of operating on an enemy's coast, and can, according to their age, maintain 10 to 12 knots for 1000 to 1200 miles.

The D class can comfortably maintain a speed of 13 or 14 knots, and might well be employed in company with the Battle Fleet, particularly

[1] Keyes was assuming here that the Royal Navy's operational strategy for a war against Germany called for the imposition of a close blockade of the German North Sea coast. For secrecy reasons, the Admiralty chose not to disabuse him (or any other officers) of this notion.

one expecting to fall in with a superior force. The E class, which will be added to the sea-going flotilla before the end of the next year, should prove very valuable in this connection for it is hoped they will attain a speed of 15 knots, and have a radius of action of 3500 miles at 10 knots. Their beam tubes also, will make them much more formidable than their predecessors from an offensive point of view, as well as greatly facilitating the operation of attacking.

* * *

Routine Training

7. The routine training of all submarines is directed towards making the crews proficient in manning their vessels, firing their torpedoes at or under moving targets, and maintaining their vessels and torpedoes in a state of repair and efficiency without outside help – (except during annual refit) – other than that available in their parent ship. The sections are organised as far as numbers permit in groups of three submarines, each group acting as a unit for docking and refitting and working, whenever possible, under the senior officer of the group whose aim is to dive and spread his group unseen in the track of the target ship.

It is submitted that this routine training, initiated and organised by my predecessor, should fit the personnel of the submarines for any operation they may be called upon to perform in time of war.

* * *

Special Training

8. The 24 submarines on the east coast are permanently stationed in the areas in which they will operate in time of war, and as they cruise continuously during summer and winter they have every opportunity of becoming intimately acquainted with local conditions. The various groups will be sent from time to time to their actual war stations ...

* * *

Attack on Battleships and Armoured Cruisers

11. The regulations which have been framed to minimise the risk of accident when submarines are engaged in attacking vessels other than their parent ship and tenders must necessarily make these operations somewhat unreal, both from the point of view of the submarines and of the ship attacked. The captain of the submarine is obliged to show his periscope to an extent which, were he attacking his parent ship, would

entail a severe rebuke for his want of skill. On the other hand, the ship is obliged to maintain a steady course and speed when she sites a periscope, whereas the parent ship is free to manoeuvre to avoid being torpedoed if the attack is so unskilful as to enable her to do so.

It is found that the faculty for judging the distance and speed of a ship through a periscope can only be acquired by constant practice, and that after an officer had been attacking torpedo craft or small tenders, he is very liable to seriously misjudge both, when attacking a larger ship. Consequently, in spite of the restrictions mentioned above, it is considered that exercises in attacking battleships and armoured cruisers are invaluable to submarine officers and it is submitted that they are also not without value to the personnel of the fleet.

[83] *Extract from Minutes taken at the 117th Meeting of the Committee of Imperial Defence*[1]

[CAB 38/21/26]

4 July 1912

THE PRIME MINISTER enquired what standard Lord Fisher would suggest for the Mediterranean supposing that whatever margin he considered necessary in the North Sea was conceded.

LORD FISHER said that a force equal to the proposed 4th Battle Squadron based on Gibraltar was sufficient. He had absolute confidence in the power of the submarine, and did not believe that any heavy ship was safe from them in narrow waters. Therefore if we had adequate flotillas of submarines and destroyers at Malta, Gibraltar, and Alexandria no battleship could move in the Mediterranean. He did not believe any trade could pass through the Mediterranean in time of war in any case, and, judging by the concluding paragraph of the Board of Trade Memorandum (C.I.D. Paper 150-B), it would make comparatively little difference if it was stopped or diverted as the case might be.

MR McKENNA said that if this estimate of the power of the submarine was correct the North Sea was equally unsuitable for battleships.

LORD FISHER said that our battle fleet would not be in the North Sea. It would be off the North Coast of Scotland or outside the Straits of Dover. If the German Fleet came out it would be attacked by

[1] Special meeting of senior political, diplomatic and military officials called by Prime Minister Asquith to discuss the Admiralty's proposal in March 1912 to withdraw the battle fleet from the Mediterranean.

submarines and destroyers, if it came out far enough it would then have to fight our battle fleet.

MR McKENNA said that that seemed to dispose of the conception of any sudden danger. Our fleet was off the North Coast of Scotland. Invasion was impossible owing to the danger from submarines. The narrow Straits of Dover could be held by submarines. In these circumstances a sudden onslaught by the whole German Fleet upon our unmobilised fleet seemed a remote contingency.

MR CHURCHILL said that the Board of Admiralty did not entirely accept Lord Fisher's views on submarines. They did not think that they could deny the open waters of the Mediterranean to battleships. But they did agree that the Mediterranean might become very precarious as a trade route.[1]

[84] *Views on Use of Submarines expressed by Commander-in-Chief, Home Fleets (Admiral Sir George Callaghan) after 1912 Summer Manoeuvres*

[ADM 1/8269]

Neptune, at Portland,
5th August 1912

*   *   *

1. The question of the sufficiency of the complement of Dreadnought battleships and battle cruisers to meet the strain of war was brought into prominent notice. The effectiveness of the modern submarine has a close bearing on the subject, and it will in future be necessary to keep the anti-torpedo boat armament manned by day and night. It will, for this reason, be impossible to spare deck hands to assist the engine room department in local trimming, as was done in many ships of the First Battle Squadron, although the amount of coal burnt was not great nor the steaming such as to call for special effort. Had the manoeuvres lasted two or three days longer and the ships not returned to coal, the number of men required from the deck would have been largely increased.

2. The complement of deck hands now allowed is nominally sufficient to man the main armament and half the anti-torpedo boat

---

[1] Privately, Churchill sympathised with Fisher but at this time his senior advisers Admirals Louis Battenberg (2nd Sea Lord) and Ernest Troubridge (chief of naval war staff) thought his strategy of flotilla defence fundamentally unsound.

armament by day, but in practice it is found that this cannot be done; at night not more than half the guns can be manned if officers and men are to be given adequate rest. In the summer months the strain on officers and men is least; in winter it would be infinitely greater owing to the long hours of darkness and more severe weather.

3. The liability to attack by destroyers and submarines may well necessitate all anti-torpedo boat guns being manned during, or at the commencement of, a fleet action, especially in misty weather, and in this case some of the crews must be taken from the main armament.[1]

4. A comparison between the complements allowed to our ships and those of foreign nations cannot be made without reference to information which is not available to me on board *Neptune*, but it is believed that, to take instances, both the Germans and Japanese base their complements on a much more liberal scale.

5. It is the opinion of a number of officers that these ships are undermanned, both as to deck and engine room ratings, and it is considered that the question of their complement should be reviewed; to this end, I am calling for reports from the ships affected and will submit them in due course.

*   *   *

8. The work of the five D class submarines attached to the Red Fleet is of particular interest as showing the increasing capabilities of these craft. In some respects they are already superior to destroyers, viz, radius of action, immunity from detection and damage from gunfire, and number of torpedoes carried. With a speed of $12^{1}/_{2}$ knots on the surface, which they can apparently rely on unless they have engine trouble, they are a great danger to ships in advanced dispositions, and might even be used in fleet actions. It is noticeable, however, that a good many engine troubles occurred, and probably improvement will result from this experience.

9. Captain [Frank] Brandt's report (attached) [not reproduced] calls attention to the desirability of increasing the usefulness of the sea-going submarine by:–

a. Providing each with a W/T set and an operator. (This is also remarked on under the heading of W/T).

---

[1] In 1913, the Admiralty authorised increasing the complements of all capital ships to provide full crews for all the anti-torpedo-boat guns rather than just half of them as hitherto. On average, this raised the number of personnel manning dreadnought battleships by between 100 and 200 seamen.

b. Adding *another officer for watch-keeping* and a stoker to their complement.

c. Providing one long range torpedo per every three carried.

These proposals are recommended for consideration.

* * *

[85] *Admiral Lord Fisher to Balfour*
[Add Mss 49712]

15 May 1913

I hope you will be able to adopt the enclosed memorandum as in your own words – there is no expert wisdom involved! *Pure common sense!*

[attached]

No means exist of preventing an enemy's submarine from coming out of their harbours and cruising more or less at will, short of mining and blocking operations on a very large scale.

Where two countries with about the same length of seaboard and an equal number of submarines face each other across a comparatively narrow sea, the waters between them will be equally dangerous to both.

In the case of war between England and France, or Austria and Italy, for example, the English Channel and the Adriatic will be swept pretty thoroughly by submarines. The case of Germany however is somewhat different in that the area desired to be infested by us, is so small compared to that desired to be similarly treated by the enemy if he wishes to play the same game. So far as our North Sea ports are concerned and not going further north than Dundee the proportion is somewhere about 5:1.

Assuming the two countries to possess an equal number of large submarines, the central open waters of the North Sea may be taken to be equally infested and dangerous to both combatants.

On approaching the German exits however the area is diminishing rapidly and the danger to German surface craft increasing proportionately, whilst on approaching English ports the reverse is the case.

The difficulty of a close investment of English North Sea ports, compared with that of investing the German exits, must be more than five times as great in our favour.

It is presumed that, if the danger of using the North Sea Ports is admitted, our ships will not be sent there, so that the difference between the Germans and ourselves is this – (considering the North Sea only for the moment) – the waters may be infested by and be equally dangerous to both sides, Germany requires many more submarines to make the conditions equal on account of her short seaboard, but whereas we do not propose to use these waters, the German must and will.

The probability is that the above and lack of numbers will cause the Germans to put their submarines to other uses; as their large submarines are being supplied with guns an attempt will probably be made to fight and destroy our submarines even at a corresponding loss of their own, providing thereby they can weaken or break the submarine blockade of German ports.

As our objective must be to keep the blockade, it will be the business of our submarines to avoid fighting the enemy's as much as possible and to exercise the submarine's sole prerogative of being able to decline a fight.

Unless the Germans take their larger submarines with their Battle Fleet to assist in Fleet Action as they are suspected of intending to do with their destroyers, the only other forecast that can be made of the manner in which they intend to use the submarines is that they will endeavour to menace our southern or western coasts and possibly commerce. When submarines have to pass through a narrow Strait such as Dover and return by it every time they are relieved, it is considered to be extremely doubtful whether any systematic or constant occupation of the English Channel can be maintained from such a distance as Germany.

*   *   *

Still it must be conceded that there is a great possibility of German submarines reaching the English Channel. If the Dover Straits blockade is made very strong and covering a large area the chance will be much lessened, but even with such precautions submarines will have a fair chance of getting through especially at night and there is also the possibility of their coming up via the North of Scotland trusting to return by Dover: though it is doubtful if the endurance of the personnel in the Atlantic in the winter months will be up to this, the risk will certainly have to be reckoned with as the submarine's arm becomes longer.

To sum up:–

The question being – what is to prevent German submarines from infesting the approaches to English parts – the answer must be:–

In the North Sea – Nothing is known that can prevent them from doing so but a large number will be required.

In the English Channel and on the West Coast – The distance from Germany with the Dover Straits cordon to pass renders this difficult but possible and the risk will have to be reckoned with.

On the general question. As submarines grow and become able to keep the sea for longer periods it will be impossible to say where they may *not* be met. They have the power to fight or evade a fight at will, so they can pick and choose their prey and can remain a constant and harassing menace to all surface craft, which at present it appears impossible to remove. Men of War will have to take the risk which decreases as the distance from the enemy's base increases and which will be greatest in the enclosed waters such as the North Sea, Mediterranean, etc.

IT WILL BECOME INCREASINGLY DIFFICULT FOR ANY OR EITHER POWER TO OBTAIN COMMAND OF SUCH SEAS AS THESE, IN THE ACCEPTED SENSE OF THE TERM; IT WILL RENDER THE DISPATCH OF EXPEDITIONARY FORCES ACROSS THEM A MORE AND MORE HAZARDOUS BUSINESS THAN EVER IT HAS BEEN BEFORE, AND THIS APPLIES EQUALLY TO THE INVASION OF ENGLAND OR TO THE DESPATCH OF OUR EXPEDITIONARY FORCE.

Considering the safety of England it would therefore appear that the development of the submarine (provided we keep an equal or larger number than prospective enemies) will result in increased safety.

[86] *Memorandum by Fisher entitled* (Submarines and Commerce)[1]
[Add Mss 49712]

28th May 1913

*   *   *

2. As to our own position (excluding the submarine for a moment), it is reasonably secure. By means of an elaborate intelligence organisation (rigidly maintained even in time of peace) the distribution of all foreign warships and armed merchant vessels likely to be used against us is accurately known. In strained relations such vessels are, and certainly will be shadowed. Also Wireless Telegraphy has added enormously to the possibilities of concentration movements of our cruisers against such ships.

[1] Dated 28 May from copy sent to Lord Esher, for which see: Esher Mss 16/13.

But most certainly the protection of commerce difficulty becomes far more acute when the potentialities of submarines as commerce destroyers are considered. It is rightly considered that the effect on freight and insurance rates must be very great when it is realised that the enemy's submarines may be met off our own great commercial ports.

It cannot now be long before this fact will become generally known to the public and it is desirable to consider fully the question of diverting our commerce to our far western ports in war time, and of developing the port and rail facilities of such harbours as Plymouth, Falmouth, Bristol Channel Ports, Fishguard, Holyhead etc.

* * *

It will be impossible for submarines to deal with merchant vessels in accordance with international law. It is presumed that they will disregard this and sink any vessel heading for an English commercial port. Our powers of retaliation will be very great in view of the large number of German merchant ships and their crews that will fall into our hands on the outbreak of war. Probably over 900 German merchant vessels will be captured if we are prompt as we should be. (That depends on the First Sea Lord.) However what else can the submarine do except sink her capture?

* * *

It must be admitted that this submarine menace is rather a desperate business for our commerce, for no means can be suggested at present if meeting it except by reprisals. All that would be known would that a certain steam ship did not arrive or that some of her boats would be picked up with a few survivors to tell the tale.

It would be an altogether barbarous method of warfare, but if it is done by Germans the only thing would be to make reprisals. Many of these reprisals suggest themselves which might cause the sinking of our merchantmen to be stopped.

One is inclined to think that in this light the arming of our English merchantmen is unfortunate for it gives the German submarine an excellent excuse (if she wishes one) for sinking her, namely, that of self defence against the gun of the merchant tramp steamer.

It would seem most desirable that the conduct of submarines in molesting commerce should be thoroughly thought out. It would be a most interesting subject for neutrals! One flag is very much like another seen through a periscope against the light! And one fears that the only thing the German submarine would be sure of would be that the vessel flying it was not German.

On quite another and even more serious grounds also it would seem necessary to make up our minds about submarines. For example, can we keep the command of the Mediterranean in their presence and should not our fleet there at once be replaced by 100 submarines at a very great saving in cost?

For the cost of one battleship you can have twenty of the biggest type of submarines!

Finally is the extreme hypothesis of stale-mate on all seas likely to be realised? If we concede this state of affairs in the North Sea now, how long will it be before the rest of the seas must be added? It is considered that this is in sight, and that the Mediterranean can be already added.

* * *

It behoves us to consider most carefully all these points in detail and to provide immediately for many more submarines in the North Sea, Mediterranean and all our foreign and colonial naval bases.

— *Remember there is no vessel in existence that can keep the sea for such a long period as the latest type of submarine*!

[87] *Extract from Report on the 1913 Manoeuvres by Admiral of the Fleet Sir William May*
[ADM 116/3381]

18 August 1913

LESSONS TO BE LEARNT

My report will hardly be complete without my views on the main lessons to be learnt, which are as follows:–

The absolute necessity of having a Port with large supplies of fuel and stores protected by land and breakwaters in the vicinity of Flamborough Head, or the Humber, where a large Fleet can lie in safety against the attack of submarines and torpedo craft. This appears to me to be an imperative necessity in the event of a war with Germany. Such a position would be on interior lines to the German Fleet in case the Germans wished to operate either in the Channel or the North Sea. Our bases at the Firth of Forth and Cromarty are too far North, and, even if this was not the case, a Fleet anchored there would not be immune from attacks of submarines. It is not for me to say whether Bridlington Bay or the Humber would be the best as I have not had the opportunity of going into the details, but on the face of it I should prefer Bridlington Bay. The expense would be great but it would be nothing in comparison with the loss of 2 or 3 Battleships in war time through the enterprising attacks of submarines.

(2) The experience gained from the raids on the Humber, Sunderland and Blyth is that provided the attack is a surprise they may be partially successful especially in misty weather. The coastal patrol, although a good protection, with proper look-out vessels and experience is not sufficient; it therefore appears necessary to have fixed defences at the principal seaports in the United Kingdom and of sufficient strength to be able to check a determined raid for some hours until a battle fleet can be concentrated on the spot and at the same time give opportunity for the submarines to act. I have already pointed out Red had unusual advantages, and when the coast patrol has more experience and practice it will be a great deterrent to anyone attempting a raid, but we must not forget the coast patrol is only organised on the east coast and it appears to me quite possible that a few transports and submarines might try and land troops on the west and south coasts. I consider the Straits of Dover may even be rushed and unless the Battle Fleet has a proper strategic base it will not be on the spot in time.

Then we must expect attacks by submarines on our commercial ports and apparently there is no protection at present. One or two submarines could go round to the Clyde or the Mersey and destroy many valuable ships.

*   *   *

I have extracted portions of the reports of some of the Flag Officers in command of Squadrons, as the points raised appear to be of sufficient importance to be brought to their Lordships' notice and in which I concur.

Rear Admiral [Doveton] Sturdee's Report
Submarine Menace

While giving all credit to the excellent management of the Submarines by the Submarine Officers, it is believed that their menace is not so serious as the Manoeuvres will indicate. No torpedoes were fired, therefore no true estimate can be formed of the danger to which ships were exposed from this arm of naval warfare. As no system of attacking these vessels has been adopted the safety of the British Navy is at the mercy of the enemy's submarines.

[88] *Captain Sydney Hall to Admiral Lord Fisher*[1]
[Fisher Papers 1/12]

[Not dated – *c.* July 1913]

The following are my impressions of manoeuvres gathered from submarine officers, also from Keyes —

The general feeling is without doubt one of general satisfaction with the vessels and of enthusiasm for the handling of the submarines particularly of the D & E classes. The Submarine service seems to be satisfied that during the short time the manoeuvres lasted they would have accounted for about 40% of the large vessels employed! I understand the claims amounted to this, but they say that the rules were a very great handicap, and that the overwhelming seniority factor was always present when a submarine claimed a surface ship.

A good example of this was the case of *King Edward VII* – a signal intercepted from her said that she had been attacked by a submarine, but as *Africa* reports torpedo passed astern I have ruled submarine "out of action".[2] One wonders at the sycophancy of *Africa* or else at his mendacity! No torpedo was fired, it was not allowed by the rules. Surely *K.E.* & *Africa* knew this, at any rate they could have asked.[3] Four times this fleet was successfully attacked and I saw an amusing letter from captain of *King Edward VII* saying they were becoming quite tired of seeing submarines rise alongside them and half clad figures climbing on to the conning tower to claim them.[4]

There was a rule which compelled a submarine to come to the surface and remain there for half an hour after making a claim after which she could not attack any vessel within 3 miles – This was a source of much annoyance to submarines and was unreal – for example if they dived at a lot of ships and found themselves close to a small one they would have to let her go by otherwise they could not attack the big ones, in this way there would have been many more casualties among fleet look outs in the real thing. I believe many claims of authentic bearings & distances from ships taken by periscope were not allowed, as the submarine did not rise.

Cornwall & Cumberland were sighted by 3 submarines two of which

---

[1] In July 1913, Adm. Lord Fisher was serving as president and Capt. Sydney Hall as secretary to the Royal Commission on Oil Fuel.

[2] HMS *King Edward VII*: Flagship of Rear Adm. Lewis Bayly commanding 3rd Battle Squadron.

[3] HMS *King Edward VII* and HMS *Africa*: both battleships of 'King Edward' class (16,350 tons) laid down 1902–1904 and completed 1906–1907. Four 12-in., four 9.2-in. and ten 6-in. guns. 18 knots.

[4] Commanding Officer: Capt. Edmond H.F. Heaton-Ellis.

proceeded to stalk them while the third remained under water.[1] After 2¹/₂ hours in spite of the cruisers' high speed & frequent alterations of course one of the two cruisers was caught, the two submarines rising quite close to her within 30 seconds of each other, meantime the third submarine had joined in the fray & was within a mile when she saw the cruisers stop and the 2 submarines rise. One of the cruisers had 'O' flag up & the two submarines also in order to do their half hour on the surface; the other cruiser was behind them.[2] Thinking it was all over the third submarine came to the surface & approached on the surface when she was put of action by the 2nd cruiser! which is rather absurd.

You will remember what I told you about the extreme importance of rapid coastal communications, it appears this has been slightly improved but is still very far from what it ought to be, so that the Blue defending submarines were badly served particularly at Grimsby and Cromer – At the former place there are loud complaints against *Duncan* she did not answer the signal claiming a successful submarine attack on her for well over an hour.[3] When she had accomplished her work, and then arbitrarily said one torpedo had been successful & reduced her speed to 12 knots. Whereas submarines say it was a sitting shot of simplest description.

It seems a fact, as a matter of gossip, that at a lecture given to C.O.'s of T.B.D.s & submarines the preface was 'I may as well tell you Red has got to win for political reasons' and among the younger officers it left a bad impression. They say they could not get permission to go out to attack at Grimsby until too late, but I don't attach much importance to this. It is also said that Red was playing manoeuvres and Blue was playing war. It seems both sides were enthusiastic for their own submarines but not so ready to allow equal capability to those of the enemy, which is natural!

The way in which destroyers claimed submarines at great distances from reading their number with only conning tower up is said to have been ridiculous and not open to argument at all. Two submarines complain also that they successfully attacked the Chief Umpire's ship & were told she was not open to attack, but having come to surface were put out of action by someone else! The story in the press of an aeroplane putting destroyers on to a submarine & capturing her was untrue, the

---

[1] HMS *Cornwall* and HMS *Cumberland*: both cruisers of the 'County' class (9,800 tons) laid down 1901 and completed 1904. Fourteen 6-in. guns. 24 knots.
[2] The O flag denoted 'out of action' i.e. sunk and no longer participating in the manoeuvres.
[3] HMS *Duncan*: 14,000 ton battleship and lead ship of class laid down in 1899 and completed in 1903. Four 12-in. and twelve 6-in. guns. 19 knots.

submarine was returning to harbour on the surface, out of action, and with 'O' flag flying. I am told the aeroplane did nothing at all. On one or two occasions cruisers went deliberately to challenge submarines knowing whereabouts they were, and with high speed & deliberately to drive them off, but that they were not successful, the submarine just waiting her opportunity & rising in right position for torpedo attack.

Much more attention seems to have been paid to avoiding submarines this year. Fleets and ships were always engaged in what became known as "Tangoing" from the waltz of that name! frequent alteration of course & high speed.

Finally I will quote verbatim a letter from the Captain of an E class submarine. The tone of it is delightful. I like the laconic way he describes loafing about the North Sea mopping up anything that comes his way. There is no mention of any superior enemy! or of his being afraid of anything, no such free lance has ever existed – here it is:

The D and E class in the first half of the manoeuvres all left the Nore with the Red Fleet, there [thence?] over to the Hanks light off the Texel and back across to a line from Flamboro' Head to about 40 miles to the east with idea of stopping Blue from interfering with landing at Grimsby. At 8.P.M. that night we went off to various billets such as off St. Abbs, Firth of Forth, Peterhead & Cromarty. E 4 & myself went back to off Yarmouth to refill with fuel as our eventual objective was Gruking Voe in Orkney, then next day took a line out to Swarte Bank and from there on to a point 40′ E of St. Abbs. Before reaching Swarte Bank we sighted two *Invincibles* and 3 of our own destroyers running South and received a wireless from them that enemy was in pursuit of them bearing N E, so dived and attacked to North. Enemy appeared in about $1/2$ an hour preceded by destroyer screen under which we dived and came up pretty well simultaneously. E 4 abreast leader, and I abreast last ship of line. Sea was very smooth and it was unsafe to have periscope up for more than 10 seconds.

During next day had two more successful attacks on *King Edward* and *Aboukir* at intervals of about 50 miles up the North Sea. On such occasion visibility was bad so had to keep diving on sighting smoke & of course several were false alarms. The E boats to my mind are very good. The engines run very smoothly and I found I could get down in about $1\frac{1}{2}$ minutes from underway with engine running – also one has so much control with hydroplanes that boat dives well with a large margin of buoyancy (positive or negative) from the ideal trim. This also enables one to dive easily on $1/2$ voltage so giving large endurance below water when avoiding destroyers &c and not actually attacking. Also plenty of water is carried and boat is very healthy, as regards ventilation. Sweating is practically nil and men in very good health on completion. The W/T installation is a great asset. I hope I have not wearied you with all this; the net result seems to me to be entirely satisfactory from submariners point of view.

PART V

ADMIRALTY REAPPRAISAL OF SUBMARINE POLICY, 1913–1914

[89] *Churchill to H.H. Asquith*[1]

[Masterton-Smith Mss, f.53, CAB 1/34]

Most Secret
Admiralty
22 October 1912

Prime Minister
Sir Edward Grey[2]

There is no doubt that Austria intends to have a great Medit[erranea]n Fleet. Our best and cheapest – perhaps our only – way of meeting this will be by a large submarine and torpedo development supported by a fast squadron.[3] Corfu is the key to the Adriatic. It is essential to effective torpedo flotilla action, and its possession w[oul]d vastly simplify our Medit'n problem in the years to come.

Opportunity may occur during the present war or at its close of regaining Corfu: but it is *now or never.*[4] Once the Austrian Fleet is built, such a step w[oul]d bring on a war.

Cyprus is useless for all purposes. It has a population of nearly 300,000, 4/5ths of whom are Greeks. These passionately desire union with Greece. The accession of so many citizens to the Motherland w[oul]d be an irresistible inducement to Greece. The gratification of their wishes w[oul]d be a liberal act. The fall of the Turks in Europe, sh[oul]d it occur, should be decisive so far as Cyprus is concerned. Cyprus sh[oul]d be free from Turkish sovereignty.

In return for Cyprus, Greece sh[oul]d *lease* us Corfu for a naval station (like Wei-Hai-Wei). Its nationality w[oul]d be unaffected.

It is asked that this project may be carefully considered.[5]

Copies to: Chancellor of Exchequer[6]
Mr. [Lewis] Harcourt[7]

---

[1] H.H. Asquith: Prime Minister (April 1908 to November 1916).
[2] Sir Edward Grey: Foreign Secretary (December 1905 to November 1915).
[3] In March 1912, Churchill announced the withdrawal to home waters of the battle squadron based at Malta. In July, however, the Cabinet forced the Admiralty to return an armoured squadron to the Mediterranean. Churchill agreed to keep a fast squadron of 3 (later 4) battle cruisers at Malta.
[4] At that time Greece was involved in the Balkan War with Turkey.
[5] Churchill's proposal was not approved and the idea of relying upon flotilla defence strategy in the Mediterranean was subsequently shelved for a year.
[6] David Lloyd George: Chancellor of the Exchequer, 1908–15; Minister of Munitions, 1915–16; Prime Minister 1916–22.
[7] Lewis Harcourt: Colonial Secretary, 1911–15.

[90] *Memorandum by Captain George Ballard, DOD,*
Naval War Staff[1]

[ADM 1/8331]

14 July 1913

A report is submitted herewith on the general duties of submarines from a War Staff point of view. If the main principles are approved a detailed organisation can be worked out on the basis of numbers likely to be built within specific periods and the personnel available.

War Staff: General Policy of Submarine Development

As the submarine has for some time definitely progressed beyond the stage of a purely local defence craft, the desirability of pressing forward the evolution of the type is fully concurred in by the War Staff. This development has been anticipated ever since the events of last year's manoeuvres and has been emphasised in frequent War Staff minutes dealing with submarine questions. Very great potentialities appear to lie in this direction.

It is not considered, however, that, as a matter of general policy, money should be diverted from the building of battleships and other types of *ocean-going* vessels towards increasing the submarine programme. The defence of the Empire as a whole requires that the present high standard of ocean-going vessels should be maintained. Submarines of any type are a special class in so far as their more immediate development seems probable. They are suitable only for special conditions, and, although there seems to be good reason for anticipating that before very long they will be practically supreme within their own sphere, that sphere is limited, and they cannot be regarded as fair substitutes for battleships or cruisers in a general review of our position. Those of the larger types may, on the other hand, be legitimately regarded as valuable prospective substitutes for a large proportion of our destroyer force of the future.

From a general point of view, there appear to be three special spheres of activity for submarines, each to a certain extent demanding special qualifications to obtain the best results. The most important of these spheres would consist in a watch of the enemy's harbours, reviving the strategy of close blockade. For this purpose, a design of vessels which could dive with safety in 6 fathoms would be essential for North Sea warfare, owing to the comparative shallowness of the water on

---

[1] Capt. George Ballard: Director of Naval Intelligence (December 1911); Director of Operations Division, Naval War Staff (January 1912 to March 1914).

the German coast. Good radius of action both on the surface and submerged and habitability would be required, but not a high surface speed as her safety would be secured by her diving capabilities if sighted by an enemy. Such a type could keep close watch on the entrances to the German rivers at any state of the tide, and force her way submerged up all the principal estuaries where hostile fleets might be lying.

It is this type of submarine which is most required to begin with. The Admiralty coastal design may possibly answer the purpose, at a cost of £75,000 per boat. This is less than the cost of a large destroyer by 20%, and the vessel provided for this sum seems on the whole likely to be the more formidable menace to our enemies. For the cost of a flotilla of 20 destroyers, a flotilla of 25 of these submarines could be produced. Such a flotilla would go a long way towards establishing close blockade where the destroyers would have to withdraw in the day time. Presumably the technical difficulty of getting them built with the plant at present available will restrict the numbers that can actually be laid down for some time to come, but all considerations appear to point inevitably to the conclusion that they should, at no distant date, supersede the destroyer very largely for North Sea warfare, although a proportion of destroyers would perhaps be required to accompany them as scouts. It is considered, therefore, that every encouragement should be given to private building firms to lay down a submarine construction plant.

The second sphere of duty for submarines would be in open water on the watch for hostile squadrons known to be at sea. Vessels designed for this purpose would to some extent take the place of light cruisers, and might be much larger than the blockade type dealt with above, as it would not be essential that they could dive with safety in 6 fathoms or even in 10. Their principal requirements would be a high surface speed with which to chase a hostile ship and get into position before diving to attack. They should carry beam tubes and possess good radius of action and habitable quarters for the crew.

It is understood that the two special large-sized submarines now building at a cost of £200,000 each approximate to this ideal. Comparing the initial cost of such vessels with the average cost of a City class light cruiser, it will be found that three of the former could be produced for the same outlay as two of the latter, and that the annual expense of upkeep and personnel would probably be considerably less. For purely North Sea duties, they would be both a cheaper and a more useful type of vessel, being able not only to watch but to threaten a hostile battle squadron. But they could not take the place of City class ships for foreign stations or the protection of trade,[1] which disability sets a limit to their value for general service. While, therefore, it is considered that the design should be adopted and developed, fewer should be laid down than in the case of the smaller blockading type of submarine. The proportion should be about 1 to 10, unless further experience suggests a different ratio.

Neither of the above types would be quite ideal for coast patrol. A coast patroller would require neither a great radius of action nor habitability for long periods. Her prime qualification should be a very high surface speed to enable her to reach a threatened point with the minimum of delay. She should also be of small size, in order that the largest possible number might be obtained for a given expenditure, numbers being of importance for this duty. For the present, this type does not seem to be so much required as the others, on account of the considerable force of fairly suitable small submarines we already possess. But the type should not be lost sight of as a probable future requirement.

The development of submarines in general towards a differentiation of types seems to be already sufficiently advanced to justify some more distinguishing official appellation for the various designs than a mere system of lettering. For example, the three types referred to above, of which two are already in hand, might perhaps be usefully designated:

Submersible Blockaders,

Submersible Cruisers,

and

Submersible Coastals,

respectively

Each title would describe accurately the primary functions of the class.

For the cost of a flotilla of 20 destroyers of the most modern type, a flotilla of 20 submersible blockaders, backed by a pair of submersible cruisers, could be built if the necessary plant became available. Such a force in itself would add very greatly to the risks of a German Fleet emerging in war from the Elbe or Wilhelmshaven. With sufficient flotillas of this nature to undertake the war duties now allotted to the 1st, 2nd, 3rd, and 5th Destroyer Flotillas as these destroyers get obsolete,[2] our command of the North Sea would be immensely strengthened at no additional cost. It would remain to be seen as to how far these flotillas

---

[1] City or 'Bristol' class unarmoured (light) cruisers: 4,800 tons. Laid down 1909 and completed 1911. Two 6-in. and ten 4-in. guns. 26 knots.

[2] War Orders called for the 1st, 2nd, 3rd and 5th Destroyer Flotillas to be organised into Force T and based at Harwich.

could perform their own scouting. Possibly a small number of destroyers would need to be included in the composition of each flotilla for scouting purposes.

As the submarines now building become available, it is considered that they should be organised in flotillas of 8 or 10 vessels each, placed under the Commodore (T), to act in conjunction with the First Fleet destroyer flotillas, which in time they would very largely or altogether supersede. Importance is attached to the two working in conjunction during the transition period.

The duty of the new submarines is no longer that of coast patrol or local defence, and they should not therefore be placed under the AOP. The above proposed organisation, if approved, can be worked out in further detail when the submarines are nearly ready for sea.

In the Mediterranean, the same types would answer requirements as in the North Sea. It is true that in most cases the water off possible hostile coasts is deeper than in the North Sea. The necessity for a type which could dive with safety in shallow water would therefore be less pronounced. But it is not desirable to over-specialise in any class of vessel, and for that reason a special design of Mediterranean submarine does not, for the present at any rate, seem desirable.

The question of the ideal design of depot ship cannot be settled without a final decision as to the precise duty that different types of submarines will undertake when the whole policy of their use has received Board approval. No reference to this question is therefore made in these remarks. It is possible that the long radius of action of the new types will enable them to work from shore depots.

It seems probable that a gun would be very useful in the first two types, that is to say the submersible blockader and the submersible cruiser, to deal not only with hostile surface torpedo craft and air craft but with merchant ships when engaged in commercial blockade. It would not need to be of anything above a very light calibre, for if a merchant ship disregarded a warning shot she would have to take the consequences of being torpedoed.

[91] *Memorandum by Commodore Roger Keyes on the Function of Submarines*[1]

[d'Eyncourt Papers, DEY 31]

Fort Blockhouse, Gosport
15 August 1913

A Committee of Submarine Officers in February 1912 recommended the construction of *two* types of submarines, after carefully considering the operations they would be called upon to perform in time of war:–

(1) The coastal: an economical vessel of small displacement embodying certain qualities which were considered in-dispensable to a submarine operating on our coast. In order that these vessels should carry out their duties efficiently in the winter months, seagoing qualities and good habitability were considered essential, and these cannot be obtained in a vessel of smaller displacement than the Scott coastal.[2]

(2) The oversea for work at considerable distances from their base, with large range of action, able to keep the sea in all weathers and habitability, so that the crews of the vessels could live on board in reasonable comfort for lengthy periods. The E class may be considered as the first of the oversea type proper, and it was decided to recommend the building of a large oversea vessel for experimental purposes to ascertain whether the working of such a vessel from a submarine point of view presented any difficulties. It was considered that this type should be capable of accompanying a modern fleet to sea and should possess the highest possible speed for strategic reasons. Certain dimensions about 100% in excess of our present experience were laid down, and it was considered that we should not be justified in exceeding these without trial.

With regard to (1):– The Scott coastal [S class] possesses the necessary qualities for the duty of the coast patrol, but is on the small side for work in the North Sea in winter months.

Vickers produced a coastal [V class] very similar in design to the Scott, possessing the same military qualities but of a larger displacement.

The Admiralty coastal design [F class] combines our own seagoing submarine experience with the best features of the two former, and on a further small increase of displacement carries a stern tube. These latter vessels on a smaller displacement possess the armament and range of action of a D and very much better habitability.

[1] Keyes had become Commodore of Submarines on 1 May 1912.
[2] The Scott coastals, designed by the Italian builders FIAT, were commissioned into the RN as the S class.

The Vickers and Admiralty coastal are of rather larger displacement than was recommended by the Committee, but this increase has given them a much larger radius of action than was anticipated, and for this reason it is considered that they are capable of operating on an enemy's coast as well as on our own; but they are on the small side for this work in severe weather and have not the offensive value of the E class.

With regard to (2):– Messrs Vickers endeavoured to design an oversea vessel [*Nautilus*] to comply with the Committee's recommendations, but found it necessary to considerably increase the displacement recommended, before they would guarantee a speed of even 17 knots with ordinary combustion engines. This was disappointing, as it was hoped to obtain 20 knots in a vessel of less displacement.

Messrs Scott were then asked to work out a design for a steam turbine submarine, [*Swordfish*] as it appears that steam is the only method of obtaining the higher power required for great speed. It was impressed on Messrs Scott that they should keep the displacement and length as low as possible. An important factor in determining the size of this vessel was the beam necessary in order to include broadside tubes. The surface displacement of the Scott oversea is 450 tons less than the Vickers and she carries almost the same armament.

I. With regard to the First Lord's minute, a statement of the types built, building and ordered, is attached.

II. The 9 A class are only suitable for harbour defence and should be replaced by B's and C's as soon as we can afford to do so.

B's and C's of which we possess 38 in Home Waters are capable of carrying out coast patrol duties, but their poor habitability and seagoing qualities prevent them from operating at any great distance from their base particularly in the winter months.

The 8 D's are suitable for coast patrol duties; the coastal were designed for these duties.

The construction of submarines smaller than the Scott coastal is strongly deprecated; when the field of production is properly opened up to competition, the price of the coastal is certain to be considerably reduced.

It is considered that for an efficient coast patrol, the Admiralty coastal is an ideal craft and is superior to any other coastal.

III. Besides the 2 large experimental submarines (Vickers and Scott's) which we have building, the D and E class are the only vessels at present capable of carrying out oversea duties. The E's are greatly to be preferred to the D's, which later should join the coastal patrols as soon as they can be replaced.

Submarines of the E displacement are considered to be very suitable to the inshore squadron work off the Elbe, but it does not appear that the depth they require to dive in (7½ fathoms) will prevent them from operating inside Heligoland. In this connection *no* submarine can dive under a large surface vessel in a less depth than 10 fathoms.

Messrs Vickers have designed a double-hulled E boat of about the same displacement. She carries 5 torpedo tubes, 1 bow 21, 2 broadside 18 and 2 stern 18, and has a speed of 15½ knots; she should be an ideal craft for this work in all weathers and she should be capable of getting there and staying there under all veather conditions. It is understood that Messrs Vickers can build this type for about £125,000.

It is a matter for serious consideration whether the extra £80,000 paid for the oversea Vickers is worth while for the two tubes and two knots gained, though it is considered absolutely necessary that we should build one vessel of this large size in order to be in a position to judge of the advisability or otherwise of laying down still larger vessels of the Ocean type. The Admiralty coastal is quite capable of carrying out in moderate weather the duties of the oversea boats as defined in this paragraph; but as previously indicated they are on the small side for work on the German coast in winter months; the offensive value of their armament compares unfavourably owing to its disposition with that of the E's although it is quite equal to that of the D's.

Regarding Convoy:– A submarine must dive before she gets within range of any suspicious craft, and for this reason a convoy to and from the area of operations would considerably relieve her anxieties, expedite her passage and save much waste of energy. It is considered that a submarine on blockade duties must take her chance. A surface scout would be in a very precarious position. The submarine herself runs some risk of being stalked and torpedoed on the surface by an enemy's submarine.

IV. Submarine officers are strongly of opinion that no submarine quality should be sacrificed for a gun. It is understood however that in the E class the presence of a gun will improve the stability. Since it will not impair submarine qualities in any way, and it is conceivable that a submarine may find herself in a condition in which she is unable to dive, a gun apart from its use against air craft will enable a submarine to die hard. Two experimental types of submarine gun are being constructed, one for a disappearing mounting, the other a light gun to pass through the conning tower. Both are being given sufficient elevation for aerial attack.

V. Concur regarding cycle reliefs.

VI. Suggestion re beam tubes will be considered. No objection is seen to this arrangement, provided the submarine possesses sufficient beam; at present this is not the case.

The Chief of Staff's minute is mainly covered by the foregoing remarks.

Concur regarding shore depots.

With regard to the provision of scouts it is considered that:–

(1) Submarines employed on our own coast patrol need surface vessels to seaward of them to give them warning; this is especially the case in heavy weather.

(2) Submarines acting on blockade cannot have scouts on account of the precarious position those vessels would be placed in.

(3) Submarines acting with a battle or cruiser squadron:– There is no doubt that submarines could be made good use of in this connection, particularly if the squadron were attacked by a superior force; the latter could be let over the submarines who would fend for themselves.

[92] *Memorandum by Winston Churchill on the Function of Submarines*

[d'Eyncourt Mss, DEY 31]

20 August 1913

NOTES ON SUBMARINES

There are three distinct types:
1. Coastal.
2. Overseas.
3. Ocean.

Of which the dominant requirements are respectively –
   (1) For Coastals – Numbers.
   (2) For Overseas – Endurance, and
   (3) For Ocean – Speed.

The Coastal Submarine is a partial substitute for the Shore battery and the Mine field.

The Overseas Submarine takes the place of Torpedo Boat Destroyers and the inshore squadron.

The Ocean Submarine is a decisive weapon of battle; and as such must count in partial substitution of battleship strength.

II. Coastals are for defence and deterrence; they can of course be recruited from the older vessels of the Overseas class; and we have already a large number of A and B boats (C's are indeterminate). But since numbers are so indispensable in this class it will be necessary to design and keep building *a small cheap type* which can be easily multiplied. You cannot expect much surface speed at the size and cost.

III. Overseas boats are for blockade. The D's and E's belong to this class though a great improvement is required. They must be able to dive quickly and in 6 or 7 fathoms – less if possible. They must be able to keep the sea continuously for 7 days, i.e. 3 days surface and the difference on the home voyage. Habitability and fuel capacity are the vital points. They do not require any supports in shore. The idea of a large submarine going to the rescue of a small is erroneous. On the spot all submarines are equal. Their differences arise only from

(a) getting there; and (b) staying there.

No relation can be established between the submarine submerged and the hostile force brought against it. A submarine cannot be overmatched nor can it be supported.

Overseas submarines proceeding on blockade service, so as to arrive fresh, should be convoyed by destroyers and cruisers and travel behind an effective screen of fast vessels until they approach the blockading area. Then their escort stands off and they go on alone. It is a matter of individual preference whether they should take a destroyer with each group for look out work or not. The pros and cons are evenly balanced. Some officers would like it, others would prefer to work alone.

IV. No class of submarines requires guns except against air craft; and all development in this direction is vicious. An anti-air-craft gun may be given to Overseas and Ocean boats in case they are pounced upon by planes when resting on the surface. The opportunities for its use will be very restricted. The power of the submarine depends on not using guns.

V. Three days will be the maximum spell of blockading duty; three days going and coming and six days rest; total a cycle of 12 days. To maintain an overseas block of the Adriatic or the Elbe, flotillas in 4 reliefs will be required – One on watch, One in transit, Two resting.

Any attempt with less will break down. With a secure base (fixed or floating) overseas, three reliefs suffice; and then Coastals could be brought over to assist the Overseas boats.

VI. 48 Overseas boats would thus be required to maintain a continuous blockade of the German rivers in 4 flotillas of 4 groups of 3 boats each. This force could be created largely at the expense of the destroyers.

VII. Surface speed is the dominant characteristic required of the Ocean submarine. This speed is not tactical but strategical. The Ocean submarine (or submarine cruiser) must have sufficient speed to overhaul a battle fleet so as to make sure of being able to anticipate it at any point, or to get ahead of it in order to dive and attack. Such vessels attack by getting there and being overtaken. 24 knots would be an ample margin of speed for Ocean submarines. These vessels cruise under escort and fight alone. They must be protected by other vessels when on the surface; and be guided by them to their point of attack. They should have no armament except the anti-aircraft gun and – the torpedo. They should have 4–21 tubes on the beam – if possible capable of firing either side[a] and at least one bow and stern tube – total 6; with 4 torpedoes for each tube – total 24.

VIII. Ocean submarines should be organised in Submarine Flotillas as follows:

3 or 4 Ocean submarines of 24 knots surface speed.

2 Light Cruisers of 30–31 knots, one of each as a small sea-going depot ship, and the other carries 3 sea planes.

This is a Commodore's command and should be considered equal as a decisive fighting unit to a first class battleship or battle cruiser.

IX. 4 Submarine Squadrons might be created for general service and stationed in the North Sea and Mediterranean. It is important to choose their ports so that the water is deep enough for the submerged cruiser to leave harbour and go to sea if necessary submerged: Cromarty, Gibraltar and Malta fulfil this condition.

[Churchill's own footnote]: [a] It ought not to be difficult to design these as we do not want to fire above 10 or 12 knots submerged speed. The outer part or mouthpiece of the tubes should be fixed to each side of the vessel, and the middle piece or carrier, opening laterally along its whole length should swivel round either way and attach to the fixed mouth piece; just as a gun might fire out of alternative gunports. But this is a detail.

[93] *Extract from Churchill to Fisher*
[Fisher Papers, FISR 1/13]

30 August 1913

*   *   *

You will discern with your penetrating eye that the root of the matter is surface speed. If the submarine is to be a partial substitute for battleship strength or battleship preponderance, and not merely a substitute for destroyers, it must possess a strategic speed which will enable it effectively to overhaul or circumvent a battle fleet, so that it can come into action without fail and be counted on as a decisive weapon. If this speed can be attained at the present time or in the immediate future by any other path except by those of size and steam, I should be delighted to learn it.

*   *   *

[94] *Memorandum by Captain George Ballard (DOD)*
Considerations as to the Best Composition of the Mediterranean Fleet
in 1915
[ADM 116/3099]

20 November 1913

The prospective strategic situation of Great Britain versus Austria in the Mediterranean is one of the questions of the near future demanding serious attention.

British requirements in those waters are purely defensive and centre on the all-important consideration of safeguarding shipping on our Eastern route and the coaling stations, including Egypt, along it, which are necessary alike to the Navy and Mercantile Marine in the Mediterranean.

The Austrian war policy might be either offensive or defensive, but is more likely to be the former. It is scarcely conceivable that circumstances should arise of a nature to induce the Dual Monarchy to enter hostilities single handed against Great Britain, and it is only as an ally of Germany in consequence that the Austrian position should be treated from a practical standpoint. If that view is well founded, it seems probable that under pressure from Germany, if for no other reason, the allied plan of operations against Great Britain could impose an offensive role on the Austrian Squadrons. An object of attack would lie before them in the trade route which it is of as much importance for Great Britain to defend and which might be threatened either by direct interception of the passing traffic or by a seizure of any of the coaling bases with which it is furnished.

The Austrian battleships capable of undertaking operations at a distance from home issues will by the end of 1915 include 4 Dreadnoughts and 3 *Radetzkys* [class battleships], while 4 more Dreadnoughts will be in various stages of building. As support to this main Squadron there will be 3 *Ferdinand Max's* and 3 *Babenbergs*. To act successfully in the defensive against the attacks of these 13 armoured ships, it would be necessary either to maintain an equivalent sea-going Battle Fleet on the threatened route, or, as an alternative, to endeavour to take advantage of the somewhat unfavourable strategic position of Austria as regards undertaking the offensive in open waters.

As regards the first of these alternatives, a fairly equivalent Fleet could be constituted by appropriating for the purpose either 6 Dreadnoughts, or 2 Super-Dreadnoughts and 3 Dreadnoughts, or 2 Super-Dreadnoughts and 4 Battle Cruisers, or 3 Dreadnoughts and 4 Battle Cruisers, or 2 Dreadnoughts, 2 Lord Nelsons and 4 Battle

Cruisers, any selection from these being supported by 6 Armoured Cruisers. In all cases the Squadrons indicated must be considered as the minimum force able to afford an equal chance of success against the Austrians in a Fleet action, and as representing therefore the lowest which could secure our interests if we adhered to an open water policy only.

But if we could make certain of reducing the Austrian Squadron before it came into contact with our own, it is obvious that a smaller armoured force would answer our requirements. This could be effected if it was possible to ensure that a Submarine or Destroyer attack could be delivered on the enemy before he reached open waters, and to attain this object certain facilities exist. With the solitary exception of Russia, no Maritime Power is so unfavourably situated for assuming the offensive in the open as Austria, because no Austrian Fleet can undertake distant operations till it has passed out through the entrance of the Adriatic, a strait only 40 miles wide, that is to say sufficiently restricted to be within the scope of sea-going Submarine or Destroyer operations, provided that they can obtain a secure base as a starting point and not more than 200 miles distant. The Island of Cefalonia would answer this purpose admirably, and if this Island was available as a base for Flotillas of 20 D class Submarines and 20 Destroyers; the Austrian Battle Squadron would be compelled to face a serious risk before encountering our own. To what extent it would actually suffer must, of course, remain a matter of conjecture, but even if only two first class units were put out of action the gain would be appreciable, and a similar danger would await the Austrians on every occasion of return to their bases and every subsequent venture into Mediterranean waters. In time they would almost certainly suffer serious reduction, and this might possibly come very quickly.

The initial cost of a Flotilla of 20 Acorn class Destroyers, inclusive of a Depot Ship, would be about £1,850,000, and of the same number of D class Submarines, with Depot Ship, about £1,650,000. The combined Flotillas would therefore cost altogether about £3,500,000, a sum equivalent to the cost of 2 *Thunderer* [class dreadnoughts] but less than the cost of a pair of any later type of Battleship. They would require the services of about 1,700 ranks and ratings, inclusive of the crews of the Depot Ships, which is about 200 more than would be required to man a pair of *Thunderers*, but 200 less than for a pair of *Iron Dukes*. On the whole, the two Flotillas would be more suitable as a provision against war with Austria than the two Battleships, in view of the peculiar strategic circumstances of the case.

The cost of equipping and fortifying a base would of course be extra, but would provide a good war anchorage for the main Battle Fleet as well as for the Destroyers in an ideal strategic position.

Assuming then that the Island of Cefalonia had been acquired and suitably defended, it would be possible and advantageous to substitute a Destroyer Flotilla and a D Class Submarine Flotilla as above for a pair of Battleships. The main Mediterranean Fleet in 1915 might then be reduced to 4 Dreadnoughts, or two Super-Dreadnoughts and 2 Battle Cruisers, or 2 *Lord Nelsons* and 4 Battle Cruisers, always allowing for 6 Armoured Cruisers in addition.

If it was ever necessary to consider the possibility of war with any enemy in the Mediterranean but Austria, this policy might be pushed to its logical conclusion or at least very much further than is suggested above. A force of 80 sea-going Submarines would cost no more to build than 3 Super-Dreadnoughts, and less to man, and would make the Adriatic entrance practically impossible if properly disposed and manoeuvred. But they would be less useful than the 3 Super-Dreadnoughts if the enemy was some other Power less handicapped in getting to sea against whose operations only a blue-water defence could prove effective, and as it is a necessary axiom of our general policy to maintain our maritime supremacy against any variety of attack, the substitution of Submarines for Battleships should be kept within strict limits until the development of Submarines has proceeded much further than it has as yet.

[95] *Julian Corbett to Fisher*[1]

[Fisher Papers, FISR 1/14]

3, Hans Crescent, SW.
30 November 1913

This is immense. It makes me feel as if I had a flash of lightning by the tail. I have made a few suggestions, but I have not dealt with it drastically as you said. To do that I should have to re-write and recast the greater part of it in my own style, and whatever you may be kind enough to think – that would not be an improvement on yours – not at any rate for ramming home your ideas.

The only big patch I offer is about submarines breaking up all our old strategic ideas. That has been worrying me for 2 or 3 years past and I have felt very strongly that the question was not really faced objectively as it ought to be. The manoeuvres this year, so far as I understand them,

[1] Julian Corbett: naval historian and lecturer at the Naval War College.

seem to me to be pantomime – so little reality did they seem to have to the actualities of futurist naval warfare.

I should be delighted to come to you any afternoon this week if I could help any more.

[96] *Memorandum by Admiral of the Fleet Lord Fisher*
[Asquith Mss 25]

5th edition printed May 1914

THE OIL ENGINE AND THE SUBMARINE
(A Contribution to the consideration of future Sea Fighting.)

The course of the Royal Commission on Fuel and Engines has brought out the fact that the only form of Internal Combustion Engine that has been so far completely successful for warships is that used by submarines. The vast advantages which a ship engined in this way possesses has consequently led to the reconsideration of the present-day position of submarines, and as their great possible advance is mainly a question of the perfection of the oil engine, and further as the great further advantage that may be thus obtained may tend to sweep all surface warships from the seas, the subject is one of the most enormous interest.

The use of submarines in the two last annual manoeuvres has convinced most of us that in war time nothing can stand against them, and broadly speaking it may be stated with confidence that –

The submarine is the coming type of war vessel for sea fighting.

But for that consummation to be reached we must perfect the oil engine and we must store oil.

There is a strong animus against the submarine – of course there is. An ancient Admiralty Board minute described the introduction of the steam engine as fatal to England's Navy. Another Admiralty Board minute vetoed iron ships, as iron sinks and wood floats! The whole Navy objected to breech-loading guns and in consequence sure disaster was close to us for years and years. There was virulent opposition to the water tube boiler (fancy putting the fire where the water ought to be and the water where the fire should be!). The turbine was said by eminent marine engineers to have an insuperable and vital defect which rendered it inadmissible as practical marine engine – its vast number of blades – it was only a toy. Wireless was voted damnable by all the armchair sailors when we put it on the roof of the Admiralty, and yet we heard what one ship (the *Argyll*) at Bombay was saying to another (the *Black*

Prince) at Gibraltar. Flying machines were a physical impossibility, said a great scientist four years ago. To-day they are as plentiful as sparrows. Submarines are only playthings! was the official remark of our Chief Admiral afloat only a little while ago and yet now submarines are talked of as presently ousting Dreadnoughts. The above texts extracted from comparatively modern naval history (history is a record of exploded ideas!) should make anyone chary of ridiculing the writer when he repeats –

The submarine is the coming type of war vessel for sea fighting.

And what is it that the coming of the submarine really means? It means that the whole foundation of our traditional naval strategy, which served us so well in the past, has been broken down! The foundation of that strategy was blockade. The fleet did not exist merely to win battles – that was the means, not the end. The ultimate purpose of the fleet was to make blockade possible for us and impossible for our enemy. Where that situation was set up we could do what we liked with him on the sea, and, despite a state of war, England grew steadily richer. But with the advent of the long-range ocean-going submarine that has all gone! Surface ships can no longer either maintain or prevent blockade, and with the conception of blockade are broken up all the consequences, direct and indirect, that used to flow from it. All our old ideas of strategy are simmering in the melting pot! Can we get anything out of it which will let us know where we are and restore to us something of our former grip? It is a question that must be faced.[1]

It is with the development of this thesis that this paper is written. Again we reiterate the statement that the oil engine (and hence our oil supply) permeates the whole question of future sea fighting – but to resume:–

It has become a habit in the development of all types of war vessels to find improvement in an increase of size. Dreadnoughts have grown into super-Dreadnoughts, cruisers have grown into battle-cruisers, torpedo boats into torpedo boat destroyers, and so on. So with the submarine. In the last eight years submarines have grown from 130 tons displacement to more than ten times that tonnage, and the question arises whether this type will follow the lead of the surface ship? Are we, in fact, to have submarine battleships and submarine cruisers?

Now to puzzle this out, we must first of all bear in mind that for at least four years past ceaseless but unsuccessful efforts have been made to find an antidote to submarines. It should also be remembered that up

---

[1] This entire paragraph was the patch written by Julian Corbett and referred to in his letter to Fisher dated 30 November 1913 [95].

to the present the submarine has been developed with one and only one object, and that is the destruction of surface vessels. These are her natural prey. No attempt has been made, as in the case of surface vessels, to pit one submarine against another; no word of a submarine destroyer has ever been heard because it has been forced upon us, by experience, that submarines cannot fight submarines, nor has any successful antidote been found even by the most bitter anti-submarine experts with unlimited means for experiments. Meanwhile, the increase in size of submarines has only had one object, namely, to render them more seaworthy and sea keeping so as to enable them to compete with their prey at ever increasing distances from their base; at the same time the greatest pains have been taken not to impair their qualities as bona fide submarines.

To this one great end the time taken to submerge and invisibility when submerged have been carefully preserved. Although an immense increase in surface qualities and advantages could have been given them by the substitution of steam turbines for their natural internal combustion engines, these have never even been seriously considered in the past – and quite rightly so – because thereby the all important advantages as a submarine would have been impaired. *In fact the development of the submarine has been entirely based and dependent upon the development of the internal combustion engine, and on that development the future great advance of the submarine must patiently wait.*

The vital qualities with which the oil engine has endowed the submarine are as follows:–

(1) Ability to start at once (like a motor car) from the engine cold. It is simply impossible to exaggerate the fighting advantage of this characteristic.

(2) Absence of smoke, so that invisibility can be maintained while their initial approach is being made upon the surface.

(3) Ability to stop on the surface and instantly dive, then proceeding by electrical power when submerged.

(4) The increase in their radius of action – or more properly in the length of time that they can remain in fighting trim on their station – their possibilities in this direction being due to their not expending fuel when lying about in wait for their enemy, while at the same time their readiness for instant action remains unimpaired. This is an invaluable attribute in war time but not so very much noticed in peace.

It is these four marvellous fighting factors which have so far made, and will always make, the internal combustion engine of inestimable advantage or value in the development of the submarine; but for the moment the advance of the internal combustion engine is hardly keeping pace with other warlike advantages with which we wish to endow the submarine; and, inasmuch as it is known that the French are now turning their attention to steam, we are compelled at this point to break off for a moment and to ask why and consider what the rôle of a submarine in future warfare may be.

The fact is that the whole question of submarines is based on three distinct functions in their employment:–

1. **Battle Functions.** – If the submarine (as some urgently and with great force and reason advocate) is to be a practical adjunct to or substitute for battleship strength or battleship preponderance, and not simply a substitute for destroyers, then the root of the matter is surface speed, and the submarine must possess a strategic speed which will enable it to overhaul or circumvent a battle fleet so that it can come into action without fail and be rightly counted on as a decisive battle weapon. This increased speed can be attained at the present time and in the immediate future by no other paths except those of size and steam, and the objections to both will appear later on in this paper. Without any doubt whatsoever a fast battle fleet which can always be accompanied by submarines under all circumstances would possess an overwhelming fighting advantage.

2. **Commerce Defence and Destruction.** – This second function calls for a type of submarine (the smallest-biggest submarine) that shall have sufficient endurance to travel as far as, say, the Argentine with an oil engine (with extra oil in the ballast tank) and carry an armament of a 3-inch gun and a large supply of small-sized Whitehead torpedoes. This type of submarine must obviously bring about a profound modification of our old ideas of oceanic strategy.

3. **Coastal Defence.** – The third function of the submarine has brought into existence the existing North Sea and coastal submarine, whose duties need hardly be entered upon here. Their value is established and admitted on all sides and they must remain indispensable.

There are thus three distinct types of submarines required for three distinct services, and any State Paper which deals with the submarine question must inevitably take cognisance of the type of construction entailed by each of these three functions. But in the consideration of the whole question it must be remembered that there is a limitation which severely restricts the field within which future developments must be sought. It is the limitation of displacement, for already the latest approved design of submarine approaches the limit of size which will permit her to dive under a Dreadnought in the shallow waters of the North Sea. Lastly, it must be ever borne distinctly and most emphatically in mind that so far the increasing size of the submarine has been wholly dependent upon the development of its engine, which has been an oil engine (an ideal one for the purpose), and specially must it be remembered that the type of oil engine that can possibly be adapted with facility for a Dreadnought may be quite impossible for use in a submarine owing to the inevitable restrictions in the direction of weight, space, and stiffness of engine foundations. Hence it is that we are now looking for a light type of oil engine.

Having thus cleared the ground by considering the past development of the submarine, its causes and certain strategic requirements of the near future, and ever bearing in mind that this form of war vessel, whether advantageous to us or not, has come to stay and will have a most profound effect on all future warship construction and naval strategy, we will proceed to consider more in detail its uses and among other things whether the submarine militates against out naval supremacy? – If it is the weapon of the strong? – whether it will compel the enemy to leave his harbours and fight us? – whether it reduces the personnel of the fleet, and so is in our favour as against conscript nations?

Note: The building of coastal submarines is not here advocated; our policy is only to build the very best and lapse of time relegates all such vessels to the second class.

The Uses of the Submarine in its present Stage of Development

So far the natural development of the submarine has not led it in the way of being an integral portion of the battle fleet for fleet fighting. It has developed itself first on the lines of an integral portion of the system of defence of our coasts and ports, and more lately on the lines of a method of regaining the lost power of blockading an enemy's coasts and ports. After ten years' incessant trial and improvement submarines have developed at present into two distinct types, and the present position is that both remain in unchallenged control of the waters they infest, so that it is perhaps not clearly recognised, even by submarine enthusiasts, what an immensely valuable and economical asset to the supreme Navy these vessels are. This is particularly so in their later types and development.

The First Type – the Large or Ocean-going Submarines. These are vessels for use off the enemy's coasts and on the high seas between. Even three years ago the distance at which it was found to be dangerous for a vessel to stay off an enemy's submarine base was demonstrated as a result of trial to be no less than 300 miles. If this distance were divided by six it may fairly then be claimed that a blockade as loose as 50 miles is impossible without a gradual but certain loss of the surface ships employed in the blockade when hostile submarines are present; or, in other words, *a blockade, however loose, is absolutely impossible for surface vessels provided hostile submarines are present.* On the other hand of war, an English blockade of the German ports is just as essential as ever, and it is with these later types of ocean-going submarines that the only escape is to be found from the above-mentioned dilemma of blockade by surface vessels being nowadays found impracticable.

These later submarines are not only, therefore, the only type of vessels capable of maintaining any form of blockade but further have sea-keeping qualities far in advance of any surface vessel, for by reason of their internal combustion engines they can remain on their station ready for full speed and immediately effective for war without any local expenditure of fuel. In this connection it is essential to remember that the internal combustion engine is the only one that can immediately go at almost full speed from cold, steam necessitates the engines being kept constantly warmed if required at a moment's notice, with a corresponding expenditure of fuel, while the internal combustion engine can start with as little delay as in the case of a motor car.

Such ocean-going submarines carrying at least 10 torpedoes (but this factor will be dealt with later) and armed with a 4-inch gun, as they could be, would not be capable of being driven below the surface or off their beat except by hostile submarines or large vessels, which large vessels in this case would then probably form but a valuable additional prey and occasion a serious loss to the enemy's fleet. In this new form, however, blockade can never be really close. When large submarines undertake a blockade they must do so on the surface, and they will become for the time being surface vessels, as far as hostile submarines are concerned, and open to attack as such. It is evident, therefore, that the blockade must not only be loose, but the appearance of any blockading submarine off an enemy's coast must be of such short duration that no hostile submarine can reach her submerged all the way. If the hostile submarines come further afield to attempt the break-up of the blockade, they in their turn must come out on the surface; if this case be taken to its logical conclusion and the enemy possess sufficient submarines, the position of stalemate will be reached, and this aspect of the case will be referred to later.

Still the fact remains that loose as these blockades must be, they will serve as a bar to expeditions, for the most determined enemy will not venture to send troop-laden transports to sea to run the gauntlet of waters known to be infested by submarines. Practically speaking, therefore, the only limit to their marvellous efficiency for blockade work is the endurance of the crews, and their endurance by a well-designed system of relief may be made practically indefinite. For such is the secrecy of submarine operations that in the future it will be more difficult than ever it was for an enemy to tell to what extent and by what force he is blockaded. Thus submarines, without exhausting themselves by a perpetual watch, but by constantly, or even occasionally, showing themselves off an enemy's ports, could maintain a blockade as efficiently and for longer periods than has ever been done with steam vessels.

The Second Type – the Small or Coastal Submarines. These are vessels designed for and stationed as an integral portion of the defence of our seaports, coasts, and over-sea bases. Being normally stationed in or off our naval and commercial harbours they incidentally establish confidence in the inhabitants of their districts against raids and invasions. Their efficiency for preventing interference with our coasts and local shipping by an enemy depends primarily upon the excellence of the system of communication along the coast; as previously stated, they are instantly ready for full speed – as is a motor car – without any expenditure of fuel while waiting or watching, are equally instantly ready for war and are capable of rapid concentration upon any threatened point where, in conjunction with the destroyers and torpedo boats of the patrol flotillas, they form an intensely valuable second line of defence, so that the most bigoted conscriptionist, did he once realise their value, would immediately grasp that in their presence raids and invasions become still more difficult than ever, and, indeed practically impossible.

Summing up the development of the submarine up to date it has already been clearly recognised that these vessels form an increasingly valuable and economical factor in our scheme of national defence. In this connection they enjoy a very special merit, which is that they do not become obsolete, but retain their full value as opposed to surface vessels until the last gallon of their fuel and the last moment of their seaworthy life, for – let us clearly realise this point – they should not be discovered, and even if they are, there is at present no known means for their destruction. Can such a statement be made of any other instrument of war?

It has further been realised that while the small type should be chiefly used as a second line of defence, and controlled by a well thought out and reliable system of rapid coastal communications, the approaches to the enemy's waters should be thoroughly infested (and known to the enemy to be infested) by the larger type, which to this end should deliberately show themselves everywhere. By this means we shall precisely re-establish on the most modern and efficient lines the old system of home defence, which was never broken through, but which is no longer practicable with surface ships. In other words we shall have the close investment of the hostile coast which is essential as a check upon the enemy's invasionary forces, ships, commerce destroyers, and mine layers putting to sea; all that it will require is a large submarine with further a large stock of ammunition; while the inner defence of our own coasts and harbour, from vessels that may have escaped the first type, may satisfactorily and surely be dealt with by the smaller type. Our own manoeuvre experience, though at present necessarily somewhat restricted, has gone far to establish the correctness of this appreciation, namely, that such a submarine blockade can be far more efficiently established and for longer periods than ever was possible with steam vessels. How far the establishment of such a blockade will operate as an effective deterrent to raids or invasion is, of course, a moral question on which manoeuvres can throw no light. It requires war experience and recent war experience gives the plainest answer.

The war experience of Italy in her invasion of Tripoli has demonstrated through competent observers the panic into which a line of but 10 miles of transports may be thrown by the report of Turkish submarines which all the time in fact were non-existent. This fact alone should lead us to realise what vast differences the possession of but a few submarines by Russia would probably have made to the course of the campaign in the case of the war with Japan when large numbers of troops had to be transported. Under these circumstances it is of the utmost importance to remember that in addition to their small cost in the first place, submarines are exceedingly economical in fuel and personnel, retain their full fighting value in relation to their natural prey on the surface however much the latter may improve, and that as regards economy, probably 20 submarines of even the E class can be built and manned at the same cost in cash and personnel as one Dreadnought.

Sea-fighting of to-day, or at any time, entails the removal of the enemy's sea forces. If, as is maintained, the submarine proves itself at once the most efficient factor for this purpose and also the most difficult sea force to remove, let us clear our minds of all previous obsessions, acknowledge the facts once and for all, and, as in the case of the Dreadnought, let us lead the way. The Dreadnought, like the planet Neptune, was not invented – it was only discovered; the calculations of science made the discovery of both inevitable. It was only a question of who would reach the goal first, and Leverrier, the French astronomer, beat our Professor Adams, while we won with the Dreadnought! England got the lead instead of having to follow! (What a business there would have been if Germany had forestalled us!) So with the submarine; we have got in first, and who knows but what our geographical position does not make it for our immense advantage! Germany has only 114 miles of coast – we have thousands!

Hostile Submarines

It has to be freely acknowledged that at the present time no means exist of preventing hostile submarines emerging from their own ports and cruising more or less at will. It is moreover only barely possible that in the future, mining and other blocking operations on a very extensive scale may so develop as to render their exit very hazardous; but it is plain that such operations would require a large personnel and an immense quantity of constantly replaceable materials.

* * *

To sum up:–

The question being what is to prevent German submarines from infesting the approaches to British ports, the answer must certainly be:–

(a) In the North Sea. – Nothing is so far known that can prevent them doing so, but a very large number indeed of German submarines would be required to do so effectively.

(b) In the English Channel and on the Western Coasts. – Nothing but the distance from the nearest German base and the difficulties of passing the cordon we might and ought to have established in the Straits of Dover, but even then it is only very difficult, not impossible. However, in this case to do so effectively the number required must be enormous.

In both cases, in fact, the risk will have to be reckoned with.

On the general question. – As submarines grow larger and become more fully capable of keeping the seas for long periods, it will become impossible to say where they may not be met. They have the power to fight or to evade a fight at will; they can pick and choose their prey, and can remain for an almost indefinite time an omnipresent, constant, and harassing menace to all surface craft, and at present there are no means for their destruction. Surface war vessels must accept this risk, and all that can be said for them is that while it is greatest and may well become intolerable in such enclosed waters as the North Sea, the English Channel, and the Mediterranean, it would most certainly decrease as their distance from the enemy's bases increases.

Does not this lead us irresistibly to the conclusion that, as stated in the introduction to this paper

The submarine is the coming type of war vessel for sea fighting. And further that:–

It will become increasingly difficult for any or either Power to obtain the command of narrow seas. It will render the despatch of expeditionary forces across them a more and more hazardous business than ever it has been before and this applies equally to the invasion of England or to the despatch of our expeditionary force oversea. Considering, therefore, the safety of England from invasion, it would appear that the development of the submarine should result in increased safety. But on the other hand, we must also recognise that since this applies equally to our prospective enemies, and that submarines are cheap, the dangers to our commerce and food supplies are very great in the narrow seas.

The Future Development of the Submarine

As has already been said, it is known that the French are turning their attention to steam driven engines for surface work in submarines, and although this fact is probably due in the first place to the slowness of the development of the internal combustion engine, yet, if a larger vessel than that at present designed is contemplated, or if it is desired that the submarine shall accompany battle fleets as an integral portion of their fighting ability, in either or both of these cases a more powerful engine than can at present be supplied of the internal combustion type is an absolute necessity.

As regards this whole policy of steam, however remarkable may be the achievements of the geared steam turbine and oil fired boiler, and even granting the immense gain in a rotary engine as compared with a reciprocating one, it is considered a retrograde step to revert to steam in a submarine owing to the overwhelming advantages which the internal combustion engine confers upon it. Moreover, though an installation of this kind may be made to work smokelessly at a more or less steady speed, it is probable that on raising steam and stopping suddenly, or in making considerable variations in speed, some smoke will be generated. Also a period of 15 minutes is stated as the minimum necessity for the steam submarine to proceed at full speed from rest. It is just these 15 minutes which may ruin her! It would anyhow restrict her immediate readiness for action, while her confrère with internal combustion engines could well be some four miles on the road in the same time. To obviate such a disability means that during the whole time the vessel is operating there must be a large expenditure of fuel to keep the engines warm, and with that expenditure vanishes one of the greatest potentialities of the present submarine. Under any circumstances it seems certain that the consumption of fuel must be more than double that in an oil engine for the same power, and the extra weight of fuel to be carried to keep the radius of action constant cannot, be made up by the saving of weight in the steam plant.

It is further considered to be open to grave doubts whether a steam driven submarine proceeding at, say 20 knots could shut down and dive within a period of three minutes. Rapidity in diving from surface work being an essential quality to save the vessel being caught and easily destroyed on the surface, it need hardly be pointed out how grave this disadvantage would be. Leaving out of the question for the moment the desirability of submarines accompanying a battle fleet, there are other cogent reasons why very large increases in surface speed – which under any conditions of engines involve a large increase in size – should be most carefully considered in submarine development. There is the question of handling the water ballast. Anyone who has trimmed in even a 600 or 800-ton submarine, which deals [sic] with 100 to 150 tons of water in three minutes, would be well aware that the construction of a vessel requiring to deal with a very much larger amount in the same time must be approached with the utmost caution. The length of the vessel alone necessitates great care in flooding arrangements or extreme angles may be taken up and the trim spoilt. It is interesting also to consider what will be the minimum depth of water in which a submarine can operate safely as her length is increased to gain surface speed. For speeds much over 20 knots it is presumed the vessel must be about 400 feet long, which necessitates a depth of 20 fathoms to enable her to pass under large ships in safety. In other words such a vessel is only available for use in depths greater than 20 fathoms, and this, to enable her to work with efficiency, debars her from large portions of the North Sea and approaches to war harbours therein.

The above are only some of the practical difficulties that must confront such a vessel even supposing that it is accepted as desirable upon general grounds to construct submarines of the larger size consequent on a desire for great speed. These difficulties to some extent dispose for the present of the very natural desire for submarines to accompany battle fleets as an integral part of their offensive power; and, if that is so, it is difficult to see exactly what is to be the rôle of the swifter larger submarine. Admitted that size means power, comfort, speed, more torpedoes (though this might be arranged for in other ways) and more ammunition for the guns, is the vessel to be considered the equal of two submarines of half her size: for she will cost very much more than double the cost of one? She may indeed become so big and such a large target that she will become a worthy prey to her own kind of a smaller, handier and cheaper variety, which, be it remembered, has no more to fear from a larger, swifter submarine than she has from the heaviest armed surface vessel in existence. Bearing in mind, indeed, the principal object of the construction of submarines at all, viz., to destroy surface vessels, a larger submarine decidedly has less value than a smaller one, for though her great surface speed will take her more quickly to the scene of action it will not help her when she gets there, while by no possibility can she be so handy in trimming or diving and she is gravely restricted by depths of water and consequently in the areas in which she can work. Without any question she cannot be the equal of two smaller submarines in her capacity for destroying surface vessels, and she cannot work at all in the shallower waters of the North Sea.

Beyond her power to accompany a battle fleet at battle speeds, the only possible justification for her construction is the sometimes erroneously held idea that she might be able to destroy submarines; but if the heavily armed cruiser (as is a fact) cannot do so, of what avail is the attempt to turn the submarine on the surface into one with a very indifferent armament? What, then, is the high speed for? Is it to run away with when on the surface? She can dive and disappear at will, and again speed to escape has already failed in surface ships. How then can it succeed in a submarine? It would almost appear that her size and clumsiness will ruin her splendid inherent qualities as a submarine, and her submarine qualities will undoubtedly ruin her usefulness as a cruiser.

Summing up:–

It is granted that a submarine might achieve a great rôle if able to accompany a battle fleet at battle speeds, but the accomplishment of such a rôle presupposes and requires great size, and this, to contain the necessary speed or any great increase in speed, militates in a much greater proportion against her true metier as a destroyer of surface vessels. It is therefore contended that with or somewhere about a submerged displacement of 800 to 1,000 tons a submarine reaches her maximum size for usefulness for war, and that that usefulness may best be improved not by steam but by the certain future improvement of the internal combustion engine, the carrying of more torpedoes, and continued sea experience to keep the personnel trained to its highest efficiency and endurance. By this it is not intended to condemn any trial of steam; in fact, as before stated, the advance of the internal combustion engine is so slow that it looks as if a temporary era of steam in large submarines may be forced upon us. But it is repeated that steam is still considered to be a retrograde step – a temporary expedient only

– for the ultimate perfection of the submarine is, for maximum efficiency, bound up with the fortunes of the internal combustion engine.

The Submarine and Commerce with some Reflection on our Food Supply in War

It has already been stated and may be accepted as fact that –

(1) There is nothing at present to prevent a hostile submarine proceeding to sea at will;

(2) A submarine of the most modern type has an enormous radius of action – probably 5,000 miles;

(3) There is at present no known means for the discovery of a submarine nor for her destruction if she is found;

(4) It is hoped – but more experience is required concerning this – that the endurance of the personnel may be found to be co-extensive with the fuel capacity.

There is therefore little to prevent, say, the Germans from stationing submarines off our principal commercial ports and indeed on the great trade routes, and most certainly the protection of commerce difficulties become far more acute when the potentialities of submarines as commerce destroyers are considered. But whereas the German ports are few and highly concentrated, ours extend over a great distance and sea area, so that the suggestion that she can occasion equal damage by her submarines to that which we can effect by means of our whole sea power is untenable. No maritime blockade, it is said, would cut Germany off from her external markets or from her sources of external supply. This may possibly be true in a war between Great Britain and Germany alone. But apart from the fact that such a war is mighty improbable, recent investigations tend to show that even in such a war neutral ports and neutral railways could not carry more than a portion of the trade of Bremen and Hamburg. German shipping would be shut up in port or captured; for British shipping to carry German trade, even to and from a neutral port, would be banned as trading with the enemy; and the remaining neutral shipping of the world would probably not suffice to carry more than a small proportion of the German trade which would still require sea transport. Again, if France and Russia were fighting against Germany and prohibiting trade, and if at the same time Austria and Italy were fighting in alliance with Germany, their own oversea trade would be stopped and production would be brought to a standstill; then Germany, for want of raw materials and a market for finished productions, would be in a very tight place indeed.

Now as regards our own position and excluding for the moment the submarine, it may reasonably be said to be fairly secure. By means of elaborate intelligence organisation (which should be rigidly maintained even in time of peace) the distribution of all foreign warships and armed merchant vessels likely to be used against us ought to be accurately known. Under strained relations such vessels certainly will be shadowed, and wireless telegraphy has added enormously to the possibility of concerted movements of our cruisers against such ships. But again we must repeat that most certainly the protection of commerce difficulties become far more acute when the potentialities of submarines as commerce destroyers are considered. Still, when it is remembered that the German seaboard is only about 114 miles and only some 300 miles average distance from our submarine bases, while our seaboard is measured in thousands of miles with numerous well found ports, all of which are over 850 miles from the nearest German submarine base, it must be allowed that there are enormously greater facilities for our trade getting in and out than hers; and, moreover, while the German trade must concentrate on arrival, ours, owing to our numerous ports, can almost equally scatter. However that may be, it is rightly considered that the effect on freight and insurance rates must be very great when once it is realised that the enemy's submarines may be met with off any or all of our great commercial ports. It cannot now be long before this fact will become generally known to the public, and it is therefore very desirable that full consideration should be promptly given to the question of diverting our commerce to our far western ports in war time, and of developing the port and railway facilities of such harbours as Plymouth, Falmouth, the Bristol Channel ports, Fishguard, Holyhead, etc. There is no doubt that if commerce can be diverted in this way, the difficulties in the way of Germany infesting the close approaches to our great commercial ports will be enormously increased.

Again, the question arises as to what a submarine can do against a merchant ship when she has found her. She cannot capture the merchant ship, she has no spare hands to put a prize crew on board, little or nothing would be gained by disabling her engines or propeller, she cannot convoy her into harbour, and, in fact, it is impossible for the submarine to deal with commerce in the light and provisions of accepted international law. Under these circumstances, is it presumed that the hostile submarine will disregard such law and sink any vessel heading for a British commercial port and certainly those who are armed or carrying contraband? If so, our powers of retaliation in the case of Germany would be very great in view of the large number of German merchant ships – probably hundreds – and their crews which, provided we are prompt, might equally be destroyed by us on the outbreak of war, for be it remembered they must pass our bases to get home. The fact remains, however, that there is nothing else the submarine can do except sink her capture, and it must therefore be admitted that (provided it is done and however inhuman and barbarous it may appear) this submarine menace is a truly terrible one for British commerce and Great Britain alike, for no means can be suggested at present of meeting it except by reprisals. All that would be known would be that a certain ship and her crew had disappeared, or that some of her boats would be picked up with a few survivors to tell the tale. Such a tale would fill the world with horror, and is freely acknowledged to be an altogether barbarous method of warfare; but, again, if it is done by the Germans, the only thing would be to make reprisals. The essence of war is violence and moderation in war is imbecility.

It has been suggested that it should be obligatory for a submarine to fire a warning gun, but is such a proceeding practical? We must bear in mind that modern submarines are faster on the surface than the majority of merchantmen, and will not necessarily need to dive at all. Therefore as the submarine would in most cases be sighted, and as she has no prize crew to put on board, the warning gun is useless, as the only thing the submarine could do would be to sink the enemy; also the apparently harmless merchant vessel may be armed, in which case the submarine may but have given herself away if she did not sink her. The subject is, indeed, one that bristles with great difficulties, and it is highly desirable that the conduct of submarines in molesting commerce should be thoroughly considered. Above all, it is one of overwhelming interest to neutrals. One flag is very much like another seen against the light through a periscope, should he have thought it necessary to dive, and the fear is natural that the only thing the officer of the hostile submarine would make sure of would be that the flag seen was not of his own country. Moreover, under numerous circumstances can a submarine allow a merchant ship to pass unmolested? Harmless trader in appearance, in reality she may be one of the numerous fleet auxiliaries, a mine-layer, or carrying troops, and so on. Can the submarine come to the surface to inquire and lose all chance of attack if the vessel should prove to be faster than she is? The apparent merchant ship may also be armed. In this light, indeed, the recent arming of our British merchantmen is unfortunate, for it gives the hostile submarine an excellent excuse (if she needs one) for sinking her; namely, that of self-defence against the guns of the merchant ship. What can be the answer to all the foregoing but that (barbarous and inhuman as, we again repeat, it may appear) if the submarine is used at all against commerce she must sink her captures.

For the prevention of submarines preying on our commerce it is above all necessary that merchant shipping should take every advantage of our favourable geographical position and that the Straits of Dover should be made as difficult as we possibly can. It is not proposed here to enter into the technical details of such arrangements, but even after every conceivable means have been taken it must be conceded that there is at least a chance of submarines passing safely through; while at night, or in thick weather, it is probable that they would not fail to pass in safety. Once through it must further be conceded that no known means exist for their destruction and but very few for their harassment. For if a submarine is hard pressed there is nothing to prevent her retiring to sea for rest and then re-appearing. The guns supplied to submarines are not to fight hostile submarines intentionally. If one tried this game the other would promptly dive and torpedo her. The guns are supplied for sudden surprise against destroyers, torpedo boats, and sea planes or for use in case a submarine is temporarily disabled from diving; and the fact that they are there completes the submarine's equipment as a commerce destroyer if it is desired so to use her. A submarine may of course be momentarily located by shipping or by sea planes, and should the latter continue to improve, we may find here a means of dropping high explosives on the submarine, which has a very vulnerable hull, and so cause destruction; but this means is not here yet, while the location by shipping would almost certainly be unfortunate for the said shipping whether an armed cruiser or the most harmless tramp.

To sum up:–

It is indubitably true that the development of the submarine must prove a terrible menace to British shipping.

Closed waters such as those of the North Sea, Adriatic, &c., must be impassable for commerce – probably neutral or otherwise – in time of war and in the presence of submarines.

Every advantage must be taken by our commerce in war time of our most favourably placed ports as regards the enemy's bases.

Against a seaworthy submarine at present the only possible means of defence is speed and perhaps in the future the seaplane.

If the foregoing is correct it will indeed be well to consider briefly the position of Great Britain as regards food and oil – the latter the life blood of our future warships of all sorts – in time of war.

There would up to the present be found but few to disagree with the famous memorandum of Admiral of the Fleet Sir A K Wilson, V.C., O.M., G.C.B., date November 19th, 1910, which incidentally laid low the invasion bogey, but also (which concerns us here) starts with these pregnant words:–

The really serious danger that this country has to guard against in war is not invasion, but interruption of our trade and destruction of our merchant shipping. The strength of our fleet is determined by what is necessary to protect our trade, and if it is sufficient for that it will be almost necessarily sufficient to prevent invasion, since the same disposition of the ships to a great extent answers both purposes. The main object aimed at by our fleet, whether for the defence of commerce or for any other purpose, is to prevent any ship of the enemy from getting to sea far enough to do any mischief before she is brought to action. Any disposition that is even moderately successful in attaining this object will almost certainly be effective in preventing a large fleet of transports, than which nothing is more vulnerable or more difficult to hide, from reaching our shores.

Now, if we accept, even in the broadest sense, the correctness of what has so far been written with regard to the development and capabilities of the submarine, it is plain that the above quoted memorandum has become startlingly upset and requires re-consideration, but the main thesis that it is not invasion we have to fear but starvation remains correct and may become still more accentuated; for, if the submarines can do what is expected of them, not only can we not prevent them from putting to sea, but, with all the will in the world, we cannot bring them to action. Under any circumstances – that is without the submarine menace – there is always a comparatively short supply of food in this country and consequent danger of a food panic, and this is equally true of oil. If this is so now, what is likely to be the case when hostile submarines can get on the trade routes unseen and untouchable? Whether rightly or not the non-arrival of but a few steamers would undoubtedly then be put down to this reason and cause a very serious rise in prices, and probably the food and oil panic that we fear.

What is the remedy?

Well, in the first place, it is absolutely necessary large quantities of oil should be stored in this country, and secondly that all food traffic coming from the Atlantic must avoid the gradually concentrating approaches to the Straits of Dover and discharge cargo at our western ports. This latter precaution alone would ensure that the hostile submarine – if German – must commence to operate at a distance of nearly 1,000 miles from his base, and although a submarine can do so, yet it remains quite true that it is a very serious disability.

General Reflections and Summary

It is broadly considered that the whole of the foregoing leads irresistibly to the conclusion that, as stated in the opening paragraphs of this paper –

The submarine is the coming type of war vessel for sea fighting.

This is further based on the axioms that the objects of the ideal war vessel are, firstly, to obtain the command of the sea with the purpose of denying an enemy the freedom of the sea for his commerce or for the despatch of his expeditionary forces; and, secondly, that this object is only attained by destruction or removal of the enemy's sea forces. It is confidently claimed that the submarine fulfils both of these objects to the letter because it is the only vessel that can do so and yet remain itself fairly safe.

It is not of course claimed that the submarine is immune from attack. Indeed, despite its advantages, it must be remembered that for all practical purposes while employed on blockade it becomes itself a surface vessel. It has, however, the corresponding advantages of comparative invisibility on the surface and of seeking and obtaining safety at any moment by diving and then it is immune from attack. Further its period under the waves is limited at present to daylight hours; but inasmuch as surface and submerged radii of action are interconvertible, provided a free time on the surface can be obtained for re-charging batteries, this disadvantage is also not so great as might appear. Lastly, there are the limit of endurance of the crew, which is the ever present personal factor, and the limit of size.

Despite all these defects, it must surely be realised that in the submarine we do very nearly attain the ideal war vessel from which battleship, cruiser or merchant vessel can only attain a modified safety by rapid flight. Without such flight (and given sufficient ammunition) it is but a question of time for the submarine to seek out, find and destroy every surface vessel.

Therefore, who can possibly deny that the submarine is the coming type of war vessel for sea fighting and as such should first of all be developed by that power whose Navy is its all in all and whose existence depends on the Navy?

On the other hand, it is cheap and manned with but a few hands and, to use a homely phrase, is within the reach of all. Consequently as the submarine grows and extends its activities, no surface war vessel of any nation can hope to fulfil its present rôle; it will be driven out of existence and submarines alone will take its place. And, moreover, being within the reach of all, sea power or command of the sea by any one nation must inevitably tend to vanish. All that can be said is that the advantage will still remain of geographical position; those countries whose outlets are in narrow waters being at a great disadvantage compared with those whose ports communicate directly with the open sea. Happily for us, Great Britain comes most distinctly within the latter category. Lastly it is believed that these principles are not yet wholly recognised by foreign nations. If we can only clear our minds of previous obsessions and build them largely forthwith we may – as in the case of turbines and the Dreadnought – again lead the way and maintain, for the present or until some antidote appears, the command of the seas and with it the pre-eminence of Great Britain.

It is possible that an antidote may be found, and meanwhile, and in that hope, it is not suggested that no more surface vessels be built, but it must be realised that for the moment an ideal oil engine is the supreme object to be desired for the submarine; the combination of these two can alone provide us with the ideal war vessel.

Note: – Given all we anticipate of the submarine era, by the advantage of our geographical position, we can entirely stop German oversea trade, while she will have difficulty – great difficulty – in making any effective impression on ours. Is not this another reason for retaining Capture of private property at sea? For at first sight we might be inclined to think otherwise. Again, if closed waters will be made impassable, as predicted, can any Power hope to have enough submarines over for effective oceanic operations against the enemy's commerce? For the vision of the submarine is limited. Neither is it safe to go ahead too fast in any dallying with capture at sea while the possibilities of aircraft against submarines are still so uncertain.

Another question: What about powerful neutrals recognising declaration of blockade by submarines only? And yet they would be surface vessels; but would it be regarded as effective, since no one could ever tell whether it was being really maintained or not, as they would be disappearing under water if anyone went to look at them! There is another consideration: Trade routes are not quite high roads, and the range of vision from the deck of a submarine is very limited, so the submarines would only be dangerous to commerce when trade closes in to enter a port or pass a strait, and that is just the position which aircraft are likely to make untenable for submarines.

On the whole, therefore, it is clear that while the development of submarine warfare will render us absolutely safe from oversea attack, it cannot possibly cripple our trade to anything like the extent to which it can be made to cripple that of our enemy.

[97] *Extract from Churchill to Fisher*
[Fisher Papers, FISR 1/14]

1 January 1914

*   *   *

There are a few points on which I am not convinced. Of these the greatest is the question of the use of submarines to sink merchant vessels. I do not believe this would ever be done by a civilised power. If there were a nation vile enough to adopt systematically such methods, it would be justified and indeed necessary, to employ the extreme resources of science against them: to spread pestilence, poison the water of great cities, and, if convenient, proceed by the assassination of individuals.

These are frankly unthinkable propositions and the excellence of your paper is, to some extent, marred by the prominence assigned to them.

*   *   *

[98] *Extract from Captain Sydney Hall to Fisher*
[Fisher Papers, FISR 1/14]

11th December 1913

*   *   *

I hear let on [*sic*] "submarines" was produced at a conference on Tuesday and caused no small commotion! Might I see a copy?

[99] *Minutes of Admiralty Conference on Submarine Policy*
[Keyes Papers, 4/10]

Tuesday, 9 December 1913

<u>Record of Conference held in First Lord's Room on
9th December [1913]</u>

(1) Nomenclature

Commodore (S) was directed to prepare a table dividing submarines built, building, and projected, into classes with regard to the services on which they could be employed.[1] Table of classification is attached. [omitted]

The class of vessel suitable for a blockade of the enemy's coast was discussed, and it appeared to be the general opinion that the Coastal class was designed for this service. Commodore (S) submitted that this was not the case. In February 1912, a committee of submarine officers recommended the construction of two classes:–

Coastal. For service in the coast patrol of our own coasts, to strengthen the existing flotillas and replace ineffective vessels.

Oversea. For service on the enemy's coast and on the High Sea.

To effectively carry out the duties required of the coastal patrol, it was necessary to design a vessel capable of keeping the sea in all weathers for two or three days at a time off our coasts in the North Sea. Such a vessel, given sufficient radius of action, would of course be capable of proceeding to an enemy's coast, but it cannot be said by those with knowledge of the conditions of life on a small submarine at sea that one of 350 ton displacement, carrying a small complement, including only two officers, is a suitable craft to steam 600–700 miles, and keep close watch on the enemy's coast for some days in severe winter weather. He recommended Es and double-hulled Es for this service and work generally which requires keeping the sea for several days.

The First Lord questioned the wisdom of building such expensive vessels as the coastal possessing a range of action of 3000 miles, for defence work on our coast, and suggested that a much smaller and more economical craft might be designed.

Commodore (S) submitted that, situated as we were, it would be false economy and undesirable to build vessels without good sea-going qualities; we already possess 38 Bs and Cs in home waters, whose poor habitability and low buoyancy makes them unfit for surface work in severe weather and some of the duties allocated to the coast patrol flotillas cannot be effectively carried out by these vessels. The committee of submarine officers is strongly of the opinion that all future construction should be on the double-hull principle, and, as we have no experience of this type, it is recommended that a FIAT submarine should be built. There is no smaller submarine built on this principle than the latter, its surface displacement being smaller than that of a B. Vickers and Admiralty constructors, in following the general idea of the FIAT design, produced a somewhat larger vessel, and in the Admiralty coastal it was found possible to carry a stern tube, thereby increasing the

[1] Captain Roger Keyes was still Commodore (S).

armament by 50%. The vessel thus produced, though larger than originally intended by the submarine committee, is considerably smaller and costs less than the D class, possessing the same armament and a large radius of action. The size of the vessel is in no way influenced by the latter, which is due to the double-hull being utilised to carry fuel. It was never contemplated that the coastal would be expected to take the place of the oversea type of which the E class submarines are at present the only satisfactory representatives. Or to be an answer to the German submarines which are all – with the exception of the first 4 vessels – of twice the displacement of our coastals.

Attention was then called to the German programme of construction, and to the fact that they have actually more large submarines built, building and projected, than we have. It was noted that their submarine vote during the last five years amounts to about the same sum as the British – theirs being devoted entirely to the construction of large oversea vessels, whereas ours includes some vessels for the coast patrol.

(2) It is understood that the policy to be worked for is the renewal of the blockade of German ports. The Chief of Staff pointed out that a considerable time must elapse before a sufficient number of submarines can be available for this service.

Commodore (S) submitted that *our* submarines should not be sent *into* the Heligoland Bight – at any rate in the early stages of a war – with the object of keeping a permanent close blockade, until we have many more available. The losses on such service are certain to be heavy, for apart from the risks the submarine would run of being caught on the surface and destroyed by gun-fire between darkness and dawn in hazy weather, they would also run serious risk of running into the enemy's minefields, and of being stalked and torpedoed on the surface by opposing submarines.

(3) and (4). The necessity of providing eventually 4 flotillas, each consisting of 12 oversea submarines, was generally agreed to.

(5) Dealt with in (1) and in the table of classification.

(6) The question was fully discussed. The 2nd Sea Lord was understood to prefer the double-hulled E on the grounds that, *to keep the sea*, a vessel of considerably larger displacement than the coastal would be necessary, an opinion which is certainly shared by all submarine officers.[1] On the other hand it was pointed out that numbers are required and the cost of a coastal is about half that of a double-hulled E. It was noted that, apart from her superior sea-keeping

[1] Vice-Adm. Sir John Jellicoe served as Second Sea Lord from December 1912 to June 1914.

qualities, her armament and its disposition makes the double-hulled E much more formidable offensively than the coastal.

In the end it appeared to be generally accepted that it would be necessary to build both types if more vessels are required for the coast patrol flotillas. Commodore (S) submitted that in order to frame our future building policy, the number of submarines required for the coast patrol flotillas and the duties they would be called upon to perform, should be definitely laid down, the situation being apparently somewhat changed as the result of experience gained during the last two years.

(7) A design for a 24 knot submarine was examined. The DNC expressed great confidence in the design and did not anticipate any great difficulty would be experienced in controlling a vessel of this displacement.[1] He remarked that if it failed as a submarine, it would still be a very formidable surface torpedo craft. In this connection the design was discussed in its relation to the late *Polyphemus*.

The First Lord remarked on the great value of speed in a submarine, in that escorted and scouted for by fast cruisers, she could overtake, work round, and submerge in the path of an enemy fleet.

Commodore (S) submitted that although the control of a such a vessel did not present insurmountable difficulties, it must necessarily be dependent to a great extent on the personal element. A bold advance on our present experience is already being made in the *Nautilus* in regard to size, and in the *Swordfish* in regard to steam propulsion. The proposed vessel is three times the displacement of an E and nearly twice the length. Its higher percentage of buoyancy necessitated the handling of six times the amount of water, and we shall be faced with the shutting down and cooling of a steam plant three times the H.P. of that of the *Swordfish* which itself is an experiment. The submarine officers who would be concerned in the design of the control and the handling of the vessel, consider that it would be advisable to await the trials of *Nautilus* before laying down a vessel of the proposed type.

No serious objection was raised by anyone present to the laying down of one experimental vessel – except that the money might be better spent. The First Lord remarked that we could not afford to delay the laying down of repeat vessels until after the first of a type had been tried. Commodore (S) submitted that in that case it would be advisable to wait until the *Nautilus* had been tried before committing ourselves to the construction of vessels of 24 knots type. It was agreed that the

[1] Sir Eustace Tennyson d'Eyncourt served as Director of Naval Construction from 1912 to 1920.

matter should be further considered towards the end of 1914, with a
view to including the type in the 1914–15 programme.

Experimental Submarines Under Construction

* * *

It was considered that we would be justified in laying down another
Swordfish in the 1914/15 programme, but that Messrs Vickers's
resources would be better employed in building double hull Es than
repetitions of the *Nautilus*.

The Third Sea Lord concurred and remarked that he had included a
Swordfish in the proposed programme.[1]

After a further discussion it was agreed to substitute a double hulled
E for a coastal, and it is understood that the Third Sea Lord's revised
programme was to include:

7 Admiralty Coastals
1 Dockyard double-hull E
2 Vickers double-hull E
1 *Swordfish*

* * *

(10) The Third Sea Lord stated that it was proposed to fit E and later
oversea submarines with a 3-inch Anti-aircraft gun on disappearing
mountings, and the D class, and possibly the coastals with a light gun
which could be brought up the conning tower. Experimental guns are in
the course of construction.

[100] *Memorandum on Submarine Policy circulated by Second Sea
Lord (Sir John Jellicoe)*
[Battenberg Papers, Chartwell Trust, 13/22B]

19 December 1913

First Lord,

The questions discussed at the Conference held in your room on
submarines a few days ago have been much in my mind since the
conference. I feel somewhat uneasy both as regards our submarine
strength as compared with Germany and as regards our future policy of
submarine construction.

[1] Rear Adm. Archibald Moore served as Third Sea Lord from May 1912 to September
1914.

At the moment we appear to require two types of submarines –

The smallest vessel which can carry out the duties of coast patrol in all weathers;

The smallest vessel that can with certainty operate and maintain herself in position off the enemy's ports in all weathers.

For the first duty, that of coastal patrol, it appears to me that we already possess in our B. and C. class submarines in almost, if not quite, sufficient numbers for the work. It is possible that they may not completely fulfil the conditions of being built to operate in all weathers but in view of our deficiencies in the oversea type of submarine, it appears to me that we can for the moment neglect the question of providing further vessels for coastal defence. I understood at the conference that the programme of Admiralty coastal vessels for next year, which has been already arranged, must necessarily be adhered to in order to complete contracts practically entered into but I suggest that when it becomes necessary in future years to add any further to the number of our submarines for coast defence we should provide a smaller type of vessel, one in effect very little larger, if at all larger, than the C class. It appears to me to be wasteful to spend so much as £75,000 on a submarine whose duties are purely coast defence.

* * *

There appeared to be an impression at the conference that the Admiralty coastal type was really capable of oversea work. It is, of course, quite impossible to give absolute positive statements in a matter of this sort when no such vessel is in existence but when one considers the displacement of the Admiralty coastal vessel and the fact that in vessels of this sort and description up to the present nothing but size will give ocean going capabilities, it appears to me that I cannot be far wrong in the opinion which I hold that the Admiralty coastal submarine will certainly not be fit for work oversea in all probable conditions of weather.

We are, of course, at the moment considering Germany alone but I would like to utter a word of caution against designing vessels in any numbers which although they maybe considered fit for North Sea work (which at the moment I dispute) will most certainly not be fit for work in the open sea against, say such an enemy as France. I am fully aware of the fact that for me to suggest the possibility of strained relations with France at the present moment will be considered a foolish proceeding, but it must be remembered that the submarines now being built will be effective for a great many years yet and there may conceivably be a change in our relations with France and Germany during the next decade. I cannot think that even the strongest admirer of the Admiralty coastal type would be prepared to assert that they would be fitted to work, say off Brest, in the winter.

* * *

I have confined my remarks above to the question which is to my mind the most pressing one, namely the necessity for developing, and developing rapidly, a really effective Oversea type of submarine. I look upon it as a matter of the first importance.

[101] *Memorandum by Winston Churchill Circulated to the Board of Admiralty together with Copy of Fisher's 'The Oil Engine and the Submarine'*
[Churchill Papers, Chartwell Trust, 13/22B]

25 December 1914

I am anxious that this most valuable and important paper should receive your earnest consideration. We may reject Lord Fisher's argument about submarines sinking peaceful merchant vessels, and certainly we have no need to construct submarines for attack or defence of commerce. On the other hand, his third classification (p.3.), coast defence, requires to be divided onto two separate branches, viz. The defence of our coasts and the blockade of the enemy's.

I see no reason for departing from the threefold division in my minute of 20 July [see [92] above]. For the ocean class we have building the *Nautilus* and the *Swordfish*. These vessels were not fast enough for the essential function of the ocean submarine, viz. Overtaking the enemy's battle fleet.

We are now at work upon a design which, if it receives board approval, will supply us with ocean submarines of the required speed and sea-going qualities, and if these are to be constructed they must be a substitute for the battleship preponderance and paid for out of the money that would otherwise have gone into battleships. We have another six months at least before a decision is required.

Since the submarine blockade of the German ports is one of the tactical objects we have in view, we must build a suitable class of vessel for that purpose. Since the proposed new programmes, both ordinary and extraordinary were put forward by the Third Sea Lord on [document number] S0367, grave doubts have been thrown upon the value of the Admiralty coastal [F] design for oversea work. On the other hand its cost is more than is needed for the defence of our coasts. I have been very unpleasantly impressed with the relative amounts spent by Great Britain and Germany respectively in the last six programmes on submarines and at the reliance of the Germans on the larger type. I am strongly drawn to the conclusion that we must build out of the ordinary programme of the year as many double-hulled Es as possible, for the present build no more coastals – whether Scotts [S class], Admiralty [F class] or W [class] – beyond what we are already committed to. The type on which we must now concentrate is a vessel big enough to maintain itself effectively on the German coasts and yet small enough to dive in German coastal waters. I assume the double-hulled E is the best design we have at present for this purpose. If time permits, however, the design should be reviewed so as to make it embody all the best features. For the present we must rate as oversea boats the following:

5 Es in commission, 13 Es building, 7 Ds in commission, 1 Admiralty coastal building, 4 Vickers coastals building – and all further double-hulled Es as they arrive.

Total overseas submarines built and building – 30. When sufficient new double-hulled Es arrive, the less suitable vessels can be relegated to the lower class. At present they are required for the blockade service and we must make the best of them.

All the rest, built and building, are required for the defence of the coasts viz. 45 vessels and 9 abroad. As the overseas need must be satisfied first, there is no immediate prospect of increasing these numbers out of the ordinary programme of 1914/15 and 1915/16.

*　*　*

Action:–

Classify the built and building submarines on the above lines.

Cease to call the 1 Admiralty and 4 Vickers coastals by the name coastal. Let them be treated as oversea boats and choose some letter which will distinguish them.

Recast the ordinary programme of 1914/15 so as to provide for the maximum number of double-hulled E's, and eliminate the new [steam fleet submarine] Swordfish (if still included) and as many of the seven Admiralty coastals as possible without breaching contracts.

Review searchingly the design of the double-hulled E's in relation to the precise tactical object for which it is to be constructed, and secondly with regard to all the improvements introduced into the Admiralty so-called coastals.

Design the best submarines for the coast defence work that can be built at a cost not exceeding £50,000.

Let everything necessary be done to enable these proposals to be carried into effect without delay. The final decision regarding placing of contracts will not, however, be taken until a conference has been held in the third week of January between myself and the 1st, 2nd, 3rd and 4th Sea Lords, members of the Board only being present.

The Third Sea Lord should also have his proposals for an extraordinary substitution programme, as verbally discussed at our last meeting, in an advanced state of readiness.

[102] *Extracts from Minutes by Winston Churchill*
[First Lord's Minutes, 3rd series, vol. 2]

14 January 1914.

Third Sea Lord.

Please recast the new [construction] programme for 1914/15 as follows:

2 repeat *Royal Sovereigns* to be completed by end of January 1916
1 Portsmouth *Queen Elizabeth*
1 Plymouth *Royal Sovereign*
Drop the torpedo-boats altogether
Drop Two light cruisers

22 January 1914

Third Sea Lord

What will be the latest dates at which fourteen submarines substituted for the fourth or Plymouth battleship would have to be begun, in order that the whole batch might be ready by June 1917, i.e. the date when this ship is required? Having fixed those dates, please distribute the costings among the financial years affected. Submarines build quicker than battleships, and the date of the completion is the governing factor.

[103] *Memorandum by Commodore (S) on Difficulties in Building*
Additional Submarines
[Keyes Mss 4/1]

CP.01202
February 1914

The inability of Messrs. Vickers to complete the submarines they are building for us within several months of the contract dates, their position in regard to the competition of other British firms, and the situation generally at their submarine works at Barrow-in-Furness were very clearly stated last September in the various remarks on G.P.43753/13.

2. The situation has not improved, and in the light of the recent decision in regard to the 1914–1915 submarine programme, has in fact been seriously aggravated, since in all probability Messrs. Vickers will before long be building four or six E class submarines for Greece.

3. Had the Admiralty order for 1914–1915 been limited, as was apparently originally intended, to two improved E class, no exception could be taken to their building later on for Greece, or any other country within certain limitations, for the importance of keeping Messrs. Vickers's submarine personnel and plant employed is fully realised, and it is obvious that the very extensive plant they have been forced to install in order to carry out the existing Admiralty contracts would have been before long very inadequately employed without foreign orders.

4. In view of the following points, however:–

(a) The progress of German submarine construction.

(b) The very limited field of production in Great Britain.

(c) The fact that construction is certain to be very slow in the case of firms building submarines for the first time.

(d) The limited supply of skilled workers, foremen and overseers experienced in submarine construction – an argument which was recently very forcibly used by Messrs. Vickers to prove that the introduction of other firms into the field would reflect on their output, since rivals were already bribing their men away.[1]

(e) The recent decision to devote nearly the whole of the sum allocated to new submarine construction in 1914–1915 to the laying down of improved E's, the majority of which must necessarily be built by Messrs. Vickers.

[1] One of the most notable pre-war submarine designers to be lured away from Vickers (to Messrs. White of Cowes) was Barnes Wallis, inventor of the legendary bouncing bomb used by 617 Squadron in 1943 to attack the Ruhr dams. See: J.E. Morpurgo, *Barnes Wallis – a Biography* (Penguin Books, 1973) p.76.

It is submitted that the firm's capacity for output should be very seriously considered in relation to our requirements, before any concession is made.

5. Messrs. Vickers' pretentious estimates cannot be accepted. The administration of the firm suffers from a most persistent and apparently incurable optimism, as their letters to the Admiralty during recent years amply prove.

6. It is not necessary to go further back than the firm's letter of the 22nd November 1913, in G.P.01439/13 herewith, (it is noted that the paper was apparently withdrawn during circulation after being minuted by E-in-C., 5 December [19]13). In this letter Messrs. Vickers make very definite statements and give an estimate of production based on the dates on which they propose to deliver the submarines under construction. The reliability of the estimate can be gauged by comparing the dates given in the table showing the capacity for output of submarines, with those given by Admiralty and Submarine Officers who have recently visited the works.

7. Submarine AE2,[1] shown as to be delivered in January, cannot possibly be ready before the third week in February. There is no prospect whatever of getting E3, shown as to be delivered in February, in the present financial year. E18 and V4 which are shown as to be delivered in May and June 1915 respectively are not yet laid down, and there is not the remotest chance of these dates being kept. The dates given for intermediate boats are equally premature, in spite of these being from 9 to 12 months behind the actual contract date of completion.

8. It is almost incredible that these very erroneous dates should have been put forward seriously as recently as the 22nd November last. The firm cannot possibly attribute these delays to alterations ordered by the Admiralty during construction, unexpected labour troubles, or indeed to anything except inability to correctly estimate their capacity for output.

9. There happens to be another paper in circulation, G.P.0785/13, covering a letter of Messrs. Vickers dated 30 August last, in which after having carefully considered the whole question of delivery, they state that AE1, which is not yet delivered, will be delivered at the end of October, and A.E.2 in November. After remarking that the contract dates for the completion of these two vessels are December 1912 and January 1913 respectively, it is considered that sufficient has been said

[1] AE1 and AE2: E class (type 1) submarines built for the Royal Australian Navy and laid down in 1911.

to show that no reliance whatever can be placed in Messrs. Vickers' estimates of output. They appear to be prepared to accept orders, British and foreign, out of all proportion to their capacity to carry them out, and if they are permitted to do so, we are bound to suffer, whether the vessels are built at Barrow or elsewhere.

10. It is considered that the Admiralty position in regard to broadside torpedo tubes should be very definitely stated and accepted by Messrs. Vickers before any further concessions are made to them.

11. It is understood that in the interests of general policy it is very desirable that the submarines, which Greece is proposing to order, should be built in England, and it is noted that Messrs. Vickers have been given permission – to build six vessels to the original E class design, except in regard to the broadside tubes which should be to our own design – S.0615/13/25958 of 19th December 1913. This would appear to be an admission that we recognise Messrs. Vickers' right to manufacture and sell broadside tubes for submarines.

12. It is quite understood that a special concession is being made to Greece, and that Their Lordships have decided to give them the benefit of our submarine experience. The value of this concession does not lie in the design of the submarine, which, as a submersible, compares very unfavourably with contemporary foreign vessels. It is entirely a question of the broadside tube which, rightly or wrongly, we consider infinitely superior to the system of using angle gyro torpedoes adopted by foreign nations.

13. It is considered that there can be no question of a Vickers design of broadside tube for submarines. It is an Admiralty secret, with the discovery of which Messrs. Vickers have in no way been associated. It is true that they are manufacturing broadside tubes for the *Nautilus*, and that in some small details the arrangements differ from those manufactured in the dockyards. The modifications are simply the result of suggestions made by Admiralty and submarine officers, based on experience in the E class.

14. Messrs. Vickers have been in no way connected with the introduction or development of these tubes, and are in no position to manufacture broadside tubes which are not a copy of ours in all essential details.

15. It is believed to be generally known abroad that our later vessels are fitted with internal broadside tubes, and there can be no doubt that other nations are experimenting in this direction, and will eventually arrive at a satisfactory solution. Until we are satisfied that this is the case, it is considered that under no circumstances whatever should Messrs. Vickers be permitted to build submarines with broadside

tubes, or to supply such tubes without the permission of the Admiralty.

16. It is not known whether Messrs. Vickers have yet replied to the letters, draft copy of which was seen in G.P.1430/12, with reference to the Vickers patents in connection with recent improvements to the Diesel engines of submarines, but it is considered that no concession should be made to the firm until the matter is satisfactorily settled.

[104] *Captain Sydney Hall to Fisher*
[Fisher Papers, FISR 1/14]

17 February 1914

There is a matter I have wanted to tell you about in connection with submarine policy, which I think important and in case you are discussing submarine matters this is a good opportunity for me to refer to it again for I have before told you about it when you were First Sea Lord and you fully approved –

It is in no way meant as an attack upon present administration, though it is in opposition to it. When Keyes has asked my opinion, I have always given it, he knows my views but does not agree with them. This is briefly what I think so important and in danger of being overlooked.

There is in submarine work both in design and in their management a strong tendency to attach a great deal of importance to 'materiel', it is particularly evident in younger officers of average capacity or below it and in those who do not have to look outside any one submarine or flotilla or submarines. A constant stream of ideas and inventions and improvements in design continuously pours in from the submarine service itself and from outside, which, unless steadily resisted involves constant alterations, tests and trials which are a waste of money and time and in my opinion detract from war efficiency – principally for the following reasons:–

There is no vessel in which the efficiency of the personnel, particularly the officers, bears such a very large proportion to the total efficiency, as a submarine.

In a battleship for example the Captain may not be absolutely first-class, but a brilliant admiral in a fleet action to lead him or a very capable navigator, good gunlayers, or an indifferent enemy may enable his ship to succeed. None of these factors are present in submarine command, no one can help or advise him, concerted action under water seems impossible, once a submarine has dived it becomes absolutely a one man show. The capability of the officers is all important, it is difficult to over state it. I have always said that 2 or 3 knots gain of speed, or any other considerable advance in materiel is not commensurate with the state of the captain's digestion – again, it seems to be that in war the unexpected is to be looked for, and that the submarine service should be prepared to be thoroughly shuffled – without dislocation of materiel – and that though a complication of types may be on many grounds a good thing, it is in a submarine service of far more effect than in surface ships in its ultimate result on war efficiency.

A surface ship of different type carries the bulk of her spares, a submarine does not. The introduction of a new type of submarine provokes tests and comparisons which cause numbers of peoples' heads to be buried in the sands of details and machinery which as I say are really unimportant.

Suppose for example the FIAT submarine building proves to be superior to our C Class. Are we any better for it? No, she will be put into a flotilla and if much superior will cause the officers in other submarines to crab their own, to attribute their own mistakes to defects in their vessels. She will require a whole set of different spare parts and should she become detached to another flotilla, in the shuffle of the unexpected, would become useless.

Submarine design should of course be improved from time to time, but the alteration should be a large one and as many possible of one type should be constructed, also departure from a size and type should not be made unless the advance is a great one and shown to be urgently required.

It is curious that my successor, though not a 'specialist', should have introduced into our submarine service what appears to me to be a regime of materiel policy.

I do not know how far he has been a free agent, but I notice in Mr Churchill's reply in the House about A7 that an 'advisory committee' has been established behind which Keyes seems to shelter. Now this complication of types is just what I would expect of such a committee. They are young officers not in a position to judge of the ultimate effect of their recommendations and just the people likely to be influenced by the advertising quacks of rival types of submarines. Whatever may be the cause, the fact remains that there seems to be eight different types of submarines under the construction as follows:–

Vickers coastal	(1)
(improved coastal same as Admiralty coastal?)	(2)
E design	(3)

improved E design   (4)
Vickers *Nautilus*   (5)
Armstrong W design   (6)
Scott's FIAT   (7)
Scott's *Swordfish* (steam)   (8)

(1) (2) & (7) are about same size (coastal)
(3) & (4) are about same size (oversea)
(6) is neither coastal nor oversea
(5) & (8) are experimental oversea about same size

You may remember that there were various types of submarines pushed at me, not only submarines but engines, batteries and all parts of submarines which I resisted with all my powers because they really do not matter. To repeat, given a reliable strong vessel and interchangeability as far as possible the all important element is personnel, in so far as introduction of new types affects or engrosses the attention of personnel, or introduces complications in stores and spare parts, it is strongly to be deprecated in itself apart from the fact that for the same money another homogenous and well tried unit might have been added to the fleet.

Naturally I take the strongest interest in the submarine service. It may be that I overestimate the effects of the change in policy inaugurated but there is no harm in my telling you this privately as you meet influential people and some of these considerations may not have occurred to them. No doubt you have noticed too, that when some officers do not succeed in existing conditions they attack or question the capabilities of those who do under conditions which do not exist. Some low fellow snarls at you in last week's *N[aval] &M[ilitary] Record* in this way[;] unable to criticise successfully your peace administration, he says 'Ah! If we had gone to war then you would have seen what I and Colomb and Freemantle would have done'. I would refuse to call anyone a great tactician or strategist until war had proved him, but there is a large following of those who cheerfully dub the peace failures as great military commanders. If a man is good at one thing I usually find he is good at another.

Keyes in writing me says the submarine service should be commanded by a senior captain who is recognised by the service as a great military commander and regrets in this connection that my last ship had the reputation of avoiding rather than confronting with the customs and traditions of the service. Well, I respect these customs and traditions only in so far as they seem to me to be applicable to modern conditions but in the main I look upon them as a sign of mental laziness on the part of those in command. There is also the 'inside of the cup' as well as the outside and I am satisfied, in fact we proved it, that I had the men with the officers and myself to a man when they were really wanted. Though I did not spend hours and hours cleaning wood and bright work, I did not scrub decks at 4.30 am at sea in the dark and I did not allow inspections on Sundays and c and c!

I hope Mr Churchill may remain long, I admire his disregard of tradition, because it is tradition and I believe his progressive spirit will do much to improve matters. It is surprising the hostility one meets if one dares to do anything new. It was said openly at C-in-C's table that *Diana* was to be shaken up, (owing to mere rumour) after a 3 days inspection more rigid than anyone had seen. He admitted that rumour had been false. My inspection report could not be bettered, but it did not kill the rumour. I was still a pirate: while they cleaned bright work my petty officers sailed boats without rudders.

In case you are not in town again I will take this opportunity of saying goodbye again with very great regret and renewed thanks for the opportunities of learning many things that I have had with you. I would like to be away most days now shifting my family to my own place at Alverstoke, in readiness for this War Course on Monday week, but I will see to what little remains to be done of course and can get up at any time should you require me.

[105] *Fisher to H.H. Asquith*
[Churchill Papers, Chartwell Trust, 2/92]

15 May 1914

I regret I am unavoidably prevented attending the meeting of the CID to which you have summoned me on Thursday, May 14th 1914, to consider (amongst others) the above three subjects and I venture to write you my views thereon:–

* * *

III Insurance of British Shipping in Time of War.

I submit to you a memorandum I have drawn up on the submarine question. I have already given a copy of it to the First Lord of the Admiralty.[1] In my opinion the statements therein contained are irrefutable and they have a momentous bearing on the question of insurance of British shipping in time of war.

[1] See [96] above.

I venture to ask your earnest attention thereto:–

Those who lecture on international law say the civilised world would hold up its hands in horror at such acts of barbarism as a submarine sinking its prey, but yet an enemy can lay mines without outraging propriety! After all, submarines can exercise discretion – mines can't!

It is patent to all that the operation of visit is attended with grave risk now-a-days. A few worthless tramp steamers sent out accompanied by one or two submarines thus! Up comes the cruiser to visit the tramps, and the submarine would give the *coup de grace* to the cruiser – therefore when declaring a blockade it will have to be stated that owing to the dangers now attending the process of *visit and search* no passes will be issued, and that any vessel breaking blockade inwards or outwards will be sunk.

[106] *Fisher to Jellicoe*
[A. Marder, *Fear God and Dread Nought*, vol. 2, pp.507–8]

Langham House
25th May 1914

We look forward to your coming down next Sunday, May 31, with Lady Jellicoe and the children. (I will play with them while you play tennis, as I am getting an expert now, having the McKenna children often here!!!)

I have burnt your letter, and its contents I will keep sacredly secret. Winston distinctly and decidedly told me on Thursday last that he was very soon going to announce your succeeding Callaghan and Callaghan going to Portsmouth.[1] He discussed about Callaghan succeeding you, but said that Callaghan wanted Portsmouth. Also he spoke of Hamilton[2] and Warrender[3] and Jerram.[4] At the moment (*and remembering what you had said to me*) I said that at the moment Hamilton (barring his very close association with the clique that now surrounds the King) seemed the best man.

[1] Jellicoe was scheduled to replace Sir George Callaghan as C-in-C in December 1914, after Sir George Warrender's appointment as commander of the 1st Battle Squadron came to an end. The reason for the delay was that Warrender was senior to Jellicoe on the flag list.

[2] Vice-Adm. Sir Frederick Tower Hamilton, Second Sea Lord 1914–16. A favourite of King George V, Hamilton reputedly owed his advancement in the service to the influence of his sister who had been King Edward VII's mistress.

[3] Vice-Adm. Sir George Warrender, Commanding First Battle Squadron, 1912–16 [1914?].

[4] Vice-Adm. Sir Martyn Jerram, C-in-C of the China Squadron, 1913–15.

Now the next thing is very private. He said Battenberg was in favour of substituting submarines for a battleship, but that you were against it.[1] It so happened that I summarised to him the very reasons you give in your letter to me:

(1) It would be fatal to Borden;[2]

(2) It would shatter the battleship standard of strength;

(3) Could the submarines be built?

Nevertheless, since I saw you last I have been hearing still further of the great efforts that Tirpitz is making SURREPTITIOUSLY to increase their submarine strength, and SO AT ANY COST I myself say: 'For God's sake, do get on SOMEHOW with building more submarines at once, *no matter what drawbacks'* ...

Old Yarrow motored 80 miles to see me on Saturday and he talked to me of our sad case in submarine building.[3] There not a single foreign order for a submarine in England, and the story is that Vickers will soon be discharging submarine workmen for want of orders (you can verify this by asking Trevor Dawson!)[4] and all this time every foreign establishment is chock-full of submarine orders: Fiume, Germany, and Scandinavian and French builders! It's the very first time in our naval history that we have not had foreign orders for every type of warship! The Greek order that Vickers did get was cancelled! WHY?[5]

PS. The Prime Minister has asked me to dine with him, but I've declined. I let fly at him about submarines, and he is evidently *greatly moved! but he entreated me to say nothing!* Burn this.

---

[1] Battenberg succeeded Bridgeman as First Sea Lord in December 1912 and served until replaced by Fisher at the end of October 1914.

[2] Robert Borden: Prime Minister of Canada, 1913–20. Borden was trying to pass a Naval Aid Bill through the Dominion House of Commons that would provide for the construction of three dreadnoughts. The plan called for these to be loaned to the Royal Navy until Canada was ready to maintain two independent fleet units.

[3] Albert Yarrow: Chairman of Yarrow Shipbuilding, Clydeside.

[4] Sir Trevor Dawson Managing Director of Vickers, Sons & Maxim Ltd.

[5] The Admiralty, as joint patent holder, refused Vickers permission to build E-class submarines for Greece.

[107] *Editorial by the Editor of* The Times *discussing Letter received*
from Admiral Sir Percy Scott[1]

[*The Times*]

Friday, 5 June 1914

THE SUBMARINE MENACE

*   *   *

SIR PERCY SCOTT'S VIEWS

*   *   *

USELESSNESS OF GREAT BATTLESHIPS

*   *   *

FUTURE NAVAL WARFARE

But the strength of navies cannot be reckoned only in Dreadnoughts,
and the day may come when it may not be reckoned in Dreadnoughts at
all. – Mr. Churchill, March 26, 1913.
The whole system of naval architecture and the methods of computing
naval strengths are brought under review by the ever-growing power,
radius and seaworthiness of the submarine and by the increasing range
and accuracy of its fatal torpedoes. – Mr. Churchill, March 17, 1914.

The communication which we print below must attract general
attention both at home and abroad, alike from the personality of the
distinguished writer and the cardinal importance of his subject. Admiral
Sir Percy Scott is a naval officer who has not only shown himself on
several occasions able to think ahead of his contemporaries, but has
made good his prophecies. To him we owed the presence of the naval
guns at Ladysmith which saved the situation, if not South Africa. He it
was who made possible the advance in marksmanship with heavy guns
which has been such an important feature in naval efficiency of late

---

[1] Rear Adm. Sir Percy Scott: leading expert on naval gunnery. Since retiring from the
service in 1911, Scott had been perfecting his 'Director' system for the control of heavy
naval ordnance.

years. To him, too, it is due that the Navy recently was provided with a director which has enormously increased the possibilities of hitting at long ranges and enabled broadside salvo firing to be carried out with a precision before unknown.

Sir Percy Scott now tells us that everything he has done to enhance the value of the gun is rendered useless by the advent of the submarine, a vessel which has for its principal weapon the torpedo. Battleships, and indeed all vessels which have not the quality of submersion, are to become obsolete. Dreadnoughts and super-Dreadnoughts are doomed, because they can no longer be safe from the submarine at sea nor find security in harbour. On the ocean, as in narrow waters, they are at the mercy of the submersible torpedo carrier.

Sir Percy Scott goes still further in his forecast of the future, for, assuming that submarine cannot fight submarine, he sees the end of sea warfare altogether. Neither number nor skill are to avail. Nothing will live afloat, for, if opposed nations have provided themselves with a sufficiency of submarines, they can destroy everything which cannot hide from these vessels below the surface. The position apparently will become one of the greatest disadvantage to the nation which depends for its existence upon water-borne supplies. Indeed, the only obvious benefit which these islands will derive from the change is the removal of all fear of invasion, seeing that, if battleships and cruisers cannot cross submarine-infested waters, neither, of course, can transports.

Sir Percy Scott brings the very serious charge against those in authority of wasting the nation's money on ships that will be unable to fight. It is for them, he suggests, to defend that policy by explaining what part the battleship will play in war, how she can be made safe from destruction by the submarine at sea or in port, and how her situation is to be kept secret from aircraft. Instead of battleships, he would have the money voted for their construction spent on building more submarines and seaplanes.

The questions thus raised by Sir Percy Scott are not, of course, new. They have, as our columns have testified for some time past, much exercised naval thought. They are directly concerned with the problem of warship design, which, as our readers will remember, formed the subject of a series of articles, published last October, by an exceptionally well-informed correspondent. He wrote: There has never been a time when the application of scientific methods to the elucidation of naval questions was so imperatively demanded as the present day. Last year also another writer in these columns pointed out that a big ship's guns were admittedly an insufficient protection against the use of the torpedo, and that, now the seaplane had given eyes to the submarine, the latter bade fair to exert a supreme influence upon the volume and flow of water-borne commerce within the area of disturbance caused by a war. This aspect, he said, demanded the attention of merchants and shipowners, and of many others not professionally interested in naval affairs.

The following is the text of Sir Percy Scott's communication:–

LARGE SHIPS OR SMALL?

*　*　*

THE NEEDS OF GREAT BRITAIN AT SEA
TO THE EDITOR OF THE TIMES

Sir, – Although I have retired from his Majesty's Navy, many people have written, and are still writing, to me as to whether we should build small battleships or large. My opinion is that we should not be building either. My reasons for holding this opinion will be found in a letter I wrote some time ago, and a copy of which I enclose herewith.

I am yours truly,
Percy Scott

52, South Audley Street,
Grosvenor Square, W.
15 December 1913

Dear Sir, – In reply to your letter I have seen the correspondence in the Press, suggesting building smaller battleships, and also, the arguments as to whether two or four battleships should be laid down in 1914.

If we have battleships we must have thick armour on them to keep out the enemy's shot, and we must have speed to give a tactical advantage in bringing our fire on the enemy; these are axioms among naval officers. For battleships our nation and all other nations have very properly decided to have big ships, big guns, thick armour, and high speed.

The other question is, are we in 1914 to build two or four battleships? The Little Navyites say two in order to save money; the Big Navyites say four to, as they think, save the country. If battleships are of use in saving the country, the Little Navyites are foolish and unpatriotic. If battleships are of no use, then the Big Navyites are wrong in putting the country to the expense of building four more; the real question to settle before talking about building more battleships is, *Are they of use or are they not?* For some thousands of years, armed vessels floating on the surface of the water have been used for attack and defence; these vessels to-day vary in size from a canoe containing one man armed with a spear, to a 32,000-ton battleship armed with 15-in. guns, and these craft, whether large or small, all float on the water and are visible. In this island, we depend upon our food supply coming from over seas; hence it has been necessary for us to have a large number of armed ships to protect our commerce and safeguard our food supply. This protecting force or insurance of our country is called the Royal Navy, and to-day consists of a large number of ships that swim on the water and can be seen, and a few that swim under the water and cannot be seen.

The introduction of the vessels that swim under water has, in my opinion, entirely done away with the utility of the ships that swim on the top of the water.

The functions of the vessel of war were:

Defensively,
1. To attack ships that come to bombard our ports.
2. To attack ships that come to blockade us.
3. To attack ships convoying a landing party.
4. To attack our enemy's fleet.
5. To attack ships interfering with our commerce.

Offensively,
1. To bombard an enemy's port.
2. To blockade an enemy.
3. To convoy a landing party.
4. To attack an enemy's fleet.
5. To attack the enemy's commerce.

The submarine renders 1, 2, and 3 impossible, as no man-of-war will dare to come even within sight of a coast that is adequately protected by submarines; therefore, the functions of a battleship as regards 1, 2, and 3, both defensively and offensively, have disappeared.

The fourth function of a battleship is to attack an enemy's fleet, but there will be no fleet to attack, as it will not be safe for a fleet to put to sea. This has been demonstrated in all recent manoeuvres both at home and abroad where submarines have been employed, and the demonstration should have made us realize that, now that submarines have come in, battleships are no use either for defensive or offensive purposes, and, consequently, building any more in 1914 will be a misuse of money subscribed by the citizens for the defence of the Empire.

As regards the protection of our commerce on the high seas, we must examine who can interfere with it. Turkey, Greece, Austria, and Italy must pass through the narrow Straits of Gibraltar to get at our commerce. Cyprus, Malta, and Gibraltar, well-equipped with aeroplanes to observe the enemy's movements, and submarines to attack him, would make egress from the Mediterranean very difficult. Spain and Portugal have ports open to the Atlantic, and could interfere with our commerce, but war with those countries seems very improbable, and they are not very far from Gibraltar. France from Brest could harass our commerce, but if homeward-bound ships gave that port a wide berth and signalled by wireless if they were attacked, fast cruisers and submarines from Plymouth could be very soon on the spot. Russia and Germany are very badly placed for interfering with our commerce; to get to the Atlantic, they must either run through the gauntlet of the Channel, or pass to the North of Scotland, and even if they get out they have nowhere to coal. America could attack our commerce, but they would have a long way to come.

If by submarines we close egress from the North Sea and Mediterranean, it is difficult to see how our commerce can be much interfered with. It has been suggested to me that submarines and aeroplanes could not stop egress from the Mediterranean, that a fleet would steam through at night. With aeroplanes that would report the approach of a fleet, and 30 or 40 invisible submarines in the narrow Strait of Gibraltar, trying to pass through them at night would be a very risky operation.

Submarines and aeroplanes have entirely revolutionised naval warfare, no fleet can hide itself from the aeroplane eye, and the submarine can deliver a deadly attack even in broad daylight. Under these circumstances I can see no use for battleships and very little chance of much employment for the fast cruisers. The Navy will be entirely changed; naval officers will no longer live on the sea, but either above it or under it, and the strain on their system and nerves will be so great that a very lengthy period of service will not be advisable; it will be a Navy of youth, for we shall require nothing but boldness and daring.

In war time the scouting aeroplanes will always be high above on the look-out, and the submarines in constant readiness, as are the engines at a fire station. If an enemy is sighted, the gong sounds and the leash of a flotilla of submarines will be slipped. Whether it be night or day, fine or rough, they must go out to search for their quarry: if they find her, she is doomed, and they give no quarter; they cannot board her and take her as a prize, as in the olden days; they only wait till she sinks, then return home without even knowing the number of human beings that they have sent to the bottom of the ocean.

Will any battleship expose herself to such a dead certainty of destruction? I say, No.

Not only is the open sea unsafe; a battleship is not immune from attack even in a closed harbour, for the so-called protecting boom at the entrance can easily be blown up. With a flotilla of submarines commanded by dashing young officers, of whom we have plenty, I would undertake to get through any boom into any harbour, and sink or materially damage all the ships in that harbour.

If a battleship is not safe either on the high seas or in harbour, what is the use of a battleship? It has been argued to me that if a foreign Power destroys our submarines we are at the mercy of his Dreadnoughts. There can be no doubt about the accuracy of this statement, but submarines are difficult to destroy, because it is difficult to attack what you cannot see. A Power that sends out ships to look for and destroy submarines will be courting disaster; the submarine when in the water must be kept away from, not looked for. Submarines will be hauled up on land, with arrangements for instantly launching them when required; they can only be attacked by airships dropping bombs on them.

What we require is an enormous fleet of submarines, airships, and aeroplanes, and a few fast cruisers, provided we can find a place to keep them in safety in war time. It has been argued to me that our enemy will seize some island in the Atlantic, get some fast cruisers there, with plenty of coal, and from this island prey on our commerce. This is ridiculous; the moment we hear of it we send a flotilla of submarines towed by an Atlantic liner, she drops them just when in sight of the island, and she brings them back to England when they have sunk everything they found at the island.

If we go to war with a country that is within the striking distance of submarines, I am of opinion that the country will at once lock up their Dreadnoughts in some safe harbour; we shall do the same; their aeroplanes and airships will fly over our country; they will know exactly where our ships are, and their submarines will come over and destroy anything and everything that they can get at.

We shall of course, do the same, but an island with many harbours and much shipping is at a great disadvantage, if the enemy has submarines.

I do not think that the importance of submarines has been fully recognised, neither do I think that it has been realised how completely their advent has revolutionised naval warfare. In my opinion, as the motor-vehicle has driven the horse from the road, so has the submarine driven the battleship from the sea.

I, am, yours truly,

Percy Scott

[108] *Extract from Fisher to Julian Corbett*
[A. Marder, *Fear God and Dread Nought*, vol. 2, pp. 507–8]
2 June 1914

*   *   *

I didn't say one single thing that I wanted to say to you yesterday. I was a fool to suggest Sunday, because always a flock of people come that day. I specially wanted to go into details over a conversation three days ago with Winston Churchill as to Percy Scott's effusion. He [was] angry, but I told him Providence had come along and helped England as usual. The effect of Percy Scott's diatribe has been to besmirch unjustly the submarine, hence Austria and Italy will continue to dig out vigorously to build Dreadnoughts against each other, and the Grand-Admiral Koster, the head of the German Navy League, will carry his point for 2 extra Dreadnoughts, so the Triple Alliance will lavish their money on vessels that will be securely blockaded by our submarines, as the Mediterranean and North Sea will be securely locked up. Blockade, as you have yourself so frequently emphasised, is the key of sea war!

*   *   *

[109] *Churchill to Battenberg*[1]
[Masterton-Smith Papers, CAB 1/34]

12 July 1914

I am sending you today a minute wh[ich] raises in the regular form the question of the changes in the new construction programme wh[ich] we have been so long examining and discussing. I am convinced that the time has come for action on these lines and although the steps are serious I do not feel any anxiety about taking them. They will add greatly to the war power of the Fleet and bring credit to all associated with them. It is my earnest hope that we shall be able to reach a full agreement upon them when they come before the Board.

[Attached Minute]
Secretary.
First Sea Lord.
As a result of our conversations, the following changes appear desirable in the new construction programme, 1914–15, as presented to Parliament:–
Substitute 15 improved E submarines for one *Resistance.*
Substitute 6 torpedo cruisers, *Polyphemus* class, for one *Agincourt.*
Substitute 4 *Calliopes* for 10 t.b. destroyers.
As an alternative to (3), Third Sea Lord suggests –
Substitute 4 extra flotilla leaders and 4 more improved Es for 10 t.b. destroyers.
The effects on requirements of men and money are shown in the attached tables.
Against a saving on Votes 8 & 9, the increased cost of personnel and maintenance must be partially set off. A note is added on the immediate extensions which will be required at the torpedo factory. Parliament would be informed early in the New Year.
The whole question must be brought before the Board at an early date.

[1] Adm. Prince Louis of Battenberg: First Sea Lord (1912–14). See also Churchill to Battenberg, 11 July 1914, reproduced in Randolph Churchill, *Winston S. Churchill: Companion Volume 2, part 3* (Heinemann: London, 1969) pp.1986–7.

[110] *Winston Churchill to Lewis Harcourt*
[Masterton-Smith Papers, CAB 1/34]
SECRET

13 July 1914

In March last I wrote the personal and private letter to Mr. Borden which I now send you. I have since received from him the enclosed telegram in reply. [Neither reproduced] Decisions have to be taken in the near future by the Admiralty in regard to the substitution of submarines and other vessels for a portion of the battleship programme of the present year. The movement of naval events and of opinion also affects the character of the advice we should give to the Canadian Government, should they be disposed to renew their Bill next year for a gift of 3 capital ships. The recent discussions which have followed upon Sir Percy Scott's indiscretion in the press have undoubtedly unsettled the basis of the arguments and advice which the Admiralty two years ago offered to Canada.

We have every reason to believe that a variation upon the original proposal of three capital ships would be acceptable and convenient to the Canadian Government. There are several alternatives which might be proposed and before the Admiralty commit themselves to any formal modifications of their previous advice, full and frank discussion with Mr. Borden is necessary so that we know exactly which alternative would be most likely to be acceptable to the Canadian Government. We therefore think it necessary that an officer fully acquainted with the naval situation in all its bearings and with Admiralty policy should go to Canada, preferably in the early part of September, and ascertain by confidential discussion with Mr. Borden what plan would be the best for him and us. Sir John Jellicoe leaves the Board of Admiralty on the 1st September next prior to becoming Commander-in-Chief of the Home Fleets in December of the present year, and no emissary could be more competent or more suitable. He would go at the invitation of the Canadian Government to consult with them on the new facts which have arisen in regard to their Emergency Naval Bill and of course his advice and experience would be at their disposal in any questions affecting their permanent policy which they might wish to discuss with him.

Mr. Perly,[1] with whom I have talked, is also strongly in favour of the plan. Whether for the purpose of a Canadian General Election, which must largely turn on the naval question, or failing a General election for

___

[1] Mr Perly: Canadian Deputy High Commissioner in London.

the debates which would ensue should the Naval Bill be introduced again next year, it is indispensable that the Canadian Government should have a policy brought thoroughly up to date and supported at every point by sound military arguments. Otherwise we may be very easily taking action with regard to our programme here which would be a very serious embarrassment to them at a critical moment.

If these views have your concurrence I should be very glad if you would make the necessary communications through official channels. I am sending a copy of this letter and the enclosures to the Prime Minister. You will see from Mr. Borden's telegram that a decision is urgent.

[111] *Churchill to H.H. Asquith*
[First Lord's Minutes, 5th series]

4 July 1914

*   *   *

As part of our general scheme for reinforcing the Mediterranean Fleet, with which you are fully acquainted, we propose during the course of the next twelve months to base 6, and later 12 additional submarines on Malta. These boats will have a considerable radius of action, and will exercise an important influence upon the strategic situation as well as greatly increasing the security of the fortress. I am looking to the development of flotilla defence in the Mediterranean as a partial substitution for battleship strength, which would entail such heavy new construction charges.

*   *   *

[112] *Extract from Draft Manuscript written by Winston Churchill[1]*

[Chartwell Trust, 8/61]

[n/d – c.1918]

The reader must now prepare himself for what looks like a reversal of policy; but which indeed had been the real policy throughout. No sooner had I won from the Cabinet the authority to order the four super-

---

[1] This manuscript was an early draft of Churchill's war memoirs published under the title: *The World Crisis*, volume 1.

dreadnoughts of the year 1914 than I immediately resumed my plans for converting two of these ships into a much larger number of smaller vessels. I proposed to treat these dreadnoughts not as Capital Ships but as units of power which could, if desirable, be expressed in any other form. I did not agree with those who considered that the days of the battleship were ended. I held and hold that the possession of a superior line of battle is an indispensable feature of the stronger navy. But the continuous progress of naval science and the revolutionary change which the torpedo and the aeroplane were causing and threatening had convinced me in 1913 [1914] that a smaller proportion of our superiority should be expressed in capital ships and a larger proportion in other forms of naval power. (I had not been able to arrive at any exact standard to govern the change, but I proposed to take the first practical step without further delay.) I pursued my enquiries even while the estimates dispute was at its height.

It was necessary to proceed in great secrecy. How could I ask the Cabinet and Parliament for four super-dreadnoughts as a vital matter in March [1914] and then transform two of these precious machines into thirty or forty submarines and torpedo-craft a few months later? The public understood dreadnoughts and the House of Commons was deeply versed in the controversy about the standard of superiority in dreadnoughts. Suppose I had broken away from the dreadnought standard, on which we had been fighting continuously for several years, and had presented instead a large and varied assortment of small craft, the types of several of which would have to be kept absolutely secret; the small craft would have been pitilessly cut down and we should have got neither the super dreadnoughts nor their equivalent.

The First Sea Lord, like myself, was convinced that the change proposed would add to our naval power. We should get better value for money out of small craft. But he and the other Sea Lords could never have been asked to give up the two capital ships for anything less than an absolute equivalent in the money available for the smaller types. (Nor would I have asked them to do so. We had to fight on the number of dreadnoughts, and we would risk compromising our agreement.)

I also intended to let the Germans lay down and be thoroughly committed to their whole dreadnought programme for the year, so that we should gain the advantage of the change at any rate one year before them. I thought it very probable that the decision of the British Admiralty to convert a portion of the dreadnought programme into other classes of vessels would lead them to follow our example. They had hitherto faithfully emulated us in all the main decisions which we had taken, following us rung by rung, always one step behind on the ladder of gun-power, speed, and size. If now we suddenly dived down into a shoal of submarines, light cruisers and torpedo craft they were almost certain to follow: but they might as well follow one year later. Accordingly, to unfold the whole story to the public at this stage would only have been to have unsettled the House of Commons and informed our rivals.

It was a very difficult path to tread, full of hazards and pitfalls; and only an overwhelming conviction of what was best for the Navy induced me to venture upon it. The First Sea Lord was in full agreement and we gave direction accordingly that the last two ships of the year were not to be laid down till the last possible moment. I only took a few thousand pounds for each in the estimates. The slips at Devonport and Portsmouth were kept ready for them, and everybody was led to assume they would be built in due course.

The next step was to agree with the Chancellor of the Exchequer. I unfolded the scheme and argument to Mr. Lloyd George and was enormously relieved to find him most favourable. Adhering to the principle that the Admiralty was not to lose money in the change, we agreed upon a total money figure at which these two ships were to be converted into their equivalent in small craft. No one else except the Prime Minister was informed. Armed with this satisfactory figure, the First Sea Lord undertook to convince his professional colleagues, and the technical departments of the Admiralty were set to work on various novel designs.

PART VI

THE WAR, 1914–1915

Preparation for War

[113] *Commodore (S) to Commander-in-Chief, Home Fleets (Admiral Sir George Callaghan)[1]*
[ADM 137/1926]

31 July 1914

I arrived at Harwich this morning with *Maidstone, Adamant,* and 10 Submarines of the 8th Flotilla, and will make that my headquarters until I receive further orders.

As it is essential to spare the submarines as much as possible while on the surface, both in regard to materiel and personnel, I have arranged for the two which will first operate in the Heligoland Bight to be towed as far as Terschelling Light vessel, in rear of the destroyer sweep which will leave Harwich on the outbreak of war. A copy of their orders is attached.

I have been informed that the 4 *Bacchantes* will take the place of the 4 *Drakes,*[2] and that the former cannot take up their station until about 4 days after the outbreak of war.

Under the circumstances, and with a view to the possibility of the German Fleet proceeding to the southward to attack the Expeditionary Force in transit, I proposed to station 4 submarines to the southward of the destroyer sweep. These will be relieved from time to time by 4 which will be held in reserve at Harwich. I hope to have two more submarines in the course of a week.

If the two selected submarines which go to the Heligoland Bight return and report favourably, I will send two more, but I look upon this operation as a hazardous experiment, and in the early stages of the war I submit that the remainder will be better employed as I have arranged, particularly in view of the small number available, and the fact that their engines are still somewhat unreliable for long surface runs.

The First Sea Lord and Chief of the War Staff concur in these proposals, and I trust you will approve.

[1] Adm. Sir George Callaghan: C-in-C, Home Fleets, December 1911 to 2 August 1914. Removed from command of the fleet on the eve of war by the orders of Winston Churchill and replaced by former Second Sea Lord, Vice-Adm. Sir John Jellicoe.

[2] The four *Bacchantes:* three of the four were the *Hogue, Cressy* and *Aboukir* sunk while on routine patrol off the Dutch coast by U-9 on 23 September 1914.

[114] *The first war patrols: War Orders for submarines E6 and E8*
[Keyes Mss 4/26]

HMS *Maidstone*
31st July 1914
No.001

1. On receipt of the order to take up War Stations E6 and E8 will leave Harwich in company with the First and Third Destroyer Flotillas under the orders of Commodore T.

2. If weather permits, E6 will be towed by *Amethyst* and E8 by a destroyer to be detailed by Commodore T. A copy of Commodore T's orders for the procedure of the First and Third Flotillas is attached for the information of the submarines.[1]

3. The flotillas will probably leave at daylight and arrive in the vicinity of the Terschelling Light at nightfall, when the submarines will slip and proceed independently to operate in the Heligoland Bight, keeping to the eastwards of Longitude 6° E when south of the 54th parallel of latitude.

4. The First Fleet cruisers, supported by the Grand Fleet, will probably carry out drives and sweeps in to the Heligoland Bight periodically at irregular intervals. Normally they will not cross a line joining the Terschelling and Horns Reef light vessels, and the submarines are not to proceed to the west of that line. It is possible, however, that our vessels may chase the enemy to the east of the line, and this is to be borne in mind.

5. The commanding officers of E6 and E8 are to arrange a plan of action dividing the area. They are to use their own discretion as to the length of time they remain there, but they should not remain in the Heligoland Bight more than three days, and, unless they find themselves very well placed for offensive operations, should return after two days. They should then proceed to Lowestoft or Yarmouth to report, and thence down the coast to Harwich where they should arrive in daylight hours.

[1] Commodore (T): Commodore Reginald Tyrwhitt commanding first fleet destroyer flotillas (Harwich) 1914–18.

[115] *Keyes to Callaghan*

[ADM 137/1926]

1 August 1914

I propose to send two pairs of submarines to patrol between the Outer Gabbard Light Vessel and the North Hinder Light Vessel.

2. One pair will remain on a line 14 miles South East from the Outer Gabbard, and the other on a line 14 miles North West from the North Hinder.

3. They will take up these stations when war is declared, and will be relieved by two more pairs as necessary.

4. On the arrival of the four *Bacchante* class cruisers, I will confer with the Rear-Admiral Commanding as to future movements in this area.

5. In the event of the First and Third Flotillas being withdrawn to join the Channel Fleet, the Commodore (T) has arranged to detail a destroyer to scout for each pair of submarines.

6. One submarine of each pair will be fitted with W.T.

7. Copies of this communication have been furnished to the Admiral of Patrols, Commodore (T), Captain (D) 6th Flotilla, and to the Chief of the War Staff.

[116] *Extract from Patrol Report by Lieutenant Commander Charles Benning*

[ADM 137/2067]

HM Submarine E5
18 August 1914

[While proceeding on the surface in the Heligoland Bight, on Monday 17th August . . .] At 4.30 am, a cloud of smoke was sighted bearing S by E., and when smoke cleared a four funnelled cruiser was seen hull down. From her appearance, and from comparison in Jane's book of Silhouettes it did not appear to be a German cruiser, but looked like one of our *Cressy* class. So certain was I that it was so, that, at about 5.30 am I put the mast up and hoisted the Demand [pennant]. Cruiser hoisted flag in answer and then fired a 6-inch salvo. I dived at once to 80 feet, but not before several salvoes had fallen round us. Cruiser then turned to Starboard going full speed in North Easterly direction. It was not until arriving at Yarmouth that I heard it must have been a German Cruiser. Arrived Yarmouth 10 am, landed one sick man, and proceeded to Harwich at noon, arriving alongside *Maidstone* at 5 pm.

[117] *Extract from Patrol Report by Lieutenant Commander Godfrey Herbert*

[ADM 137/2067]

HM Submarine D5

23 August 1914

At 4.0 pm 6 columns of smoke about 1 mile apart were sighted to eastward. I dived and remained in my position, as I soon discovered that I was in the centre of their line of approach. This proved to be a four funnelled cruiser (*Roon* (?) with three destroyers on either bow, the nearest one being about 1500 yards from her. I attacked and had very little distance to proceed before coming within 500 or 600 yards immediately before her Starboard beam. I fired both bow tubes, but deeply regret that neither took effect. She appeared to have sighted me only a few seconds before I fired, and must have been very much on the alert, as shots were falling round me immediately after the first torpedo had left. I fired the second at once but am of opinion that as they were only set to 5 feet and the sea was very calm, she must have been able to avoid them. The cruiser was not going more than 10 knots, but I had allowed for 14. I retired to the bottom after steaming for 3 miles in a westerly direction loading my tubes, but on reaching the surface found one destroyer two miles astern of me apparently looking for me. I then sat on the bottom until dark in 20 fathoms.

[118] *Extract from report by Keyes to Chief of the War Staff*[1]

[ADM 137/2067]

23 August 1914

The reports of the commanding officers of E4, E9 and D5 are attached. No possible excuse can be offered for the latter missing the German cruiser [confirmed as the *Roon*] on the afternoon of 21st August, and her commanding officer readily admits that the cruiser was a gift and that he acted contrary to orders in firing both torpedoes simultaneously. Lieutenant-Commander Herbert is, however, a very gallant and determined officer, and will do better next time.

---

[1] Chief of the War Staff: Vice-Adm. Sir F. Doveton Sturdee.

[119] *Decorations for submarine personnel: Telegram from Admiralty to Commodore (S)*

[ADM 137/1949]

16 September 1914

Your report of 26th August action in Heligoland Bight, submit names of warrant officers and ratings recommended for notice, with a view to consideration for the Conspicuous Cross and Conspicuous Gallantry Medal respectively, up to two of the former and six of the latter.

Your submission should be communicated in the form of a supplement to your former report, so as to reach the Admiralty tomorrow.

Reply from Commodore (S):

Sir,

1. With reference to Admiralty Telegram Number 76 of to-day's date. I have the honour to submit the enclosed supplement to be attached to my report dated 28th August on the proceedings of the submarines engaged in the operations in the Heligoland Bight.

2. No warrant officers are borne in submarines.

[Attached document]

Secretary of the Admiralty

1. Submitted: The commanding officers of all the submarines which took part in the operations in the Heligoland Bight on the 28th August, and those engaged in the various reconnaissance's prior to the operations, have unanimously expressed to me their admiration of the cool and gallant behaviour of the officers and men under their command.

2. When a submarine is submerged, her captain alone is able to see what is taking place; the success of the enterprise and the safety of the vessel depend on his skill and nerve and the prompt, precise execution of his orders by the officers and men under his command.

3. Our submarines have been pioneers in waters which might well have been mined. They have been subjected to skilful and well thought out anti-submarine tactics by a highly-trained and determined enemy, attacked by gunfire and torpedo, driven to lie on the bottom at a great depth to preserve battery power, hunted for hours at a time by hostile torpedo craft, and, during the engagement on the 28th August, they were forced to dive under our light cruisers and battle cruisers in order to avoid interfering with the latter's movements.

4. Sudden alterations of course and depth, the swish of propellers

overhead and the concussion of bursting shells give an indication to the crew of the risks to which they are being exposed, and it speaks well for the morale of these young officers and men, and their gallant faith in their captains, that they have invariably carried out their duties quietly, keenly and confidently under conditions which might well have tried the most hardened veteran.

5. These duties in no way differ from those in a peace exercise, and it is only when an accident occurs that it is possible for a junior officer or man in a submarine to stand out above his fellow.

6. The commanding officers of the submarines are of the opinion that it is impossible to single out individuals when all performed their duties so admirably, and in this I concur. If six Conspicuous Gallantry Medals are to be awarded, I can only suggest that the crews of the 8 submarines which took part might be permitted to ballot for them – I believe there is more than one precedent for this in the annals of the Victoria Cross.

7. I would, however, submit as an alternative that if a naval medal is eventually given, a special clasp for submarine work in the Heligoland Bight would be highly appreciated.

[120] *Keyes to Sturdee*

[ADM 137/1926]

20 September 1914.

1. Submitted, reports of the proceedings of submarine D.1, D.7, D.8, E.3, and E.10, which returned from the Heligoland Bight last evening and during today are forwarded herewith.

2. During the past week, these submarines, and also submarines D.3, D.5, E.7, E.8, and E.9 have experienced very heavy westerly gales.

3. The brief reports of the Commanding Officers do not adequately express the strain and hardship to which they and their crews were subjected. Their position, on a lee shore, within a few miles of the enemy's coast, in the notoriously high steep seas which accompany westerly gales in the Heligoland Bight was undoubtedly precarious, and it was creditable to the Commanding Officers that they should have maintained their position in the hope that the weather would moderate sufficiently to make submarine work possible.

4. I do not consider, however, that the damage which the submarines are nearly certain to sustain and the risks they run under such conditions can possibly be repaid by a military success, and I am giving directions that, in future, submarines are to return towards the British Coast when severe westerly weather threatens.

5. Briefly, the position was as follows:–

A short steep sea which made it impossible to open the conning tower hatch, vision limited to that through periscopes, i.e., only a cable or two between the seas which continually broke over them. The submarines were thus an easy prey to any surface vessel falling in with them and it was necessary to keep submerged; also, to make an offing, and there were no means of ascertaining the position except by sinking to the bottom and obtaining soundings. There was no rest on the bottom even at a depth of 22 fathoms as the submarines were rolling and bumping with considerable negative buoyancy, and, therefore, it was necessary to keep under way, at a depth clear of the keels of possible ships. At this depth, motion was considerable and bumping, i.e., vertical motion 20 to 30 feet. When battery power became low, it was necessary to come to the surface, since lying on the bottom was dangerous.

6. On the surface, it was necessary to keep a ventilator open to run the engines in order to keep head to sea, through this much water was shipped.

7. To sum up, no good purpose can be served by maintaining a close blockade of the Heligoland Bight in such weather. Even if the enemy emerged which is unlikely, it would be almost impossible to bring off a successful attack.

Widening the Area of Operations.

[121] *Keyes to Commander-in-Chief, Home Fleets (acting Admiral Sir John Jellicoe)*[1]
[ADM 137/1926]

23 September 1914[2]

The attached copy of my submission No. 029 of 23rd addressed to the Chief of the War Staff, Admiralty, as submitted for your information.
Commodore (S)

To Chief of the War Staff, Admiralty.

In compliance with your telephone message of yesterday morning directing me to consider the question of establishing a submarine patrol on the 'Broad Fourteens', I beg to submit the following remarks:–

(1) If submarines are required to patrol the 'Broad Fourteens' they can of course do so, but I consider the few oversea submarines we possess might be very much better employed elsewhere.

(2) If the object of the patrol is to attack the enemy's vessels proceeding to the southward, the chances of one of the few submarines we have available being in the right places at the right moment would be very small, and I consider they would be better stationed off the Sandettit Shoal – a position which commands a narrow approach and ensures the enemy being attacked. Further, there would appear to be no particular reason why the enemy should select the 'Broad Fourteen's' route.

(3) If the 'Broad Fourteen's' patrol is for observation, I consider that submarines are unsuitable in that they must necessarily dive if an enemy appears, and they will consequently be unable to report what they have seen for more time, probably not until nightfall.

(4) The objection to using destroyers designed for offensive operations, wearing themselves out in such a service, is no doubt fully recognised. If destroyers so employed are supported by their flotilla cruiser, the latter will most surely be torpedoed by a submarine before many days elapse. The area is infested with foreign fishing vessels, and the Germans will continue to obtain definite information as to the movements of our vessels in those matters.

(5) I would suggest that an observations patrol could be carried out by trawlers fitted with W[ireless] T[elegraphy]. Their presence will of

---

[1] C-in-C Home Fleet: Adm. Sir John Jellicoe, 1914–16.
[2] On this date U-9 sank the *Hogue, Cressy* and *Aboukir.*

course be reported to the enemy, who will no doubt send a cruiser occasionally to raid them. Therefore a few submarines working with the trawlers would be invaluable, though their chance of being in the right place at the right moment is not great, their presence will soon become known to the enemy, and they may act as a deterrent. It is understood that the French are anxious to send their submarines into the North Sea, and I would suggest that they might well be employed on this service.

(6) An offensively employed submarine's main difficulty is to find target ships. Her opportunities will be few and far between if regular, well-defined patrols are avoided.

(7) The following is a point for consideration:– After the raid of the 28th August, many of the enemy's large submarines were undoubtedly kept within reach of their ports, seven or eight submarines of the latest types being seen on patrol by our submarines working in the Heligoland Bight. Prior to that date, no large submarines had been sighted in that area.

(8) After a period of inactivity on our part, their submarines have again emerged, and, from today's reports, are proceeding to the northward as well as to the southward.

I submit that this emphasises the value of a fairly frequent incursion into the Bight.

[122] *Keyes to Jellicoe*

[ADM 137/1946]

10 October 1914.

In compliance with your H.F.0088 of the 6th October, I beg to submit the following remarks:–

THE STATE OF THE FLOTILLA

1. Although the Submarines of the D and E classes can undertake long cruises in any weather, they are often out of action for a few days, and occasionally for lengthy periods.

2. During the heavy weather experienced recently several vessels have suffered severe straining of hydroplane shafting, and have developed leaks in the locality of the hydroplane guards. Those defects have necessitated docking, and in two cases lengthy visits to Sheerness Dockyard. The heavy hydroplane guards have always been a source of weakness and leakage in rough weather. Those which have given trouble are being removed and replaced by a slack wire jackstay between the fore end of hydroplane and a belt in the bow. This

arrangement should throw a mine mooring clear, prevent an occurrence such as that experienced by E.6, and thus enable a Submarine to dive under a mine-field, if absolutely necessary, with some prospect of success. The later E class have fooling hydroplanes.

3. Clutches of a certain type have given a great deal of trouble, and it has been arranged for the vessels so fitted to be taken in hand, one at a time, for an alteration which will take about a fortnight. This work is being carried out night and day with the assistance of an Engineering Firm at Ipswich – a much quicker proceeding than would have been possible had the vessels been sent to a Dockyard.

4. When these alterations have been completed, the main causes of breakdown and delay will have been removed, and it is hoped that a high percentage of the Submarines in commission will be maintained efficient.

* * *

At present there are eight D class and eleven E class in commission, and two more E class are expected before the end of the month. Of these, fourteen are ready for service; two are laid up for clutch, and two for hydroplane defects, and one is completing a long annual refit. At present, there are eight at sea, five available at short notice, and one resting, having returned from the Heligoland Bight today. The other which returned today is being taken in hand for clutch defects.

5. The reason for the large proportion at sea is given in my 041 of the 10th October, a copy of which is forwarded herewith. The two Submarines at Zeebrugge are really resting, and will be available for service elsewhere when relieved. To maintain five or six Submarines incessantly in the Heligoland Bight, I think twelve to fifteen should be allocated to this service; this would release, say three, for service elsewhere, in the course of a few days.

PROPOSED OPERATIONS

6. I understand that we cannot send vessels through the Sound without compromising Denmark, but I submit that it is very much to Germany's interests to maintain Denmark's neutrality, and the latter could hardly be held responsible for the passage of a Submarine without a Danish pilot, following in the wake of a neutral mechantman through the Sound. In Naval Notes of the 4th October, it is reported that the two German cruisers patrolling the Southern entrance of the Sound have recently been joined by eight Torpedo Boats. The addition of the latter is probably due to the visit of E.1 and E.5 to the Kattegat, the object of the Torpedo Boats being to act as an anti-submarine screen. I consider

that a Submarine attack on these vessels presents no great difficulty, and, if it could be carried out without compromising Denmark, should be attempted. The moral effect would be great.

7. In Naval Notes of the 7th October, it is stated that the Germans, alarmed by the appearance of British submarines in the Kattegat, stopped all exit of merchant shipping from Lubeck during 24 hours. I would submit that the enemy might be given good cause for alarm, and loss might be inflicted on his trade, and on neutral shipping carrying contraband, with little or no risk to ourselves. Even if vessels are not captured, our presence in the Kattegat examining ships would cause anxiety and inconvenience, and would certainly raise the shipping insurance. At the commencement of the war, a great deal of trade passed down past the Horns Reef inside Heligoland; from our Submarines' reports, this trade has almost entirely ceased. On the other hand, E.1 and E.5 report a great many vessels, flying the Norwegian, Danish and Swedish ensigns, in the Kattegat; many of them were doubtless carrying contraband; some may have been German under a neutral flag.

8. I would suggest the occupation of the Kattegat for a few days at a time by Destroyers and Submarines. The entrance to the Sound and Belts would be watched by the Submarines by day. This duty might be carried out by Destroyers by night. Both would be well placed to attack the enemy's cruisers should they emerge. Or if it is considered advisable to withdraw the Destroyers by night to avoid all risk of their being cut off, the Submarines could watch by night, provided moonlight nights are selected. The chief risk the Destroyers would run would appear to be that of being caught to leeward of their supports in a strong Northerly blow sufficient to reduce their speed below that of the enemy's cruisers, should the latter emerge, get past the Submarines and chase. If good judgement is exercised by the Destroyers, there should be no risk of this.

9. I would suggest the stationing of two Submarines off Horns Reef during the operations, with orders to watch for and attack, any vessels proceeding from the Heligoland Bight to the Northward; their primary object, however, being to report by Wireless Telegraphy if any considerable force proceeds to the Northward. As their Wireless Telegraphy is not reliable for sending more than about fifty miles, I propose that some vessel should cruise within W/T reach of them to receive reports.

10. From Submarines' and other reports, a Zeppelin cruises off the Jutland coast.

11. A combined Submarine and Destroyer operation, supported at a distance by Cruisers, on the lines I have indicated would surely cause

some annoyance, and might well inflict considerable loss to the enemy, and, if you approve, I would like to take part in it, using the *Lurcher* and *Firedrake* to link the Submarines off the Belts with the Destroyers acting in the Kattegat. I would suggest the latter should keep clear of land during daylight, when approaching the Kattegat and arrive at their stations so as to commence operations at dawn.

12. The *Lurcher* and *Firedrake* and other Destroyers would require oil, but it is presumed that there would be no difficulty in supplying them outside territorial limits in fine weather. The Submarines can look after themselves for at least a fortnight.

13. In the event of the enemy coming out of the Heligoland Bight in force, I propose to proceed with all available Submarines to wait off his ports for his return. As mines have been laid and the mine-fields are without doubt masked by buoys, I submit that an aerial reconnaissance should be carried out without delay and repeated from time to time, as it is very important that the Submarines should know the position of the buoyed channels which the enemy will make for.

14. The Submarines will probably be the first to know of the enemy's exit, and they can only report by proceeding to within W/T reach of some vessel or station. To ensure important information being reported as soon as possible I would suggest that in future a few Destroyers or a Cruiser should be within W/T touch of the Submarines at stated times during the night and day. If the enemy are about, the Submarines may not be able to rig their W/T installations until nightfall.

[123] *Keyes to Sturdee*

[ADM 137/1926]

12th October 1914.
No. 043

Submitted with reference to my 029 of 10th instant, addressed to the Commander-in-Chief, Grand Fleet, a copy of which was forwarded to you for information, if the proposal suggested in paragraph 6, to send two submarines into the Baltic is approved, the following procedure is submitted:–

The towing of submarines at night and in thick weather is not recommended; therefore, in order to tow them as far as possible to save fuel, I propose that the submarines should leave Yarmouth when the weather is fine and likely to remain settled for two or three days. The submarines will leave at daylight, in tow of two destroyers, with a destroyer to look out ahead and another on the starboard flank.

At nightfall, the submarine will proceed independently; their object will then be to arrive at the entrance to the Sound unseen, and follow a neutral ship through the Sound into the Baltic; when there, to attack the enemy's fleet which is said to be carrying out Gunnery practice in the Baltic.

The conduct of the Commanding Officers of the Submarines must to a great extent depend on their initiative and judgement, but I will impress on them the importance of avoiding any action which might compromise Denmark.

If the proposal contained in paragraph 7 of my submission referred to is carried out, it should be deferred until the submarines are in the Baltic as it is important that they should get as far as possible unsuspected. They are quite able to carry out their operations without assistance, but it would undoubtedly be an advantage to the submarines to find friends in the Kattegat when they return, and if the temporary occupation of the Kattegat by destroyers and submarines is approved, I would suggest that it commences on the seventh day after the departure of the submarines from Yarmouth.

[124] *Keyes to Jellicoe*

[ADM 137/1926]

12 October 1914

1. I was sent for yesterday with reference to your telegram of 6 p.m. 10th instant which crossed my submission No. 029 of that date, and in compliance with the Chief of the War Staff's directions I have submitted further proposals to him. These have been approved.

2. A copy of my minute to the Chief of the War Staff of even date is enclosed for your information. [See [123] above]

[125] *Copies of Telegrams between Keyes and Jellicoe*
[ADM 137/1946]

13–16 October 1914

FROM: Commodore (S)
TO: Commander-in-Chief, Grand Fleet
DATE: 13th October 1914.
2355: Suggested three Submarines should proceed to Baltic and use Libau as base for some weeks. Admiralty have approved. Submarines E.1, E.9, E.11 leave Gorleston tomorrow, 14th October.

FROM: Commander-in-Chief, Grand Fleet
TO: Commodore (S)
DATE: 14th October 1914.
0846: Your 2355, wish it all success from me.

From: Commander-in-Chief, HF, HMS *Cyclops*.
To: Commodore (S)
Date: 15th October 1914.
Your 089 of 10th October. Situation altered by despatch of submarines and I await their report as to chance of a T.B.D. raid into Baltic getting themselves clear of mine-fields. Stoppage of trade is best effected in vicinity of Orkney Islands and Shetland Islands and is now being carried out. The difficulty of searching in the Kattegat and of escorting to British ports makes operations against trade undesirable in that vicinity. Concur in proposal in paragraph 13 of your letter. Think C Class Submarines should relieve later vessels off River Schelde. Are you supplied with Code A.

FROM: Commander-in-Chief, Grand Fleet
TO: Commodore (S)
DATE: 16th October 1914.
0025: Are movements of Submarines as stated in your letter 043 of 12th October, or as in your telegram 2355 of 13th October?

From: Commodore (S)
To: Commander-in-Chief, HF, HMS *Cyclops*
Date: 15th October 1914.
Your telegram today, Submarines off Schelde have been withdrawn by order of Admiralty. I am not supplied with Code A, but will apply for it.

FROM: Commodore (S)
TO: Commander-in-Chief, Grand Fleet
DATE: 16th October 1914.
Your telegram 0025 of 16th October, Submarines are acting in accordance with my telegram 2355 of 13th October; a copy of their orders was posted to you on 13th October. Your telegram 0840 of 14th October was conveyed to them before sailing. They left 15th October, full of buoyancy and confidence.

[126] *Telegram from Jellicoe to Keyes*

[Keyes Mss 4/11]

25th October 1914

With reference to your submission No. 029 of 10th October, the Admiralty now inform me that the submarines in the Baltic will remain there. There is certainly a more likely field for them than in the Heligoland Bight, which is boycotted by larger ships. I fully realise of course the valuable work carried out in the Heligoland Bight.

[127] *Commander Hugh Grenfell to Admiralty via Sir George Buchanan*[1]

[ADM 137/271]

Petrograd
6 November 1914

I have the honour to inform your Excellency that last week I paid two visits to Admiral von Essen, commanding the Russian naval forces in the Baltic, at Helsingfors. Owing to the large staff of the Admiral, there was no room for me on board of his flagship, the *Ryurik*, but accommodation was given me in the hospital ship *Ariadne* taken over from the Finnish Steam Navigation Company. On the second occasion Admiral von Essen wished me to meet our submarines, and for that purpose sent me in a destroyer to Lappvik on Friday the 30th. October. The vessels arrived thither at 6 in the evening of that day, and the following morning in company with our commanding officers I returned to the Admiral at Helsingfors, thereafter the same night leaving for Petrograd, as the chief of the Naval general Staff, Vice Admiral Roussin, wished to hear from me about the doings of and the arrangements made for the submarines.

The Admiralty, and Admiral von Essen, are greatly pleased by the dispatch of these boats to the Baltic, where it is hoped that they can produce considerable effect; if not immediately, on account of the lateness of the season, at any rate next spring. At the same time Admiral von Essen confided to me that he would have been even more pleased had he received timely notice of their coming, or been informed beforehand as to whose orders they were intended to be subordinate, since through ignorance on these points his own plans for a full

[1] Cmdr Hugh Grenfell: British naval attaché to Russia 1913–17; Sir George Buchanan: British Ambassador to Court of St Petersburg.

fortnight were entirely upset, and he seemed to speak with more regret because the weather at that time had been unusually favourable (calm and fog) for their execution. As a matter of fact, he told me that his intention had been to lay mines in the vicinity of Danzic, when the sudden and quite unexpected news that the British Submarines had arrived in the Baltic, coupled with his want of knowledge of their movements and his inability to issue directions, rendered him powerless to carry it out. He was, in consequence, much gratified when instructions finally arrived placing them under his immediate orders. Meanwhile the Russian naval authorities are doing all in their power for the boats themselves, and for the comfort of the crews. The old cruiser *Ruinda* had been specially arranged as a parent ship exclusively for them, and a lieutenant particularly appointed to her as executive officer on account of his own very considerable experience with submarines and good knowledge of English.

The boats themselves on Monday last, the 2nd November, proceeded to Revel to have certain defects made good at the Volta works which are expected to take about 10 days, whereupon Admiral von Essen will have a programme ready for them. The latter, however, depends on some degree upon the weather, because the signs of a possible early winter, and the strong frosts that have already prevailed during the last fortnight, may perhaps so quickly bring about the presence of floating ice as to make the employment of submarines extremely difficult, although in this respect the Germans are in even worse case as their activities of necessity take place in the Gulf of Finland where the ice will be greater in quantity and thickness as well as earlier in its appearance than off Danzig or further to the westward.

Arrangements have also been made to supply our men with warm clothing, to heat the boats, to victual our sailors as near as possible to the manner in which they are accustomed, and to provide them with money. The latter is being issued by Admiral von Essen's paymaster upon the requisition of our senior officer at the rate of 10 roubles to the pound, which seems the most suitable plan for the present, whilst the final adjustment can later be made between the two admiralties.

*   *   *

[128] *Keyes to Chief of War Staff (Vice-Admiral Henry Oliver)*[1]
[ADM 137/225]

1 November 1914
NO: 059.

1. In accordance with the First Lord's verbal directions, I beg to submit the following remarks regarding the employment of Submarines against an enemy attempting a raid or invasion, and on the work of Submarines generally.

2. They are based on the experience gained during the Grand Manoeuvres of the last two years and various Patrol Flotilla exercises which were carried out on a large scale under the orders of the Admiral of Patrols during 1912 and 1913. These latter were particularly valuable, as their object was to test the vessels of the Patrol Flotillas in their proper functions, and to arrive at the best means of dealing with an enemy attempting:

(1) The disembarkation of a Military Expedition.

(2) To attack by long range gun fire our more or less weakly defended ports, such as Newcastle, Hartlepool and Harwich.

(3) To force a passage through the Straits of Dover by day or night.

Finally, I will endeavour to apply the lessons of this war to the experience gained in those exercises.

3. Peace exercises have been misleading in some respects, for in them it has been difficult to put a proper value on, for instance

a. The military qualities of a Submarine, which have hitherto been untried in war.

b. The dispositions and procedure of Submarine and other Flotillas, which in such exercises are only tested over a period of a few days.

c. The moral effect of the Submarine menace on the conduct of an enemy.

4. In regard to (a):–

(1) During the last two or three years, Submarines have been exercised and trained very approximately under war conditions, and war experience has brought little to light which was not anticipated by those who have worked in and with them, but the rules under which they were umpired in peace exercises have been proved to be altogether unreal.

[1] Vice-Adm. Henry Oliver: Rear Adm. 1913, Vice-Adm. 1917, Adm. 1923, Adm. of the Fleet 1928. Director Intelligence Division 1913–14; chief of Naval War Staff 1914–17; 1st Battle Cruiser Squadron 1918; Vice-Adm. Home Fleet 1919; Adm. of Reserves 1919–20; Second Sea Lord 1920–24; C-in-C Atlantic 1924–27; retired list 1933.

(2) For example, if a Submarine was sighted for two or three minutes on the surface, or even if her periscope was sighted prior to her attack, she was put out of action. War has proved that a well-handled Submarine is more immune from attack than even Submarine Officers anticipated. Our experience, and that of the enemy, has shown that it is exceedingly difficult to put a Submarine out of action, unless she can be caught unaware on the surface and rammed, or stalked and torpedoed while on the surface by a hostile Submarine.

(3) On the other hand, war has proved, as anticipated by Submarine Officers, that it is extremely difficult for a Submarine to find targets, and, provided the field of operations is large and the movements of the enemy are unknown, it is to a very large extent a matter of luck whether she happens to be in the right place at the right moment. It has always been contended by Submarine Officers that vessels acting on definite patrols in well-defined areas would be easy prey to a hostile Submarine, given time and patience. Although some successes against vessels so employed have been admitted in peace exercises, the period of the exercises has generally been too short to furnish the opportunity, and, on this account, possibly, the danger of exposing vessels in this manner has not been fully appreciated by those who have based their opinions on Manoeuvre results.

(4) To take an opposite example:– During peace exercises, a very large percentage of successful attacks have been delivered by Submarines on torpedo craft proceeding at high speed. In these exercises, Torpedoes which, in order to ensure success, have been fired at very close range, have necessarily been set to run beneath the vessel; they have undoubtedly done so, and consequently faulty conclusions were drawn. The difficulty of getting a Torpedo discharged at a depth of about 30 feet to pick up the shallow depth necessary to strike a torpedo craft within the short range essential to ensure success against a small vessel manoeuvring at high speed was not appreciated by our Submarine Officers, or indeed by those of the enemy, judging by the number of unsuccessful attacks the latter have delivered. It is now realised that torpedoes must be fired at much longer range at such vessels, and with a good look-out and a prompt use of the helm, torpedo craft manoeuvred at high speed can be considered very fairly safe from Submarine attack.

(5) It may be taken for granted that when the enemy emerge from their defended ports, and when they approach our coasts, they will be preceded and covered by a host of Destroyers pursuing the exceedingly aggressive and unpleasant tactics they have been

employing against our Submarines in the Heligoland Bight. The latter have fortunately exercised under similar conditions for the last two years and will not hesitate to attack through such screens, but these must necessarily militate against success and add considerably to the difficulties, particularly in water too shallow to admit of the submarine diving under her objective in order to escape ramming. The question of shoal water cannot be ignored when considering the value of Submarines in relation to invasion. We have recently had a lesson which is not likely to be disregarded by the enemy, – I refer to the Naval action on the Belgian coast, and the fact that the enemy's Submarines did not succeed in attacking even such a heavy draught ship as the *Venerable*, of whose presence they must have been well aware.[1] At the same time, I would like to place on record that, in accordance with my orders, C.38 watched Ostend for several hours on the 25th ultimo and during his reconnaissance Lieutenant Commander [Geoffrey] Layard closed to within a mile of the entrance, his vessel being aground, with six feet of periscope showing at low water. It was a creditable performance, and in my opinion he and very many other Officers under my command would have successfully attacked the *Venerable* and other vessels, had they been enemy. Whether a similar attack delivered on transports, after they have reached such shallow water, would inflict much loss or prevent the majority of their troops reaching the shore is a matter of doubt.

(4b)

(1) Dispositions which were considered the best to meet every likely action on the part of an enemy compelled to act within the short period of a peace exercise, and which had only been previously tested for a few days at a time, have been maintained for several weeks, and I have viewed with some concern the amount of seawork, and consequent wear and tear of machinery, which the majority of the Submarines of the Patrol Flotillas have been carrying out.

(2) It is obviously impossible with the force at our command to be ready for the enemy everywhere, particularly when one does not know within several months when, and within 300 miles or so, where he is likely to deliver his attack, and, in my opinion, the time has arrived to reconsider our position and to employ our Flotillas sparingly, with a view to preserving the efficiency of the vessels, concentrating them as far as possible in readiness in positions where they can best prevent the enemy from inflicting injury of

[1] HMS *Venerable*: a '*Formidable*' class 15,000 ton battleship. Four 12-in. and twelve 6-in. guns. 18 knots. Used as guardship to cover landings of Naval Brigade at Ostend in September 1914.

vital importance. Some risks must necessarily be taken elsewhere.

(3) In view of the revised terms of my appointment, I have visited the various Admirals under whose orders the Submarines of the Patrol Flotillas are acting, and have made submissions to them for the disposition and employment of these vessels. A detailed report on this subject will be forwarded when certain outstanding points have been settled.

(4c)

(1) The moral effect of the Submarine menace has been rather neglected in Peace Manoeuvres, and in my opinion greater risks have been run than would have been justified, or taken, had very heavy loss of life and the destruction of valuable vessels been the actual, rather than theoretical result of failure.

(2) It is exceedingly hard to place a proper value on moral effect. In the light of the enemy's action on the Continent, there can be little doubt that he will not hesitate to take great chances, under certain circumstances, and will face the possible loss of a great many men and much obsolete materiel in order to achieve success with a reasonable portion of his expedition. In my opinion, the moral effect of the Submarine menace can be almost neglected in relation to invasion, as far as the Submarines of the Patrol Flotillas operating on our open coasts are concerned.

(3) The moral effect of the Submarine menace on the high seas and off the enemy's own ports, where ships of high military value are concerned, cannot be exaggerated. Of this there is ample proof at hand on both sides. That it is an exaggerated menace on the high seas, where the field of operations is large and the number of submarines small, can hardly be dispatched. At least twenty-five German Submarines have had the freedom of the seas for three months, and during this time scores of targets have been at large. In no case has a Submarine achieved success on a vessel proceeding at a fair speed protected by actively manoeuvred screens as the enemy's ships of military value will undoubtedly be protected when they eventually emerge. Presumably the enemy's Submarines have been off our harbours fairly constantly, but up to the present, they have had no success, probably because, as a rule, our Fleet puts to sea at night.

(4) Hitherto, the enemy's light cruisers have followed a similar course, but by constant mining he should be made to emerge with his Fleet or Expedition by day, since he would hardly attempt the passage through a swept channel by night. In the deep water off his swept channel I would apply the Submarine menace. There, the moral effect would be real in relation to his transports, as well as valuable ships.

On our open coasts, I submit again, it is no menace to an invasion in force, and the enemy is astute enough to know it.

5. In the Patrol Flotilla exercise referred to, a section of the coast was tested; light cruisers and destroyers from other sections, and the numerous depot and attached ships acted as the enemy, representing transports, mine-layers, cruisers etc. Sometimes over 100 vessels were engaged. The conditions were more favourable to the defenders than they are likely to be in this war, since the defending Commander knew that his section would be attacked within a defined limit of time. In every case, without exception, a landing on an open beach was successfully carried out according to the Umpire's ruling. I do not know whether the rules were too favourable, but they were similar to those laid down in the Grand Manoeuvres. It is not to be supposed that the invader exercised any brilliant strategy, or that the defender was inept. They both did the obvious thing; the invader arrived before dawn with a number of torpedo craft, which swept towards the enemy's Submarine station in order to make the Submarines dive at a considerable distance, 20 miles or even more from their objective. The distance of the raid from the Submarines' base and the latter's submerged range of action in relation to time are the deciding factors, unless the defender is sufficiently strong to drive in the invader's screen and cover the approach of the Submarine on the surface. In this latter case, the passage can be made at about 11 knots; submerged, it is not likely to exceed 4 to 6 knots.

These facts should provide, as I have previously submitted, that the Submarines of the Patrol Flotillas cannot be relied upon to inflict loss on enemy's transports landing troops on an open beach at a distance from their base, unless sufficient warning can be given to enable them to be in the vicinity when the transports arrive, or in a position to attack them in daylight, at sea, during their approach. It has been suggested that the removal of buoys and lights will prevent the enemy arriving at night, but an enemy so well served by spies and spy craft should have no difficulty in arranging the necessary leading lights. During Peace Manoeuvres Submarines have sometimes been extended along the coast with the object of dealing with such raids as that delivered at Filey in 1913 Manoeuvres, but a scattered disposition obviously cannot be maintained during a long war.

6. I am ignorant of the views of the Military authorities in regard to the landing of an Expedition on an open beach. Presumably only an advanced force of infantry, cavalry and light artillery will be disembarked in the open; heavy artillery transport etc being taken to a harbour with quays.

7. It is proposed to station the available Submarines in the principal harbours, to extend the gunfire of those which are defended and protect others, such as Yarmouth and Blyth, which are not defended. In my opinion, they will be invaluable in this connection, morally, and also effectively if they get sufficient warning and are not caught unawares. I do not know whether the Humber raid in the 1913 Manoeuvres was really regarded seriously as a success. But I am still strongly of the opinion that the few transports and the Battleship which entered the Humber would have been torpedoed by the numerous Submarines which were put out of action for being *seen* on the surface at a considerable range by hostile Destroyers, which they took to be friends. The Battleships and Cruisers which cruised about outside, regardless of the Submarines which were also put out of action for being seen would either have retired or suffered greater loss than was admitted. In the 1913 Manoeuvres and in Patrol Flotilla exercises, vessels attacking ports where Submarines have been concentrated have almost invariably suffered loss. Whether the loss will be sufficient if the enemy comes in great force is a matter of opinion.

8. There are 24 Submarines for the East Coast patrol and a redistribution of these was recently approved, the allocation now being six for the Thames defences, six in the Firth of Forth, six in the Humber area, and six in the Tyne area. There are 14 Submarines in the Dover Patrol; when the situation on the Belgian coast is relieved. I would suggest that five of these should be saved to the East Coast – three to Yarmouth and two to Hartlepool. These and one or two other small changes will be submitted shortly; in the meantime I propose with your approval, to move the *Adamant* to Yarmouth with three E class Submarines. They will also be conveniently situated to assist Submarines which make use of Yarmouth occasionally, prior to proceeding to and returning from the enemy's coast.

9. Many exercises have been carried out to test the efficiency of the Destroyers and Submarines of the Dover patrol to dispute the passage of Battleships, Cruisers and Submarines of the oversea classes. The latter have had no difficulty in torpedoing the Flotilla Cruisers of the patrol after submerged runs of 20 to 30 miles; they have fired torpedoes into Dover Harbour without being interfered with, and have dived through the Straits into the Channel unreported. Vessels representing Battleships and Cruisers have occasionally made the passage safely, at night, and invariably in safety in the twilight. The latter is a condition of light which makes a submerged attack through the periscope impossible and enables the attack of Destroyers to be avoided. Vessels and Squadrons passing through the Straits of Dover during daylight

have generally been successfully attacked by one or two Submarines, but the long line to be guarded precludes more being brought into action. It can hardly be said therefore that the Straits of Dover are closed to an enemy by the Patrol Flotillas, or that a determined enemy preceded by Destroyer Flotillas and proceeding at high speed, under favourable conditions of weather and light, would not have a fair chance of getting through unscathed. At present, however, there are 86 British and French Submarines, and a large number of Destroyers operating in the Straits, and their moral effects must be enormous.

10. To sum up:–

It is presumed that some warning will be received of the embarkation in the enemy's ports.

It is certain that he will not attempt to land on the open beach, unless the weather is set fair and westerly.

On receipt of the information I would send some Submarines of the D and E classes to cruise off likely landing places while the weather is favourable for disembarkation, others to the Heligoland Bight to watch off the ports from which an expedition is expected to leave.

The submarines of the Patrol Flotillas would remain off the harbours ready to attack the enemy by day or night, should he try to force an entry. One or two transports sunk in the entrances might well block the channel for the remainder. In this connection, the provision of a few block ships held in readiness to be sunk in the channel or foul of the quays is worth consideration.

I am convinced that no considerations of shallow water, mines, screens etc will deter the Commanding Officers of our Submarines from driving home an attack by day or night, if opportunities offer, and I have no doubt whatever as to the ultimate result of an attempt at invasion. At the same time, I desire to place on record that, in my opinion, we have not a sufficient force of Submarines to seek invasion in every possible locality, and that the long winter nights before us are all against the Submarine.

11. I am conscious that the views I have expressed in regard to the Submarines of the Patrol Flotillas in the foregoing remarks, and have previously submitted on more than one occasion, are unwelcome, but I submit it is best to realise the limitations of these small Submarines and Destroyers of the Coast patrols and avoid placing a fictitious value on their capabilities. I am absolutely convinced that my conclusions, which are based on much practical experience, are correct; they are certainly the result of much thought and discussion, and in drawing them up I have been greatly assisted by Captain [Arthur] Waistell, an Officer who has had considerable experience in War Staff duties at the War College.

12. I understand that it has been decided to lay mines in the Heligoland Bight on the lines I suggested in my 046 of the 14th October, as the result of Submarine reconnaissance which located two hostile mine-fields between Horderney and Heligoland, and reported the area North and East of Helysland as being free from mines. As Submarines acting under my orders will be watching off those mine-fields, I submit that I may be permitted to lead the mine-layers into the selected position, in order that I may satisfy myself that they are correctly placed.

[129] *Keyes to Oliver*

[ADM 137/225]

5th November 1914
No. 060

*   *   *

2. Experience in this war has proved that submarines on patrol in areas where they are liable to be attacked by the enemy submarines must either manoeuvre throughout the day at high speed on the surface or remain submerged.

3. In the present stage of the war, while the enemy submarines are actively aggressive, and until there is some indication of their vessels attempting a raid on the coast or an invasion, it would seem advisable to withdraw our submarines and keep them in readiness in positions secure from attack by hostile submarines, with the object of preserving their efficiency with a view to the future. Under the conditions in which they were being worked in some patrols, they were suffering considerable wear and tear, without, in my opinion, commensurate military advantage.

4. The Flag Officers concerned have generally concurred in these views, and the Admiral Commanding the Coast of Scotland raised no objection to the transfer of three submarines from his command to that of the Admiral of Patrols, for service in the Tyne area; only three submarines had previously been allocated to the whole of this area, involving the protection of Newcastle, Blyth, Sunderland and the Tees.

5. The new disposition of the flotillas, which has been approved, is shown on the enclosed table. [not reproduced]

6. Our experience in the early days of the war brought out the vital importance of submerged endurance. On this account it was realised that a C class boat would run great risks of being caught on the surface

or on the bottom with her battery down, if subjected to the violent anti-submarines tactics employed by the enemy in the Heligoland Bight. It has, however, been found that, by placing the motors of the B and C class submarines in series instead of in parallel, the submerged speed of these vessels can be considerably reduced and their endurance almost doubled.

7. We have no superiority in Overseas submarines, and for the moment, very little new construction on which to fall back. Our C submarines may very well prove invaluable before the end of the war for operations in the North Sea and off the enemy's coast. Their range of action on the surface and their submerged endurance will now admit of their visiting the Heligoland Bight with a stay of two or three days in moderate weather.

8. I have not yet had an opportunity of meeting the Admiral of Patrols in the Humber Area, but, on his return there, I will do so, and forward a detailed report on the subject of the employment of the Patrol Flotillas Submarines in the various areas.

The Emergency Construction Programme

[130] *Minute by Winston Churchill on Emergency War Programme*
of New Construction
[ADM 1/8390/256]

10 August 1914

3rd Sea Lord[1]
Please prepare forthwith an emergency war programme of new construction in destroyers and submarines: the latter sh[oul]d be the maximum wh[ich] our yards can manage without hampering existing work of an urgent character. S.M.'s have been already ordered.

[131] *Extract from Memorandum by Tudor on Spare Capacity in*
Warship Building Industry
[ADM 1/8390/256]

11 August 1914

*   *   *

The number of Submarines which can be turned out in the immediate future depends almost entirely on Vickers' capacity for turning out the engines, and a careful review of the work in hand leads to the conclusion that the maximum programme which can be safely counted upon for rapid execution is *12 Improved E Class*, of which,
8 would be ordered immediately, and,
4 would be ordered at the end of the year,
delivery varying from 18 to 20 months from date of ordering.
Of these twelve, two will probably be engined by Scotts with FIAT engines.

[132] *Minute by Churchill*
[ADM 1/8402/419]

31 October 1914

Secretary,
First Sea Lord, [Admiral Lord Fisher][2]

[1] Rear Adm. Frederick Tudor: Third Sea Lord 1914–17; C-in-C China 1917–19.
[2] On 28 October 1914, Adm. of the Fleet Lord Fisher returned to the post of First Sea Lord.

I. I shall be much obliged if you will give this matter your personal attention, and issue the necessary orders to obtain 20 submarines additional to those now ordered in the shortest possible time. Keep me informed of your progress and proposals. But there must be no delay.

II. Let me also have your proposals for accelerating to the utmost those in hand.

[133] *Memorandum by Fisher distributed at Meeting held at the Admiralty on 3 November 1914*
[Fisher Papers, FISR 5/121]

There is no doubt that at this moment the supply of additional Submarine Boats in the shortest possible time is a matter of urgent national importance. They will not be obtained unless the whole engineering and shipbuilding resources of the Country are enlisted in the effort, and the whole of the peace paraphernalia of red tape, routine and consequent delay be brushed on one side. I have carefully studied the submarine question during my retirement and have had many opportunities of keeping in touch with the present position and future possibilities, and am convinced that 20 submarines can be commenced at once, and that the first batch of these should be delivered in 9 months and the remainder at short intervals completing the lot in 11 or 12 months.

To do this, however, cheapness must be entirely subordinated to rapidity of construction, the technical departments must have a free hand to take whatever steps are necessary to secure this end without any paper work whatever. Apparently this matter has been under consideration at the Admiralty already for a considerable time but *nothing has yet been ordered* and the First Lord has concurred that a fresh start be made independently of former papers, and the matter placed under my sole supervision without any other officers or departments intervening between me and the professional officers. I will give instructions as to the work, and direct that if any difficulties are met with, they be brought to me instantly to be overcome. The Professional Officers' reports as to acceptances to tenders or allocation of work must be immediately carried out by the Branches.

Only in this way can we get the boats we require. To ensure the completion of the 20 boats steps are to be immediately taken to order the parts for the engines for 25 boats. We know from experience that it is in the machinery parts that defects and failures occur in manufacturing of castings, forgings etc., causing great delay. The parts for the extra

5 sets of engines will be available for these replacements and eventually the 5 extra sets can be fitted in five further hulls. I propose to review the progress being made once a fortnight in the hope that it may be feasible to order still further submarines beyond these 20 now to be commenced at once.

The training of sufficient officers and men for manning these extra boats must obviously be proceeded with forthwith, and those responsible must see to it that the officers and crews are ready.

[134] *Minutes of Meeting held at the Admiralty*
[ADM 116/3454]

Tuesday, 3 November 1914

The First Sea Lord (Lord Fisher) presided at a Conference this day at the Admiralty.

[Also] *Present:*

Second Sea Lord, Third Sea Lord, Additional Civil Lord, Parliamentary and Financial Secretary, Secretary, Naval Secretary to First Lord, Engineer-in-Chief, Assistant Director of Torpedoes and another representative of the Director of Naval Ordnance, Commodore (S) and Assistant, Naval Assistant to First Sea Lord, Director of Naval Construction and an Assistant, Superintendent of Contract Work, Superintending Electrical Engineer, Director of Dockyard Work, Director of Navy Contracts and an Assistant

Lord Fisher explained to those present that this Conference had been summoned with the approval of Mr. Churchill, primarily with the object of expediting the delivery of 20 submarines which were to be at once commenced, but in the second place a big further building programme for a special purpose had been decided on. The question of placing orders for submarines had been under consideration for some time past. The First Lord, however, had assented to the cancellation of all existing papers on this subject, and a fresh start was to be made immediately on the lines of a special war routine. All red-tape methods – very proper in time of peace – were now to be abandoned, and everything must be entirely subordinated to rapidity of construction. It was desired to impress upon all present the necessity of avoiding paper work, and of proceeding in the manner indicated in the secret memorandum which would be circulated next day in regard to the matter. Arrangements would be made in due course to obtain additional vessels of other types in a similar manner.

NOTE – After this, a meeting of all the shipbuilding firms of the

United Kingdom took place at the Admiralty under the presidency of Lord Fisher, and the programme mentioned above was parcelled out there and then.

[135] *Keyes to Fisher*
[Keyes Mss 4/13]

3 November 1914

*   *   *

Submitted in view of your remarks this morning as to the vital importance of providing as many submarines as possible in the shortest possible time, regardless of cost and departmental restriction, I submit as a first action that every endeavour should be made to accelerate the completion of the submarines under construction and recently ordered.

[136] *Memorandum by Fisher to Churchill*
[ADM 1/8402/419]

5 November 1914

First Lord:

The situation was explained at the Conference on November 3rd, at which all those interested were present, and my colleagues on the Board also attended. I think, so far as I could gather, no difficulties are likely to arise (I put in this remark for the First Lord's feeling of security that his wishes will be carried out). The first boats ought to be completed ready for trials in eight months, and the whole in eleven months. At least these dates must be strenuously worked for. To enable this to be done, engines for 25 boats will be commenced. The extra five will feed the 20 if defective parts are developed and so prevent delay from this cause. These will be eventually fitted in five further hulls, if so decided later on. As *TIME* must be the primary consideration, cost will of course be higher than with peace procedure. [marginal comment by WSC: Hurrah!]

All work will be spread over engineering.and other firms throughout the country, so that a large number of manufacturers will be simultaneously employed. Supply of identical parts will with advantage be organised at the Admiralty and supplied to the builders complete. Preliminary steps have already been taken respecting batteries, main motors, periscopes, torpedo tubes and similar parts, so that these will all be ordered within a fortnight, unless there are very special reasons, which I will personally examine at once the moment a hitch occurs. If batteries, periscopes, etc., cannot be obtained in time from the usual firms, others must be brought in and energetic steps taken to provide them with the necessary facilities and information to manufacture – (Mr. Schwab,[1] for instance, volunteers to obtain periscopes in America).

If building E type hulls, instead of G, will reduce time of construction by even so short a period, this will be done; and as on questions of design will be involved when copying existing boats, local Overseers should have full powers to settle matters. If reference to the Admiralty should be necessary, it should be direct to Heads of Departments. The firms competent to build should be sent for, given the drawings and all other necessary information and told to go straight on with the work with all possible despatch. As the work involved is difficult for new firms to estimate, the net cost and percentage system will be advantageous and will be adopted, as time will also be saved thereby. Preliminary terms are to be arranged at the time of giving orders to proceed.

To save time and to facilitate rapid construction, the Heads of Departments will settle all matters, and all difficulties they experience are to be immediately referred to me. The clerical departments will execute without any further references. The Second Sea Lord is taking steps for the training of the personnel required for these new boats. Heads of Departments not to write minutes, but to come to me at once personally if difficulties are met with, however trivial, – so that there may be no excuse whatever hereafter for delay. As the First Lord says in his minute: THERE MUST BE NO DELAY.

[Attached minute (8 November 1914) by Captain Sydney Hall][2]
Third Sea Lord,

Replies from all departments concerned are now attached. Balance of evidence is that E design will be quicker than G, and that it is not advisable to defer completion of V; it only remains to settle the orders for the 20 additional E Submarines. SCW concurs as follows:–

·   Vickers 6); Armstrong 2); Scott 1); White 1); Thorneycroft 1); Beardmore 2); Brown 1); Fairfield 1); Yarrow 2); Palmers 1); Laird 1); Swan Hunter 1). (=20)

If approved, submit drawings be prepared at once and firms *wired* to send representatives to Admiralty on Tuesday, 10th.

[1] Charles Schwab: American industrialist. President of Bethlehem Steel Corp.
[2] In November, Fisher appointed Capt. Sydney Hall to the Admiralty as Captain Supervising Submarine Construction.

[Attached minute (8 November 1914) by Tudor]
Approved

[Attached minute (10 November 1914) by Tudor]
First Sea Lord,
I have now dealt with the whole of the Firms, and they have all consented to take the number of boats allotted to them, and to work to their utmost to produce them in the times you named.

Six firms, however, represented to me that they could build 2 boats each almost as quickly as 1 boat, perhaps not a fortnight to a month between the two. Further, Vickers are very anxious to build their own engines, which would release six of the sets we have ordered.

Under the circumstances, I should like to know whether we could increase the programme to 26 boats instead of 20 – this would be the number I originally proposed.

I am having a report of the proceedings drawn up, so that they may be placed on record and the firms have proper authority to carry on – they are now doing so on my verbal authority.

[Attached minute (10 November 1914) by Churchill]
Approved. This is additional to the 8 extra ordered 6 weeks ago.
$26 + 8 = 34$, + the normal programme of 1914–15 (10*), + 20 U.S.A.
$= 64$. (Please check figures).

[Attached minute (11 November 1914) by Tudor]
[At *] this number should be 9 – making total 63.

[137] *Memorandum Circulated by Director of Contracts*
[Keyes Papers]

CP 01458/14
Contracts Department, Branch 8
11 November 1914

Secret
The following orders for submarines boats have been placed:–

Messrs. Vickers Ltd   for 6 E class submarines   (Hull and Machinery)

Messrs. Armstrong-Whitworth for 2 E class submarines (Hull) ⎫ Machinery
        and Co.   ⎬ to
Messrs. Beardmore and Co.   for 2 E class submarines (Hull) ⎭

Messrs. Yarrow and Co.	for 2 E class submarines (Hull)	be
Messrs. Thorneycroft and Co.	for 2 E class submarines (Hull)	supplied
Messrs. J. Brown and Co.	for 2 E class submarines (Hull)	by
Messrs. Fairfield and Co.	for 2 E class submarines (Hull)	the
Messrs. Palmers and Co.	for 2 E class submarines (Hull)	Admiralty
Messrs. Cammell Laird	for 2 E class submarines (Hull)	
Messrs. Swan, Hunter and Co.	for 2 E class submarines (Hull)	
Messrs. J.S. White and Co.	for 1 E class submarine (Hull)	
Messrs. Scotts	for 1 E class submarine (Hull)	
The Bethlehem Steel Corporation of 111, Broadway, New York, USA.	For 20 submarines complete – United States Navy type – to be delivered in sections and put together in this country at a dockyard	

[138] *Minute by J.B Marshall (Director of Dockyards) discussing New Construction that can be undertaken in the Dockyards*
[Fisher Papers, FISR 1/17]

31 December 1914

With reference to the directions of the First Sea Lord to consider the question of undertaking in HM Dockyards the further construction of Submarine Boats, representatives from the three Large Yards and Pembroke have attended conferences at this Office to-day. Captain SS Hall, Engineer Rear Admiral Goodwin, and Mr. Johns, Constructor of DNC's Department, present.

In view of the discussion which took place it is thought the following Boats could be laid down at the periods stated and *all would be completed in twelve months from the date of laying down.* This has been drawn up on the assumption that the Boats to be constructed are in the main to be of G Class and built from battleships and cruiser [building] slips but if a special boat is to be constructed at each Yard it is submitted it be; substituted for other of those herein specified and laid down with the G's as soon after design &c is settled and drawings and materials are available.

As Portsmouth, Devonport and Pembroke have had no previous connection with the construction of Submarines it is submitted to obtain the whole of the machinery for the boats to be built there by Contract, but each Yard to assemble at least one set after delivery of parts by Contractors in order to gain experience in the machinery for these boats. In the case of the Switchboards also although the bulk of these are ex Chatham and proposed to be obtained from Contractors it is thought Yard Officers should undertake for the sake of experience the manufacture of one or more of these boards.

The following are therefore submitted as a basis of what the Yards can undertake:

PORTSMOUTH – 12 boats

Dates for laying down	Dates for completion	Remarks
April '15	January to March '16	The machinery for the whole of
June '15	April to June '16	the 12 boats to be obtained by
October 1915	July to September 1915	Contract but Yard to assemble that
January 1916	October to December 1916	for 4 boats preferably the later
		ones. As regards Switchboards
		these to be obtained by Contract
		for all except 2 of the last batch.

The boats will be launched about six months after date of laying down and completed at varying intervals between periods quoted against them.

DEVONPORT – 12 boats

2	March '15	March '16	Machinery for all boats to be
4	April '15	March to April '16	obtained by Contract but that for 2
4	May '15	April to May '16	of the latter boats to be assembled
2	June '15	June '16	at Yard. Switchboards to be
			obtained by Contract except two,
			to be made in Yard for last 2
			boats.

CHATHAM – 12 boats

6	1st June 1915	15th March 16 to June 16	The machinery for 2 of the first 6
4	1st Nov 1915	15th Aug 16 to mid Oct 16	and 2 of the second four to be
2	1st Jan 1916	October to Nov '16	manufactured in the Dockyard,
			that for remainder to be supplied
			and assembled by Contract. All
			Switchboards for the Chatham
			boats will be constructed by that
			Yard.

PEMBROKE – 6 boats

2	April '15	April '16	Machinery to be obtained by
2	June '15	June '16	Contract but Yards to assemble set
2	Nov '15	Nov '16	for last boat in order to gain
			experience. Switchboards to be
			obtained by Contract except that
			for last boat.

(These will be launched 8 months after date of laying down)

The dates given by the Yards for laying down are the earliest that can be worked to in view of the New Construction now completing and repairs to ships in commission and a total of 42 boats so far as can at present be seen can be taken in the Yards with the men and facilities existing or projected.

If it be approved to lay any of these boats down action will at once be taken to order the necessary materials and work to the dates above given.

The approximate cost of the dockyard work involved in building these 42 boats of the G Class under the foregoing conditions is £3,665,000.

[Attached minute (31 December 1914) by Engineer in Chief]
The approximate estimated cost of the machinery is £950,000.

[Attached minute (7th January 1915) by Churchill]
We have 77 s[ub]m[arine]s in commission and 75 building. This is a proposal to build 42 more. I do not see any relation between this and our tactical requirements. None of these vessels can be ready till 1916, and it is the duty of the Admiralty to endeavour to secure a good result in 1915. The existing resources in labour and *material* are fully employed. To issue new orders is not to get new work done, but only to produce a paper effect, at the expense of existing contracts. It is much more important to concentrate energy and attention upon the rapid and punctual delivery of the immense programme now under construction than to enlarge it. I understand that this programme was the maximum possible. If more labour is available it should be turned to securing an acceleration of current work.

On the other hand I see no objections to forming a submarine construction yard at Portsmouth and Devonport. Two G [class] boats might be allocated to each to begin with. But I require to be assured that men will not be withdrawn from other Admiralty work, repairs especially: and the trade will not be burdened by demands for materials which will only delay their existing work.

[139] *Copy of Office Memorandum circulated within Admiralty*
[ADM 137/294]

9 February 1915

COMMODORE (S) AND CAPTAIN (S): APPOINTMENT OF
1. Captain Sydney S Hall CB has been appointed Commodore S in succession to Commodore Roger JB Keyes CB MVO ADC and will take over the duties hitherto carried out by that officer with the exception of those to be undertaken by the Captain S as stated below.

2. Captain Arthur K Waistell has been appointed Captain (S). He will be in command of HMS *Maidstone* and of all Submarines of the Harwich Striking Force.

3. A light cruiser will be placed at his disposal by the Commodore (T), when required for active operations.

4. These appointments will take effect from 8th February.

[140] *Copy of orders circulated by Captain (S) Arthur Waistell to officers commanding HM Submarines prohibiting unrestricted attacks on enemy merchant ships*
[ADM 137/294]

HMS Maidstone
25th March 1915

MEMORANDUM: No 0058

1. Submarine E4 is to leave Harwich, if the weather is favourable, on the morning of the 31st March, for the Kattegat, in order to attack any enemy's War Vessels that may be operating there.

2. Your attention is called to the fact that neutral Submarines and other neutral Men-of-War may be met with, and particular care must be exercised not to mistake them for enemy vessels and fire at them.

3. Enemy merchant vessels are not to be interfered with, as you have not sufficient men to spare for a prize crew. The only method of dealing with enemy merchant ships countenanced by the British Government is the legal one of capture, and subsequent Prize Court proceedings.

4. On the way to the Kattegat, or on the return, should fuel considerations permit, it will be advisable to pass near the Naze, – it is a likely point for meeting German Submarines.

5. You are not to pass through the Belts or The Sound.

6. You are to return at any time on account of bad weather, or should other circumstances render this desirable; otherwise you are to remain in the Kattegat for four days, leaving for Harwich on the afternoon of the fourth day.

7. Care should be taken that sufficient fuel is left in case of your return being delayed by bad weather.

8. Various Notices to Mariners in regard to the Skagerrak and Kattegat are attached, also a sheet giving other Hydrographic information.

9. Your orders contained in my Memorandum dated 22nd March 1915, No 0058, are hereby cancelled.

(signed) A Waistell

Submarine Operations off the Dardanelles and in the Sea of Marmora

[141] *Lieutenant Norman Holbrook VC to Captain Roger Keyes,*[1] *on Receipt of the* Victoria Cross *for sinking Turkish Battleship*
[Keyes Mss 4/36]

HM Submarine B XI
Dardanelles
17th January 1915

I am writing to thank-you very sincerely for the kind letter of congratulations you sent me. I feel that the great distinction conferred upon me, is too much for the small service I have rendered, as the *Messudiyeh* was a very old ship and not much of a loss to the Turks. Winn wishes me to thank-you very much for your kind congratulations to him.[2] It was very good of you to have taken so much trouble about my crew. I should have been very worried had they been forgotten but they were not. The signal we received here from the Admiralty on December 23rd included the crew as well as the officers, it stated that the crew were to receive the CSC or medal according to rank, and then on New Year's Day was changed to the DSM.

* * *

I expect you have read my report I forwarded to the Admiral which was not very interesting, but perhaps you would like to hear how the boats behave out here diving in a tideway. Before going up the Dardanelles I took particular care in trimming and to start with the boat dived very well taking very little helm to keep her at any depth. As soon as I got inside the Dardanelles she took full dive helm at 300 on two to keep her down at sixty feet. Often she came up as far as forty feet then went down again without altering the speed or helm. When I wished to bring her up I had to give her full rise helm and speed up to 500 on two and even then sometimes remained at twenty feet for quarter of an hour or more, before she would come up the remaining five feet to see. When I sighted the *Messudiyeh* I altered eight points to starboard to attack her, the boat immediately sank to eighty feet and remained there, and nothing would bring her up till I blew two auxiliaries for five minutes.

[1] In February 1915, Capt. Roger Keyes was appointed Chief of Staff to Adm. Frederick Carden commanding the fleet blockading the Dardanelles.
[2] Lt S.T. Winn: second in command HMS/m B11.

I think the cause of this was the sudden change of tide from ahead to the beam. Up to the time of firing the diving was very erratic, the depth varying from fifteen to forty feet. On firing the boat sank to forty feet (I made men run forward) and I took some time with 500 on three before she came up, then she refused to dive till I flooded the auxiliaries I had previously blown. When I eventually got back again into the main channel with the tide astern the depth ranged from between sixty and forty feet. And I had no trouble to bring her up. I hear from the French they have the same difficulty with diving.

* * *

Please don't believe my letter published in the papers, it has been somewhat enlarged by the press, but still owing to my sister's folly I have now £300 for the crew and I would be very grateful if you would advise me what to do with it. It is too difficult for me to decide.

* * *

[142] *The First Sea of Marmora Patrol by HM Submarine E11, 19 May to 7 June 1915*
[private collection]
Original draft of Patrol Report compiled by Lieutenant-Commander Martin Nasmith, Lieutenant Guy d'Oyly Hughes and Lieutenant Robert Browne
HM Submarine E XI

May 19th, 1915 – (1)

1.10 am: Left Imbros Island, in company with Torpedo Destroyer *Grasshopper*.

2.45 am: Arrived off Cape Helles. Parted company with *Grasshopper*, and proceeded into Straits.

3.10 am: Passed through trawler patrol line.

3.20 am: Passed through Destroyer line. Heavy rifle fire and artillery fire taking place on shore. On approaching, hostile searchlights on Kephes Point and Suandere. Dived whilst abreast of Achi Baba.

4.0 am: At 80 feet. Course and speed as requisite to make passage.

5.15 am: Rounded Kelia Bhar, touching bottom off point in 9 fathom.

6.10 am: At Nagara Point. Observed two hostile battleship *Targut Reis* and *Heredin Barbarossa* and several hostile Destroyers, who opened fire. The former retreated up the Straits, and were lost to view in a cloud of smoke. (NB) The sun was very bright and low, just behind them, making it impossible to follow their movements. Destroyers continued to attack at every exposure of our periscope. The conditions of light, together with speed at which the vessel was travelling, rendering the periscope exceptionally visible. Stood well up into Khelia Leman before rounding Nagara.

6.40 am: After rounding Nagara Point, whilst still being attacked by Destroyers, observed *Targut Reis* and *Heredin Barbarossa* proceeding at full speed to the Westward, keeping close to the Southern Shore. It being impossible to attack owing to presence of Destroyers. Course being continued up the Straits at various depths.

9.30 am: Arrived off Gallipoli. Proceeded to the North East. Sighted several trawlers to the Northward of Gallipoli.

1.45 pm: Diverted to bottom in 14 fathoms. Position at Lat 40°28′ N. Long 26°51′ E.

9.0 pm: Rose to surface – commenced to charge.

9.45 pm: Signalled to *Jed*, reporting successful passage through Straits. Dived on the appearance of hostile Destroyer to the Northward.

10.0 pm: Rose to surface and continued to charge.

20th May, 1915 (2)

0.30 am: Dived on the appearance of Destroyer from the Westward.

0.40 am: Rose to surface, continued charging, Destroyer still in sight, disappearing to the Eastward.

4.0 am: Finished charging, dived towards line between Marmara Is and Kodja Burnu, and continued to patrol between these points.

10.0 am: Observed armed trawler.

Noon: Observed small torpedo boat, having the appearance of a French submarine.

4.0 pm: Proceeded towards Rodosto, and examined anchorage, but harbour proved to be void of ships.

7.0 pm: Rose to surface, commenced charging batteries, hands to bathe.

21st May, 1915 (3)

3.0 am: Completed charge and dived.

6.0 am: Rose to surface. Hands to bathe.

7.0 am: Continued on patrol towards the Northward.

11.30 am: Observed small coastal sailing vessel, laden with small logs of timber. First Lieutenant boarded same to inspect her, and stole four chickens, offering in payment the enormous amount of a 1/-. The same being refused by a much frightened and extremely polite Turkish skipper.

12.0: Made fast alongside, and trimmed down, using vessel as screen, and proceeded on patrol, weather being at this time very foggy.

5.30 pm: Observed the high land at Deirmen Burnu, also an armed coast watcher. By keeping the sailing vessel between ourselves and his view, was able to observe him without being observed. Turned away from the coast. The weather remaining foggy until 8.0 PM.

8.0 pm: Cast off the sailing vessel, and proceed towards the Westward. Continued to charge batteries on passage.

22nd May, 1915 (4)

1.20 am: Observed hostile destroyer, and dived.

2.00 am: Rose to surface, and proceeded.

3.00 am: On signalling billet. Rigged wireless mast. From 3.00 Am until 6.0 AM attempted to get into wireless communication with *Jed*, but were unsuccessful.

6.6 am: Dived and proceeded to the Eastward.

10.30 am: Observed small Gunboat on patrol, and also several small sailing vessels.

4.0 pm: Rose to surface, but were observed by small hostile Destroyer, and forced to dive.

9.30 am: Rose to surface, proceeding towards the Eastward.

23rd May, 1915 (5)

3.0 am: Observed Oxia Is, altered course towards Constantinople.

4.15 am: Observed several small sailing ships, also the houses of Constantinople being quite plainly in view.

4.50 am: Whilst approaching small sailing vessel in order to inspect her, observed transport approaching from the Westward (three masts, one funnel, clipper bow) dived and proceeded to attack her.

5.10 am: Transport observed our approach, and turned round in Constantinople, and escaped.

5.30 am: Returned to surface, and returned to complete examination of vessel mentioned above.

5.50 am: Whilst alongside sailing vessel, observed Turkish Torpedo Gunboat at anchor off Constantinople dived and proceeded to attack her.

6.30 am: Fired port bow torpedo, which struck hostile vessel amidships on the starboard side. Vessel was observed to dip by the bow, and heeled over to port, finally sinking by the bows in about five minutes from being hit. Before sinking, firing at us with rifle and six lb gun. A shot from the six-pounder striking our foremost periscope, and putting it completely out of action. After watching the vessel sink, which was assumed to be either the *Peik-i-Shevket* or *Birki-Satvet*.[1]

---

[1] The ship was actually the gunboat *Peleng-I Derya* (775 tons). Sunk.

Course was made in the direction of Panderma.

10.30 am: Rose to surface, and the damaged half of the foremost periscope was removed, after having a fire round it to loosen the joint. Crew having prayers, Swedish exercises, and bathe.

2.30 pm: Small steamer observed, proceeding NE dived to avoid same.

4.30 pm: It being too late to examine Panderma, a course was made for the signalling position.

24th May, 1915 (6)

2.0 am: Arrived on signalling billet. Rigged wireless mast. Communication obtained with *Jed*.

5.0 am: Finished signalling, lowered mast, and proceeded towards North Channel.

6.0 am: Smoke observed ahead, dived and proceeded.

10.30 am: Observed small steamer proceeding to Westward. Examined vessel through periscope. Rose to surface and ordered her to stop. Vessel endeavouring to escape in the direction of Marmara Is. Proceeded to chase vessel, and fired several rounds of rifle ammunition at vessel, which stopped. Ordered crew to leave the vessel, which they did, in three boats, considerable panic taking place amongst the crew, which caused the capsizing of one boat, and several people being thrown into the water. This being due to the vessel still going ahead, and lowering the boats before the way was taken off. Every man was wearing a cork life-belt, so no one was in any danger of drowning. Although the panic still continued amongst the portion of the crew that still remained, whilst endeavouring to lower last boat, until the appearance of one [Silas Q.] Swing. The war correspondent of the *New York Sun*, a typical American both in manner and appearance, for this same gentleman we have a great admiration, and consider that he deserves full marks for coolness, not being the slightest bit perturbed. After asking us to wait a minute and receiving an answer in the affirmative, he restored order amongst the gentlemen who were still struggling to lower the boat, and then placed himself at our disposal by introducing himself in a manner used in the best circles, and caused us much amusement, by shouting Glad to make your acquaintance, my name is Swing with accent and drawl both complete. Received information from him that the vessel was a small passenger steamer, bearing a name that sounded something like a cross between a cough and a sneeze, was going to Chanak, and so far as he knew, had no stores on board. By this time the Turkish Crew have succeeded in lowering the last boat, our American friend, discovering that she was pushing off

without him, rushed over to the other side of the vessel, shouting Now
then, wait for me, wait for me, and on the boat clearing the vessel's side,
gaily waved his hand to us in a parting greeting. We then boarded the
vessel and discovered that our American friend was either loyal to the
Turks, or short sighted, as a nice big 6 inch gun was laying diagonally
across the fore deck, and the fore hold filled with gun mountings, and
possibly smaller guns. While the after hold was full of ammunition of
all kinds, including about 50 charges for big 15 guns. After having
discovered the ammunition in the vessel, could quite understand the
extreme haste to leave the vessel, that the crew evinced, and their
evident reluctance to remain on the vessel, whilst there were great
possibilities of being hit with a torpedo. Smoke being then observed to
the Eastward, a few souvenirs were hastily removed, and a demolition
charge placed in the after hatch. The fuse fired and the boat proceeded
full speed astern, until a safe position was reached, then stopped and
waited for the fuse to reach the charge, which it did in four minutes, this
being as set. The charge blew up with a loud explosion, a great flame,
and a lot of smoke, seeming to blow up the decks. In the space of about
a minute, the vessel heeled over, and cocking her bow into the air, sank
rapidly by the stern, almost perpendicular, and in the words of the
Prophet, all things considered, it certainly was some sink.[1]

The smoke mentioned above, having been made out to be a
somewhat similar steamer, dived to attack her, but was observed, and
she made for Rodasto. We then rose to the surface and leisurely pursued
her. Observing her to be full of stores, etc, piled high on deck. When she
reached Rodasto, she made fast to the pier. Whilst we still continued our
pursuit. Great excitement being noted in the town, also several armed
soldiers mustering on the pier. Dived and approached the vessel. The
water shoaling rapidly, ran aground, being then about 2000 yards away
from the target. A torpedo was fired from the port bow tube, which
struck the vessel amidships.[2] We then gently retreated to sea, our
departure being accompanied with a hail of rifle bullets from the shore,
one of which struck the lower part of our one remaining periscope, but
failed to penetrate. The Turks seem to have a fondness for firing at
periscopes, and seemed to be specially trained in the hitting of them. In
addition to the vessel being destroyed, it is also assumed that the pier is
damaged. Whilst diving away from the scene of our labours, more
smoke was observed, so a course was made towards it. It was
discovered to come from a small paddle steamer, proceeded to

[1] Naval Auxiliary *Naga* (480 tons). Sunk.
[2] SS *Hunkar Iskelesi* (512 tons). Sunk.

challenge her. She endeavoured to escape, proceeding towards the shore. After firing several rifle shots at her, she stopped for a few moments, and then realising the fact that we had not a gun, proceeded to steam full speed for the shore, cleverly keeping her stern towards us, and attempting to ram us, every time we closed up to her. Observing that she had horses on board, and also large bundles of barbed wire entanglements, a hot rifle fire was kept up upon her. She eventually ran ashore, her crew jumping overboard and swimming to beach. The boat was then trimmed down and the vessel approached carefully, it being the intention to place a demolition charge on board, and blow her up. Just as the boat reached shallow water, two mounted soldiers were observed galloping at full speed towards us, followed by 50 to 100 more cavalry, who dismounted from their horses, and opened up a hot fire upon us, and caused us to retreat. An attempt was then made to destroy the vessel with a torpedo, but owing to the shallowness of the water which made it impossible to approach to a closer range, and the smallness of the target, the only part of the vessel presenting to our view being the stern, the torpedo missed its mark.[1] We then dived out on a South Easterly course.

5.0 pm: Rose to surface, and proceeded to recharge batteries.

10.30 pm: Dived and proceeded slowly towards Constantinople.

25th May, 1915 (7)

3.0 am: Rose to surface, charged batteries, course being made towards Constantinople.

6.0 am: Dived on approaching Oxia Is, course continued towards Constantinople.

12.30 pm: After having entered the Bosphorus, and reached the entrance of the Golden Horn, without being observed from the shore. Two transports were observed laying at the Arsenal Wharf, and an attack was made on both these vessels. Firing both bow tubes. The port bow heater torpedo failed to run, and sunk immediately after having been fired, cause assumed to be, the tail plug still remaining in position. The starboard torpedo observed to be running straight towards the larger vessel, and an explosion was also heard, but owing to presence of a Brennan Torpedo,[2] and being swept ashore by a strong tide, were unable to observe the results of the shot.[3] The boat was being rapidly bumped to the surface, and was only prevented in so doing by going full speed

---

[1] SS *Kismit*. Missed.

[2] This in fact was E11's first torpedo circling back.

[3] Torpedo hit and damaged SS *Istanbul* (3559 tons) which managed to beach in shallow water before sinking (see [142a]).

astern, and flooding all internal ballast tanks, until she became stationary. The way out being then felt along the bottom until vessel was in a safe position. A course was then steered towards the centre of the Marmora, with many sighs of relief for a lucky escape.

[142a] *Deck Log of USS* Scorpion: *entry by Commander James P. Morton*
[U.S. National Archives, RG 74]

off Tophane, Constantinople
25 May 1915

12.40. Sighted periscope of a submarine projecting about one foot above waterline and distant about 330 yards on port beam (towards Seraglio Point), which travelled in a northerly direction for about 1800 yards then submerged and fired two torpedoes, one to the northward direction towards Dolam Magteke – a surface run – and the other towards the south west, just below the surface, ran past *Scorpion* about thirty yards distant and struck lighters moored alongside of steamer *Stamboul* (off Shikedji wharf) blowing up the lighters and tearing large hole in starboard quarter of the *Stamboul* on waterline. Four torpedo boats with tubes charged opened fire with several guns in the general direction on which the submarine submerged.
12.50 Hoisted American ensign at main.
1.25 SS *Stamboul* in tow of two tugs was taken up the Bospherous and anchored off Calataki, stem on beach.

3.30 pm: Rose to surface, stopped, hands to bathe.

4.30 pm: Proceeded on various courses, charging batteries until daylight.

26th May, 1915

6.0 am: Remained stopped on the surface. The day being spent in getting spare torpedoes into position for firing. This being completed, hands to bathe, and the remainder of the time, make and mend, it being necessary for everyone to have a little rest.

7.30 pm: Proceeded towards signalling billet.

27th May, 1915 (9)

0.30 am: Communication having been established with the *Jed*, and signalling exercises completed, a course was made to return towards the Eastward.

1.30 am: A large battleship, presumably of the *Targut Reis* class, accompanied by two destroyers, were observed ahead, steaming towards Westward, boat was turned round and speed reduced. The boat being then trimmed down, and waited for the flotilla to pass. They appeared to be steaming at about 12 knots. The attack proved unsuccessful, owing to being in the moonlight, being forced to dive whilst on the point of firing, by one of the accompanying destroyers, who passed immediately over us, when we were at 30 feet. The course was then steered to the Eastward to a position about midway between Marmora Island and Constantinople.

8.0 am: On billet, the day being spent on the surface, cleaning up the boat. It being also the official washing day, all members of the crew had a wash, and certainly not before they needed it, it being nine days since the last one.

5.0 pm: A small steamer, having the appearance of a yacht, heaving in sight, it was decided to challenge her, and blow her up if possible, but she fired at us with a gun, so decided not to bother.

7.0 pm: Proceeded to signalling billet.

28th May, 1915 (10)

1.0 am: Communication having been established with the *Jed*, and signalling exercise being completed a course was then made towards the Eastward, towards the Gulf of Ismid.

6.0 am: Several patches of smoke being observed to the North East a course was made towards them.

6.30 am: It could now be seen that the smoke was caused by five vessels, escorted by a destroyer. Vessels assumed to be supply ships or transports. The convoy consisting of one large vessel and four small ones. We then dived and proceeded to attack.

7.30 am: Fired the port beam torpedo at the largest vessel, which was struck on the port side aft. The explosion making a very loud report and nearly frightened scribe out of his skin, who had fallen asleep during the attack. The stricken vessel seemed to be completely lifted up out of the water, aft, and heeling over to starboard, sunk in less than a minute after being hit.[1] It had been noted that the escorting destroyer was making a zig zag course, and preceded the convoy. After the sinking of her charge, we dived to 70 feet, having in mind the ability the wily Turk seems to possess in the hitting of periscopes. When a safe distance was reached, examined the situation through the periscope, and discovered the destroyer hunting vigorously for us, whilst the remainder of the ships continued on their course. Continued diving until the destroyer was hull

[1] SS *Bandirma* (474 tons). Sunk.

down, then rose to the surface, and proceeded to the Gulf of Ismid.

11.30 am: Arrived on position, and remained on the surface charging batteries.

12.0 am: Observed steam vessel proceeding towards us from the direction of Constantinople.

12.30 pm: Dived and proceeded to attack her.

1.45 pm: Fired starboard beam tube at her. No explosion was heard, but the vessel was observed to stop, and then proceeded on course again. By some slight hitch in the arrangement of the sinking valve, we discovered the torpedo floating when we went to look for it. The second hand gallantly removing the pistol in the water, the torpedo was hoisted on board, the evolution being performed with creditable despatch. It was then discovered why the steamer had temporarily stopped, and also that a miss was no miss, the war head of the torpedo being crushed in slightly, and in all probability struck the vessel low down, and passed on underneath her bottom.[1] Friday is evidently not an unlucky day for that ship to sail.

4.30 pm: Boarded a small sailing craft, and the second hand rummaged through her with his accustomed skill. She had no cargo on board, but he removed from her all the delicacies that she possessed, and we then parted with many expressions of goodwill.

7.30 pm: Proceeded to signalling billet, and established communication with the *Jed*.

29th May, 1915 (11)

4.0 am: Proceeded towards Gallipoli and dived on the approach of smoke from the Eastward.

7.0 am: Vessel proved to be a store-vessel, but our attack failed, and boat breaking surface, enemy's vessel escaped. Spent the whole of the day patrolling the Eastern entrance of the Dardanelles, but with the exception of two or three hostile destroyers, no other vessels were observed.

8.0 pm: Proceeded towards the Eastward.

30th May, 1915 (12)

8.0 am: Spent this day in clearing up the boat as much as possible, crew washing and bathing. We are beginning to have trouble with the state of the atmosphere whilst diving. The air soon becoming oppressively foul. This being probably due to the fact that there is so much dirty linen etc about, and in consequence of the amount of sweat falling in the boat, most of the clothing in the boat is damp. These

---

[1] SS *Dogan* (216 tons); torpedo hit but failed to explode.

things, in addition, to the fact of the crew constantly eating and sleeping in the boat, and that only a minimum amount of cleanliness is possible, tend to make the boat anything but sweet smelling.

8.0 pm: Course made towards the Southern end of Marmara Is. The boat being well trimmed down. A watch was kept on the Southern passage, but nothing was observed.

31st May, 1915 (13)

4.0 am: Dived, and a course made into Panderma.

8.0 am: A large vessel was observed laying anchor in Panderma Roads. She was evidently a German vessel, being one of the latest vessels of the Rickmers Line, and was apparently engaged in the embarkation of troops, as several small boats were observed in the vicinity of the vessel, and a camp of considerable size observed to the right of the town.

9.20 am: Having approached to within range of vessel, fired port bow tube torpedo at her, which struck on port side of vessel amidships, and made an exceptionally loud report on exploding. Vessel was observed to list heavily to port, but before sinking, enemy managed to beach her.[1] Did not consider that it was worthwhile to use another torpedo on her, as she was evidently too badly damaged to be of any further use. A course was then made towards the North East, the remainder of the day being spent in charging batteries, etc. Small tug observed proceeding to Panderma.

8.0 pm: Proceeded to position South of the Gulf of Ismid.

1st June, 1915 (14)

4.0 am: Dived to 20 feet and patrolled the entrance of the Gulf of Ismid all day, but with the exception of several small coasting sailing vessels, nothing whatever was sighted.

8.0 pm: Rose to surface, and commenced to recharge batteries, a course being made towards the signalling billet.

2nd June, 1915 (15)

4.0 am: Communication having been established with the *Jed*, a course was then made towards the Eastward.

8.10 am: Smoke was observed to the Westward, which eventually proved to be a small destroyer proceeding towards the Eastward. Dived to avoid same. Smoke towards the Eastward observed just before diving.

9.0 am: Rose to surface, and steered to intercept the vessel from the Eastward.

[1] SS *Madeline Rickmers* (3431 tons). Sunk. (The wreck was not recovered.)

9.20 am: Dived and attacked vessel (store ship).

9.40 am: Fired starboard bow tube torpedo, which struck vessel on the port side just before the bridge. She immediately began to sink by the bow. She completely sank in about 3 minutes.[1] Observed more smoke towards the Eastward and approached her. Dived and attacked.

10.50 am: Fired port beam torpedo at vessel, who proved to be a small store ship, but the torpedo missed.[2] The ship steaming towards the shore. She approached the shore quite closely, then anchored, the crew landing in a boat. Rifle fire was opened upon us, when on rising to the surface to look for our torpedo, which had evidently gone right inshore towards a small town on the beach. Nothing was observed of the torpedo, and it was impossible to proceed further in the matter of the vessel owing to the rifle fire. A course was then made towards the Eastward.

12.30 pm: More smoke was observed towards the Eastward, and was eventually made out to be a small two funnelled vessel escorted by two destroyers.

1.15 pm: Dived and attacked same.

2.15 pm: Fired port bow torpedo at vessel. Torpedo observed to be running quite straight, but was evidently a miss under.[3] We then cruised about in the vicinity until the convoy had disappeared, and then proceeded to look for the lost torpedo, which we had great hopes of finding, as care had been taken to get inshore of the convoy and the torpedo fired seawards, in the hope of the same mistake being made with regard to the sinking valve, and also that deplorable result which took place again, it being considered the limit to lose a torpedo by it being in too close a proximity to the shore to allow for its recovery, after our studied carelessness with regard to the sinking valve. However to our delight we soon observed the lost sheep, and after removing the pistol, proceeded to float it into the boat by means of the stern tube, which evolution was performed with much celerity and expressions of delight. This method of recovery being considered to deserve full marks. The remainder of the day being spent charging batteries and cruising about.

3rd June, 1915 (16)

AM: Remained on the surface all day, drying clothes etc.

3.0 pm: Observed smoke towards the North Eastward. Dived and steered towards it. It was eventually discovered to come from a vessel

[1] SS *Tecielli* (390 tons). Sunk.
[2] SS *Basangic* (400 tons); torpedo observed from target ship to pass under keel.
[3] Gunboat *Samsun* (450 tons). Missed.

having somewhat the appearance of a yacht. Having decided that we were not closing rapidly enough underwater, rose to the surface and proceeded to gaily chase the stranger very rapidly. When within 2000 yards of each other, suddenly discovered that instead of running away, our friend was making straight towards us, as hard as he could go. We treated him to a most spectacular disappearance, diving at full speed, from the surface to 20 feet in one act, to be treated in turn, with a disappearing trick from our friend. Rising to the surface when he had gone.

4.0 pm: Hostile destroyer appeared, apparently searching for us, so dived and remained below until midnight.

4th June, 1915 (17)

AM: Rose to surface, making a course towards the signalling billet, and charging batteries.

3.0 am: Communication having been established with the *Jed*, course was then made to the Eastward, remaining cruising on the surface during the morning.

2.0 pm: Course was made towards Oxia Is and patrolling to Southward of same. Hostile destroyer observed during afternoon and evening, evidently the same one; she is apparently detailed for our benefit. The remainder of the day being spent in patrolling to the Southward of Oxia Is recharging batteries at nightfall.

5th June, 1915 (18)

4.0 am: Spent the day in bathing, and ventilating the boat, also in topping up batteries, an earth having been discovered in one of the main motors. This in addition to having a cracked intermediate shaft, has decidedly cramped our style.

8.0 pm: Course was made towards the signalling billet, and communication having been established with the *Jed*, permission was asked to return. Course was then made to the Eastward. Charging batteries as required.

6th June, 1918 (19)

4.0 am: Having arrived on billet – the day was spent in the usual way, according to our Sunday routine, prayers, Swedish exercises, and bathing. During the afternoon a destroyer being observed, and several sailing vessels. The batteries being fully charged during the afternoon.

9.30 pm: Course was then set towards the Northern entrance of the Dardanelles. The boat proceeding slowly on the surface.

11.0 pm: Signalling billet was reached, and communication established with the *Jed*, but nothing of any importance was obtained, owing to the difficulties of signalling, it taking an hour to get four words through. The aerial sparking very badly all the time.

7th June, 1915 (20)

3.40 am: Dived and proceeded to enter the Straits, keeping a watch through the periscope.

6.30 am: Passed Gallipoli at 90 feet. Proceeded down towards Nagara Point, examining all anchorages carefully, but failed to find any battleships. Observed large vessel, apparently troopship, anchored off Moussa Bank, and few small vessels, and sailing ships in Ak Bashi Leman [*sic*]. On reaching Nagara Point and having been disappointed with regard to a target, turned round and attacked the large vessel off Moussa Bank.

Noon: Fired port bow torpedo at vessel, which struck her on the port side forward, she immediately heeled over to port, and commenced to settle down by the bow.[1] We had previously turned round to come down again, having passed the vessel on the way up, so we continued our course towards Nagara Point.

1.30 pm: Passed Nagara Point at various depths and turned down towards Chanak.

2.0 pm: Passed Chanak and dived to 70 feet and steered a course towards the entrance.

4.0 pm: Rose to surface, and by going full speed astern, and rising to the surface stern first, managed to shake clear a large mine which had been hanging to the port foremost hydroplane since passing Chanak. On rising to the surface we were met by the *Grampus* who escorted us to Port Mudros.

[143] *Officer Commanding Naval Force at the Dardanelles (Vice Admiral John de Robeck) to Admiralty*

[Keyes Mss 4/36]

<u>Submarine E11 – Proceeding 5th August to 3rd September 1915</u>

10 September 1915.

Secretary of the Admiralty.

In forwarding the attached report of the services performed by HM submarine E11 in the Marmora from 5th August to 3rd September 1915, I have the honour to bring to Their Lordships notice the exceptional work performed by this boat.

---

[1] SS *Ceyhan* (3590 tons). Sunk.

2. As is well known and recognised throughout the service the operations of a submarine are almost entirely due to the efforts of her commanding officer. Commander Martin E. Nasmith VC has proved himself to be a submarine officer of great skill, initiative and daring, and in addition to this he possesses to an exceptional degree all those qualities which go to produce a leader of men. I strongly recommend him for promotion to Captain at the earliest possible moment.

3. Lieutenant Guy d'Oyly Hughes carried out voluntarily a most dangerous service on 21st August, when he landed ashore and blew up a low breakwater support to the Ismid railway line, in spite of the presence of an armed guard within 150 yards of him. After a running fight of about a mile, he dived into the sea and was finally pulled on board the submarine utterly exhausted, having had to swim nearly a mile in his clothes. I strongly recommend him for the Victoria Cross.[1]

[144] *Second Patrol of the Sea of Marmora by HM Submarine E11*
[private collection]

H.M. Submarine E.XI
4 September, 1915

Sir,

I have the honour to forward the following report of the proceedings of H.M. Submarine E.11 while in the Sea of Marmara between the 5th August and the 3rd September.

5th August

1.30 am: Left Kephalo and was escorted to the entrance of the Dardanelles by *Basilisk*.

4.7 am: Dived abreast Suan Dere Point.

4.20 am: While still at 20 feet after periscope fouled a wire apparently stretched between two buoys. This was cleared by stopping and lowering periscope. Came to the surface and found no damage. Dived again.

4.45 am: Mine was heard to bump heavily along the starboard side while at a depth of 70 feet in the Kephes Mine field.

6.30 am: Rounded Nagara Point. Dived to 110 feet.

6.50 am: Caught net across the bow – the boat was lifted to 90 feet and her weigh much reduced. A crack was then heard which was either the wires parting or slipping up clear of the stem which was

---

[1] Lt Guy d'Oyly Hughes was awarded the DSO.

subsequently found to be brightly polished from the top to a depth of seven feet.

7.0 am: Torpedoed transport with three masts and one black funnel in Ak Bashi Liman. When last seen vessel was down by the bows.[1]

11.20 am: Passed Gallipoli.

12.30 pm: Rose to surface and proceeded to the North Eastward. Attempted to communicate with *Astor* but could obtain no reply.

1.20 pm: Forced to dive by Gunboat.

2.20 pm: Gunboat having drawn away came to the surface and proceeded. Gunboat returned to the attack but our superior speed kept me out of gun range none of the shots coming within 500 yards although a large number were fired. During the chase again attempted to communicate with *Astor* – unsuccessful.

6.20 pm: Gunboat gave up chase.

10.20 pm: Having charged batteries returned again to the South West and endeavoured to communicate with *Astor* at dawn but was again unsuccessful.

6th August

6.30 am: Forced to dive on wireless billet by aeroplane which approached silently by means of a [?] [glide] from a considerable height dropping two bombs within 100 yards of the boat.

3.0 pm: Met E. 14 at rendezvous. Shortly afterwards observed smoke both boats spreading to the attack. Smoke proved to be Gunboat of the *Berki-Shevket* class.

4.30 pm: Torpedoed her amidships off Silivri – Her trim did not alter and she was beached stern first. Owing to the slight damage apparently done fired second torpedo at her when aground. This being rather an end on shoot unfortunately missed the torpedo passing close to her stem.[2]

5.30 pm: On rising to the surface some four miles off the gunboat opened fire shots however all fell short.

7th August

5.0 am: Dived by Dohan Aslan buoy keeping a watch on road.

11.30 am: Observed troops on road heading towards Gallipoli. Rose to surface and opened fire. Several shots dropping well amongst them caused them to scatter.

---

[1] SS *Halep* (3684 tons). Sunk. *Halep* was raised on 13th August but promptly sunk again by a torpedo dropped from an RNAS aircraft. She was raised again on 25th August and sunk on the same day – for the third and last time – by a torpedo from HMS/m E11.

[2] Torpedo-cruiser *Perk-I Sevket* (775 tons); one torpedo hit that broke the ship's back but failed to sink her.

12.20 pm: Observed column approaching along same road. Rose to the surface again and dropped several shells amongst them – the range of the road now being known from our position at Dohan Aslan Buoy. Column took cover in open order.

1.40 pm: Large column observed on road nearer Gallipoli marching at high speed. Opened fire but failed to stop progress of column – although a large number of dead and wounded appeared to be left alongside the road. The column was under fire for about half an hour when we were forced to dive by shore guns.

3.30 pm: Rose to surface and opened fire at a considerable body of troops apparently resting. They immediately dispersed and subsequently opened a well directed fire with a field gun. Dived.

6.0 pm: Observed hostile destroyer.

7.20 pm: Rose to surface and charged batteries. Attempted to establish wireless communication with *Astor* but failed.

8th August

4.40 am: Sighted Turkish battleship escorted by one destroyer about 5 miles N.E. of Gallipoli.

5.0 am: Torpedoed battleship starboard side amidships. She immediately took up a list about 10° to starboard altered course towards the shore and opened a heavy fire on the periscope.

5.20 am: A large flash was observed forward after which she rolled over and sank.[1]

5.20 am: A second destroyer was observed to approach from Gallipoli. Attacked and fired torpedo at her which passed immediately underneath.[2] Battleship subsequently proved to be the *Harridin Barbarossa*.

9.0 am: Established wireless communication with *Jed*.

10.10 am: Observed party of troops ashore but on closing to open fire were put under by shore guns.

10.45 am: Observed two masted – one funnelled steamer to the North Eastward. She was attacked by E.14 and ran ashore, where she was subsequently torpedoed by E.14 and set on fire by gunfire from both boats. The last round fired caused the upper half of E.11's gun mounting to fracture – the gunlayer being thrown overboard and the gun very nearly following him. Examination proved the cause to be a flaw in the metal Gun was dismounted – upper portion of pedestal removed and the gun replaced in lower position. The gun was ready for action in 24 hours.

[1] Battleship *Barbaros Heyreddin* (10060 tons). Sunk.
[2] Destroyer *Basra* (500 tons); torpedo ran under target.

9th August
Met E. 14 at Rendezvous. Received 2 torpedoes from her.

10th August

[144a] *[Naval Signal received from Flagship at 0121 hours, 10 August 1915]*

Large merchant ships reported off Ak Bashi Liman evening of 9th. Enquire in the morning if still there. E2 will bring as much ammunition as possible. Excellent news from Home. Ends.

4.30 am: Burnt empty sailing vessel.[1]

9.0 am: In company with E. 14 held up small hospital ship proceeding towards the Dardanelles. Directed her to send a boat. Sent Lieutenant D'Oyly-Hughes and party of three hands onboard to carry out examination. Before boarding the entire crew were ordered to one end of the ship and the boat's gun was kept trained on them. The inspection was then carried out – nothing contraband being found. The ship was the *Zia* Red Crescent No.70.

4.0 pm: Dived for small destroyer – failed to attack but observed her to be armed with nothing heavier than a 6pdr gun and Torpedo tube which latter was apparently in all readiness with the crew closed up.

5.0 am: Burnt small sailing vessel.

11th August

9.0 am: Sighted small destroyer of yesterday close to Stephano Point. Closed her until she sighted us. Then altered course away from land and went on to fourteen knots drawing her away from shore guns. Opened fire at 7000 yards. She returned the fire all her shots falling well short. Owing to the difficulty of spotting due to her constant alteration of course we failed to hit her, and in view of the gradual close in range it was considered necessary to dive. She patrolled over head for some time and then returned to Constantinople.

[144b] *[Naval Signal received from Flagship at 0926 hours, 11 August 1915]*

Reported on good authority that Antaki is being used as port to disembark goods from Constantinople. Small steamers arrive at night only. Ends

---

[1] Turkish dhows typically displaced approximately 20 tons.

10.30 am: Came to surface, overhauled and burnt six small sailing vessels.

9.30 pm: Dived to 70 feet in Gulf of Mudania.

12th August

4.0 am: Rose to surface and bombarded Mudania Railway Station. Struck the station three times before being put under by the shore guns.

7.0 am: Left Mudania.

10.30 am: Burnt small sailing vessel laden with timber.

7.30 pm: Off Stephano Point. Dived on sighting hostile aeroplane, which dropped two ineffective bombs when boat had reached a depth of 40 feet.

9.0 pm: Proceeded towards Gallipoli.

13th August

9.0 am: Communicated with *Astor*.

11.0 am: Held up large Hospital Ship. Sent Lieutenant D'Oyly-Hughes and party onboard for examination. She proved to be the old Great Eastern Steamer *Cambridge*. No contraband was found onboard.

Proceeded to Gulf of Artaki. Inspected Harbour and Bay. Found Bay empty and one small steamer alongside slipway. Rose to surface and opened fire which was immediately replied to from shore.

11.30 am: Dived and opened range. Rose and fired three rounds at Gun which did not fire again. Fired several rounds at steamer damage unknown.

6.0 pm: Dived out through the Rhoda Channel.

14th August

11.20 am: Met E. 2 at rendezvous and received ammunition from her.

15th August

5.0 am: Proceeded slowly towards the entrance of Constantinople.

9.0 am: Whilst in the entrance observed steamer alongside Haidar Pasha Railway Pier – under cover of the breakwater. Continued watch on the entrance, proceeded slowly towards her.

10.20 am: Torpedoed her from the North Westward, the torpedo striking her on the port side abreast the mainmast. She immediately settled down by the stern.[1]

12.30 pm: Rose to surface abreast of Oxia Island. Burnt two empty sailing vessels.

5.30 pm: At rendezvous with E.2. Lashed rifle on 12pdr gun and

[1] SS *Isfahan* (843 tons). Sunk.

carried out aiming rifle practice with E. 2. The spotting being done by wireless.

7.0 pm: Observed smoke of small steamer proceeding from Constantinople towards Panderma. E.2 commenced the attack with her gun. Steamer altered her course towards the shore guns on Stephano Point. After a few rounds E.2 gun mounting carried away. The attack was continued by E. 11 the vessel having turned back when E.2 ceased firing. Opened fire at 6000 yards range when vessel turned again and ran in towards the shore. On being struck twice with common shell she again altered course and opened a very accurate fire with a number of guns. Dived quickly.

9.0 pm: Surface – observed enemy returning to Constantinople. Proceeded into the Gulf of Ismid.

16th August

4.30 am: Rose to surface in position for bombarding Viaduct of the Baghdad Railway. Fired fifteen rounds before being put under by shore guns. Several shells hit the bridge supports. Dived out of Ismid.

6.30 am: Came to the surface in the entrance to destroy sailing vessel but was forced to dive whilst doing so by a hot fire from the shore.

8.0 am: Surface – proceeded towards rendezvous.

9.30 am: Sighted hostile aeroplane – submerged until conning tower only was above water. On his getting quite close – waved to him and then dived to 40 feet. Since then no aeroplane has attacked.

17th August

10.30 am: Observed dirigible Air Ship over Constantinople. Proceeded on the surface to the Western end of the Sea of Marmara.

18th August

7.0 am: Rose to surface near Dohan Aslan Buoy to bombard troops but they scattered before fire was opened.

8.30 am: Rose to surface and opened fire on large convoy, several shells falling amongst them before they managed to scatter.

9.0 am: Observed fire springing up where our shots had fallen. This rapidly increased in size until in the afternoon and evening it had assumed very large proportions.

19th August

9.0 am: Dived into Artaki Bay but found nothing except one small sailing vessel which was afterwards searched and burnt.

12.30 am: Returned to position off Sarkioi and lay on surface watching Marmara Channel for the remainder of the day.

[144c] *[Naval Signal received from Flagship at unknown time
19 August 1915]*

[Destroyer] *Berk-I-Savuet* reported to have arrived in Constantinople badly damaged. Seaplane has torpedoed one small ship at *Ak Bashi Liman* and one has been torpedoed in Fals Bay on Wednesday 17th daylight. *Marmona Pasha* possibly ship torpedoed and set on fire by you and Boyle. Her position not known yet. Steamer torpedoed 15th by seaplane is close inshore just west of Injeh Burmin. She was painted black and has one funnel and four masts. Ends.]

20th August

5.0 am: Proceeded to the Eastward.

3.30 pm: Stopped off Kalolimno Island and constructed raft capable of carrying one man and a demolition charge. The raft was tested while the hands were bathing.

5.30 pm: Proceeded towards Gulf of Ismid arriving as the moon was setting.

21st August

Lieutenant D'Oyly-Hughes having volunteered to make an attempt on the Ismid Railway the following plan of attack was arranged: The boat to approach the shore half a mile to the Eastward of Eski Hissar village. Lieutenant D'Oyly-Hughes to swim ashore with raft carrying charge (16¼ pounds Guncotton) and proceed to railway line, there to place charge in a convenient position for breaking the line. If however the watch kept on the line appears to be inefficient he should proceed to Viaduct and place charge in the best position for demolishing same. In the event of meeting a vigilant watch en route to return to a position on the line if possible adjacent to the boat and there explode the charge making as rapid a return as circumstances permit. The boat will remain as close to the shore as possible.

The following signals to be made on landing:

    1 flash – About to start Boat invisible

    2 flashes – About to start Boat visible

    3 flashes – Returning at once

On returning when two or three hundred yards from the shore blow one blast on the whistle or show one flash. Boat to reply with one red flash. This to be repeated as necessary.

Trimmed boat down till conning tower only was above water.

Proceeded slowly towards shore until the nose just grounded three yards from the rocks, the cliffs on either hand being sufficiently high to prevent the conning tower being observed. In order to prevent boat being swept broadside on to the rocks it was necessary to keep her going ahead Port and astern Starboard with the helm hard to Port. Lieutenant D'Oyly-Hughes dropped into the water abreast of the conning tower and pushed the raft carrying the charge, his accoutrements and clothes to a spot some 60 yards on the Port bow of the boat. His weapons consisted of an automatic service revolver and a bayonet sharpened in order to silence detached sentries without noise. He also carried an electric torch and a whistle.

The Cliffs proved unscaleable [sic] at the first point of landing, he therefore re-launched the raft and swam along the coast until a less precipitous spot was reached. Here after a stiff climb the top was arrived at, no coast watchers apparently being in the vicinity. Half an hour later after a considerable advance he reached the railway line. He then proceeded very slowly with the charge towards the Viaduct, keeping a little above the line on the Northern side. Having advanced some five or six hundred yards voices were heard ahead and shortly afterwards three men were observed sitting by the side of the line talking quite loudly. After watching them for some time he decided to leave the charge which was very heavy and cumbersome and go forward making a wide detour inland to inspect the Viaduct. This detour was successfully carried out the only incident being an unfortunate fall into a small farm yard, disturbing the poultry but not rousing the household.

From a distance of about 300 yards the Viaduct could easily be seen as there was a fire burning at the near end of it. A stationary engine could be heard on or just beyond the viaduct and men were moving about incessantly. He decided that it was impossible to destroy viaduct so he returned to the demolition charge and looked for a convenient spot to blow up the line. He found a low brickwork support over a small hollow and placed it underneath. Unfortunately it was not more than 150 yards from the three men sitting by the line, but there was no other spot where so much damage could be done. He muffled the fuse pistol as tightly as possible with a piece of rag but the noise was very loud on such a still night and the men heard it and instantly stood up. They then came running down the line so a hasty retreat was made. After running a short distance he turned and fired two shots to try and check the pursuit but these proved ineffectual. Soon after two or three ineffectual shots were fired from behind.

In view of the fact that speed was necessary Lieutenant D'Oyly-

Hughes decided that to return down the cliffs at the place of ascent was impossible so he followed the railway line to the Eastward for about a mile till it came out close to the shore. He plunged into the water about three quarters of a mile to the Eastward of the small bay in which the boat was lying. The Charge exploded as he entered the water – fragments falling into the sea near the boat although the distance between the boat and the charge was between a quarter and half a mile. After swimming some four or five hundred yards straight out to sea he blew a long blast on his whistle but the boat being in a small bay behind the cliffs did not hear it. Day was breaking very rapidly, so after swimming back to the shore and resting for a short time on the rocks, he commenced swimming towards Bay in which boat was lying. At this point he discarded his pistol, bayonet and electric torch, their weight making his progress very slow. It was not until he had rounded the last point that the whistle was heard and at the same time he heard shouts from the cliffs overhead and rifle fire was opened on the boat. As the boat came astern out of the Bay the early morning mist made her appear to him to be three small moving boats, the bow, the gun and the Conning tower being the objects actually seen. He swam ashore and tried to hide under the cliffs but on climbing a few feet out of the water realised his mistake and shouted again before entering the water. I picked him up in an extremely exhausted condition about 40 yards from the rocks he having swam the best part of a mile in his clothes.

5.5 am: Dived out of rifle fire and proceeded out of the Gulf of Ismid.

10.30 am: Overhauled and burnt three small sailing vessels laden with fruit and vegetables.

5.0 pm: Met E.2.

7.30 pm: Proceeded – E. 2 towards Mudania, E. 11 towards Constantinople.

9.0 pm: Sighted convoy consisting of one destroyer, three steam tugs and eight small sailing vessels in tow of the tugs. Having reconnoitred carefully with low buoyancy I decided that the chances of a successful night attack poor, observing that the position of the moon was entirely in favour of the enemy's disposition. Station ahead of the convoy was taken up and maintained until dawn. Their course appeared to be direct from Constantinople to the channel between Marmara Island and the speed of the convoy rendered it impossible for them to close the land on this course before day break.

22nd August

4.30 am: Dived to attack destroyer who started zigzagging as the light increased.

Failed to approach her in first attack. Turned to attack again and when just arriving in position to fire my periscope was unfortunately dipped owing to an inequality in the boat's depth line and although this only lasted a minute the destroyer had altered course away when the next sight of her was obtained. On speeding up and turning in for a third attack it was observed that she had turned round and was proceeding to the assistance of a dhow and the third tug which had apparently broken down. I therefore kept within easy gun range of the convoy and having opened the range from the destroyer sufficiently rose to the surface and opened fire on one of the tugs. Hit her twelve times and damaged several dhows in tow before destroyer was able to return to their assistance.

7.45 am: Dived – Both tugs now proceeded towards the shore having left the convoy. Destroyer having put me under, closed the tugs and apparently directed the undamaged one to proceed to the assistance of the broken down tug not dhow. I followed her and arrived in time to find her with both vessels in tow. Rose to the surface at close range with the intention of sinking them by gunfire. An accurate fire was however opened by the second tug which forced me to again submerge. Immediately on submerging the leading tug slipped her charges and proceeded at full speed to rejoin the remainder of the convoy. I then rose to the surface at a range of 6000 yards and on dropping a few shells near them the dhow was observed to sail away towards the shore. When she had reached a position outside the tug's gun range I closed to within 50 yards and sank her by gunfire.[1] The crew consisting of twenty men jumped overboard at the first shot. These I picked up. Amongst them was a German bank manager who was taking a quantity of money to Chanak Bank. The dhow was otherwise laden with ammunition. Having stowed the prisoners below dived with the intention of torpedoing the apparently helpless armed tug. On closing however it was observed through the high powered periscope that she had been deserted with the exception of one man who was hiding under the gunwhale. On rising to the surface to sink her fire was opened by another tug apparently coming to the rescue. She was however not in time, the tug being sunk by gunfire in a few moments.

During the afternoon overhauled a sailing ship laden with a cargo of fruit. The prisoners were placed on board and made to discharge the cargo overboard which duty they carried out with a willing hand, apparently much surprised at being granted their lives.

[1] Turkish naval tug *Dofen* (124 tons). Sunk.

23rd August

1.30 pm: In wireless communication with *Astor* (Distance 60 miles). Received information of the presence of a number of Transports in the Dardanelles. Failed to meet E. 2 on rendezvous.

24th August

7.0 am: Returned to Westward. Topped up battery preparatory to making an attack in the Dardanelles.

25th August

3.45 am: Proceeded with low buoyancy on the surface to within 8 miles of Ak Bashi Liman – making one short dive in the vicinity of Gallipoli to avoid detection by destroyer.

7.0 am: Fired torpedo at Gunboat in Ak Bashi Liman. Torpedo ran under gunboat and exploded among some shipping immediately behind her.[1] Damage not observed owing to ships in the foreground. Gunboat and destroyer proceeded to chase us passing several times overhead. Proceeded slowly to the Northward and returned to the attack close to the shore.

10.15 am: Fired both bow tubes, hitting two large transports both of which listed over and settled down.[2] It is understood they subsequently sank.

10.20 am: Proceeded towards False Bay.

12.0 am: Fired torpedo at large transport but track of torpedo could not be seen and no explosion was heard.[3] A large number of small craft were patrolling to seaward of her.

12.30 pm: Turned and fired second torpedo which struck her by the foremast. She settled down by the bows and was last seen with her propeller revolving out of the water.[4] Proceeded to Chardak Liman.

3.0 pm: Fired stern tube (the only remaining torpedo) at large transport hitting her under the forecastle. She was observed to settle down by the bow and it is understood was subsequently sighted on shore by E. 2.[5]

6.20 pm: Met E. 2 five miles East of Gallipoli and arranged that she should proceed to Ak Baski Liman the following day.

26th August

8.0 am: Overhauled and burnt small sailing ship laden with grain.

---

[1] Gunboat *Burrkat Reis*. Torpedo ran under target to hit and sink SS *Kios* (3304 tons).

[2] Torpedo fired from upper bow tube hit and sank (for the last time) the SS *Halep* (3364 tons); the torpedo from the lower tube hit and sank SS *Tenedos* (3564 tons).

[3] SS *Sam* (3662 tons). Missed.

[4] SS *Sam* (3662 tons). Sunk.

[5] SS *Lilly Rickmers* (4690 tons); damaged and beached.

Washed clothes and cleaned out boat.

27th August

Dived into and carefully inspected Gulf of Mudania, but found nothing.

28th August

5.0 am: Rose to the surface at dawn and opened fire on Mudania Railway Station. Put under by shore guns.

10.0 am: Proceeded to attack by gun fire small steamer in the entrance to the Gulf. She immediately however returned a sufficiently accurate fire to necessitate diving. Proceeded to a position 6000 yards from Railway Station and there met E. 2. Both boats carried out bombardment of Station and Magazine being outside range of Shore guns. Considerable damage must have been done although no fire was caused.

29th August

5.0 am: Proceeded towards Gulf of Ismid.

9.0 am: Burned sailing vessel laden with fruit. Proceeded towards Constantinople to investigate position of Zeppelin Shed but could arrive at nothing definite.

5.0 pm: At rendezvous but failed to meet E. 2.

30th August

Burnt four small sailing ships in the Gulf of Mudania. Having observed that the line of traffic to Constantinople followed the shore closely till reaching the entrance to the Gulf of Ismid, decided that there was the place to operate after dark.

9.0 pm: Rounded up three sailing vessels, secured two of them the third escaping in the dark. Both were laden with coke and coal. Burnt the larger of the two and owing to the number of prisoners already onboard it was necessary to release the other after discharging a considerable amount of the cargo.

31st August

Proceeded to the East of Prinkipo Island.

7.20 am: Rose to surface and opened rifle fire across bows of four sailing ships. The crews hauled down their sails and deserted their vessels at once, but after firing one round into the nearest was forced to dive by shore guns. Their first round pitched within ten yards of the after hydroplanes.

4.0 pm: Bombarded three masted sailing ship off Katirli village. Hit her with a large number of rounds.[1]

[1] Barque (750 tons). Sunk.

9.0 pm: Proceeded into the Gulf of Ismid.

1st September

5.0 am: Rose to surface and carried out deliberate bombardment of Railway Viaduct for over an hour. Range 6000 yards this being just clear of the fall of shot from shore guns. A large number of shots were observed to hit and considerable damage must have been done. At the close of the bombardment a shore gun was brought up with a range of at least 7000 yards.

10.30 am: Overhauled and burnt two small sailing ships taking their crews on board.

11.0 am: Proceeded towards Western end of Marmara and discharged the prisoners to a sailing vessel lying under the lee of Arablar Island.

2nd September

Charged batteries, dismantled gun, fitted extra jumping wire and prepared for the return journey through the Dardanelles.

3rd September

2.0 am: Proceeded with low buoyancy on the surface passed Gallipoli diving at daylight eight miles to the eastward of the net.

6.25 am: Ran through the Nagara net at depth of 80 feet. Increased speed to 8 knots on touching the net and broke through. Boat was pulled up to 60 feet before net parted. The course was only deflected a few degrees. Lieutenant D'Oyly-Hughes who was placed in the conning tower with the deadlights open to observe described the net as follows: A number of 2½ inch wires crossed and securely joined together forming about a ten foot mesh. He also observed a dark object hanging down the Port side which might well be a sinker. It is anticipated from this that the net might be safely passed without encountering obstruction if taken between two buoys and at a depth of 120 feet or more; observing that on the passage up a very stout horizontal wire was met at a depth of 110 feet. It is supposed that this wire was the lower jackstay supporting the sinkers.

9.15 am: Came to surface off Helles and was escorted to Kephalo by *Bulldog*.

[145] *Extract from Minute attached to Patrol Reports from HM*
Submarine E11 by Arthur Balfour[1]
[ADM 137/382]

10th September 1915

* * *

It is worth considering whether some episodes of this remarkable story might not be published verbatim ...

[146] *Memorandum by Commodore of Submarines*
[ADM 137/1115]

15 October 1915

45 Lieutenants or Sub-lieutenants will be required to man submarines now under construction. 6 Lieutenants, 20 Sub-Lieutenants and 2 Midshipmen have volunteered, some of whom are obviously unsuitable. 5 Lieutenants (E) [Engineering], who are very desirable volunteers cannot be spared from (E) duties.

It is suggested that the service afloat, and particularly the Grand Fleet know nothing as to the employment of Submarines during the war, and that if this was known plenty of volunteers would be forthcoming.

I submit that a selection of the Baltic and Dardanelles reports from submarines may be printed and issued to all ships of the Grand Fleet for the information of Executive Officers, and that when this has been digested names of volunteers for submarines may be called for from Sub-lieutenants and Lieutenants up to one year's seniority.

[Attached minute (22 October 1915) by Captain Thomas Jackson][2]
These reports from submarines have been considered as very confidential and have only been seen by a few officers in the Admiralty. The publication for the information of officers of these reports, or of parts in them, will be almost tantamount to publishing them in the Gazette and it will be difficult to avoid matters becoming known generally which have hitherto been considered as secret.

---

[1] Arthur Balfour: former Prime Minister (1901–1905) served in the coalition government as First Lord of the Admiralty from May 1915 to November 1916.
[2] Capt. Thomas Jackson: a/DNI 1908–14; Director of Operations Division, Naval Staff, 1914–17.

[Attached minute (25 October 1915) by Admiral Sir Henry Jackson][1]

Let the reports be prepared and examined and [the] decision as to issue can be then considered.[2]

---

[1] Adm. Sir Henry Jackson: First Sea Lord, May 1915 to November 1916.
[2] Ultimately the print was not circulated.

PART VII

TAKING STOCK: WARTIME EXPERIENCE, 1916–1918

[ADM 137/2077]

30th August 1916

After two years of war I beg to put before Their Lordships a general survey of the work of the Submarine Service.

Coastal Submarines

With the exception of a few C Class detailed for anti-submarine work away from their bases, of which two were lost with all hands, the whole of the coastal flotillas have been employed defensively. No opportunity has occurred for meeting the enemy, and no loss has been incurred.

This portion of the Submarine Service has no doubt had a certain moral effect upon enemy raids and bombardments, but its main use has been as a training ground for officers and crews for new submarines. From the coastal flotillas there have been supplied 130 trained officers and 64 trained crews for oversea submarines. The flow of new entries from volunteers has kept pace with this demand, and the standard obtained appears to be high. Fourteen officers have reverted to the General Service through not coming up to standard as commanding officer of a submarine or from being of unsuitable temperament.

The coastal flotillas have been kept constantly on their local patrols, which consist of a portion of flotilla being actually at sea every morning at daylight, the remainder being ready for sea and standing by. This has been monotonous and trying in the extreme to young officers burning for active service, but it has been regularly and cheerfully carried out. In addition to the patrol work, training and practice has continued at every opportunity, 530 torpedoes having been fired during 920 practice attacks by the coastal flotillas during the last quarter. Constant practice is one of the foundations upon which we base efficiency, and I wish there could be more. Enemy mines restrict it, also weather on account of recovering torpedoes, and these causes are unpreventable. The chief restriction, however, is shortage of tenders; the want of one is much felt in [depot ships] *Vulcan* and *Alecto*. As soon as older destroyers are available it is hoped one may be allotted to each of these depots.

Oversea Submarines

Custom, established before submarines were used in war, has confined despatches broadly speaking to incidents during which one belligerent or both have come under gun or torpedo fire. In such despatches individual successes of submarines have been reported and there is no need to refer to them again in this paper, they are

331

included, however, in Appendix I [not reproduced] to make this survey complete.

In submarine warfare the torpedo has little effect and the gun none at all on a submarine officer; his chief enemy is the mine, followed in order of merit by fleet anti-submarine craft fitted with explosive sweeps or depth charges, passive obstructions such as nets with mines in them, aeroplanes and zeppelins with bombs. All ships are in danger from mines, but no other class of ship is asked to run the gauntlet of mines on the enemy's coast to anything like the same extent as the oversea submarines. When submarines go into enemy waters they do so as an operation, the actual period of exposure is short, and when the operation is concluded the force is withdrawn.

Submarines, however, on the great majority of their cruises are all the time in the close neighbourhood of known minefields and in areas most likely to hold new mines and those that have drifted out of position. They are harassed continuously by destroyers, trawlers, and special anti-submarine vessels fitted with sweeps and depth-charges, by enemy submarines, and particularly by aircraft, which in these waters have the advantage of being often able to see the submarines even at 60 feet. The area the enemy has to defend is so small that it is seldom possible to come to the surface in daylight, the navigational difficulties among the minefields are great and the rapidly changing densities of the water on enemy's coast make the trimming and depth control a constant anxiety.

Positive results under such conditions, where no precaution is ever neglected by the enemy and targets are rare, must necessarily be few, and these results are no measure of the work done or the risks incurred by submarines in war. Their patrols have been kept up throughout winter months when the gales and weather experienced in the Heligoland Bight are severe, on many occasions necessitating their being shut down for long periods.

It is only after going onboard a submarine on her return from one of these cruises that one realises what a tremendous strain is imposed on the personnel. They are all young men in the prime of life who have undergone rigorous selection for fitness, but they are obviously much tried after seven or eight days during which they are continually in what constitutes action to a submarine. It is fair to remember that the sighting of a surface enemy is a relief to this strain which unfortunately is seldom obtained.

Owing to the submarine suddenly receiving a great deal of notice in the press and some irresponsible booming, I fear there has been a tendency to overrate the results likely to be obtained from them. It seems to be considered that if a submarine gets within torpedo range of an enemy she should certainly torpedo her, and if she does not, that the fault lies with the commanding officer. I do not believe that this will ever be the case. There must always be a great difference between theory and practice due to the periscope eye being monocular or very limited field and so close to the water; the means of obtaining grasp of a situation are very poor. There is also the psychological effect on the officers after several days shut up in a submarine. This is assuredly one of the reasons for the poor results obtained by German submarines in spite of the targets they have had, and the only remedies are a very highly trained personnel and the employment of as many submarines as possible in the area of operations.

The percentage of hits to torpedoes fired which has been obtained by our overseas submarines is 32.5[%], and this I consider is not likely to be improved. If expectations run too high disappointment is sure to follow, and I am aware that there have been three occasions lately when keen disappointment has been experienced.

(1) [The first] was a failure of the submerged tube mechanism when a hit should have been certain. The constant additions to the intricate mechanism of submarines is in one sense responsible for this, and I hope we have touched bottom in this respect. These additions, all of which require constant attention, have been:–

1. Wireless.
2. Gyro compass.
3. Fessenden signalling.[1]
4. Hydrophonic receivers.
5. Forbes logs.
6. Bounding machines.
7. Air purification.
8. Masts worked from inside.
9. Guns (Wet).

At the same time this failure was preventable, and strong disciplinary action was taken. I believe it to have been the only case where more should have been accomplished by the personnel.

(2) On one occasion a submarine lying on the bottom at night off Norderney heard a number of ships pass on the surface and did not rise to attack. The officer concerned is one of. the best we have, he has during this war taken his submarine over 20,000 miles looking for just such an opportunity. I am absolutely certain he remained where he was with greatest reluctance; as a fact the submarine was, fortunately for

---

[1] Fessenden: underwater telephone/signalling device.

herself, in the only 13 fathom patch in the swept channel, the ships not heard until very close and their wash was causing the submarine to roll 15° on the bottom. The vessels were accompanied by sweepers and the humming of the sweep wires was so loud as to drown the roar of the ships passing overhead, the submarine being actually struck by one of the sweeps. It was his opinion that the night was so pitch dark that it would have been impossible to come to the surface amongst these vessels at the speed they were going with any prospect of anything but being run over. Further the onus of establishing a ship as an enemy and not a friend is entirely on the submarine, and I consider the commanding officer was justified in this instance.

(3) One submarine arrived in vicinity of Horns Reef and was obliged to go to the bottom at 0.20 a.m. on 1st June owing to a zeppelin coming over low down. At 0.45 a sweep passed along his side, and from 2.15 to 5.30 eleven explosions were felt close to. At 4.15 something was dragged over the jumping wire. No ships were heard at all. It is believed that enemy ships must, however, have been in his vicinity, and judging after the event it is regretted he did not rise at the same time, however, the commanding officer, who had made many previous cruises, had no idea enemy ships were out.[1] As he had not heard any he presumed he was being hunted by anti-submarine craft in the usual way. These are the only three cases in the course of 370 cruises undertaken in which I have ever had occasion to enquire closely into the action of the submarines of this flotilla and so I judge it advisable to give them in some detail.

Two submarine minelayers have been added to the Harwich flotilla, E.24 and E.41. E.24 was lost from an unknown cause on her third trip. E.41 has done five successful minelaying trips into the Heligoland Bight. When this flotilla is not at sea, they are, like the coastals, kept constantly at exercise, the volume of this amounted to 236 torpedoes and 258 attacks last quarter.

The percentage of losses of our oversea submarines has been 33%, probably heavier than in any other of H. M. Forces.

21 were in commission on 4th August 1914.

41 have been commissioned up to 4th August 1916.

22 have been lost; 15 with all hands; in 3 others about a quarter of the crew were saved; in the remaining 4 the crews were saved and taken prisoners.

It is satisfactory to record that the keenness to get into the oversea

---

[1] The enemy ships referred to were the battleships of the German High Seas Fleet retreating to port after the Battle of Jutland fought the previous evening (31 May 1916).

flotillas from the coastals has not abated. These losses, however, bear out my contention that the oversea submarines, particularly those of the Harwich flotilla, are always in action when in enemy waters, though the actions have not been made the subject of despatches and the losses have not been announced.

* * *

[148] *Commander Francis Cromie to Commodore Sydney Hall*[1]
10 October 1917.

Many thanks for your letter of 21/9/17. As regards the iron ore I went into the whole position very carefully with the [Russian] Chief of Staff when the Foreign Office telegram came out. The entire Swedish coast from Lulea to Oland has the three mile limit buoyed, and ships navigate safely inside these.

Neutrals pass directly across the Hano bight, but the Germans follow the shore, except they sometimes cut across Kalmar Sound under strong escort. Boats have been sent several times to Hano bight and Utkippen without result. E.19 did see several ships (empty) west of Bornholm, but apparently laden ones stick close to the Swedish and Danish waters, which we are not permitted to violate. Russian boats have been operating off Landsort and in Bothnia, but [had] only one success, when an empty northbound tramp cut a corner. Lately the Russians have had such bad luck with breakdowns, due to the crews having chucked out most of the mechanics and P.O.'s, that we have been reserved for the important patrol. And now we are suffering: E.8's field coils burnt out and one propeller dropped off – nuts, boss, and all in deep water; E.19: badly damaged hull after running aground in the Strategic fairway through the shears, owing to the weather having broken up the buoys; E.9: also breaking [down?] from the same cause. It is an awful shame, and I have put it strongly before the C.-in-C. about E.19 being allowed [to] use a passage they knew was dangerous. I have sent minutes of the courts of inquiry to you. Out of seventeen Russians there are five fit for immediate use, others being damaged or broken down; so at present the remainder are kept more or less in reserve for defence against the threatened attack by the enemy fleet.

I quite understand the spirit of your letter, but I think you have forgotten that I am placed under the Russian C.-in-C., who has changed

[1] Francis Cromie: senior officer Baltic Submarine Flotilla, 1916–18. Cromie Letters – Submarine Museum, HMS *Dolphin*.

four times so far this year. I am by no means a free agent, even though professional jealousy has died down; it is difficult for you at home to imagine what a part the latter played out here in 1915–16. I come under the Admiral (S.), though I have always stuck to my right of direct access to the C.-in-C., and so we go when and where we are sent. You seem so disturbed over the matter, if you will excuse my saying so, that perhaps it is better to run over events as shortly as I can, so that you may better understand the peculiarities that would not occur if the Russians had a flotilla in England.

In 1915 we had such an extraordinarily successful year (I never came back empty-handed from a trip) that the Russian submarine and other officers became as jealous as women over our success and popularity, and like women, spread every sort of scandal about us. When Admiral von Essen died we were placed under the Com. S. by Kanin, who did not like us, and our opportunities were reduced. In 1916 we were kept idle for months at a time and I got positively rude about it, but [I] was always put off saying that the plans were not complete, until I said, "if they did not see fit to use my thirteen years' submarine experience in forming the plans, that I should be more useful at home than sitting down in Reval". We were kept waiting for the great landing in Riga Gulf which never came off. Nepenin, who was then N.I.D. and a great friend, did his best, but became C.-in-C. too late in the year to do much, and I confess 1916 was a wasted year, but not from want of asking till I became rude on the matter. A change in Commodore (S) and Nepenin as C.-in-C. gave me a great pull, which I worked as hard as I could till the Revolution, which has upset all. The C.-in-C. and Commodore (S) changed again, the whole plan of campaign was abandoned; all officers were only concerned with politics and discipline in the Fleet – the worst enemy was their own Fleet. At one time the T.B.D.'s and ourselves were the only forces to be relied on, and we were reserved for emergencies. And although we cannot show material results as to the value of the information this flotilla has brought home, I think even your worse enemy would be satisfied. As it is my command I ought not to blow, but the fact remains that, since Nepenin's death, the intelligence has gone to pot and the [Russian] D.N.I. relies very greatly on our reconnaissances, and those made by C.26 and C.27; you will hear of [this] shortly from the C.-in-C.

*   *   *

Time and time again I have begged to go out after Fritz., and every time I hear of a Fritz submarined [sic] at home I report, and rub it in to the Staff.[1] But this year we have really gone quite a lot, and [after] a long talk with Admiral Vladislaveff after lunch yesterday, he stated that he thought that if no move was [made] against Riga Gulf in a fortnight it would be over for this year and he agreed to use us offensively. I put forward a scheme combining submarines and T.B.D.'s against patrols and trade which he was much taken with, and has gone to the C.-in-C. about [it]. I also tried to revive the old bombardment of Libau scheme too. The submarine defence of the Gulf of Riga was altered without a word to me, so I went direct to Admiral Starck in the Riga Gulf and explained my views, which were immediately adopted. Lately we have had great difficulty with provisions and have been going to sea on our emergency rations, of which we had hoarded up ten days in each boat. I take it that it is up to me to keep the flotilla going with stores until the Admiralty decide to withdraw us, and that question is better decided by the diplomats (?) and liaison officer. My private opinion expressed in March was that it were better for us to give the Russians the boats and stores and clear out. However, things have gone better than I expected, and we have done far more this year than all last year. I don't see how this country can go on, and personally I am convinced they must make peace next year – I hope they won't forget us when terms are discussed – unless the Allies take charge as the Huns do in Austria and Turkey.

* * *

Have you yet considered relieving me? I am not applying for it, but I am ready to go. I get on all right with the powers but can't stand this navy as a whole, since the Revolution, also I don't look forward to a more or less idle winter for English and Russians to fall out in.

Terischenko, Minister for Foreign Affairs, suggested I should become N[aval] A[ttache], but I think I nipped it in the bud; anyway I look to you for protection if it goes any further.[2]

If (as rumoured) Admiral Pilkin becomes C.-in-C. I want to come home, as the squabbles in the Fleet will be more than I care to have any dealings with; in this case I recommend that a Captain be sent out, if the flotilla remains.

---

[1] Cromie was referring here to his repeated to requests to deploy his flotilla on 'hunter-killer' anti-submarine patrols.

[2] Francis Cromie was appointed naval attaché and promoted acting Captain at the end of 1917.

[149] *Memorandum from the Captain (S), Harwich,*[1] *to the Chief of the War Staff, Admiralty, enclosing Narrative by Stoker Petty Officer William Brown explaining his Method of Escape from Wreck of Submarine E41*

[ADM 137/1922]

31st August 1916

1. With reference to my submission of, 18th August 1916, No.0170, the report by Stoker Petty Officer William Brown, Official Number 306130, of the method of his escape from Submarine E41, after she had sunk, is forwarded herewith.[2]

2. Although the man was fighting for his life, it is a wonderful example of indomitable courage and perseverance, and of refusing to acknowledge defeat.

He was by himself, in almost complete darkness, with the gradually rising water, receiving electric shocks and, towards the end, suffering from the effects of chlorine gas and a badly crushed hand, and yet, in spite of continual disappointments, he worked on for nearly two hours, keeping his head to the last, and at the seventh attempt at opening the hatch, succeeded and escaped.

3. I would strongly recommend that Stoker Petty Officer Brown may be advanced to Chief Stoker, for which rating he is fully qualified.

(Signed) Arthur K. Waistell

REPORT BY STOKER PETTY OFFICER WILLIAM BROWN OF THE METHOD OF HIS ESCAPE FROM HM SUBMARINE E41.

1. About 10.30 am on Tuesday, 15th August 1916, something was heard to come in contact with the bottom of the Boat forward, twice in quick succession. Immediately after the Engine Room telegraph rang to Out Clutches.

2. I took out the Port Clutch and then closed the muffler valve, then it was reported that the Ship was making water. I proceeded forward to ascertain the position of the leak. Finding no leak above the Battery Board, came to the conclusion that she was holed low down.

3. First impulse was to close the lower Conning Tower hatch and put a pressure in the Boat, but the Men were going up the Conning Tower.

4. At this time, Sewell, ERA, spoke to me and asked my opinion. I replied we would have a chance if we could close the hatch and get a

---

[1] Captain (S) at Harwich (HMS *Maidstone*) was Capt. Arthur Waistell.
[2] HMS/m E41 was sunk after an underwater collision with HMS/m E4 off Harwich, 15th August 1916.

pressure in the Boat. He thereupon stood by the air valves, and I waited to close the hatch. At this point, Bullock, Chief ERA, enquired if all Hands were out of the Engine Room. I replied I would find out; on going aft, I found one man coming forward and I ordered him to put on a lifebelt and keep his head till he could get a chance to get up the Conning Tower hatch.

5. On ascertaining there was nobody else aft, went forward and put on a lifebelt. Then went back and closed the valve on the air trunk through the Engine room bulkhead, as at this time I thought I would have to use the Engine Room as a way of escape.

6. I then went back to try and close the lower Conning Tower hatch, but before I reached it water began to come down through it, and the Boat took a decided dip forward. I went aft once more, closed the Rear Engine Room bulkhead scupper and shouted to the Hands forward to come aft to the Engine Room. There was however no response. Repeated efforts brought no reply, the midship compartment being in darkness and partly flooded, therefore it was impossible to ascertain if there was anyone alive, beyond a low moaning there was no sound.

7. It was impossible for me to leave the door, as it would have closed behind me and would have been impossible to open again, owing to an increase of pressure in the flooding compartment. I remained there hoping for some of them to come aft, until the water rose 18 inches above the sill of the door and chlorine gas began to come through from the midship compartment. I was then reluctantly forced to close the door, and proceeded to unscrew the clips of the torpedo hatch above me.

8. At this juncture the Engine Room was in complete darkness with the exception of the Port pilot lamp, which appeared to be burning through earth. The water was slowly rising in the Engine room through the voice pipes, which I had left open to relieve excessive pressure on the bulkhead of the Engine Room.

9. I then proceeded to disconnect the torpedo hatch from the gearing, which necessitated the removal of two split pins and two pins from the links. Before the foremost one could be removed however, I had to unslip the strongback and wait till there was sufficient pressure in the Boat to ease off the strongback.[1]

10. The heat at this time was excessive, therefore I rested awhile and considered the best means of flooding the Engine Room, and eventually came to the conclusion that the best way was to flood through the stern

[1] Strongbacks were removable girders that braced the underside of the torpedo loading hatch.

tube or the weed trap of circulating system, or by dropping exhaust and induction valve and flooding through the muffler valve.

11. I tried the stern tube first, but could neither open the rear door nor stern cap. I then came forward to the forepart of the Engine Room and considered the problem once more. Whilst passing the switchboards, however, I received several shocks owing to the water from the voice pipes running over them and on to the deck. Then came to the conclusion that the next best thing would be to try the weed trap of the circulating inlet, so went aft again, but could not get back the butterfly nuts, as the weed trap was in an awkward position, and also water from the voice pipes was pouring down on top of me. So proceeded forward again and opened muffler valve, also the two test-cocks on the two groups [of] exhaust pipes; tried them and found water was coming in.

12. I then got on top of the Engines underneath the torpedo hatch, in order to drop the exhaust and induction valves, but discovered that the pressure inside the Boat was equalising the external pressure, and that the hatch was rising off the strongbacks. I then proceeded to unslip the strongback, in order to drive the pin out of the link.

13. This was accomplished by means of a medium Vandangel's spanner, which I had carried with me from the time of entering the Engine Room. I now proceeded to knock out the pin securing the hatch to the gearing but found that the rubber jointing was springing the hatch up, the strain being so carried on the pin wedging it, that it was impossible to drive out.

14. I then dived down under the water and eased back the wheel of the gearing. After some little trouble I eventually managed to get the links in line, and was enabled to drive out the pin.

15. I then came to the conclusion that it would give me more clearance whilst getting out of the hatch if the other strongback was removed, so I therefore removed it without any trouble. I was now ready for flooding the Boat completely.

16. I have always held the theory that the pressure in a sunken air-locked vessel can be greater than the external pressure, deciding factors being the weight and shape of the sunken vessel. The shape of a Submarine appeared to lend itself to obtaining this increase of pressure. I then discovered that the Boat was flooding very slowly and I decided as a last resort to open the scupper in the Engine Room bulkhead.

17. I had previously closed this from inside the Engine Room, as I was of the opinion that if I flooded through the exhaust and induction valves, the induction valve would possibly close owing to the pressure behind it. So proceeded to ease back the butterfly nuts on the deadlight, open it and allow the water to come through. I only used this method of

flooding as a last resort, as I anticipated chlorine generating from this water, obtained from the midship compartment. This proved to be the case, but I then discovered that as the water came in, the air was escaping through the hatch. So I tried three times to open the hatch, succeeding in opening it about halfway, but the air rushed out and the hatch fell down again.

18. So I then dived down and retrieved the clip bolts and slipped two of them and lightly secured them to the end of the dogs, the idea being to get a sufficient pressure in the Boat, then knock the bolts away, anticipating being blown out by the pressure.

19. I then proceeded to put this idea into execution; the hatch flew open, but there was not sufficient pressure to blow out, nor yet time for me to escape before the hatch came down again.

20. I tried once more to lift the hatch with my shoulder, but it descended on my hand. I managed to raise the hatch sufficiently to clear my hand and let it come down again.

21. I now considered it was impossible to attempt to blow myself out by means of internal pressure. Therefore, I knocked the dogs off the deadlight and allowed the Boat to flood as quickly as possible, with the idea of flooding the Engine Room completely and then raising hatch and escaping.

22. I allowed the Engine Room to flood till the water was up to the covering of the hatch. I then raised the hatch and escaped, rising to the surface and being picked up by HMS *Firedrake*.

Correspondence between the Commander-in-Chief, Home Fleets, and the Board of Admiralty on better Utilisation of HM Submarines.

[150] *From the Secretary of the Admiralty, Sir W. Grahame Greene, to Commander-in-Chief, Home Fleets*[1]
[ADM 137/1926]

Admiralty
29th July, 1915

With reference to your submission of the 24th July, No. 1496/H.F.0022, proposing that a force of submarines should be based on the Tyne in order to support the Grand Fleet during a fleet action, I am commanded by my Lords Commissioners of the Admiralty to acquaint you that owing to the necessity of having a strong force of submarines in the southern part of the North Sea, and to submarine requirements for other operations, it is not possible to give effect to your proposal at present. When, however, more oversea boats become available this question will be reconsidered.

[151] *Jellicoe to Admiralty*
[ADM 137/1926]

Iron Duke
8th November, 1915
No. 2535/H.F.0010

1. In reply to Admiralty Letter of 4th November, 1915, M.08120, be pleased to represent to the Lords Commissioner of the Admiralty, as regards the allocation of E class submarines to work with the Grand Fleet, that it was not proposed that they should accompany the Grand Fleet on passage south, owing to their insufficient surface speed. My suggestion was that they should be based on the Tyne in order that they might be given rendezvous at which they should meet the battle fleet, in order to be available for a fleet action.

2. There is no doubt the speed of the submarines would be sufficient for them to meet the battle fleet at any probable rendezvous, and it is considered possible to make such arrangements after the meeting as to ensure their being available for the fleet action.

3. It is quite certain that the German battle fleet will be accompanied

---

[1] C-in-C, Home Fleets: Adm. Sir John Jellicoe (August 1914 to November 1916).

by submarines, and we shall be at a great disadvantage if our own submarines are not in a position to take offensive action against the German battle front.

4. I am aware that, should the High Sea Fleet leave their ports to accept action, or to carry out operations off our coast, it is the intention to endeavour to attack the enemy by submarines whilst on passage back to their ports, but I would submit that an offensive against the battle fleet during the action is far preferable to an attack on them after the action, since the submarines might conceivably play a very important part in the fleet action itself, and our losses from this cause might conceivably be so heavy as to turn the balance of gun power in favour of the Germans.

5. If it is not possible to allocate 12 E class submarines to the Grand Fleet before the J and K classes are completed, I submit for earnest consideration that at least six should be so allocated.

6. There is no reason why these submarines should not be employed in a manner similar to the present employment of the Harwich force, when not otherwise required, but unless certain submarines are definitely allocated to the Grand Fleet, it is quite impossible for me to convey to those in command any intentions during a fleet action, and the dispositions which I desire that they shall assume.

7. I trust that their Lordships will see fit to reconsider the determination arrived at in the letter under reply.

8. In regard to the three C class submarines that were temporarily attached to the Grand Fleet for the summer, and the Admiralty decision on this point, I have, in my telegram, No. 359 of the 7th November, 1915, begged for a reconsideration of this matter. I have stated my reasons fully in the telegraph.

[152] *Admiralty to Jellicoe*

[ADM 137/1926]

17 November 1915

1. With reference to your letter of the 8th November No. 2525/H.F.0010, I am commanded by My Lords Commissioners of the Admiralty to acquaint you that the Eleventh Flotilla of E and G Class Submarines to be stationed at Blyth will be an Oversea Flotilla and will carry out similar duties to the Eighth Flotilla at Harwich but in a different area. It was always intended that the Eleventh Flotilla should co-operate with the Grand Fleet, although the vessels composing it are too slow to work in company with the Grand Fleet.

2. The Eleventh Flotilla will be placed under your orders.

3. In detailing Boats for cruises, you are to note that they should not be sent to the Southward of a line joining Flamborough Head and a position in Latitude 56° N., Longitude 8° E., without special arrangements being made with the Admiralty. The Admiralty will give orders that the Eighth Flotilla Boats are never to cruise North of the above line. This will obviate the liability of boats of different Flotillas being not acquainted with each other's movements and possibly attacking each other by mistake.

4. The Eleventh Flotilla will also have to co-operate in defensive measures in case of raid or invasion North of Flamborough Head, and the Captain (S) Blyth will have to keep the Rear Admiral Commanding, East Coast of England, informed of the movements of his vessels and the times when boats are expected back from cruises, and the Captain (S) Blyth and the Rear Admiral should concert measures to avoid mistakes occurring between their respective vessels.

5. A copy of this letter has been sent to the Rear Admiral Commanding, East Coast of England.

[153] *Memorandum by Jellicoe*

[Keyes Mss 4/20]

Iron Duke
14th October 1916

SUBMARINE COMMITTEE

The following Officers are requested to form a Submarine Committee, and important questions relating to the employment of submarines will be referred to this Committee by the Commander-in-Chief.

Any suggestions which the Committee may make on submarine subjects will also be welcomed by the Commander-in-Chief.

Captain Roger J. B. Keyes, C.B., C.M.G., M.V.O., D.S.O., A.D.C.
  H.M.S. *Centurion*
Captain Algernon H. C. Candy, H.M.S. *Boadicea*[1]
Commander Charles J. C. Little, H.M.S. *Fearless*[2]

---

[1] Capt. Algernon Candy: Cmdr 1909; executive officer HMS *Diana* 1910–12; CO Portsmouth submarine flotilla 1914; acting-Capt. 1915; Capt. 1916; Assistant Director of Torpedoes 1918.
[2] Cmdr (later Admiral Sir) Charles 'Tiny' Little: see biographical appendix.

[154] *Jellicoe to Admiralty*

[ADM 137/1926]

Iron Duke
16th October, 1916

1. Be pleased to submit for the consideration of the Lords Commissioners of the Admiralty that the recent activity of enemy submarines off the coast of the United States of America indicates that this form of attack on trade will certainly be adopted in the Spring when the weather conditions become favourable for it.

2. It is also quite possible that the operations of enemy submarines may be extended to the South American ports where the facilities for the establishment of submarine bases are far greater.

3. The most effective counter appears to be the employment of our own submarines to locate and attack those of the enemy if possible. Torpedo boat destroyers could not be spared in sufficient numbers to work in such open waters, but decoy vessels if available, particularly if accompanied by one of our submarines should prove of great use.

4. It is submitted that our submarines of the J and E classes are required in Home Waters, and that those of the D and G classes should therefore be selected for this service.

I hope shortly to lay before their Lordships for consideration detailed proposals for these operations.

5. Meanwhile in order to obtain submarines quickly I beg to submit for earnest consideration that twelve submarines of the H class should be ordered secretly from Mr. [Charles] Schwab, and that these submarines should be constructed in sections and sent to Canada for assembly in order to avoid difficulty with the United States Government. An alternative might be to order H class submarines as commercial submarines similar to the *Deutshland* [*sic*] etc.,[1] but to so arrange the interior as to admit of torpedo tubes being fitted at Halifax after delivery. The tubes to be built in England and sent out for assembly.

6. It is assumed that if an order were given now the submarines might be ready by April or May, 1917, having in view the rapidity with which H 1–10 were built.

7. If their Lordships entertain this idea, it would seem that the quickest method to adopt would be to send an Agent to the United States of America to place the order personally.

[1] A reference to the U-155 that in 1916 evaded the British naval blockade, crossed the Atlantic, entered New York harbour with a small commercial cargo, and returned safely to Germany.

[155] *Commander Charles Little to Commander-in-Chief, Home Fleets*[1]

[ADM 137/1926]

H. M. S. *Fearless*
18 January, 1917

I have the honour to attach hereto, Notes for the Employment of H.M. Submarines during the Summer Months of 1917, in accordance with your orders.

NOTES FOR THE EMPLOYMENT OF H.M. SUBMARINES DURING THE SUMMER MONTHS OF 1917

1. It is generally recognised that the principal role of the British Navy during the forthcoming Summer will be to combat the German Submarine menace to our food supplies and overseas trade generally.

2. In these notes it is proposed to investigate in general terms whether H.M. Submarines can be of use to the Fleet in this respect, to what extent, and to indicate a general disposition.

3. The submarine is not primarily intended to fight the submarine, but at the same time if surface craft targets are not available, the submarine can be employed to advantage on this service. Under favourable conditions a submarine can deliberately attack and destroy an enemy submarine which is unaware of its presence. This is a man to man fight as both submarines start on the surface, and the one that observes the other first has all the advantage on his side. It cannot be doubted our submarine officers have had more experience than the Germans, and should come off well in this class of warfare. The diving patrol in this case should not be permitted.

4. No other vessel can attack a submarine during daylight with much chance of success if the submarine wishes to evade the attack, and at night only on rare occasions. I am speaking now only of H.M. Ships, and not decoy vessels or other anti-submarine craft. It is to be regretted, but at the same time it is true, that H.M. Ships cannot be used with any hope of success to attack enemy submarines. If they attempt it, it is only a question of time before they in turn become the attacked, and losses are incurred without the desired result being achieved.

5. Before suggesting any disposition of our submarines to meet the forthcoming menace, it is as well to state broadly how they are at present employed.

---

[1] From November 1916 to 1918, the post of C-in-C, Home Fleets, was held by Adm. Sir David Beatty.

6. We have three distinct types of submarines, i.e.

Fleet Submarines

Patrol Submarines

Coastal Submarines

7. The Fleet Submarines are now in the process of being formed into a new arm of the Battle Fleet.

8. The Patrol Submarines are engaged chiefly in watching the Heligoland Bight for German men-of-war putting to sea or returning to their bases.

9. The Coastal Submarines are distributed on the East Coast as part of a defence scheme in case of Invasion, or Hostile Raids by the enemy Battle Cruiser Fleet.

10. Is this disposition making the best use of our submarine weapon at this stage of the War? In my opinion it is not.

11. It is suggested that in the rare event of the German Fleet or units of it putting to sea with an offensive object in view, our own Fleets are capable of dealing with them effectively, and so far as submarines are concerned the Fleet Submarines (12th and 13th Flotillas) are available also for this purpose.

12. The *Fleet Submarines* are designed to accompany the Fleet at sea and on account of their great size (for a submarine) they cannot be used with advantage for any other purpose under the present conditions. It is therefore proposed to leave them with the Grand Fleet and not to consider them in this discussion.

13. Secondly. If my contention in paragraph 11 is admitted this places the *Patrol Submarines*, i.e. D. E. F. G. H. J. and V Classes ([blank] vessels when all E. class are completed and repaired, which should be before the Summer) at our disposal; but at the same time it will be seen from the disposition of submarines proposed later that a portion of these will be well placed for their proper role of attacking the enemy ships at sea in the Heligoland Bight, in addition to their anti-submarine duties. The J. Class are included under the patrol heading for this purpose as it is considered they can be spared from the North Sea and their good habitability speed, and enormous radius of action, suit them for work on distant stations, such as the South East Coast of America.

14. Thirdly *Coastal Submarines*. It is respectfully submitted that these are now being utilised to very small advantage as an Invasion is highly improbable. They comprise the C. Class submarines.

15. We have 30 of these available if the three are towed home from Hong-Kong. These vessels can be relied upon to operate in the North Sea 200 miles from their base in the Summer months, and are on account of their small size, the best suited for anti-submarine work generally.

16. Speaking broadly, how can these 107 Patrol and Coastal submarines be best employed against the submarine menace. As pointed out previously this work is not the role of the submarine and great results cannot be expected as regards numbers of submarines destroyed, but at the same time the moral effect among the enemy will be of great value, and our submarines will act as a deterrent and save many merchant ships from destruction.

17. The most advantageous places in which to attack commerce destroying submarines are close to their own base, where the areas are comparatively small, and again when they are in the act of attacking the trade on the Trade Routes or other waters, such as among the fishing fleets, etc.

18. As regards enemy submarine exits, there are three in Home Waters, Zeebrugge, the Heligoland Bight, and the Skagerrak.

19. If we could seal the three home exits it would be the complete answer to the submarine menace but unfortunately this is now only possible with Zeebrugge, and it is hoped that it will be done.

20. As regards the Bight, although the rivers cannot be blocked now, it is possible to mine extensively further out and it is understood that this matter is under consideration.

21. The mine is the best weapon against the submarine in this connection.

22. The areas outside the minefield, and on the probable enemy tracks, are where our submarines must be disposed.

23. Their areas of activity should be frequently changed so as to harass the enemy boats as much as possible.

24. The third exit for the German submarine is the Skagerrak, this is a much more closely defined channel and our submarines can be employed to advantage there.

25. To sum up, the North Sea is best divided into two anti-submarine areas.

Area 1, North of 54°N, including the Skagerrak
Submarines Proposed
   6 G. Class
   6 E. Class
Based on *Titania* at Blyth
   11 C. Class
Based at Leith and Tyne with *Hebe* and *Bonaventure*
   8 G. Class
   4 E. Class
   9 C. Class
Based at Tees with *Lucia* and *Thames*

Area 2, South of 54°N

Submarines Proposed

   6 D. Class

Based with *Vulcan* at Humber

   5 H. Class

   3 F. Class

   4 V. Class

Based with *Alecto* at Yarmouth

   10 C. Class

[Remaining coastals to be] based on Dover, Portsmouth, or Plymouth, to be used on the enemy submarine tracks in the southern portion of the North Sea, or in the Channel depending on where the enemy submarine activity is most marked.

26. This scheme leaves 6 J. Class, 20 E. Class and 3 H. Class for services abroad and in addition to these there are L. Class (improved E.) and more H's under construction.

27. This also liberates [depot ships] *Maidstone*, *Forth* and *Pandora*, for depots abroad, in addition to *Adamant* and *Ambrose*.

28. Speaking generally, the submarines in the North Sea would be employed outside the minefield and on the enemy's tracks outwards and inwards. The patrol submarines taking the outer billets and Coastals (C. Class) inner billets.

29. The general idea being to so dispose our submarines that an enemy submarine while passing through the North Sea should be attacked at least once in daylight, i.e. our submarines should be 40 to 50 miles apart on a line parallel to enemy's probable course, the lines of submarines being well separated. It is also proposed to use the C. Class towing scheme.

30. Northern Area submarines would be available for work off the Norwegian Coast, the Skagerrak, and the Shetlands if enemy were active there.

31. These would be controlled by Captains (S) Blyth and Tees.

32. Southern Area by Captain (S), Humber.

33. 50% of the submarines should be at Sea during the Summer months. That is we should have about 30 submarines at Sea in the North Sea at one time. This leaves ample at the depots in case of emergency for raids etc.

34. As regards the 6 J, 22 E, and 3 H class and new vessels, these are for work on the West Coasts, in the Mediterranean, and abroad, their sphere of operations can best be allocated by the Admiralty, who have all trade information etc.

35. With the depots available very good use can undoubtedly be made of this large number of submarines, the majority of which are at present wasted in the North Sea.

36. They would probably be well scattered and the five depot ships would not be any too many.

37. The French and Italians must be asked to co-operate with us in the Mediterranean off the Austrian exits and Dardanelles in a similar manner.

38. There is no doubt that our submarines, belonging as they do to the Stronger Power are unable to carry out the role which they are primarily designed for, at this stage of the Naval War. This being the case it is suggested that they are better employed as I have attempted to indicate.

39. They will be assisting the Fleet in its most difficult task.

[156] *Beatty to Admiralty*

[ADM 137/1926]

Iron Duke,
18 January 1917

1. Be pleased to submit to the Lords Commissioners of the Admiralty that I may be informed as to the policy which governs the organisation and distribution of our submarine flotillas around the coast.

2. It would appear that nine-tenths of these valuable craft have been used entirely for defensive purposes, and consequently have not been in a position to enable them to do anything during the $2^1/2$ years we have been at war.

3. No doubt when the fear of invasion was always present this was desirable. In view of altered circumstances, however, and the many changes of ideas, coupled with the increase in enemy submarine activity, I would submit that the time has arrived to change the policy governing their employment and to consider more active projects.

[157] *Admiralty to Beatty*

[ADM 137/1926]

30th January 1917

1. With reference to your letter of the 18th instant, No. 132/H.F.0022, relative to the policy governing the organisation and distribution of Submarine Flotillas around the coast, I am commanded by My Lords Commissioners of the Admiralty to acquaint you that it is understood

from your telegram No. 485 that you refer to submarines of C and D classes.

2. The D Class Submarines are at present much reduced in numbers, but under ordinary conditions are employed on oversea patrol work. The C Class Submarines of the Flotillas mentioned in your telegram are unfit for work far from the coast during the winter and are mainly employed against raids, although they have been used offensively and will be so used to an increased extent when weather admits.

3. It must be borne in mind that Submarines constitute our principal defence against raids of all kinds, as the basing of the Fleet in the North renders it impracticable that the heavy Ships can intervene in time.

4. A Submarine Patrol against enemy Submarines is about to be established off St. Kilda, and later on, when weather permits, Submarines of C Class will be based on the Shetland Islands for work against enemy Submarines on passage. Experience shows that it is a very difficult matter for a Submarine to get within range of enemy Submarines in the North Sea, but that the latter relax some of their vigilance when out of the North Sea.

[158] *President, Submarine Committee to Beatty*
[ADM 137/1926]

H. M. S. *Centurion*
2nd February, 1917

Submitted:

1. In accordance with your memorandum H.P. 0022/542 of 26 January, 1917, I have discussed the re-organisation of the submarine flotillas, and submarine matters generally with Captain [Algernon] Candy and Commanders [Charles] Little and [Ernest] Leir,[1] and the attached memorandum represents our views as to the submarine policy best calculated to meet the existing naval situation.

2. Proposals for re-organising the submarine flotillas and their disposition, with a view to carrying out the policy recommended, are contained in paragraphs 25 to 35 of Commander Little's letter of 18 January, 1917. These proposals are concurred in as amended in a marginal note to paragraph 28.

3. The papers referred to in paragraph 4 of H.F.0022/542 are returned herewith.

[1] Cmdr (later Vice-Adm.) Ernest 'Light-fingered' Leir: Commander 1914. CO E4 1913; Senior Submarine Officer 8th Flotilla 1914–15; Capt. Portsmouth training flotilla 1915; spare submarine officer 8th Submarine Flotilla 1916. Awarded DSO 1917.

REMARKS ON SUBMARINES

(1) Policy and proposals, future organisation of Submarine Flotillas

1. Many naval officers, both with and without practical submarine experience, who thoroughly appreciate the value of submarines, and have sound ideas as to their employment under normal conditions, seem to lack the imagination to apply their knowledge or practical skill to the extraordinary conditions which now prevail. One has so often heard it said that Like must fight like; The answer to the submarine is the submarine, on the one hand: and on the other, Submarine cannot fight submarine, they were not designed for the purpose – It would be waste of time and effort to use submarines to hunt submarines.

2. There can be no doubt whatever that the greater proportion of our submarines are not being fully or wisely employed at present, and it is proposed to review the whole submarine question with the object of arriving at a policy which will meet the existing naval situation (and incidentally to prepare for the criticism which is likely to be levelled at a proposal for drastic re-organisation).

3. Under the conditions which existed at the commencement of the war, and for which we trained before the war, the object of our larger submarines was to attack the enemy's vessels of war at sea, or off his ports. If while carrying out a sea patrol, or blockading a port, one of our submarines sighted an enemy's submarine *on the surface* and was able to manoeuvre unseen and unsuspected into a position from which she could fire a torpedo she had fair prospect of destroying the enemy. In the early days of the war several encounters between submarines occurred. They generally sighted one another more or less simultaneously, both submarines promptly dived, each was afraid to remain on the surface for more than a few moments for fear of giving the other the chance of a shot, and stalemate ensued, probably without a torpedo being fired. In these days one or two good opportunities were missed by both sides, owing to the attack being delivered at very close range, too close to allow the torpedo, fired from the depth of a submerged submarine's tube to rise sufficiently soon to hit such a shallow draft craft as a submarine on the surface. Later on both our submarines and the enemy's scored successes, but these encounters made the submarines very wary, and very loath to risk remaining on the surface in the vicinity of the enemy's ports, or in localities where the presence of an enemy's submarine was suspected. Consequently opportunities for attack have become increasingly rare in the limited field in which our submarines operate.

4. As the war proceeded, mines, nets, depth charges, and other anti-submarine devices made the blockade of the enemy's ports increasingly

difficult and dangerous. The threat of being stalked by an enemy's submarine, assisted probably by aerial reconnaissance, imposed continuous diving on our patrols, which were gradually withdrawn from the Bight. It is understood, however, that our submarines are still maintained in positions in which they are subjected to risks, and suffer losses, out of all proportion to the military results it is possible for them to attain under the new conditions. Service in submarines so wastefully employed cannot but have a detrimental effect on the morale of their personnel.

5. The inactivity imposed on a large number of our smaller submarines must also have a disheartening effect on their crews, and seriously affect their efficiency, since proper training cannot be carried out in most cases owing to the threat of mines. At the commencement of the war these small submarines were, and still are, divided between various strategic points on the East Coast to repel invasion, and at Dover to deny the Straits to the enemy! It was amply proved in a number of patrol flotilla exercises, before the war, that no reliance can be placed in submarines employed on such services, since the enemy will naturally not elect to arrive at an hour favourable for submarine attack, or choose a locality in the vicinity of our submarine bases. Moreover the number available is quite insufficient to guard every likely landing place or to inflict any appreciable loss on a determined attempt at invasion.

6. These facts could not have been more forcibly brought to the notice of the Admiralty, but it is understood that the disposition was the result of an ancient undertaking on the part of the Admiralty to maintain submarines for coast defence, presumably when they persuaded the War Office to abandon defensive mining! (and forego the effective fortification of important harbours?!). Under prevailing conditions there would seem to be ample justification for the abrogation of this agreement if such an agreement exists. In any case the release of the submarines should be insisted on.

7. It has always been maintained that submarines can co-operate effectively in the defence of a port protected by a comparatively weak fortress, such as the Humber, the Tees, Hartlepool, and the Tyne. The fact that submarines are stationed at those ports is no doubt known to the enemy, and has probably acted as a deterrent. He was probably unaware that a submarine was stationed at Hartlepool, (she only arrived a few days prior to the raid), the only place of those attacked by the enemy's battle-cruisers which could be called a defended port. Had the submarine been employed as ordered she would probably have torpedoed an enemy ship, or at least, caused an immediate withdrawal,

as it was, directly the submarine dived the enemy hauled off. Attack on such places as Scarborough and Whitby was of course not anticipated and submarines cannot be maintained continuously off places which possess no sheltered harbour. The presence of submarines at Yarmouth and Blyth have probably acted as a deterrent, and those at Yarmouth no doubt contributed to the brevity of the enemy's bombardments of that place and Lowestoft. It would be advisable therefore to continue to base submarines at Blyth, Tyne, Tees, Humber, and Yarmouth. It is not suggested for a moment that the operations of any of our submarines should be linked to coast defence, but one or two of the resting submarines could be held in readiness in case of attack.

8. From the foregoing remarks it will be seen that our submarines cannot be expected to inflict serious losses on the enemy's submarines. Opportunities for attack will become increasingly rare, as the enemy is forced to remain submerged through the fear of our submarines, decoy ships, and the guns of our merchant men. We are, however, very strongly of the opinion, that every submarine, not actually required for service with the Grand Fleet, should be withdrawn from her present allocation and employed on the trade routes, in the vicinity of fishing fleets, and generally speaking, in areas in which the enemy's submarines are at present so active. Their presence will add enormously to the anxieties and difficulties of the enemy, will tend to limit his vision to the range of field of his periscope, and his offence to the torpedo. The activities of our submarines in the Marmora were very considerably checked by the arrival of the enemy's submarines in that sea. The advantage is all with the hunter, and bold and confident submarine officers have no hesitation in saying that it would be difficult to exaggerate the discomfort and anxiety of being continually stalked, particularly after they realised that the enemy was skilful enough to stalk and torpedo E.20.[1]

9. If it is still considered in some quarters that it would be waste of time and effort to employ submarines to hunt submarines, this opinion is not accepted by the present First Sea Lord,[2] or shared by the Captains of submarines, who, in the absence of capital targets, and after a long spell of dangerous and unprofitable employment, or enforced inactivity, would be only too keen for the opportunity of hunting their opposite numbers in the open sea, clear of the minefields which have taken such heavy toll of our submarines without the attainment of commensurate results. It is hoped that the proposed reorganisation will be put into

[1] E20: torpedoed and sunk on first patrol in Sea of Marmora.
[2] Adm. Sir John Jellicoe.

force at once. There will be a fine field for initiative and enterprise and the best man will win. Boldness, patience, and a skilful stalk may well be rewarded by the destruction of an enemy, on the other hand, carelessness, or lack of skill, is likely to suffer disaster. In any case there can be no question that our submarines can be valuably employed in the campaign against the attack of the enemy's submarines on our trade, and when he is reduced in his offensive to attack by torpedo, losses will become comparatively negligible, for ocean-going submarines are not handy for submerged attack at the close range so necessary for accurate shooting at a single ship.

10. We are of the opinion that little can be expected from our diving patrols in the open sea. It is understood that the submarines employed on these diving patrols dive continuously throughout the day and are consequently limited to a very small field of vision, particularly in bad weather. The odds against their seeing an enemy submarine on passage, at any rate soon enough to manoeuvre into a position to attack, would seem enormous. It is hoped that these diving patrols will be withdrawn, or otherwise conducted. Commander Leir, who is second to no one in submarine skill and experience is very strong on this point.

11. Paragraph 10 of the Submarine Committee's Memorandum Proposed action against hostile submarines operating off the Atlantic Coasts, sums up views generally in regard to anti submarine tactics. The enemy submarines are, and likely to become increasingly suspicious of hidden armaments. It would seem advisable to disguise all decoy ships most carefully as Neutrals frequenting the same trade routes. Decoy ships have been seen fairly recently which have their character written all over them and which would certainly never take in an enemy submarine.

12. The value of mines as a means of destroying the enemy's submarines cannot be exaggerated. Most of our submarine losses have probably been due to mines. It is important however, when possible, to make the enemy dive when passing a minefield as she is likely to pass safely over moored mines at high water unless there is a considerable seaway.

[159] *Beatty to Admiralty*

[ADM 137/1926]

Iron Duke
6th February, 1917

Sir,

1. With reference to Admiralty letter M.0753 of 30th January, 1917, relative to the organisation and distribution of submarine flotillas around the coast, be pleased to lay before the Lords Commissioners of the Admiralty the following further remarks on this subject.

2. In putting forward these recommendations I would inform their Lordships that the opinions of the Captains (S) of the Grand Fleet and a number of selected submarine officers have been obtained. Further, I have had the advantage of the deliberations of the committee formed by my predecessor under the presidency of Captain Roger Keyes, C.B., &c., and which has lately been considering the special questions relating to the employment of submarines which I have placed before them.

3. One is impressed with the opinion universally held by officers in every way competent to judge, that our submarines are not being employed to the best advantage; that in fact their general employment is unsuited to their capabilities and that at this critical juncture we are not making the fullest possible use of the highly-skilled personnel and excellent material at our disposal.

4. In this connection it is to be observed that the conditions of submarine warfare have entirely changed since the outbreak of hostilities. The submarine was built to sink the enemy's heavy ships, the High Sea Fleet being considered the principal menace. Actually, however, at this present moment, it is not the High Sea Fleet but the enemy submarines which threaten our existence. Our submarine dispositions to meet this new situation require modification.

5. It is contended that the present conditions make it imperative to reorganise our submarine flotillas to carry out offensive operations against the enemy submarines, recognising that although this is not the primary duty for which our submarines were built, it is their primary duty at this moment.

Mines remain the principal offensive weapon against the enemy submarines. Our own submarines should be used to back up the minefields and to attack the enemy submarines which escape the barrage.

*   *   *

[160] *Admiralty to Beatty*

[ADM 137/1926]

23rd March 1917

My Lords Commissioners of the Admiralty have had under their careful consideration your letter of the 6th February, No. 297/H.F. 0022, recommending a re-organisation and distribution of submarine flotillas in home waters.

2. The disposition of submarines depends on many considerations. In your proposals due weight was, in the opinion of Their Lordships, not given to the necessity of disposing a sufficient number of submarines on the South and East coast. The East Coast of England, and especially the part South of Lowestoft, is open to bombardment or invasion with the Grand Fleet based as at present, and the presence of an adequate number of submarines in Southern waters gives us the only opportunity we possess of damaging or sinking vessels of the High Sea Fleet when carrying out operations in localities in which the Grand Fleet cannot touch them. Offensive operations against enemy submarines are highly important, but provision against the menace of the High Sea Fleet or raiding Squadrons or ships must be made. Moreover, a very large proportion of the German submarines which go to sea take the Southern Route and there is also always a large submarine flotilla based upon Zeebrugge.

3. The Harwich and Yarmouth submarine flotillas must be kept, in Their Lordships' opinion, numerically strong, and My Lords could not agree, as suggested by you, to six submarines only being stationed on the Coast between Lowestoft and Dover. Harwich will not be reduced below twelve E Class submarines (in addition to minelayers), or Yarmouth below ten submarines. It has to be recognised that, owing to refits and other causes, the number of submarines actually available is, in any emergency, considerably lower.

4. My Lords also are unable to approve of the formation of a flotilla of C boats based on Swarbacks Minn, to work between the Shetlands and the Norwegian coast. All experience in their possession goes to show that C Class submarines would be unfit for this overseas work and could not carry it out successfully. C Class submarines can, however, be employed to advantage against submarines in the Southern part of the North Sea, where the conditions are much more suitable for them.

5. Again, it is very doubtful whether much success can be obtained against enemy submarines on passage in the North Sea. The experience

of many attempts in this direction during 1915–1916 showed that there was very small chance of success. Enemy submarines on passage in the Southern and Central portion of the North Sea are very much alive to the danger of attack, and never relax a most vigilant lookout when on the surface.

6. As regards your suggestion that a submarine patrol be established in fairly close proximity to our Eastern Coast, the objection is that these vessels would be working in the midst of our surface patrols and the submarines would be continually harassed and possibly sunk by our own patrol vessels.

7. Your proposal that a force of submarines should be formed for service on the Trade Routes in the approaches to the Channel, Ireland, and other local points has already been partly adopted by the formation of a flotilla based on Queenstown.[1] It is of course fully realised that although operations of our submarines against those of the enemy may not meet with great success in the sinking of hostile vessels, the mere knowledge that British submarines are working against the enemy submarines has a great moral effect upon the enemy, and cramps very much the activities of German submarines. A further flotilla is being based on Lough Swilly for anti-submarine work.

8. After full consideration, My Lords have decided to distribute the submarines as shown on the attached sheet A. [not reproduced] In this organisation the K class submarines are not included.

9. A copy of Admiralty Letter M. 01504 of 21st March to the Rear Admiral Commanding, East Coast of England, is enclosed, [not reproduced] and attention is called to the arrangements to be made for the protection of Blyth and the Tees.

[161] *Admiralty to Beatty*

[ADM 137/1926]

21st October, 1917

Their Lordships have had under consideration your submission of the 25th ultimo, No. 2360/H.F.0022, forwarding a paper on the concentration of British Submarines for attack on enemy submarines in the North Sea.

2. Without going into detail Their Lordships feel that there are several considerations which militate against the adoption in full of the policy outlined in the paper, and I am to offer the following observations:–

---

[1] The *Ambrose* flotilla under the command of Capt. Martin Nasmith VC.

3. In submarine v submarine warfare the element of surprise is the predominant one. A submarine is at all times a very difficult torpedo target on account of its small size and the difficulty of estimating the inclination correctly. When on passage in the North Sea, enemy submarines are evidently very much on the alert and are very frequently zig-zagging. This is only to be expected considering the number of attacks that have been made on them, and that they are probably aware that we know their tracks within certain limits. A high degree of vigilance must very much reduce the chance of successful attack.

4. On the other hand, when in their operation areas submarines cannot continue to be so fully on the alert for a period of several weeks. They also know that their opportunities for successful attack on trade are much more numerous if they remain on the surface, and will probably do so unless such tactics become obviously dangerous.

5. If they keep constantly under way at any speed whilst on the surface the wear and tear on their engines is very much increased, which involves a longer time out of action on return to Germany. Their fuel consumption is also increased to an extent which may limit the length of each cruise.

6. Consequently there is a strong inducement, when operating on the trade routes, for submarines to remain stopped, or to cruise slowly about on the surface.

7. During 1917 the following successful attacks on enemy submarines by British Submarines have taken place:–

March 9th	G.13	North of Muckle Flugga
April 5th	C.7	Off Schouwen Bank (Flanders Flotilla)
May 12th	D.7	Off N. of Ireland
September 12th	D.7	Off N. of Ireland

It is noticeable that E.54's success followed shortly after the establishment of a new patrol line in that area, and D.7 when she succeeded was the first submarine to occupy that particular patrol line, which had only just been established.

8. Although there have been a large number of sightings of submarines by submarines in the North Sea, and about 60 of our submarines (exclusive of K. Boats) have been operating in that area, only two successes have been scored. The 14 submarines (now 13) operating in the Atlantic since March 1st have also scored two. It must be taken into account that the *Vulcan's* flotilla included 6 D boats which have been laid up for repairs considerably longer than the average refitting periods.

9. At present it is apparent that enemy submarines when operating against trade spend a large part of their time on the surface, even in

areas close to the coast. For the time being we are prevented from operating our Atlantic submarines in areas where enemy submarines are most concentrated, owing to there being no satisfactory recognition signal which can be used submerged. This restriction will however be shortly removed.

10. The effect of further developing our offensive submarine patrols in the West Coast areas would be either to force enemy submarines to work submerged, thereby limiting their capacity of doing damage, or compel them to work further out in the Atlantic. In the process of producing this effect we might hope to destroy some of the enemy's best submarines.

11. Accepting the difficulties of submarine v submarine warfare with the types of submarines available, My Lords consider it advisable at present to maintain the present submarine force in the Atlantic and possibly to strengthen it by the substitution of later type boats for the 'D' class, which are not suitable for the long Atlantic Sea.

12. As regards the distribution and operations of those submarines stationed in the North Sea, this question has, as you observe, to be considered in relation to the general policy of mining and surface patrols.

13. The suggestion to work submarines by W/T from the base appears to present very great difficulties of execution. Better results would probably be obtained by organised patrols in areas through which the [enemy] submarines are known to pass. The matter is engaging the attention of the Naval Staff, and a further communication will be made to you.

The principle of making the flotillas as homogeneous as possible is concurred in.

Submarine Operations at the End of the War

[162] *Extract from Report by Commodore (S) Sydney S. Hall*
[ADM 137/2077]

5 October 1917

*   *   *

The total losses during the war are now:–
73 officers.
630 men.

These have been almost entirely confined to the oversea submarines and are about 10% per year of those employed.

Though these losses are sufficiently high to warrant, as has been previously acknowledged, the statement that the oversea submarines are always in what constitute action to them when on patrol, they are not published or recorded in any way, so that unless some recognition is made, the feeling which is apt to arise will be justified that they are suffering these losses without any result and that they are incurring the risks daily without serving any useful purpose.

I believe that definite moral effect is undoubtedly produced by these anti-submarine patrols apart from the numbers of submarines actually sunk and that tangible results are obtained from the minelayers and it is in connection with these unrecorded actions that I ask for recognition for the officers and men given below.

The diving patrols carried out are most arduous. In summer they are submerged for 19–20 hours after 12 hours of which the air is bound to be oppressive in spite of purifiers; certainly not even the head of a match will burn. In winter the North Sea weather and cold, and at all these times the anxieties from mines and our own patrols, are a great trial of patience and endurance, the worst part of which is that there has been little hope during the last year of any target beyond the extremely difficult one of a submarine.

The exhilaration of an encounter with the enemy is only very rarely obtained to sustain them. What is required and given by these officers and men is 2 o'clock in the morning courage for the whole of the time they are at sea.

The two American submarine officers who have recently been on a week's patrol in our submarines owned that they were in their own language all out and fit for nothing at the end of it, though they both had an encounter with the enemy to cheer them up, in one case sinking a German ship, and the cruises were not what our officers call trying ones.

[163] *Lieutenant Anthony B. Lockhart to Admiralty*
[ADM 137/2071]

H.M. Submarine V1
5th January, 1917

Sir,

I have the honour to report the proceedings of Submarine V1 on patrol from 27th December 1916 to 4th January 1917:–

27th Dec: 1 p.m. Left *Alecto* and proceeded to billet North of Haaks Light Vessel via G.G. Channel.

28th Dec: 2 a.m. Arrived on billet. Diving patrol all day. Slight sea. 11 a.m. Sighted Dutch Cruiser of *Koningen Regentes* class in shore steering South. Noon position 53°10´N., 4°30´E.

29th Dec: Diving patrol all day. Nothing sighted. Rough sea. Noon position (D.R.) 53°9´N., 4°9´E.

30th Dec: Diving patrol all day. Nothing sighted. Moderate sea. Noon position 53°14´N., 4°9´E.

31st Dec: Diving patrol all day. Nothing sighted. Heavy sea. Noon position (D.R.) 53°14´N., 4°5´E.

1st Jan: Diving patrol all day. Nothing sighted. Slight sea. Noon position (D.R.) 53°7´N., 4°13´E.

2nd Jan: Diving patrol all day. Nothing sighted. Heavy sea. Noon position (D.R.) 53°12´N., 4°7´E.

3rd Jan: Diving patrol all day. Nothing sighted. Slight sea. Noon position (D.R.) 53°15´N., 4°0´E. 4.30.pm. Surface. Shaped course for Yarmouth via North Hinder Light Vessel.

4th Jan: 1.30 p.m. Secured to *Alecto*.

(signed) Lieutenant AB Lockhart

[164] *Patrol Report by Lieutenant Commander Robert Raikes to Vice-Admiral Commanding, West Coast of Ireland*[1]
[ADM 137/2076]

H.M. Submarine E.54,
May 3rd 1917

I have the honour to report, that when on passage to patrol, April 28th and May 2nd, I carried out attacks on 3 enemy submarines under the following circumstances.

---

[1] Adm. Commanding Coast of Ireland (Western Approaches): Vice-Adm. Sir Lewis Bayly.

Report of proceedings on April 29th

8.40 a.m., when in Lat 50° 28 ́N. Long 9° 23 ́ W., sighted enemy submarine 6–7 miles distant, bearing (rough) N.N.W., which appeared to be steering about W.S.W. Dived to attack immediately. Steered N.W. Could not see submarine through periscope till 8.59 a.m., when altered to 290° and at 9.8 a.m. to 250°, which left enemy on a slightly closing bearing (from 73° to 65°). Continued on this course closing enemy until 9.30 a.m., when on putting up periscope, enemy was seen to have altered towards us, putting boat fine on his port bow 1500 yards. Altered course to 160° at full speed and stood by starboard beam tube to fire as she passed. On putting up periscope again, however, enemy was seen to have continued his alteration right round to about 95°, and was slightly on our port quarter (boats head 180°). Thinking that I might not get another opportunity of firing, and although the range was great, about 2500 yards, I followed round and fired the port beam tube 9.42 a.m. Estimated speed of enemy 6 knots (boats head 95°). Torpedo did not hit, and apparently enemy saw neither periscope, not track of torpedo. Proceeded to attack at full speed to get in with bow torpedoes. The sea was very calm and the surface was glassy. I therefore did not like to close too much, when I should otherwise have done so, for fear of being seen. The enemy also again altered course, to the southward, which brought sights on sooner than was expected. I gave the order to fire both bow torpedoes at 9.59 a.m. Estimated speed of enemy 4–5 knots, distant 800–900 yards (boats head 105, beam shot). The starboard torpedo was fired by me from the pistol grip at the periscope. The tubes' crews had orders to fire the 2nd torpedo as soon as the 1st one went, if it was not fired from aft as well, but for some reason they thought and reported that both had gone. I did not discover that the port torpedo had not gone until it was too late to fire again. Both torpedoes were angled 1 1/2 outwards. The starboard torpedo appeared to be going to pass just ahead of the enemy and must have gone close as the enemy altered course at about the time it would have reached him. It is considered that if the port torpedo had gone (which was angled the other way) it would have had a very good chance of hitting. After the torpedo had reached him, the enemy altered course and disappeared at full speed. Do not think he saw periscope. He was a large boat of the later U type.

11.08 a.m. When in position Lat 51° 34 ́N. Long 13° 12 ́W., on the surface, sighted enemy submarine about 6 miles 3–4 points on the port bow. Dived to attack. Steered 275° at an average speed of about 7 knots and maintained a steady bearing by 50°. Estimated I must have been just abaft the enemy's beam, going slightly faster and gradually closing. Continued like this until 1.20 p.m, when I came to the conclusion that the enemy was altering course towards us. I altered straight towards him and on putting up periscope at 1.30 p.m. found him nearly bows on about 500 yards off, having suddenly altered course to about 190°. Put helm a starboard and dived to 60 feet to cross his bow. On coming up again at 1.40 I found I was on his starboard beam and altered to 180°. He appeared to be going very slowly and to be altering to starboard again. Attacked at 6 knots, in order to close as quickly as possible in view of possible further alterations of course. At 1.51 raised periscope and found I was about 700 yards off and sights not quite on. I lowered periscope in order to close as far as I could, to make more certain of hitting and altered course in order to bring my sights on. I raised the periscope again at 1.52^1/2 ready to fire, and found that the enemy had altered course right away from me and that I was fine on his starboard quarter. I fired the starboard bow tube as I thought there might be a faint chance of hitting at that range, although the target was very small and going away from me. I regret I did not have time to prevent the port torpedo being fired as well, according to the order previously given. The starboard torpedo broke surface just outside the tube and I saw no track, though this might have been due to the boat swinging. The boat had been to 60 feet with the bow cap open during the attack, which might have caused water in buoyancy on balance.

I consider that the enemy, in all probability, saw my periscope when it was put up at 1.51 p.m., 1^1/2 minutes before firing, although it was only up for 15 seconds at the most. The enemy turned N.E. after altering, and then to S.E. in which direction he disappeared. He was a very large boat of the later U type.

3.40 p.m. Heard an under water explosion and observed a column of smoke 3 points to Port Bow (course N). Came to the surface and saw that the smoke was a very long way off, but sighted the mast and funnels of a steamer right ahead. She was blowing off steam and did not look normal. Closed at 11 knots on surface as the battery was low after the last attack, and soon saw that the steamer was down by the bow and stopped.

4.22 p.m. When about 3^1/2 miles off I dived and continued to close. 4.50 sighted enemy submarine on starboard bow apparently just come to the surface and proceeding towards the steamer which appeared to be abandoned. Proceeded to attack.

5.0. When about 1500 yards off enemy altered to port and passed to southward of steamer (same side that I was) and then round the stern. I altered to port and placed it round the bow sighting him again 4 minutes later. Steering about 90 (my course 50°) just before I reached the bow of the steamer. Attacked on this course until 5.7 when enemy submarine starboarded, at first I thought he was going away, but he altered through about 220° and steered towards the stern of the steamer again.

I altered to port to attack on the new course going 6 knots to intercept him before he reached the stern.

5.11½ raised periscope and fired both bow torpedoes at about 400 yards range 6 points on enemy's bow one hit midway between conning tower and bow, the other midway between conning tower and stern. Enemy submarine sank. About ½ minute later a third explosion was heard which shook the boat a good deal and which, the German Officers afterwards suggested was their own torpedoes, the pistol firing gear being operated by the pressure.

I picked up survivors, the Captain and 2 other Officers and 4 men. (The Captain of U.81 also was nearly sinking when picked up and was saved by Lieutenant Aylmer who went overboard after him with a line), and then followed the steamer life boats and brought them back to the steamer, which the Captain informed me he thought he could get into Bantry. I dived near the steamer (S.S *Dorvie*) until dark and then proceeded to Queenstown to replenish torpedoes and land prisoners.

I should like to bring to your notice that the behaviour of all officers and men was excellent and entirely as expected. I should like to particularly mention Lieutenant C.A. Aylmer, 1st Lieutenant, observing that this is the second occasion that he has been of the utmost assistance to me in the sinking of an enemy submarine, and that the excellent work of all the crew is greatly due to his efforts – also; – Joseph P Morris, P.O. 1-Cox. and James Smith, E.R.A. Chief E.R.A. of boat whose work on this and all occasions has greatly increased the efficiency of the boat as a whole.

(signed) R Raikes,

[165] *Captain Martin E. Nasmith VC to Vice-Admiral Sir Lewis Bayly*
[ADM 137/1946]

H.M.S. *Ambrose*
7 March 1918

I regret to report that Submarine H.5, having failed to return from patrol, is considered to have been lost with all hands. It is further considered that she was the Submarine referred to in the following message from Vice Admiral, Milford Haven; observing that her line of patrol was in Lat. 53°6′ N. between Long. 4°30′ and 4°50′ W.

Message begins: Master of S.S. *Rutherglen* reports that his Vessel rammed Submarine 2030 2nd March when in position Lat. 53°4′ N. Long. 4°40′ W. Submarine was crossing bow at considerable speed. After collision cries were heard and men seen in the water, also there was a strong smell of petrol vapour. Forepeak of *Rutherglen* is flooded. Ends.

Her Commanding Officer, Lieutenant AW Forbes, D.S.O. was an officer of considerable Submarine experience and one for whom I had the greatest admiration, and in whom I placed complete confidence. I am convinced with my knowledge of this Officer that he at all times took every possible step, first for the destruction of the enemy, and secondly for the safety of his ship, and that whatever the circumstances of the collision were, that no possible blame can be attributed to him. He was specially noted for the command of one of our larger Submarines, and his loss to the Submarine Service, together with that of his Officers and men who have performed excellent work in these waters, is very much felt. It is deeply regretted that Ensign EWF Childs, USN, of US Submarine AL.2, who was making an instructional cruise in H.5, was also lost.

With regard to the S.S. *Rutherglen*, it is submitted that she should not be informed that the rammed Submarine was British, but should receive the usual reward for sinking an enemy, since the success of the campaign must largely depend upon immediate hostile action being taken by any Merchant Vessel finding herself favourably situated for attacking a Submarine. The question of recognition between Merchant Vessels and Allied Submarines is not considered feasible, and the risk of such an accident happening on a dark night, although deeply to be regretted, must be accepted as a necessary war risk.

[166] *Lieutenant Frederick A.P. Williams Freeman DSO to Admiralty*[1]
[ADM 137/2071]

H.M. Submarine H9
31st March, 1918

I have the honour to report as follows, on the circumstances under which I was heavily fired on by the S.S. *Benarty* on the morning of Saturday, March 31st.

When four miles South of the Haisboro' Light Vessel, steering 155,

---

[1] Frederick Williams Freeman retired as Cmdr in 1927. Awarded DSO in October 1914 for defusing a mine fouling hydroplane guard on HMS/m E6.

speed 11 knots, visibility 5 miles, a merchant vessel was sighted just on the Port bow, steering approximately opposite course. Two patrol vessels were in sight on my Starboard quarter and had been challenged. When the merchant vessel closed to approximately 2¹/2 miles she turned to Port under hard helm and almost immediately opened fire at a range of about 4000 yards. Two shots fired in rapid succession passed very close directly over me. I stopped and went astern, at the same time making the auxiliary challenge and making certain the ensign was blowing clear broad on to him. He continued firing and at least four of his shots fell within 50ft of me, two of which exploded. The nearest shot pitched about 10ft from the abreast my bridge. I could not turn away as his range was so exact and the shots were falling so close that he would certainly have hit me as I turned broadside to him. At least 15 of his shots fell close to me. As a last expedient I was forced to dive although I considered this dangerous in view of the fact that three patrol vessels were now approaching me, and the fact of any diving would naturally establish, in their view, nature of hostility, and owing to their proximity they would have been likely to have destroyed me with depth charges etc. By remaining submerged for as short a time as possible and proceeding at full speed I was able to come to the surface and establish my friendly character before the patrol craft were near enough to take action.

I would submit that under the circumstances the action taken by the merchant vessel in firing at me, and continuing to do so, was nothing short of criminal. She can have had no possible reason for supposing I was hostile, but had every reason for assuming I was friendly. I was flying a *new six-breadth* ensign on the mast, which was blowing broad on to her and was not obstructed in any way by bridge or periscope. This must have been very plainly visible as I could see her flag which was much smaller. At the time I was in sight of two of our own trawlers which were obviously patrol craft and it must have been obvious to the merchant vessel that had I been hostile these trawlers would have taken action. I was cruising on the surface with full buoyancy, bridge screen, mast, etc. up and proceeding down the war channel in broad daylight, which very obviously a hostile submarine would not do. Had she been suspicious of me she had only to turn 8 or 16 points to avoid me and obtain assistance, which was in sight.

In view of the above circumstances I submit that action may be taken against the Master of S.S. *Benarty*.

LIST OF SOURCES

Admiralty Papers (ADM class) Public Record Office, Kew, London

Additional Manuscripts (Add. Mss) British Library, London

Cabinet Papers (CAB class) Public Record Office, Kew, London

Private papers of Winston S. Churchill (Chartwell Trust Papers)
Churchill Archives Centre, Churchill College, Cambridge

Private papers of Admiral of the Fleet Lord Fisher (Fisher Papers),
Churchill Archives Centre, Churchill College, Cambridge

Private papers of Admiral of the Fleet Lord Keyes, (Keyes Papers)
British Library, London

Private papers of Sir James Masterton-Smith (Masterton-Smith Papers)
Public Record Office, Kew, London

Private papers of Reginald McKenna, (McKenna Papers) Churchill
Archives Centre, Churchill College, Cambridge

Private papers of third Earl of Selborne, (Selborne Papers) Bodleian
Library, Oxford

Records of the Admiralty Constructors Department (Ships' Covers)
National Maritime Museum, Brass Foundry, Woolwich, London

LIST OF DOCUMENTS

1. Letter from Sir Edmund Monson (British Ambassador) to Marquis of Salisbury (Prime Minister) in 'Trial of French Submarine Boat *Gustave-Zede* and Other Submarines', FO, 26 January 1899, ADM 1/7422A.

2. *Navy Debates*, Session 6 April 1900, comprising extracts from *The Parliamentary Debates* of all questions, proceedings, and debates relating to Navy Affairs, (Wyman and Sons, 1900) p.515. Copy in Admiralty Library.

3. Discussion on the Use of Contact Mines for Defence Against Submarines, in 'Principal Questions dealt with by the Director of Naval Ordnance', 5 February 1900, ff.105–8, ADM 256/39.

4. 'Submarine boats in the United States' in, '1900 Submarine Boats Considered by USA House Committee', Admiralty 18/5/1900, ADM 1/7462.

5. Extract from letter by Rear Admiral Lord Charles Beresford to Vice Admiral Sir John Fisher, 12 June 1900 enclosed in Beresford to Balfour, 21 June 1900, ff.92–104, Add Mss 49713.

6. *Navy Debates*, Session 17 July 1900, comprising extracts from *The Parliamentary Debates* of all questions, proceedings, and debates relating to Navy Affairs, (Wyman and Sons, 1900) p.767.

7. Private Letter from Lord Nathaniel Rothschild to George Goschen, 'Holland Type Submarines – Offer by US Firm Holland Torpedo Boat Co. to build for Admiralty', 23 July 1900, Admy 15/1/1901, ADM 1/7515.

8. '1900 Submarine Boats Considered by USA House Committee', 3 August 1900, Admiralty 18/5/1900, ADM 1/7462.

9. Isaac Rice to Secretary of the Admiralty, 'Holland Type Submarines – Offer by US Firm Holland Torpedo Boat co. to build for Admiralty', 17 September 1900, Admy 15/1/1901, ADM 1/7515.

10. Minute (23 October 1900) by Controller, 'Holland Type Submarines – Offer by US Firm Holland Torpedo Boat co. to build for Admiralty', Admy 15/1/1901, ADM 1/7515.

11. Extract from Memorandum to Cabinet by Lord Selborne, 'Naval Estimates, 1901–1902: Memorandum on Shipbuilding', 17 January 1901, CAB 37/56/8.

12. Copy of Private memorandum by Financial Secretary (H. Oakley Arnold-Forster) to First Lord (Selborne) 10 January 1901, f.4, Add. Mss 50294.

13. Memoranda and Minute by Rear Admiral Sir Arthur Wilson dated 21 January 1901, 'Holland Type Submarines – Offer by US Firm Holland Torpedo Boat co. to build for Admiralty', Admy 15/1/1901, ADM 1/7515.

14. Private letter from Arnold-Forster to Selborne, 8 August 1901, f.6, Add Mss 50294.

15. Extract from Memorandum to Cabinet by Lord Selborne, 'The Navy Estimates and the Chancellor of Exchequer's Memorandum on the Growth of Expenditure', 16 November 1901, p.15, CAB 37/59/118.

16. Private letter from Lieut F.D. Arnold-Forster to Captain C.G. Robinson, 'Submarine Boats', 7 May 1901, ADM 1/7522.

17. Memorandum by Inspecting Captain of Submarines to Controller on subject of 'Submarine Boat Number 6', 3 July 1902, cuts 20&21, Ships' Covers 185.

18. Attached minute (16 August 1902) by Captain Reginald Bacon to Rear Admiral William May, in 'Hulk for Crews of Submarine Boats,' ADM 1/7605.

19. Minute (20 December 1902) by Inspecting Captain of Submarines in 'Appointment of a Commander for Service with Submarine Boats', 20 December 1902, ADM 1/7605.

20. Minute (10 January 1903) by Inspecting Captain of Submarines in 'Convoy of three Submarine Boats from Barrow', 10 January 1903, ADM 1/7605.

21. Inspecting Captain of Submarines to Commander-in-Chief, Portsmouth (Adm. Sir Charles Hotham), 31 May 1903, in 'Copies of reports on Tactical and Other Exercises by Submarine Boats up to 31 December 1903', D307/04, ADM 1/7725.

22. Inspecting Captain of Submarines to Commander-in-Chief, Portsmouth, 'Submarine A1 report of Inspecting Captain of Submarine Boats on passage from Barrow to Portsmouth', 3 August 1903, A730/03, ADM 1/7644.

23. Extract from Medical Report enclosed in: 'Tactical and Other Exercises of Submarine Boats 1 June to 31 December 1903', A307, ADM 1/7725.

24. Minute by Director of Naval Intelligence, 26 February 1903, on

'Royal Engineers Submarine Mining School: Submarine Mines in Naval Warfare', WO 15 January 1903, AMD 1/7717.

25. Private letter from H.O. Arnold-Forster (Secretary of State for War) to Lord Selborne, 2 November 1903, f.1, Selborne Mss 34.

26. Private letter from Lord Walter Kerr to Lord Selborne, 4 November 1903, f.3, Selborne Mss 34.

27. Draft of private letter from Lord Selborne to H.O. Arnold-Forster, 14 November 1903, f.7, Selborne 34 (see also copy sent in f.9, Add Mss 50308).

28. Private letter from H. O. Arnold-Forster to Lord Selborne, 16 November 1903, f.9, Selborne Mss 34.

29. Private diary of H. O. Arnold Forster, entry for 22 November 1903, f.97, Add Mss 50335.

30. Acquisition From the Army of Fort Blockhouse for Use as Submarine Base. Minute (14 December 1903) by DNI, in 'Royal Engineers Submarine Mining School: Submarine Mines in Naval Warfare', WO 15 January 1903, ADM 1/7717.

31. Private letter from Kerr to Selborne, 6 January 1904, f.3, Selborne Ms 41.

32. Meeting of the Board of Admiralty. Minute by First Lord, 13 January 1904, on 'Royal Engineers Submarine Mining School: Submarine Mines in Naval Warfare', WO, 15 January 1903, ADM 1/7717.

33. Extract from comments written c. November 1903 by Admiral Sir John Fisher (C-in-C, Portsmouth) on a memorandum by the Prime Minister (Arthur James Balfour) circulated to the Cabinet Defence Committee in November 1903 entitled: 'The Possibility of Serious Invasion', f.56, Add Mss 49710.

34. Private letter from Admiral Sir John Fisher to Jack Sanders (Private Secretary to Prime Minister, Arthur Balfour), 5 December 1903, f.57, Add Mss 49710.

35. Private letter from Admiral Sir John Fisher to Jack Sanders, 29 December 1903, f.59, Add Mss 49710.

36. Memorandum by Admiral Sir John Fisher, c. late November 1903, ADM 116/942.

37. Private letter from Arthur Balfour to Admiral Sir John Fisher, 3 January 1904, f.71, Add Mss 49710.

38. Private letter from Arthur Balfour to Lord Selborne, 7 January 1904, f.1, 5, Selborne Mss 39.

39. Extract from private letter from Admiral Sir John Fisher to Arthur Balfour, 5 January 1904, on the purchase of additional submarines, f.75, Add Mss 49710.

40. Memorandum by Inspecting Captain of Submarines on New 'B type Submarine', 7 November 1903, cut 4, Ships' Covers 185.

41. Memorandum (19 December 1903) by Captain Reginald Bacon and subsequent correspondence relating to the Appointment of a Naval Constructor to Assist the Inspecting Captain of Submarines in the Design of Submarine Boats, in 'Staff for Submarine Boat Design', ADM 1/7745.

42. Private letter from Sir Arthur Wilson (C-in-C, Channel Squadron) to Lord Selborne, 24 February 1904, f.1, Selborne Mss 21.

43. Telegram (18 March 1904) from Commander-in-Chief, Portsmouth (Adm. Sir John Fisher) to Admiralty, in 'Loss of Submarine A1', A555, ADM 1/7718.

44. Telegram (19 March 1904) from Commander-in-Chief, Portsmouth to Admiralty, 'Loss of Submarine A1', A555, ADM 1/7718.

45. Note from Admiral Lord Walter Kerr to Lord Selborne, 19 March 1904, f.79, Selborne Mss 41.

46. Telegram (29 March 1904) from Commander-in-Chief, Portsmouth to Admiralty, ADM 1/7718.

47. Private letter from Admiral Sir John Fisher to Lord Selborne, 31 March 1904, f.130, Selborne Mss 24.

48. Extract from Umpires' Report on 'Manoeuvres Between Home Fleet and Submarines', March 1904, enclosed in *Second Annual Report of the Submarine Flotilla – 1904*, A.861/05, ADM 1/7795.

49. Private letter from Rear Admiral Reginald Custance to Lord Selborne, 31 August 1904, f.47, Selborne Mss 23.

50. Printed letter from Admiral Sir John Fisher to Rear Admiral William May, 20 April 1904, ADM 116/942.

51. Secretary of State for War (Arnold Forster) to Army Chief of the General Staff (Gen. Sir Neville Lyttleton), 19 May 1904, f.4, Add Mss 50308.

52. Extracts from the private diary of H. O. Arnold-Forster, entries for 22, 23, 25 November and 2 December 1904, ff.108–16, Add Mss 503412.

53. Extract from 60th Meeting of Committee of Imperial Defence, 2 December 1904, CAB 37/6/117.

54. Unattributed memorandum probably Captain Reginald Bacon on 'The Training of Officers and Men for Submarine Boats', April 1903, enclosed in *Naval Necessities*, volume 2, pp.454–6, Admiralty Library, Ministry of Defence.

55. Inspecting Captain of Submarines (Bacon) to Commander-in-

Chief, Portsmouth (Fisher), 8 May 1904, in 'Complements and Training of Crews for Submarine Boats', A681/03 ADM 1/7644.

56. Inspecting Captain of Submarines to Admiralty via Commander-in-Chief, Portsmouth, enclosed in 'Modifying the System for Obtaining Officers for the Submarine Service', 2 August 1905, A1088/05, ADM 1/7795.

57. Memorandum on the Offensive use of Submarines by Admiral Sir John Fisher (First Sea Lord) sent to Arthur Balfour (Prime Minister), 24 January 1905, ff.165–77, Add Mss 49710.

58. Memorandum by First Lord of the Admiralty, the Earl of Cawdor, circulated to selected members of the Cabinet. Printed at the Foreign Office, March 1905, CAB 37/75/57.

59. Private letter from Admiral Sir John Fisher (First Sea Lord) to the Earl of Cromer (Consul-General in Egypt), 22 April 1905, Fisher Papers FISR 1/4.

60. Minutes taken at 'Meeting of Submarine Boat Design Committee on 23rd June 1905', f.1, Ships' Covers 290.

61. Further remarks on 'Meeting of Submarine Boat Design committee on 23rd June 1905', f.1, Ships' Covers 212.

62. Memorandum (26 August 1905) by Bacon discussing validity of the 'Holland Company' patents, and renewal of monopoly agreement with Vickers, cut 4, Ships' Covers 290.

63. Extract from minute (17 November 1905) by Captain Reginald Bacon on memorandum by Captain Edgar Lees dated 16 November urging building of D class, cut 12, Ships' Covers 212.

64. Decision to further delay the adoption of the D type Submarine. Attached minute (18 December 1908) by Controller, cut 43, Ships' Covers 290.

65. First Sea Lord (Fisher) to First Lord of the Admiralty (Reginald McKenna), 24 September 1909, f.78, FP 413, Fisher Papers FISR 1/8.

66. Draft of memorandum by Admiral Sir John Fisher, n/d, November 1908, FP 4238, Fisher Mss 5/13. A later version was enclosed with above letter, Fisher to McKenna, 24 September 1909.

67. Views of Rear Admiral Sir John Jellicoe. Copy of letter from Controller to First Sea Lord (Fisher), 18 April 1909, FP 413, ff.79–81, Fisher Papers FISR 1/8.

68. Inspecting Captain of Submarines to Commander-in-Chief, Home Fleet, 'Exercises Carried out by Submarines during month of July 1910', 5 August 1910, ADM 1/8128.

69. Inspecting Captain of Submarines to Commander-in-Chief,

Portsmouth, 'Submarines: Scheme for Allocation to Various Bases', 5 February 1907, in A1568/07 ADM 1/7921.

70. Secretary to the Admiralty to Commander Sydney S Hall (Inspecting Capt. of Submarines designate), 6 November 1906, in 'Admiralty Committee on Submarine Service', Admy 6 November 1906, ADM 1/7880.

71. Minute by Assistant Director of Mobilization Division, in 'Submarine Service – recruiting for service in submarines', n.d., ADM 116/1122.

72. Report by Inspecting Captain of Submarines on the pay and conditions of service for submarine personnel, in 'Submarine Service – recruiting for service in submarines', 19 May 1910, ADM 116/1122.

73. Letter by Inspecting Captain of Submarines on the conditions of service of submarine personnel, contained in 'Submarine Service – recruiting for service in submarines', 17 February 1913, ADM 116/1122.

74. Correspondence relating to the eyesight of submarine officers. Commodore (S) Roger Keyes to Admiralty via the Admiral of Patrols (Rear Adm. John de Robeck), 20 February 1913, Keyes Mss 4/13.

75. Report on the Swedish Submarine *Hvalen*, and discussion of its merits in comparison with British and French types of Submarines, 19 November 1909, Keyes Mss 4/22 (M 01374/1909).

76. Private letter from Captain Sydney Hall (former ICS) to Captain Roger Keyes (serving ICS), *c*.11 February 1911, Keyes Mss 4/1.

77. Memorandum (1 September 1911) by Constructor H.G. Williams to Controller, cut 31, Ships' Covers 291.

78. Note from Constructor Harris G. Williams to Captain (S) Roger Keyes, 22 November 1911, Keyes Mss 4/4.

79. Private letter from Captain Sydney Hall to Captain Roger Keyes, 7 October 1911, Keyes Mss 4/22.

80. Private letter from Captain Roger Keyes to Captain Sydney Hall, 19 October 1911, Keyes Mss 4/22.

81. Extract from Report by Submarine Committee on Future Material Requirements, in 'Development of British Submarines', 29 February 1912, ADM 1/8374/93.

82. Memorandum by new Inspecting Captain of Submarines (Roger Keyes) to Admiralty, 3 June 1911, Keyes Mss 4/13.

83. Extract from minutes taken at the 117th meeting of the Committee of Imperial Defence, held on 4th July 1912, CAB 38/21/26.

84. Views on Use of Submarines expressed by Commander-in-Chief, Home Fleets (Adm. Sir George Callaghan) in 'Manoeuvres 1912: General remarks by Flag Officers and Captains of Red Fleet', 5 August 1912, X2669/12, ADM 1/8269.

85. Private letter from Admiral Lord Fisher to Arthur Balfour, enclosing memorandum on Submarine Warfare, 15 May 1913, f.95, Add Mss 49712.

86. Memorandum entitled 'Submarines and Commerce' enclosed in private letter from Admiral Lord Fisher to Arthur Balfour, 28 May 1913, f.105, Add Mss 49712.

87. Extract from report by Admiral of the Fleet Sir William May to First Lord (Winston Churchill) on 'Naval Manoeuvres, 1913', 18 August 1913, ADM 116/3381.

88. Private letter from Captain S.S. Hall, former Captain (S), to Admiral Lord Fisher (Chairman of Royal Commission on Fuel and Oil) Summer 1913, FP 648, Fisher Papers FISR 1/12.

89. Copy of letter from First Lord of the Admiralty to Prime Minister H.H. Asquith, 22 October 1912, Masterton-Smith Mss. f. 53, CAB 1/34.

90. Memorandum by Director of Operations Division, Naval War Staff, 14 July 1913, in 'Submarines: Report by Naval Staff on War Duties of', ADM 1/8331.

91. Memorandum on the Function of Submarines by Commodore of Submarines, 15 August 1913, d'Eyncourt Papers DEY 31.

92. Memorandum on the Function of Submarines by First Lord of the Admiralty, 20 August 1913, d'Eyncourt Papers DEY 31.

93. Extract from private letter from Winston Churchill to Admiral Lord Fisher, 30 August 1913, FP 720, Fisher Papers, FISR 1/13.

94. Memorandum entitled 'Considerations as to the best composition of the Mediterranean fleet in 1915', by Captain George Ballard (DOD), 20 November 1913, f.77, ADM 116/3099.

95. Private letter from Julian Corbett to Admiral Lord Fisher, 30 November 1913, f.53, FP 752, Fisher Papers, FISR 1/14.

96. Memorandum by Admiral of the Fleet Lord Fisher (5th edition printed May 1914), f.192, Asquith Mss 25.

97. Extract from private letter from Winston Churchill to Admiral Lord Fisher, 1 January 1914, FP 763, Fisher Papers, FISR 1/14.

98. Extract from Private Letter by Captain Sydney Hall to Admiral Lord Fisher, 11 December 1913, FP 758, Fisher Papers, FISR 1/14.

99.   Minutes taken by Commodore Roger Keyes at Admiralty Conference on Submarine Policy held on Tuesday, 9 December 1913, Keyes Mss 4/10.

100.   Memorandum on Submarine policy circulated by Second Sea Lord (Sir John Jellicoe), Battenberg Mss. MB1/T49/25. Untitled memorandum on Submarine Policy by First Lord of the Admiralty addressed to 1st, 2nd, and 3rd Sea Lords, 25 December 1913, enclosing copy of Lord Fisher's 'Oil Engine and the Submarine', f.261, Chartwell 13/22B.

101.   Minute (25 December 1914) by Winston Churchill to Board of Admiralty attached to Fisher's 'Oil Engine and Submarine', Chartwell 13/22B.

102.   Extracts from copy of minutes by First Lord of the Admiralty taken from docket since lost, in 'First Lord's Minutes', 14 January 1914, 3rd Series, volume 2, Admiralty Library, Ministry of Defence.

103.   Difficulties in Building Additional Submarines. Memorandum by Commodore (S) on 'Vickers Request for Permission to build for other nations', CP01202, February 1914, Keyes Mss 4/1.

104.   Private letter from Captain S.S. Hall to Admiral Lord Fisher, 17 February 1914, FP.783, Fisher Papers, FISR 1/14.

105.   Copy of letter from Admiral of the Fleet Lord Fisher to Prime Minister H.H. Asquith, 15 May 1914, f.75, Chartwell 2/92.

106.   Private letter from Admiral Lord Fisher to Vice-Admiral Sir John Jellicoe (Second Sea Lord), 25 May 1914, printed in Arthur Marder, *Fear God and Dread Nought: the Correspondence of Admiral of the Fleet Lord Fisher of Kilverstone*, (3 volumes) London 1952–59, ii, 507–8.

107.   Editorial by the editor of *The Times* discussing letter received from Admiral Sir Percy Scott, *The Times*, Friday 5 June 1914, p.9, column 6 to p.10, column 1.

108.   Extract from private letter by Admiral Lord Fisher to Julian Corbett, 2 June 1914, printed in *Fear God and Dread Nought*, ii, 507–8.

109.   First Lord of the Admiralty to First Sea Lord, 12 July 1914, Masterton-Smith Papers ff.116–18, CAB 1/34.

110.   Private letter from Winston Churchill to Lewis 'LouLou' Harcourt (Secretary of State for the Colonies), 13 July 1914, in Masterton-Smith Papers f.154, CAB 1/34.

111.   Extract of letter by First Lord of the Admiralty to Prime Minister H.H. Asquith, 4 July 1914, in 'First Lord's Minutes', 5th Series, p.7, Admiralty Library.

Admiralty on 'Emergency War Programme of New Construction in Destroyers and Submarines', f.6, Admy 11 August 1914, ADM 1/8390/256.

131. Extract from memorandum on spare capacity in warship building industry, by Third Sea Lord, 11 August 1914, f.7, ADM 1/8390/256.

132. Attached minute (31 October 1914) by First Lord on 'Additional Orders for Submarine Boats', Admy 11 November 1914, ADM 1/8402/419.

133. Memorandum by Lord Fisher on laying down further numbers of Submarines beyond those already under construction, distributed at meeting held at the Admiralty on 3 November 1914, FP.4305, Fisher Papers, FISR 5/121.

134. Minutes of meeting held at the Admiralty on Tuesday, 3 November 1914, ADM 116/3454.

135. Extract from Commodore (S) to First Sea Lord (Adm. Lord Fisher), 3 November 1914, Keyes Mss 4/13.

136. Memorandum (5 November 1914) by First Sea Lord in 'Additional Orders for Submarine Boats', Admy 11 November 1914, ADM 1/8402/419.

137. Memorandum Circulated by Director of Contracts, dated 11 November 1914, Keyes Mss 4/11.

138. Minute (31 December 1914) by Director of Dockyards, on S.019/14, 'Submarine boats: New Construction that can be undertaken in the dockyards', FP 891, f.70, Fisher Papers, 1/17.

139. Copy of Office Memorandum circulated within Admiralty, 9 February 1915, f.4, ADM 137/294.

140. Copy of orders circulated by Captain commanding oversea submarines to all commanding officers prohibiting unrestricted attacks on enemy merchant ships, 25 March 1915, f.35, ADM 137/294.

141. Private letter from Lieutenant Norman Holbrook VC to Commodore Roger Keyes, on receipt of the Victoria Cross for sinking Turkish battleship, 17 January 1915, Keyes Mss 4/36.

142. The First Sea of Marmora Patrol by HM Submarine E11, 19 May to 7 June 1915, Draft (Original Version) of Official Report compiled by Lieutenant-Commander Martin Nasmith, Lieutenant Guy d'Oyly Hughes and Lieutenant Robert Browne [Private Collection].

142a. Deck Log of USS *Scorpion*, 25 May 1915, RG74, NARA, College Park, Maryland, USA.

143. Officer Commanding Naval Force at the Dardanelles (Vice-Adm. John de Robeck) to Admiralty, 10 September 1915, Keyes Mss 4/36.

144. Second Patrol of the Sea of Marmora by HM Submarine E11, 4 September 1915 [Private Collection].

145. Extract from minute attached to Patrol Reports from HM Submarine E11 by First Lord, 10 September 1915, ADM 137/382.

146. Memorandum (15 October 1915) by Commodore of Submarines included in file of correspondence relating to Publication of Submarine Patrol Reports, ff.504–19, ADM 137/1115.

147. Memorandum (30 August 1916) by Commodore of Submarines on the Performance of the Submarine Service 1914–16, ff.53–79, ADM 137/2077.

148. Commander Francis Cromie to Commodore (S) Sydney Hall, 10 October 1917, in 'Printed Letters from Captain Cromie', RN Submarine Museum, HMS *Dolphin*.

149. Memorandum (31 August 1916) from the Captain (S), Harwich (HMS *Maidstone*) to the Chief of the War Staff, Admiralty, enclosing narrative by Stoker Petty Officer William Brown explaining his method of escape from wreck of Submarine E41, 31 August 1916, ff.500–503, ADM 137/1922.

150. Admiralty to Commander-in-Chief, Home Fleets, 29 July 1915, f.43, ADM 137/1926.

151. Commander-in-Chief, Home Fleets, to Admiralty, 8 November 1915, f.48, ADM 137/1926.

152. Admiralty to Commander-in-Chief, Home Fleets, 17 November 1915, f.51, ADM 137/1926.

153. Copy of memorandum by Commander-in-Chief, Home Fleets, directing the creation of Home Fleets Submarine Committee, 14 October 1916, Keyes Mss 4/20.

154. Commander-in-Chief, Home Fleets, to Admiralty, 16 October 1916, ff.87–8, ADM 137/1926.

155. Commander Charles Little (member of Home Fleets Submarine Committee) to Commander-in-Chief, Home Fleets, (Beatty), 18 January 1917, ff.102–11, ADM 137/1926.

156. Commander-in-Chief, Home Fleets, to Admiralty, 18 January 1917, f.112, ADM 137/1926.

157. Admiralty to Commander-in-Chief, Home Fleets, 30 January 1917, ff.114–15, ADM 137/1926.

158. President Submarine Committee to Commander-in-Chief, Home Fleets, 2 February 1917, ff.127–8, ADM 137/1926.

159. Commander-in-Chief, Home Fleets, to Admiralty, 6 February 1917, f.115, ADM 137/1926.

160. Admiralty to Commander-in-Chief, Home Fleets, 23 March 1917, ff.119–21, ADM 137/1926.

161. Admiralty to Commander-in-Chief, Home Fleets, 21 October 1917, ff.170–71, ADM 137/1926.

162. Extract from Report (5 October 1917) by Commodore (S) Sydney S. Hall on the Performance of the Submarine Service, ff.77–9, ADM 137/2077.

163. Lieutenant Anthony B Lockhart to Admiralty, 5 January 1917, f.53, ADM 137/2071.

164. Patrol Report by Commanding Officer of HM Submarine E54 (Lieutenant Commander Robert Raikes) to Vice-Admiral Commanding Coast of Ireland (Lewis Bayly), 3 May 1917, f.115, ADM 137/2076.

165. Report from officer commanding the submarines patrolling the Western Approaches (Capt. Martin E. Nasmith VC) to Commander-in-Chief, Queenstown, (Vice-Adm. Sir Lewis Bayly), 7 March 1918, f.664, ADM 137/1946.

166. Lieutenant F. Williams Freeman to Admiralty, 31 March 1918, f.371, ADM 137/2071.

BIOGRAPHICAL APPENDIX

ARNOLD-FORSTER, H. Oakley: MP 1892–1909; Parliamentary and Financial Secretary to the Admiralty 1901–3; Secretary of State for War 1903–5. Died 1909.

ASQUITH, Herbert Henry: MP 1886–1918, 1920–24; Chancellor of Exchequer 1905–8; Prime Minister 1908–16.

BACON, Reginald: Captain, 1900; Rear Admiral 1909; Vice-Admiral 1915; ICS, 1901–4; Private Secretary to First Sea Lord 1904–5; CO HMS *Dreadnought*, 1906–7; Captain of HMS *Irresistible* 1907–8; DNO 1907–9. At the end of 1909 offered post of Controller but instead quit the Navy to become Managing Director of Coventry Ordnance Works (1910–15); recalled to service and appointed Flag Officer, Dover Patrol 1915–18.

BALFOUR, Arthur: MP 1874–1922. First Lord of Treasury and Leader of House of Commons 1891–2, 1895–1902; Prime Minister 1902–5; leader of HM opposition 1905–11; First Lord of the Admiralty 1915–16; Foreign Secretary 1916–19.

BALLARD, George: Captain, 1904; Rear Admiral 1914; a/DNI 1903–5; chairman amphibious warfare projects committee 1906–7; DNI 1911 (for one month); DOD 1911–14; Admiral of Patrols 1914–15.

BATTENBERG, Prince Louis of: Captain 1891, Rear Admiral 1904; Vice-Admiral 1908; Admiral 1912; Admiral of the Fleet 1921; Director of Naval Intelligence, 1902–5; 1st Cruiser Squadron 1905–7; C-in-C Atlantic Fleet, 1908–10; 3rd and 4th (reserve) Battle Squadrons 1910–11; Second Sea Lord 1911–12; First Sea Lord 1912–14. Changed family name to Mountbatten 1917; created Marquis of Milford Haven 1917.

BAYLY, Lewis: Captain 1899; Rear Admiral 1908; Vice-Admiral 1913; President of War College 1908–11; 1st Cruiser (later renamed 1st Battle Cruiser) Squadron 1911–12; for Special Services at the Admiralty 1912–13; 3rd Battle Squadron 1914; C-in-C Channel 1914–15; C-in-C Queenstown (west coast of Ireland) 1915–19. Retired list 1919.

BEATTY, David: Captain, 1900; Rear Admiral, 1910; Vice-Admiral,

1914; Admiral 1916; Admiral of the Fleet 1919; Naval Secretary, 1911–13; 1st Battle Cruiser Squadron 1913–15; Vice-Admiral Battle Cruiser Fleet 1915–16; C-in-C Home Fleets 1916–18; First Sea Lord 1919–27.

BERESFORD, Lord Charles: Captain 1885; Rear Admiral 1897; Vice-Admiral 1902; Admiral 1906. Rear Admiral Mediterranean Fleet 1900–1902; C-in-C Channel Squadron 1903–5; C-in-C Mediterranean 1905–7; C-in-C Channel Fleet, 1907–9. Four times elected MP: for Waterford (1874–80), East Marylebone (1885–9), Woolwich (1902–3), and Portsmouth (1910–16).

BETHELL, Alexander: Rear Admiral 1906; Vice-Admiral 1913; Admiral 1916. A/DNO 1904–6, Rear Admiral Home Fleet 1906–8; DNI 1909–11; C-in-C East Indies 1912; President Naval War College 1913–14; 7th Battle Squadron 1914; C-in-C Channel 1915; C-in-C Plymouth 1916–17.

BRIDGEMAN, Francis: Rear Admiral 1903; Vice-Admiral 1907; Admiral 1911; Rear Admiral Channel Fleet 1904–5; Rear Admiral Mediterranean Fleet 1906–7; C-in-C Home Fleet 1907–9; Second Sea Lord 1909–11; C-in-C Home Fleets 1911; First Sea Lord 1911–12.

BURNEY, Cecil: President ASW Committee 1909–10; 5th Cruiser Squadron 1911; Atlantic Squadron 1911–12; 5th (reserve) Battle Squadron 1913–14; C-in-C Channel 1914; 2nd in command Home Fleets 1915–16; Second Sea Lord 1916–17; C-in-C Scotland 1917–19.

CALLAGHAN, George: Captain 1894; Rear Admiral 1905; Vice-Admiral 1910; Admiral 1913; Admiral of the Fleet 1917; Captain of Portsmouth Dockyard 1904; Rear Admiral Channel Fleet 1906–7; 5th Cruiser Squadron 1907–8; Rear Admiral Mediterranean Fleet 1908–10; 2nd Battle Squadron 1910–11; C-in-C Home Fleets 1911–14; C-in-C Nore 1915–18.

CHURCHILL, Winston S.: Undersecretary of State Colonial Office 1906–8; President Board of Trade 1908–10; Home Secretary 1910–11; First Lord of the Admiralty 1911–15; Minister of Munitions 1917; Secretary of State for War and Air 1918–22; Chancellor of the Exchequer 1924–9; First Lord of the Admiralty 1939–40; Prime Minister 1940–5 and 1951–4.

CLARKE, George: Governor of Victoria 1901–4; member of War Office Reconstitution Committee 1903–4; Secretary to CID 1904–7; Governor of Bombay 1907–13. Created Lord Sydenham.

CUSTANCE, Admiral Sir Reginald: Rear Admiral 1899; Vice-Admiral 1904; Admiral 1908; naval attaché to USA 1893–5; DNI

1899–1902; Rear Admiral Mediterranean Fleet 1903–4; Vice-Admiral Channel Fleet 1906–8.

D'OYLY-HUGHES, Guy: Commander 1925, Captain, 1932. Joined submarines 1913; Lieutenant HMS/m E11 1915–16; Lieutenant HMS/m J4 1916–17; CO HMS/m C3 1917; CO HMS/m E35 1917–19; attached to RAN 1919–21, staff of Submarine School 1922–25 and CO HMS/m *Oberon*, attached for staff duties to Admiral commanding reserves 1925–27, half-pay thereafter, CO HMS *Glorious*, 1938–40. DSC for first patrol in Marmora 1915; DSO for commando raid during second Marmora patrol, bar to DSO for sinking U154 in 1918. Killed in action, 8 June 1940 after sinking of carrier HMS *Glorious* by German battle-cruisers *Scharnhorst* and *Gneisenau*.

ESHER, Viscount Reginald: Secretary to Carnarvon Commission 1879; Chairman War Office Reconstitution Committee 1903–4; permanent member of CID 1904–18; Cabinet liaison French General HQ 1914–18.

FISHER, John Arbuthnot: Captain 1874; Rear Admiral 1890; Vice-Admiral 1896; Admiral 1901; Admiral of the Fleet 1905. Director of Naval Ordnance, 1885–9; Admiral Commanding Portsmouth Dockyard 1890–91; Controller, 1892–7; C-in-C North America and West Indies Station 1897–9; British representative to Hague Peace Conference 1899–1900; C-in-C Mediterranean 1899–1902; Second Sea Lord 1902–3; C-in-C Portsmouth, and member of War Office Reconstitution Committee 1903–4; First Sea Lord 1904–10; permanent member CID 1910–16; Chairman Royal Commission on Fuel Oil 1912–14; First Sea Lord 1914–15; Chairman Board of Invention and Research 1915–18.

GREENE, William Grahame: private secretary to First Lords of the Admiralty 1887–1902; assistant Secretary to the Admiralty 1907–11; Permanent Secretary 1911–17; Secretary Ministry of Munitions 1917–20.

HALL, Sydney: Captain 1908; Rear Admiral 1919. ICS 1906–10; Captain HMS *Diana* 1910–12; secretary to Royal Commission on Fuel Oil; Captain HMS *Roxburgh* 1914; assistant Naval Secretary and Captain Supervising Submarine Construction 1914–15; Commodore (S) 1915–18. Retired list 1919.

HAMILTON, Frederick Tower: Rear Admiral 1907; Vice-Admiral 1913. Inspector of Target Practice 1907–9; 5th Cruiser Squadron 1909–11; Vice-Admiral commanding 3rd (reserve) Fleet 1911–13; Second Sea Lord 1914–16; C-in-C Rosyth 1916–17; died 1917.

HERBERT, Geoffrey: Lieutenant 1905; Commander 1917. CO HMS/m A4 1907, HMS *Monmouth* 1908–10; CO HMS/m C36 1910–13; CO HMS/m D5 1913–14 (sunk 3 November 1914); British liaison officer French Submarine Service 1914; captain of Q ship HMS *Baralong* (branded war criminal by Germany for sinking of U.27 in August 1915); CO HMS/m E22 1915–16 (sunk 1916); CO submarine K13 1916–17 (sunk 29 January 1917); attached to staff of Admiral Commanding at Queenstown 1917–18; half-pay 1919. Managing director Daimler Cars from 1920; recalled to active service 1939; captain armed merchant cruiser *Cilicia* 1939–43. Retired list 1943. Awarded DSO (13 September 1915) for sinking of U.27.

HORTON, Max: Lieutenant 1905; Commander 1914; Captain 1920; Rear Admiral 1932; Vice-Admiral 1936; Admiral 1941. CO HMS/m C8 1908–10; HMS *Duke of Edinburgh* 1910–12; CO HMS/m D6 1912–14; Junior member, Submarine Committee, 1912–14; CO HMS/m E9 (Baltic Flotilla) 1914–16; CO HMS/m J6 1916–17; CO HMS/m M1 1918; CO 3rd Submarine Flotilla 1918–19; Rear Admiral 2nd Battle Squadron, 1932–4; Rear Admiral 2nd Cruiser Squadron, 1935–6; Rear Admiral Reserve Fleet 1937–9; Flag Officer Submarines 1940–1; C-in-C Western Approaches 1942–5. Retired 1945. Awarded DSO for sinking cruiser *Hela* 1914, bar to DSO for service in Baltic 1916, second bar to DSO for service in Baltic during Allied intervention in Russia 1919.

JACKSON, Henry: Captain 1896; Rear Admiral 1906; Vice-Admiral 1911; Admiral 1914. Naval attaché in Paris 1896–9; Captain of torpedo school HMS *Vulcan* 1899–1901; a/DNO 1902–3; Controller 1905–8; President Naval War College 1912–13; Chief of War Staff 1913–14; nominated C-in-C Mediterranean Squadron 1914; Admiralty War Council 1914–15; First Sea Lord 1915–16.

JELLICOE, John R.: Captain 1897; Rear Admiral 1907; Vice-Admiral 1910; Admiral 1915; Admiral of the Fleet 1919. DNO 1905–7; Controller 1908–10; C-in-C Atlantic Fleet 1910–11; 2nd Battle Squadron 1911–12; Second Sea Lord 1912–14; C-in-C Home Fleets (Grand Fleet) 1914–16; First Sea Lord December 1916–December 1917; Governor General of New Zealand 1920–24.

KERR, Admiral of the Fleet Lord Walter: Captain 1872; Rear Admiral 1889; Vice-Admiral 1895; Admiral 1900; Admiral of the Fleet 1904. Naval Secretary 1885; Junior Naval Lord 1892; 2nd Naval

Lord 1893–5; C-in-C Channel Squadron 1895–8; Senior Naval Lord 1899–1904.

KERR, Mark E: Captain 1902; Rear Admiral 1912. Flag Captain to Battenberg 1909–11; Head Naval Mission to Greece 1913–15; C-in-C Adriatic 1916–17; Deputy-chief of Air Staff (RAF) 1918.

KEYES, Roger J.B.: Captain 1905; Rear Admiral 1917; Vice-Admiral 1918; Admiral 1926; Admiral of the Fleet 1930. Naval attaché Rome 1905–8; CO HMS *Venus* 1908–10; Inspecting Captain (Commodore 2nd class from 1912) of Submarines 1910–15; Chief of Staff for Naval Operations at the Dardanelles 1915; Captain HMS *Centurion* 1916–17; Director of Plans Division, Naval Staff 1917–18; Flag Officer, Dover Patrol 1918; DCNS 1921; C-in-C Mediterranean 1925–8; C-in-C Portsmouth 1929–31; Con. MP Portsmouth 1934–43; Director Combined Operations 1940–1; baron 1943.

LAMBTON (surname changed in 1911 to Meux), Sir Hedworth: Captain 1889; Rear Admiral 1902; Vice-Admiral 1907; Admiral 1911. Naval Secretary 1894–7; Naval Brigade South Africa 1900–1901; Royal Yacht 1901–3; 3rd Cruiser Squadron 1904–6; C-in-C China 1908–10; unemployed 1910–12; C-in-C Portsmouth 1912–16. MP for Portsmouth 1916–18.

LAWRENCE, Noel: Lieutenant-Commander 1912; Commander 1914; Captain 1919; Rear Admiral 1932; Vice-Admiral 1936; Admiral 1940. Joined submarines in 1904; CO HMS/m E1 1912–16; Senior Officer Baltic Submarine Flotilla 1914–16; CO HMS/m J1 1916–17; CO HMS/m K2 1917–18; Commander (S) 8th Submarine Flotilla 1918; Commander (S) 2nd Submarine Flotilla 1919–20; staff of War College 1920–23; Flag-captain East Indies Squadron (HMS *Chatham*) 1923–5; Captain HMS *Eagle* 1929–31; Flag Officer Submarines 1932–34; Vice-Admiral Aircraft Carriers (HMS *Courageous*) 1935–7; Admiral Commanding Reserves 1938–40; naval liaison to Ministry of Aircraft Production 1941–2. DSO for torpedo hit on battle cruiser *Moltke* 1915, bar to DSO for torpedo hits on battleships *Grosser Kurfurst* and *Kronprinz* 1916.

LEES, Edgar: Captain 1904. ICS 1904–6. Retired from active service in 1906 to become managing director of Whitehead Torpedo Factory.

LITTLE, Charles 'Tiny': Commander 1913; Captain 1917; Rear Admiral 1929; Vice-Admiral 1933; Admiral 1937. Joined submarines 1903; CO HMS/m D1 1908–11; Commander (S) 4th Submarine Flotilla (guarding Dover Straits) 1911–15; staff of

Commodore (S) 1915–16; Captain of HMS *Fearless* and 12th Submarine Flotilla 1917–18; Captain HMS *Cleopatra* 1919–20; Director Trade Division (Naval Staff) 1920–2; Captain of Fleet, Mediterranean Fleet 1922; staff of War College 1924–6; Captain HMS *Iron Duke* 1926–8; Director Naval Staff College 1928–30; 2nd Battle Squadron, Home Fleet 1930; Flag Officer Submarines 1931–2; DCNS 1932; Fifth Sea Lord 1933–5; C-in-C China Station 1936–8; Second Sea Lord 1938–41; Head, British Admiralty Delegation, Washington 1941–2; C-in-C Portsmouth 1942. Retired list 1947.

MADDEN, Charles: Rear Admiral 1911; Naval Secretary 1908–10; Fourth Sea Lord 1910–11; Rear Admiral Home Fleet 1911–12; 3rd Cruiser Squadron 1912–14; chief of Staff to C-in-C Home Fleets 1914–16; 2nd in command Home Fleets 1916–19; C-in-C Atlantic Fleet 1919–22; First Sea Lord 1927–30.

MAY, William: Captain 1887; Rear Admiral 1901; Vice-Admiral 1905; Admiral 1908; Admiral of the Fleet 1913. Director of Naval Ordnance 1900–1901; Controller 1901–5; C-in-C Atlantic Fleet 1905–7; Second Sea Lord 1907–9; C-in-C Home Fleet 1909–11. Unemployed until placed on retired list in 1913.

McKENNA, Reginald: Chief Secretary to the Treasury 1905–7; President Board of Education 1907–8; First Lord 1908–11; Home Secretary 1911–15; Chancellor of the Exchequer 1915–17; Chairman Midland Bank 1919–43.

MILNE, Admiral Sir Berkeley: Captain 1891; Rear Admiral 1904; Vice-Admiral 1908; Admiral 1911. 2nd Battle Squadron 1908–10; unemployed 1910–12; C-in-C Mediterranean 1912–14. Court-martialled for escape of the *Goeben* in 1914.

MOORE, Rear Admiral Archibald: Captain 1901; Rear Admiral 1911; Naval Assistant to First Sea Lord 1907–8; DNO 1909–12; Controller and Third Sea Lord 1912–14; 2nd Battle Cruiser Squadron 1914–15; relieved of command at insistence of Admiral Sir John Jellicoe.

MURRAY, Oswyn: Secretary to the Admiralty 1917–36.

NASMITH, Martin E. (from 1923 Dunbar-Nasmith): Lieutenant-Commander 1914; Commander 1915; Captain 1916; Rear Admiral 1928; Vice-Admiral 1934; Admiral 1937. Junior member of Submarine Committee and assistant to Commodore (S) 1912–14; CO HMS/m E11 1914–16; CO HMS/m J4 1916; Captain HMS *Ambrose* Flotilla (west coast of Ireland) 1917–18; Captain *Lucia* Flotilla (Russian Intervention) 1919–20; Captain HMS *Vindictive* 1921; Flag-captain (HMS *Iron*

Duke) Mediterranean Fleet 1921–3; Director of Trade Division (Naval Staff) 1923–5; President Britannia Royal Naval College 1926–9; Flag Officer Submarines 1929–31; C-in-C East Indies 1932–4; Second Sea Lord 1935–8; C-in-C Plymouth 1938–40; C-in-C Western Approaches 1939–41; Flag Officer London 1942–6. Awarded Victoria Cross for first Marmora patrol, 1915.

NICHOLSON, Field Marshal Sir William: Director of Military Intelligence 1902–4; Quartermaster-general 1905–7; Chief of General Staff 1908–12. Appointed member of Dardanelles Commission 1916.

OTTLEY, Charles: Captain 1899; naval attaché Washington DC 1899–1901; a/DNI 1902–4; DNI 1905–7; retired 1907. Secretary CID 1907–12; Board of Directors Messrs Armstrong-Whitworth 1912–19.

SCOTT, Rear Admiral Sir Percy: Inspector of Target Practice 1905–7; 1st Cruiser Squadron 1907–9; unemployed 1909–11; retired list 1911. Inventor of numerous gunnery control instruments.

SELBORNE, third Earl: First Lord 1900–1905; Governor of South Africa 1905–9.

SLADE, Edmond: Captain 1899; Rear Admiral 1909; Captain of Portsmouth War College 1904–7; DNI 1907–8; C-in-C East Indies 1909–11; for special services at the Admiralty 1912.

STURDEE, Fredrick Doveton: Captain 1899; Rear Admiral 1908; Vice-Admiral 1914; Admiral 1917. a/DNI 1900–1902; Flag-captain to Beresford 1906–8; Rear Admiral 1st Battle Squadron 1909–10; President Anti-Submarine Committee 1910–12; 2nd Cruiser Squadron 1912–13; Chief of the War Staff April–November 1914; Flag Officer commanding detached battle cruiser force South Atlantic 1914–15; 4th Battle Squadron, 1915–18; C-in-C Nore 1918–21.

TROUBRIDGE, Rear Admiral Ernest C: Naval Secretary 1908–11; Chief of War Staff 1912–13; 1st Armoured Cruiser Squadron 1913–14; court-martialled in September 1914 for escape of the German battle cruiser *Goeben*; Admiral commanding Danube Flotilla 1918.

TUDOR, Frederick: Rear Admiral 1915. Director of Naval Ordnance 1912–14; Controller 1914–17; C-in-C China Station 1917–19.

TUPPER, Reginald: Rear Admiral 1910; Captain HMS *Excellent* 1908–10; ASW Committee 1910–13, refused post as head of naval mission to Turkey 1913; unemployed 1913–14; 10th Cruiser Squadron 1915–17.

TWEEDMOUTH, first Earl: First Lord of the Admiralty 1906–8; removed from office for mental illness in April 1908; died 1909.

WAISTELL, Arthur: Captain 1914; Rear Admiral 1923. Captain (S) 8th Submarine Flotilla 1914–15; Commodore commanding destroyers Atlantic Fleet 1922–3; assistant Chief of Naval Staff 1922–3; 1st Cruiser Squadron 1924–6; C-in-C China 1929–30; C-in-C Portsmouth 1931–4.

WATTS, Sir Philip: DNC 1901–12.

WHITE, Sir William: DNC 1887–1901.

WILSON, Sir Arthur Knyvet: Captain 1880; Rear Admiral 1895; Vice-Admiral 1901; Admiral 1905; Admiral of the Fleet 1907. Controller 1897–1901; C-in-C Channel Squadron 1901–4; C-in-C Channel Fleet 1904–7; retired from active service March 1907. Recalled to active service November 1909; First Sea Lord 1910–11. Retired List 1912. Permanent member of CID 1909–14. Admiralty War Council 1914–18. Awarded Victoria Cross for action with Naval Brigade in Sudan at Battle of El Teb 1884.

INDEX